AGAINST THE CURRENT

AGAINST THE CURRENT

Reform and Experimentation in Higher Education

Edited by
Richard M. Jones
and
Barbara Leigh Smith

SCHENKMAN PUBLISHING COMPANY, INC.
331 Broadway
Cambridge, Massachusetts 02139

Schenkman Publishing Co., Inc.
190 Concord Avenue
Cambridge, MA 02138

ISBN: 0-87073-648-5
ISBN: 0-87073-649-3 paper

Library of Congress #83-15066

Printed in the United States of America.

We dedicate this book to the memories of
John Dewey
and
Alexander Meiklejohn

Acknowledgements

We are grateful to the Alexander Meiklejohn Experimental College Foundation, the Koppers Foundation and the Metropolitan Life Foundation for their generous support of this project.

Manuscript preparation was greatly assisted by the careful work of a number of individuals. Leslie Gatton, Anne Seidner and Leo Daugherty provided editorial assistance. Naia McClelland, Betty Hatter, and Joanne Jirovec patiently typed and re-typed the manuscript's several drafts. Finally, Malcolm Stilson, Debbie Robinson and Bob Dana provided critical assistance in compiling the bibliography for the book.

Table of Contents

Introduction*

by

ERNEST BOYER

Eleven years ago I was invited to travel to Olympia, Washington to work intensively in a motel room with Charles McCann to help plan a new institution called The Evergreen State College. At that time Evergreen was just a dream, a dream committed to excellence and innovation. In coming back tonight, I am enormously impressed. An exciting innovative program has taken shape, and more to the point, it has been nurtured and kept vital during the past ten years. And needless to say, a beautiful campus has been built and Dan Evans, a distinguished president, brings to this institution the rare combination of vision, intelligence and common sense. As Byron Youtz says in his splendid paper on Evergreen State, this institution is a magnificent survivor; well, he said "survivor," I've added the word "magnificent." I'm convinced that Evergreen has survived, and more than that, it has flourished because of two ingredients. It has had the good fortune of having outstanding leadership and clear vision. No institution that chooses to innovate can long endure without those two essential and enduring ingredients.

I am also delighted that this conference overlaps with the 50th-year reunion of the Alexander Meiklejohn Foundation. Meiklejohn is a giant in American education. His intelligence, his integrity and brilliant innovations remain an inspiration to us all and to the members of the Meiklejohn Foundation who have helped support this conference. We are enor-

*Dr. Ernest Boyer, president of the Carnegie Foundation for the Advancement of Teaching and formerly U.S. Commissioner of Education, has maintained an active interest in alternative higher education throughout his career. He, in fact, had a hand in the initial planning of The Evergreen State College. The introduction is based on Dr. Boyer's keynote address to the Conference.

mously in your debt for keeping the vision of Meiklejohn burning brightly in our midst.

The theme of this conference is alternative education. When Dan Evans called me some months ago, I reflected that my own introduction to so-called experimental education goes back to 1957, when I participated in a conference at Goddard College in Vermont. On that occasion I met a remarkable man named Tim Pitkin, a college president, who argued with great vigor that college was not a *place;* it was a *process*, and students were at the center of it all. I found Tim Pitkin and his arguments enormously compelling. I also liked the way he would shake up his fellow presidents by saying our biggest problem is not the lack of money, but the lack of deep convictions about what we are doing. He was not popular in those days. "Pitkins's Law"—that says we need ideas more than money—has stuck with me to this day. President Pitkin has shaped my professional life more than any other person, and I am deeply in his debt. It was because of Tim that I mucked around a bit with the 4-1-4 calendar at a funny little college called Empire State. It was because of Tim that I tried to start a college for prisoners at Bedford Hills in New York (it was shot down by the legislature because of Attica), and I can say in reflection that all the troubles I have had over the years go directly to Tim Pitkin and Goddard College. Some day I will return the favor.

Back in the 1950's we had a cluster of institutions that clearly could be identified as experimental: Reed College, Antioch, Monteith, Goddard, Bennington, New College of Hofstra, Sara Lawrence and Shimer. There was, as Art Chickering says in his splendid paper, a "beleaguered band of adventurous administrators" who were inspired by Meiklejohn and were led by Ralph Tyler, their intellectual mentor—presidents who were not interested in change for the sake of change but wanted change for the sake of students.

During those ambivalent days of the 1950's these were voices in the wilderness. Higher learning was living in the happy buoyancy of the G.I. Bill and colleges were smugly riding the crest of the baby boom. Experimenters were looked upon as odd irritations in the corner of the vineyard; and yet, this is what has intrigued me as I reflected on our history. If you were to stop any college president in the hallowed corridors of ACE or AAC as it assembled in the nation's capitol, and said "Name some experimental colleges," the same list would have been repeated time and time again. In spite of their offbeat nature and in spite of the fact that they were not members of the inner club, everyone knew that something was going on—even though their messages were quite frequently ignored.

There are no such vivid convictions in our midst today. Most educators would be hard pressed to name a dozen or more experimental institutions, save perhaps for the host institution here tonight and a few others attending as participants. But something fascinating has happened in the last twenty or thirty years, and I think that is what is the root behind this conference. These experimental colleges didn't have much impact on their colleagues; but what I find enormously ironic is the fact that the probing questions Tim Pitkin asked twenty or thirty years ago, which were inspired by the conviction that students be at the center of the enterprise, were not answered in the classroom, but in the barricades across the campus.

In the 1960's, this smugness of the 50's was dramatically shattered. The free-speech movement exploded on the campus. New slogans were blowing in the wind. The Beatles replaced the Kingston Trio and placards appeared announcing "I Am A Human Being; do not fold, spindle or mutilate," the very thing Pitkin was shouting about at Goddard fifteen years before. I shared with Dan Evans the agony of those days. I was shouted down, locked out and sneered at. The four-letter words were often jarring, but there was no denying the fact that beneath the screaming there was an authentic core. The agony of my own leadership was that I more often supported the *students* than I did the institution. The truth became agonizingly clear—*students* were at the center of the campus. The messages of the innovators had been ignored and now the students shouted their frustration for all to hear. At the same time, another revolution swept across the campus. An historic 1954 Supreme Court decision struck at school desegregation, and college students marched off to Jackson, Mississippi, to Selma, Alabama. When they returned to campus they were impatient with what they considered to be "academic games." Then came the long shadow of Vietnam. The revolution that had demanded free speech, open dorms, more academic options and then Civil Rights, now challenged the power of the Pentagon.

Now, tonight I recognize this all sounds like ancient history except to those of you who lived through it. I have recounted it here because I am convinced we cannot know where we are today or where we should go tomorrow unless we understand clearly where we have been. And while the radicalism of the 1960's stands in stark contrast to campus mentality today, the influence lingers on. We only need to look as far as the haircut of David Stockman. I am convinced that the legacy of the past cannot be undermined. I point you towards any college catalog. Just for fun, several weeks ago I pulled down a Kent State catalog—not only because it is symbolic of the trauma of the 1960's and 1970's, but because Kent State is solidly placed in Ohio, where I was born: mid-west America, safe, secure, bland, unimaginative, predictable. I quote to you from the catalog: They have pass/fail options at Kent State University; they have something called "forgiveness" policies; they have individualized majors; they have off-campus study; they have weekend and evening college at Kent State; they have cross-disciplinary majors.

And then I picked another catalog, Manhattanville College: conservative Catholic women's college, Westchester County, New York, where they have off-campus study, credit for life experience and degree programs for adults. I could go on. I'll wager that you could randomly select the catalog from almost any campus and discover programs that were unheard of thirty years ago, except at the few "offbeat" colleges mentioned earlier.

This leads to my central point: Is it possible that, in fact, during the past twenty or thirty years the message of the experimentalist—driven home with vivid accuracy by the protesting students—has now become a way of life? Experimentation is, in fact, the norm. Today we have endless academic options, we have non-campus education, and we have finally accepted the fact that learning never ends. Viewed from this perspective, tonight should be a victory celebration. All the stuff Tim Pitkin preached twenty years ago can now be found in college catalogs from coast to coast.

However, there is a difference. As I look at these innovations and the motivations behind them, I am increasingly impressed that most colleges today are not driven by conviction. They have become academic "supermarkets" without a sense of mission. Many of the so-called innovations reflect more form than substance. They are not deeply rooted in an educational philosophy with students at the core. They are driven by the conviction that the institution must survive, and "We will do whatever it takes to keep us in the academic supermarket business." We should not be beguiled. Change for the sake of change, for survival, does not represent the kind of authentic innovation of which this conference speaks and to which the experimental colleges of the 1950's were wedded. And so it seems to me that we urgently need a new innovative agenda—one in which the challenges of the future and not the battles of the past will be clearly faced. And in the remaining moments I should like to give you three examples that represent the challenge of experimentation in the decade just ahead.

First, I'm convinced that in the 1980's those of us who care about education must find ways to better educate traditionally by-passed students. For a decade or more we have heard lots of talk about the demographic shift. We've been told that we are moving from a baby boom to a baby bust. And that's true, of course. The youth generation in America will drop 23% by 1990. Schools and colleges in most sections of the country will confront the struggles of retrenchment. But the real demographic story is not the overall decline, but what is going on just below the surface.

In the United States today, 28% of all white Americans are 18 years of age and under; 37% of all blacks are in that age group, and 42% of all Hispanics—nearly 1 in 2—are 18 years of age and under. Today, America is the fourth largest Spanish-speaking nation in the world. In Los Angeles County this fall 50% of all kindergarten children are Hispanic. In the State of Texas, 50% of *all children* enrolled in public schools are of Hispanic origin. Now put that up against another cluster of statistics that are equally significant. In 1979, 80% of all white young people age 19 had graduated from high school; 63% of all blacks had graduated, and only 60% of all Hispanic 19-year-olds were high school graduates. 40% of Hispanics had not completed high school. Consider also that for the population as a whole, only 17% of Hispanic adults here attended college. For blacks, the rate is 20%, while 32% of whites have gone to college. The face of young America is changing and the new students who increasingly will dominate the schools and later on the colleges are comprised precisely of those who have been *least* well served by the nation's colleges and schools.

And this changing demography affects us in another way as well. Consider the number of households with school-age children. In 1960, 50% of all American households had children of school age. Today among the white population, only 39%—a little over ⅓ of all white households—have school-age children. By contrast, almost 50% of all blacks have school-age children and 61% of all Hispanic households have children of school age. As I look at America I think we are developing what will be a terrible tension where we are divided not only by age but by culture, too. As white America is aging—white America that traditionally has had the power, the influence to control the schools—it demonstrates less interest in the schools because it has less children in the schools.

On the other hand, the youth of America, increasingly comprised of black and Hispanic children, will have less power, but these are precisely the children who have been least served by our formal institutions. It seems clear to me that serving a changing student body is an urgent agenda for the 1980's. Yet, rather than act constructively to the new immigrants in our midst, we have become frightened and defensive. At the very time when we need a strong public education institution, we hear talk of "forsaking" the public schools, as if somehow the poor people in our midst will find their way into a network of privately-funded institutions.

More disturbing is the fact that we have begun to politicize the Spanish language and view it as a threat to our survival. Simply as a matter of record, let me say that I have found no issue during my term in Washington that was more political and less rational than bilingual education, which became a code word for hostility and fear. And instead of understanding the importance of bringing a new generation into the mainstream of American life, we turned our backs on language. We made it the whipping boy of a political debate. Very quickly, I'm afraid, the public schools could be a battleground in which America divides itself not only on the basis of age but on the basis of culture, too. The agenda for the innovators goes far beyond our insular theories of individual development. It requires us to engage the individual in the social context. As I look ahead to America in the 1980's and beyond, the transcendent education question we all face is the simple issue of whether we will be able to educate responsibly a new generation of Americans—not for the sake of the nation alone, but because they are human beings who need to be well served. This, to me, is the essential obligation of experimental education.

Second illustration, on quite another front: As I look to the social context, I believe those who care about innovation must confront the enormous impact of non-classroom education. I first saw television when our high school class took a senior trip to New York City. We went to the RCA Building in Rockefeller Center and saw a marvelous demonstration on a 10-inch screen in which they told us that the snowy figure was actually three floors below.

Today, children are introduced to television four-and-a half-hours a day before they ever go to school, have watched television 6,000 hours. By the time they graduate they have watched television 16,000 hours and listened to classroom teachers only 11,000 hours. These statistics are so familiar that they numb us; yet the point is clear that we are entering an era in which the classroom teacher is no longer the central figure and the school is not seen as the window to the world.

Christopher Evans, in his new book, *Micro Millenium*, writes about the impact of another form of language. During the 1980's he says the "book" will begin a slow and steady slide into oblivion. Computers will take over because they store more information which can be more readily retrieved. He goes on to paint a picture in which books will be tiny silicone chips which can be slipped into small projectors and read from viewing screens against the wall in the home. My point clearly is that we confront a communication revolution that will dramatically change our notion of how people teach and how they learn.

Several weeks ago a survey came to me. I was intrigued that 20 years ago when American teenagers were asked, "What influences you the most?", number one was parents; number two was teachers; number three was peers. Today—1980 the question is repeated, "What influences you the most?" This time parents have been replaced by peers as number one; next comes parents; third comes television (which jumped from 8 to 3 in just 20 years); and finally, classroom teachers. If you look at those shifts, there is a powerful message to be drawn. It seems clear to me that in the last decade or two, the influential teachers in our culture have shifted from the predictable transmitters of tradition to the more ambiguous, more immediate, more transient senders of messages through peers and mass communications.

In my view, the strengths of the traditional and the non-traditional teachers in our culture must somehow be combined. It is foolish to flail away at what have become the most dramatic possibilities of communication. After all, television can take students to the moon. Through television we can go to the bottom of the sea. It's true, also, calculators can solve problems faster than the human brain; computers can retrieve instantly millions of information bits. But I'm old-fashioned enough to suggest that calculators and computers cannot and will not make discriminating judgments. They cannot and will not teach students wisdom. And the challenge of the future is not to fight technology nor to ignore it, but rather to teach about the new instruments of communication and to build a partnership between traditional and non-traditional education, letting each do what it can do best.

Thus far I've spoken about education in the context of the changing student and in the context of the changing teacher. I should like to close by asking questions about the "substance." The harsh truth is that we confront a world where all actions are inextricably interlocked, and yet many of our students do not see those fundamental connections. Several years ago, when I was in the Office of Education, Joan Gance Cooley of Children's Television Workshop came and asked if we would help support a new TV series for junior high students, focusing on science. I said, "Joan, we'll support you with two requirements: one, I don't want a course on science alone. I'd like a course that deals with the application of science to technology and its social implications. I also think we need a television course that is linked into curriculum for the classroom and the teacher." She concurred. We now have a course on public broadcasting called "3-2-1 Contact." In doing background research for that little children's program, television researchers went to New York City and asked junior high school students some simple questions. In response to the question "Where does water come from?" about 20% said the faucet. And when asked, "Where does light come from," they said the switch. "And where does garbage go?" down the chute. Is it true, perhaps, that we are educating children to their ignorance of their immediate surroundings and that we are so preoccupied with the wants and needs of individuals that we fail to understand that individuals are, in fact, connections, and that there is no way to separate the individuals from the interconnectedness and interdependency of our world? Simply stated, those of us in education must concern ourselves not only with the *process*, but with the *substance*, too.

In 1979 millions of American sat in front of TV sets and watched the Three-Mile Island crisis unfold. We listened to strange talk about rehms and cold shutdowns. As I listened, I felt as if I was hearing a foreign language. The truth is it *was* a foreign language, because most of the viewers had no reference points to give meaning to the terms that suddenly were of grave concern. As a nation and perhaps as a human race, we are becoming civically illiterate. Unless we find better ways to educate ourselves as citizens, I believe we run the grave risk of drifting unwittingly into a new kind of dark age, a time when a small band of specialists will control knowledge and tell the rest of us what we should and should not believe and how we should and should not act. In the 1980's innovators must tackle the toughest of all assignments: we must somehow find a way to preserve individual differences and acknowledge the uniqueness of each student while also building a greater social understanding which gives meaning to individual lives. We must help students to confront their separateness and recognize their togetherness.

I am convinced that these new challenges cannot be met without close cooperation between the nation's colleges and schools. Education is a seamless web. Whether we find a way to teach beyond the classroom authentically is a problem for the colleges and schools, and whether we develop greater civic understanding must begin in the early grades as well. The truth is that a century ago educators understood far better than we do today that we cannot have excellence in education unless we have excellence in the schools. It's such a simple point—the need for close collaboration—and yet in recent years, the school/college relationship has been essentially ignored. Higher education institutions have pretended that quality education could be achieved without working with the schools, which are, in fact, the foundation of everything we do. I believe the time has come to end this isolation. The nation's colleges and universities have a responsibility to help solve the crisis in the schools, which is, a problem they have helped create.

There are signs that are reassuring. Just one month ago I was pleased to help to host a meeting in Colorado Springs, where all 50 chief school superintendents met at their own request with 50 college and university presidents, one from every state. And they spent the week talking, not about governance and politics, but about the central questions I have just discussed: Who are the students? Who are the teachers? *What* are we teaching and *how* can we serve the individuals in our midst? There are no panaceas, but if a new generation of young Americans is to be educationally well-prepared, the primary obligation for excellence rests with the colleges who work closely with the schools. And rebuilding quality is important not because it is a school crisis, but because it is a "people" crisis; young men and women whose lives will be forever diminished or enriched by the programs we provide.

Well, what does all of this have to do with this conference? Let me recite the ways: There was a moment of high drama 20 or 30 years ago when "experimentation" had the central message. Few listened, except the students, and the centrality of that message burst into fury in the Berkeley campus and spread across the nation. I do not believe that the experimentation agenda of the 1980's is the same one articulated in the 1950's, save for one essential issue: *the centrality of the education is the student*. In the 1980's, I believe that agenda must be put in social context, and the social context that I see is the changing demography of this country, the changing impact of technology and the important possibilities of educating towards civil responsibilities. And I believe that there are many educators in this nation, and certainly a host of educators in this room, who will be responsible to that challenge.

Editors' Preface

When we first began to think of commemorating the tenth birthday of The Evergreen State College by hosting a national conference on alternative higher education, we were unsure of what to expect in the way of response. Judging from the number of our sixties-siblings around the country which had either folded or returned to traditional ways, we feared we might find ourselves trying to give a party for folks to whom a wake might seem more appropriate. The coolness we met from the first foundations we approached for support confirmed this fear. "We don't want to pay for a conference in which people sit around and congratulate each other for merely still being alive," was the general tenor of the coolness.

With encouragements from our president, former Washington Governor Dan Evans, and from Alfred S. Schenkman, President of the Schenkman Publishing Co., we continued our search for funds. The Metropolitan Life Foundation, the Koppers Foundation and the Alexander Meiklejohn Experimental College Foundation came through, and we proceeded.

In response to one small "Call for Papers", in the *Chronicle of Higher Education,* we received 220 proposals! We invited twenty-five of these to be written for presentation and discussion at the conference. Of these, twenty chapters make up the book before you.

First, some impressions drawn from the 220 proposals:

1. The innovational impulse of the sixties and early seventies was felt and expressed nationwide. Almost every faction of American higher education—public and private, small and large, new and established—seems to have acted on the impulse in one form or another.
2. The strength of the impulse, and the extent to which it was expressed, was unique in the history of American higher education.

This exuberance is now spent, and will not be re-experienced in the imaginable future.

3. The future of American higher education is bleak. The depression has set in, and it will get worse. Predictions of the effects that this general depression is likely to have on the fortunes of *alternative* higher education emerged, however, as controversial, and the articulation of this controversy proved to be among the more illuminating aspects of the conference. Some seasoned innovators saw little ahead but a search for some conservative trench in which to hunker and reminisce. Others found hope in the opposite view. In paraphrase of one proposal: Experimentation out of freedom was nice, but experimentation out of desperation may be better.
4. Many proposals feared that the conference might amount to no more than a cry in the wilderness. All went on, though, to express interest in adding their voices to the cry. The strongest fear, expressed in a large number of the proposals was: Worse than that the legacy of the 60's and early 70's should prove to be uninherited is the possibility that it should prove to be uninheritable—for lack of articulation. We decided, therefore, to limit the conference selections to those proposals which sought to articulate past experience in terms of its probable relevance in the future.
5. Strong interest was expressed in analyzing failures as well as successes.
6. While the cultural conditions which inspired—perhaps intoxicated—innovational impulses in the 60's and 70's have ceased to exist, the talents and interests which those conditions schooled are still virile. Among those who possess these (now more informed) interests and talents, awareness of our society's needs for continued experimentation in alternative education is keener than ever. There is also awareness that the days in which opportunities for such experimentation came *to them* are over, that they must now add to their innovative savvy the knowing of how to make their own opportunities.
7. In some of the proposals there was an interesting note of guilt, straining, it appeared, to become responsibility. For example:

> To the degree that some of the experiments that we tried in the 60's and 70's were ill-conceived, mindlessly romantic, or academically specious, we who made these errors must face our responsibilities and make sure that we don't repeat them . . . Emperor's wardrobes are cheap and easy to come by, alas, and we need some reliable mirrors to keep us honest . . . I think your conference should insure at least a bit of Satanic advocacy.

So much for the early fears of some of the foundations that our conference might only invite a group of good old boys to tell each other bedtime stories.

8. We invited all of the major foundations which supported the educational experiments to be reported at the conference to submit proposals of their own. Only one (FIPSE) responded. We don't know how to interpret this.

As to the organization of this book, there are four parts to it.

Part I focuses on the possible destiny of disciplinary professionalism. Disciplinary professionalism has dominated the policies and practices of American higher education for a century. Most experiments in alternative higher education have sought to change these policies and practices. The future of disciplinary professionalism would probably influence the future of alternative higher education more than any other single development. Thus, the debate on this subject by Professors Hahn and Weaver, and the response to that debate by Professor Euben made a pertinent starting point for the conference.

Had Professors Hahn and Weaver been able to design the definitive experiment to test their differing views on the role of disciplinary professionalism they could not have improved on the contrast in the early developments of two of the most dramatic institutional innovations of the sixties: The Santa Cruz Campus of the University of California and The Evergreen State College. Part II, therefore, focuses on this contrast, and proceeds to highlight different facets of the contrast from a variety of political, economic and philosophical perspectives.

The three chapters which comprise Part III describe significant innovations developed in very large universities.

Part IV came as something of a surprise. Although we designed a futuristic thrust into the conference (and succeeded), one of the most dramatic realizations to emerge was how organically related many of the innovative ventures of the 60's and 70's were to two generative forerunners dating to the 20's and 30's: Goddard College and The Experimental College of the University of Wisconsin and the legacy of John Dewey and Alexander Micklejohn. This realization was amplified by the personal participation in the conference of Dr. Royce Pitkin, founding president of Goddard, and of thirteen alumni of the Alexander Meiklejohn Experimental College. Part IV focuses on several tracings of this re-discovered heritage.

PART ONE

Disciplinary Professionalism: Two Views of the Developing Context For Alternative Colleges

I. Disciplinary Professionalism: First View

by

FREDERICK STIRTON WEAVER

In this examination of current tendencies and likely changes in undergraduate liberal arts education, I will focus on the nature of academic disciplines. Disciplines are the principal organizational form in liberal arts curricula. I believe that some of the most far-reaching impending changes in colleges can be best understood through the study of academic disciplines and the peculiar type of academic professionalism they represent.

THE PROFESSIONAL CHARACTER OF ACADEMIC DISCIPLINES

While we all know that disciplines are a set of conventional categories of knowledge, it is less well appreciated that these conventions embody and rely upon a system of power relationships. That is, disciplinary conventions are defined and enforced by departments, learned societies, scholarly journals, degree structures, and granting agencies; academic disciplines are professional organizations. Directly analogous to other professions, such as medicine and law, disciplinary professionals organize and create specialized knowledge and transmit it to others; and, in the name of those services, they control the training and certification of disciplinary competence, reserve a range of jobs for certified practitioners, work to maintain standards by dispensing sanctions and rewards, and insulate themselves from the judgments of outsiders in all of these activities. The Ph.D., awarded by university departments, is the reigning certificate, and through control mechanisms like journals, learned societies and degree structures, disciplines sustain internal hierarchies and define legitimacy as a particular set of intellectual activities.

The institutional foundations of disciplinary professionalism were laid during the middle and late decades of the nineteenth century, propelled by the rise of the urban middle class and their ambitions and career expectations. These new social forces rapidly consolidated into what Burton J. Bledstein so aptly calls the "culture of professionalism."[1] The traditional professions of medicine and law, after the antebellum disintegration of elitist, local guilds, reorganized themselves into state and national professional groups based on what they saw as meritocratic principles; the ministry, as a profession and as an influence in colleges, continued to decline; and a whole range of middle class occupational groups actively and self-consciously sought to become professions. Morticians, dentists, pharmacists, librarians, veterinarians, school teachers, engineers, architects, social workers, and public administrators are examples of occupational groups that made concerted efforts to control their occupations in the name of eliminating quackery and establishing authority for sound, professional practice. The historical reasons for these widespread efforts at professionalization have recently begun to be explored in suggestive ways, but in this surge of scholarly interest, the significance of the differences between the professional projects of academics and those of other occupational groups has not been sufficiently recognized.

A necessary first step, however, is to note that I define a profession by the special set of institutionalized occupational controls that regulate the means of entry, standards of practice, and competition both within an occupation and between that occupation and others.[2] It is further necessary to refine this definition, and the clearest and most useful means is to identify bachelors and/or advanced degrees from colleges and universities as entry requirements by which professions distinguished themselves from other occupations (e.g. trades) that also are formally controlled.

The successful professional projects were those that fastened onto the emerging university as the means to train and certify a standardized competence; and the most successful were those able to enforce graduate degrees as necessary vehicles for entry into the profession. Centralizing professional training in colleges and universities entailed struggling simultaneously against amateurism, apprenticeship systems, and proprietary schools. These struggles were more successful in some cases than in others, depending only in part on the character of the occupations, and the rewards for driving out amateurs and rival training systems were substantial for those in a position to reap them.

All of this, however, is only one side of the professional projects. Vesting training and certification in universities, monitored by professional associations, was possible and effective if and only if the resulting symbol of competence was honored by employers, clients, patients and other customers for the professional services. There is little point in controlling the supply of a quality service if the demand for that type of service is not ensured. This was a problem, because even though aspiring professional groups magnified and exploited people's fears and insecurities about health, social order, sex, race, and culture, they could not rely on the unprofessional public to respect the professional certificate to the proper extent.

If the public could not be adequately convinced, state legislatures were capable of being persuaded to enforce the needed recognition by closing off whole sets of activities to all but the certified.[3] In some cases, occupational licensing was the prior condition for raising standards, i.e., requiring college and university degrees. All levels of government contributed significantly to a considerable number of professional projects by creating demand for appropriately certified professionals, either directly by employing them or indirectly by creating procedures and requirements which forced others to employ them.

The drive for professionalization was a major impetus for the creation and expansion of the modern university and for the transformation of undergraduate colleges in the late 19th and early 20th centuries.[4] Not only did this expansion of higher education require more teachers, but the new importance attached to these institutions by aspiring professions and professionals meant that the functions of training and culling students required *qualified* educators. Thus academics were able to manipulate to their own advantage the same symbols of competence, merit, and specialization used by others.

Nevertheless, despite similar aspirations the leaders of the newly-founded national disciplinary associations conceived of their professional projects inharmoniously with the aspirations of students and non-academic professional groups: academics managed to define competence, merit, and specialization in terms appropriate for professionalizing *research* rather than teaching. As a consequence, teaching generally and undergraduate teaching in particular remain low status professional work.

It is no surprise, then, that the organization of disciplinary graduate programs, designed to train research professionals, began to influence undergraduate curricula as early as the late 19th century. During the early decades of the 20th century, undergraduate majors and minors rapidly constrained the elective system, which had already nurtured the development of disciplinary departments. This was a key step in the domination of the undergraduate curriculum by disciplinary professionalism, although the corresponding changes in administration did not occur until the 1930s.[5]

It is especially important to understand that in this process *each academic discipline* came to constitute a distinct professional body.[6] While adequate for some purposes, the usual "academic profession" category is too general to identify some of the most interesting features of academic professionalism.[7] Although disciplines were housed side by side in educational institutions and played similar roles in the preliminary training of nonacademic professionals, the disciplinary particularism of highly professionalized faculty members was already a strong trend in the 1920s and 1930s. By the late 1940s and early 1950s, the department had become the point of intersection between disciplines and institutions. The avenue of professional advance and recognition was outward from the department to national disciplinary associations, journals, and colleagues—far from students, class schedules, college committees, academic deans, and other irritating institutional demands that promised no professional payoffs. The proper role of the institution in this scheme of things (and one which institutions increasingly came to accept and encourage in order to enhance their reputations) was to support, honor, and compete for individuals whom disciplinary bodies had accorded professional recognition.[8]

The achievement of autonomy by disciplinary departments in colleges and universities required more influence than was available to fragmented disciplines. In the first decades of the 20th century, several national disciplinary associations vainly tried to establish the primacy of purely professional criteria in faculty personnel decisions, but their impotence was unequivocally demonstrated in some notorious cases of faculty firings.[9] Cooperation was clearly necessary to dilute the power of college and university administrations and governing boards. In 1913, representatives of the American Economic Association, the American Political Science Association, and the American Sociological Association took a preliminary step towards founding what emerged two years later as the American Association of University Professors (AAUP), encompassing all disciplines. The AAUP's central purpose was clearly expressed in the classic 1915 Report of its Committee on Academic Freedom and Tenure:

> The responsibility of the university teacher is primarily to the public itself, and to the judgment of his own profession; and while, with respect to certain conditions of his vocation, he accepts a responsibility to the authorities of the institution in which he serves, in the essentials of his professional activities his duty is to the wider public to which the institution itself is morally amenable.[10]

General civil libertarian convictions did influence the formation of the association; nevertheless, its central thrust was professional, reserving certain crucial realms (curriculum, research, and personnel) to the judgment of professionally certified competents—the disciplinary faculty. These professionals, and *not* administrators, trustees, or legislators, were seen to be the only qualified interpreters of the interests of the "wider public."

The political struggle by academics for professional autonomy within colleges and universities corresponds to the licensing efforts of other occupational groups, but in sharp contrast to the predominant situation in other professions, the employers of academic professionals are academic professionals. As soon as the AAUP's principles of academic freedom and tenure became general practice, it was professional historians, biologists, economists, philosophers, etc., who trained and subsequently hired new professional historians, biologists, economists, philosophers, etc. Thus, the demand for as well as the supply of certified professionals came under the immediate control of each disciplinary profession. As a consequence, there are no bases for continuing conflicts between professional associations and professional schools, nor is overt political intervention (e.g., licensing) required to ensure the market for the certificate. This almost pure form of professional colleague-orientation (as opposed to client-orientation) obscures the professional character of academic disciplines, even to academic disciplinarians.[11]

The professional model offers a much more satisfactory explanation for academic disciplines' evolving and overlapping intellectual content than do efforts to define disciplines by intellectual essence. The attempt to list distinctive intellectual characteristics of disciplines (e.g., subject matter, methodology, etc.) are directly analogous to the 1940s and 1950s scholarship on the sociology of the professions, in which so much effort went into defining professions by finding sets of traits specific to certain occupational activities.[12] While this approach has lost some favor in the sociology of professions, it seems to be alive and well in scholarship on academic disciplines, in spite of the trouble people have in applying it.[13]

Like the sociologists' traits of professions, such a definition of disciplines begins by implicitly accepting at face value disciplinary professionals' assessments of their own activities and worth. Moreover, such an approach consistently fails to represent accurately how disparate are the specialized activities which are lumped together under general rubrics like history, philosophy, sociology, and biology, or to discriminate adequately between, for example, astronomy and physics, mathematics and philosophy, historical sociology and social history, anthropology and sociology, and even economics and business administration. In a similar vein, are ecology, urban studies, American studies, and geography *really* disciplines? These problems are considerably less formidable when one considers academic disciplines to be primarily professions, a large part of whose activities center on controlling the supply of and creating demand for qualified practitioners.

The conception of academic disciplines as professions does not deny the distinctive intellectual character of academic disciplines; the various disciplines obviously do address different types of knowledge in different ways. Nor does this conception deny the progressive movement represented and furthered by the establishment of disciplinary professions in the late 19th and early 20th centuries.[14] It does suggest, however, that questions of each discipline's intellectual coherence and utility are important only to the extent that they serve the interest of research professionals. These interests require a definition of what a particular category of disciplinary professionals does, and the more sharply this line can be drawn around a specialized expertise, the more convincing a case can be made for those research professionals within the boundary. But even in the upper reaches of disciplinary professionalism, standards of precision have not been very high. Boundaries remain amorphous and subject to rapid redefinition when a growing field of inquiry, with promise of substantial employment and grant opportunities, looks as though it might fall outside the discipline. Occasionally these developments, whose genesis is seldom from within the academy, lead to the birth of a new discipline.

Definitions of disciplinary content are flexible, intellectually arbitrary, and change over time, but they do exist. The disciplinary departments of major universities are the principal arbiters of disputes about which side of the boundary particular questions, issues, methods, and views are located, and these departments exert a profound influence on what is or is not legitimate at a particular time. The curricula of the leading graduate departments are the nearest we have to explicit definitions of professional legitimacy.

Academic disciplines, therefore, are categories of knowledge fashioned by the interests of research professionalism. Even if one accepts current disciplinary categories as useful for research purposes, the substance of disciplines is intellectually arbitrary and pedagogically awkward for undergraduate education. *Disciplines simply were not developed to help undergraduates organize their thinking about the world,* and there is certainly nothing in their constitution to suggest that pedagogical usefulness has been an unexpected by-product. Yet undergraduate curricula continue to look like watered-down versions of graduate programs designed to train research professionals, even in colleges where the ethos of faculty research has always been weak.[15] Undergraduates' academic work is, by and large, an introduction to one or more disciplines, and disciplinary definitions prevail in discussions about such central educational principles as breadth, depth, coverage, and rigor.

In my opinion the research orientation of academic professionalism has had the most deleterious effect on undergraduate education through its influence on the organization and content of the liberal arts curriculum. This conclusion is significantly different from most critiques, which emphasize the academic reward system and the way it favors research activities at the expense of undergraduate teaching. The reward system is indeed strongly tilted towards research, but there are serious problems with making this argument the center of a critical analysis.[16]

An undue emphasis on the potent effects of research incentives necessarily carries with it the implication that those who are exclusively undergraduate teachers are not sufficiently smart, creative, or self-disciplined to succeed in research careers. This assessment comes from even critical commentators, who thereby accept the disciplinary professions' definition of who are the "best people" and bemoan the loss of these quality individuals to undergraduate instruction.[17] This tacit acceptance of conventional criteria of excellence results in an unwarranted undervaluing of the large numbers of talented men and women who are committed to undergraduate education and have chosen to make it the center of their careers. As soon as one acknowledges the peculiar and self-serving nature of the disciplinary professions' standards of faculty merit, there is no more reason to argue that the potentially most able undergraduate teachers are diverted away from undergraduate teaching. Nor is its equally dubious converse arguable: those who have made it to the very top of their disciplinary professions are precisely those least suited for effective undergraduate teaching.

Moreover, the empirical evidence consistently indicates patterns of faculty work in which teaching, and mostly undergraduate teaching, is the activity to which faculty devote by far the greatest amount of time and effort, irrespective of institutional type, faculty rank, gender, and discipline.[18] So, at least in terms of reported behavior, it appears that the effect of the biased reward system is not as important in directing faculty effort as might be thought.

The principal point is that independent of relative rewards, the overwhelming proportion of faculty committed to teaching undergraduates do their teaching in disciplinary curricula.

PROSPECTS FOR CHANGE

These implications are intrinsically important, and a clear interpretation of current practices is necessary for plausible speculation about future directions. For this speculation, I will rely on the fundamental elements of the professional model; the hegemony of disciplines in undergraduate curricula depends on the research orientation of academic professionalism, which in turn is based principally on institutional power relationships.

As I have already mentioned, the research ethos of disciplinary professionalism was already established, at least as a strong tendency, by the 1930s. But it was during the twenty-five years after World War II, with the rapid increase in enrollments, public faith in higher education as a means of upward mobility, large-scale research projects funded by public and private sources, and shortages of qualified faculty, that the place of academic disciplines was developed and crystalized.[19] To attribute this development and crystalization directly to these factors, however, analytically short-circuits the line of causation by missing the mediating linkage—the unparalleled rise of faculty power within institutions. Disciplinary professionalism was already sufficiently established. The shift in power, leading to greater faculty autonomy in matters of curriculum and personnel, resulted in its being expressed in the hegemony of academic disciplines.[20]

In predictable dialectical fashion, these changes also produced their own negations, principally in student revolts against the types of education they were receiving, the loss of public confidence, and the alternative institutions and programs most of us here represent. But the irony of the student reaction is that its most important consequence was to dismantle general education and breadth requirements. And while there probably was little educational loss associated with their demise, their abolition left the disciplinary major virtually unchallenged as the most coherent and systematic format of liberal education. Institutions and programs whose organizations were non-disciplinary or anti-disciplinary exercised, alas, very little influence on the direction of academic life, remaining rather polite alternatives to what continued to be the mainstream.

This perspective suggests that the research orientation of faculty professional life is likely to be severely challenged in the next couple of decades. As the number of academic job opportunities relative to certified professionals continues to decline (along with research funding), there are good reasons to expect that institutions will reassert their control over faculty work at the expense of disciplinary research emphases.

Growing faculty unionization may mitigate some of the effects of the shift of internal political power from faculty to administrators, but even this may not be of much help in retaining the hegemony of academic disciplines. Faculty unions are definitely not disciplinary organizations; like faculty senates, they can be most effective when they are perceived by their members to be neutral in respect to intra-institutional struggles among disciplinary groups. Moreover, the rise of collective bargaining on campuses is one of the contributing factors leading to changes in the character of college and university administrators. The need to deal with unions, chronic budgetary crises, and governmental regulations are already leading to the supplanting of faculty-oriented administrators by labor relations specialists, lawyers, fund raisers, financial experts, information specialists and others with similar skills.[21] The faculty, as a consequence, will have less direct influence over them than over their more academic predecessors, and this new breed of higher education manager will be considerably less sympathetic to or impressed by traditional symbols of institutional quality, a good number of which rely on a high degree of disciplinary professionalism.

Therefore, as the size, financial health, and even survival of more institutions become increasingly dependent on recruiting and retaining students from smaller cohorts and differing backgrounds, the terms of faculty-administration struggles are likely to shift towards accepting the principle that the faculty's primary responsibility is to design and implement instructional programs attractive to students.[22] Teaching and other client-oriented activities will become more vital facets of faculty work than publishing books and articles on issues whose major importance is internal to the disciplinary professions.

If we simply project current intra-institutional power relations into this new environment, one might expect a strenthening of disciplinary professionalism and an exacerbation of weighting research over teaching. Those arguing this conclusion can point to three important processes stemming from a sharp and sustained decline in the number of faculty positions: (1) Young people with Ph.D.s from elite universities will increasingly have to accept jobs lower down the institutional pecking order, thereby heightening disciplinary professionalism in places heretofore less affected by it. (2) As promotion and tenure opportunities continue to narrow, making standards more stringent, departments may well lean more heavily on the seemingly tangible criteria of scholarly publications than on difficult-to-assess teaching effectiveness. (3) Financial pressures on institutions will enable ("require") disciplinary faculty and academic administrators to jettison parts of the curriculum which are not of "core" disciplinary stature.

I am not denying the effect of these forces, and we can see them operating now. Nonetheless, I believe that they are short-run and will be transformed by changing configurations of power within institutions. The stark fact is that colleges and universities will have to cater to students rather than to faculty, and it is extremely doubtful that research-oriented disciplinary professionalism is going to have much influence in institutional changes during the next two decades. Trustees, state legislators, and, above all, administrators are going to be setting the directions in this new context, particularly if faculty try to retain professional work patterns.

Colleges and universities in the United States, compared to those in other nations, have always been sensitive to changing consumer demands, but we will see something new in this regard; instead of change coming by expanding into new areas, as in 1880–1930 and 1945–1970, colleges and universities will try to reallocate resources to meet the interests of a changing type of student. This will lay bare the conflicts of interests between students and professionalized faculty at a time when the faculty market position is very weak, institutions' need for students is very strong, and the availability of public fiscal resources is, at best, uncertain.

This pressure will no doubt be felt most strongly in those institutions lower down in the standard rankings of quality, but it certainly will not be restricted to them. Even at the very top, major universities will continue to be squeezed by reduced governmental research funds and the difficulty of finding positions for their graduate students, but pressures will be considerably less harsh on these few institutions. This form of professionalism, therefore, may survive more or less intact in some elite universities and colleges, but without followers, these leading institutions' disciplinary professionalism may simply become an artifact of an earlier era.

THE PLACE OF ALTERNATIVE COLLEGES

From my reading of current trends, I believe that there are at least three areas in which alternative colleges must improve their performance if they are to survive the next two or three decades with integrity to their principles and meeting their responsibilities to students and society.

1. It is imperative that we refine our thinking about the intellectual and pedagogical purposes of interdisciplinary education. If my projections have any validity, we will see the rise of interdisciplinary courses and programs throughout higher education, especially tailored to what are perceived to be the interests of particular segments of potential students. The chances are, however, that these endeavors will not be of the type in which most of us desired to be involved when we chose to go to an alternative institution. The unfortunate fact is that we as a group have done a very poor job in articulating the purposes of interdisciplinary teaching. With the notable exception of St. Johns, most of our presentations of interdisciplinary purposes have not gone beyond the argument of "coverage:" that is, the contention that disciplines overemphasize specialized rigor at the expense of breadth, and that there exist important lumps of information which have fallen into the cracks between disciplines.[23] There have always been a number of serious problems with this argument:

a. It not only reifies disciplines, it portrays them inaccurately. When sociologists, historians, philosophers, anthropologists, biologists, physicists, geographers, and many, many others convincingly demonstrate how such a portrayal seriously misrepresents the range of legitimate work within their disciplines, and rigor has already been conceded, this case for interdisciplinary education is not especially compelling.

b. The pedagogical consequences of this "coverage" rationale are based on the same positivistic conceptions of knowledge as most disciplines are, and therefore this line of argument supports the disciplinary style of pedagogy: the teacher as authority filling empty students with information and techniques. This promotes unfortunate habits of mind among students, who too easily accept their prescribed role as passive consumers of objectified knowledge.[24]

I believe that alternative colleges must break out of the organizational forms and pedagogical practices consistent with positivistic conceptions of knowledge, and in doing so become true alternatives to conventional conceptions of education.

2. Faculty at alternative institutions are in the best position to demonstrate that undergraduate teaching is first and foremost an intellectual

activity and to show that it can and should be the principal basis for professional growth. Good teachers are made, not born, but the converse proposition has for too long supported the ideology of disciplinary professionalism and the reluctance to consider teaching as a serious part of professional development.[25] Are some types of curricula more conducive to teaching development than others? I suspect so, but there has been very little effort to discuss this in systematic ways.

Closely related to the above, it is important to show that any instructional development effort which implicitly assumes that the *content* of teaching is either fixed or not of central importance offers neither a feasible nor desirable conception of faculty development.

3. In a curriculum in which the principal intention is to develop habits of interesting, systematic, and independent thinking, the distinction between "liberal" and "pre-professional" education is irrelevant. This supposedly qualitative distinction between types of education possessed only a dubious validity when it was used by nineteenth century proponents of the classical curriculum in their struggle against the incursion of the disciplines, and now it is virtually empty of meaning. Undergraduate major curricula in liberal arts disciplines make sense only in terms of their decisive preprofessional nature. The remainder of students' study programs are made up of breadth requirements, formulated through political compromises among disciplinary departments, and for the most part rely on introductory disciplinary courses and electives, which can be chosen on the same bases by any student, liberal arts or not. Nevertheless, much of the debate about higher education seems to have been cast in this false dichotomy, and we in alternative colleges ought to be able to use it to our advantage.

* * * * *

While my prescriptions are slanted in very specific ways, my major conclusion is that alternative colleges cannot afford to remain mere "alternatives" in the next few decades. Although probably in a variety of ways, we all will have to take the very risky step of defining ourselves as critics of conventional forms of higher education, a step we have too long been reluctant to take. I realize that this will entail even more work for faculty and administrators in institutions whose major unifying characteristic is overwork, but our place in higher education now requires that we aggressively demonstrate to all that our institutions are definitely not merely places for students and faculty who cannot make it in the mainstream. We represent very different, active visions of higher education, and along with that, correspondingly different visions of the society in which we will live in the next few decades.

NOTES

1. Burton J. Bledstein, *The Culture of Professionalism: The Middle Class and the Development of Higher Education* (New York: W. W. Norton, 1976), Magali Sarfatti Larson, *The Rise of Professionalism: A Sociological Analysis* (Berkeley and Los Angeles: University of California Press, 1977), especially pp. 104–207, and Thomas L. Haskell, *The Emergence of Professional Social Science: The American Social Science Association and the Nineteenth-Century Crisis of Authority* (Urbana, Ill.: University of Illinois Press, 1977) are important interpretations of the historical relationship between higher education and professionalization.

2. See Terence M. Johnson, *Professions and Power* (London: McMillan, 1972), pp. 43–45, for this definition of profession.

3. *Occupational Licensing Legislation in the United States* (Chicago: Council of State Governments, 1952), pp. 23 and 78–80 are valuable tables, showing occupational licensing by occupation, state, and date.

4. Three especially useful sources on the organizational and intellectual changes in higher education during the last century are Laurence R. Veysey, *The Emergence of the American University* (Chicago: University of Chicago Press, 1965); Christopher Jencks and David Riesman, *The Academic Revolution* (Garden City, N.Y.: Doubleday, 1968); and Alexandra M. Oleson and John Voss (eds.), *The Organization of Knowledge in Modern America, 1860–1920* (Baltimore: Johns Hopkins University Press, 1979).

5. In addition to the citations in footnote #4, see Frederick Rudolph, *Curriculum: A History of the American Undergraduate Course of Study Since 1636* (San Francisco: Jossey-Bass for the Carnegie Council on Policy Studies in Higher Education, 1977), pp. 202–244.

In the 1930s, the central position of disciplinary departments was acknowledged and made administratively rational by gathering groups of them into divisions. Laurence Veysey, "The Humanities in American Universities Since the 1930's: The Decline of Grandiosity" (Santa Cruz, Calif.: mimeo) is a provocative study of the least coherent of these new units.

6. The visual and performing arts are the newest and least professionalized of the liberal arts disciplines, and they are constantly subject to criticism about standards from colleagues in more established disciplinary professions. For a good discussion of the place of visual and performing arts in higher education, see James S. Ackerman, "The Arts in Higher Education," in Carl Kaysen (ed.), *Content and Context: Essays on College Education* (New York: McGraw-Hill for the Carnegie Commission on Higher Education, 1973), pp. 219–266.

7. Most of the works cited in the earlier footnotes refer to an undifferentiated "academic profession". For other examples of this, see Harold L. Wilensky, "The Professionalization of Everyone?" *American Journal of Sociology*, Vol. 70, #3 (September 1970), p. 141, and the articles collected in Walter P. Metzger (ed.), *Reader in the Sociology of the Academic Profession* (New York: Arno Press, 1977). A partial exception is Peter M. Blau, *The Organization of Acadmic Work* (New York: Wiley, 1973), p. 12, who uses conventional sociological criteria and tentatively concludes that disciplines might be professions.

8. Donald W. Light, Jr., "The Structure of the Academic Professions," *Sociology of Education*, Vol. 47, #3 (Winter 1974), pp. 2–28 [also included in Metzger's anthology, *Reader in the Sociology of the Academic Profession*] is a clear statement of this character of the disciplinary department in colleges and universities. Additional useful works on this are P. H. Dressel and D. J. Reichard, "The University Department: Retrospect and Prospect,"

Journal of Higher Education, Vol. 41 (May 1970), pp. 387–402; R. Straus, "Departments and Disciplines: Stasis and Change," *Science* (November 30, 1973), pp. 895–897; and the concise expression of different opinions by the first four contributors in Dean E. McHenry (ed.), *Academic Departments: Problems, Variations, and Alternatives* (San Francisco: Jossey-Bass, 1977), pp. 1–62.

9. The principal source on this subject is Walter P. Metzger, "The Age of the University," in R. Hofstadter and W. P. Metzger, *The Development of Academic Freedom in the United States* (New York: Columbia University Press, 1965), pp. 407–605.

10. Metzger, "The Age of the University," p. 409.

11. In a frequently reprinted article, Reuben A. Kessel, "Price Discrimination in Medicine," *Journal of Economics and Law*, Vol. 1 (October 1958), pp. 20–53, argues that the patterns of medical practice made the cultural homogeneity of physicians important for coordinating and maintaining their professional monopoly in the national market. Therefore, there were tangible pecuniary reasons for making it more difficult for anyone who was not a white Protestant male from an upper-middle class background to enter the profession. It is somewhat surprising that the peculiar type of market control exercised by disciplinary professionals in the academy did not enable them to be considerably bolder in opening their professions to others.

12. Johnson, *Professions and Power*, pp. 22–23, cogently criticizes the traits approach in scholarship on professions. This approach is older than functionalism in sociological theory and should be considered as an important forerunner of it. For the congruence of these conceptions, compare the formulation in Alexander Flexner's address to the National Conference on Social Welfare in 1915, entitled "Is Social Work a Profession?" and published in *The Social Welfare Forum: Official Proceedings* (1915), pp. 576–590, with the functionalist classic by Kingsley Davis and Wilbert Moore, "Some Principles of Stratification," *The American Sociological Review*, Vol. 10, #2 (1945), pp. 242–249.

13. The difficulties of trying to identify disciplines by internal intellectual characteristics are discussed and illustrated by Jonathan Broido, "Interdisciplinarity, Reflections on Methodology", in J. J. Kockelmans (ed.), *Interdisciplinarity and Higher Education* (Penn State Pa.: Pennsylvania State University Press, 1979), pp. 244–305, and Charles B. Fethe, "A Philosophical Model for Interdisciplinary Programs," *Liberal Education*, Vol. 59, #4 (December 1973), pp. 490–497.

14. The rise of research and the academic disciplines was instrumental in giving colleges and universities their current intellectual definition and purpose. We can argue about the extent to which this has actually been realized, but certainly compared to early nineteenth century institutions, in which classes were devoted mostly to students' recitations of memorized texts and faculty were recent graduates desperately trying to maintain a semblance of discipline inside and outside the classrooms, modern higher education institutions appear intellectually very serious. A large part of this change is due to the professionalization of the faculty through disciplinary training. In addition to the citations in footnote #1, Oscar and Mary Handlin, *The American College and American Culture: Socialization as a Function of Higher Education* (New York: McGraw-Hill Book Co. for the Carnegie Commission on Higher Education, 1970), pp. 5–42, describe the strongly non-intellectual character of older colleges in the U.S.

15. Rustrum Roy, "Interdisciplinary Science on Campus", in Kochelmans (ed.), *Interdisciplinarity and Higher Education*, pp. 163–166, and Neil J. Smelser, "The Social Sciences", in Kaysen (ed.), *Content and Context*, pp. 129–144, discuss this influence on undergraduate curricula in different areas of study.

16. See Blau, *The Organization of Academic Work*, p. 106; Carol Herrnstadt Shulman, *Old Expectations, New Realities: The Academic Profession Revisited*, AAHE-ERIC/Higher Education Research Report, No. 2, 1979 (Washington, D.C.: AAHE, 1979), pp. 26–35: and Howard P. Tuckman, *Publication, Teaching, and the Academic Reward Structure* (Lexington, Ma.: Lexington Books, 1976), pp. 70–94, for the pattern of rewards favoring research.

17. For instance, this form of criticism is predominant in the introductory essays in McHenry, *Academic Departments,* pp. 1–62.

18. J. Victor Baldridge, et al, *Policy Making and Effective Leadership* (San Francisco: Jossey-Bass, 1978), pp. 102–110 and Shulman, *Old Expectations, New Realities,* pp. 26–28 report such findings from a variety of surveys.

19. Baldridge, et al, *Policy Making and Effective Leadership,* p. 95, discusses the influence of these forces on strengthening disciplines after World War II.

20. Shulman, *Old Expectations, New Realities,* pp. 9–10, relying mostly on Ladd's and Lipset's surveys, argues that the rise in faculty salaries and general status during this period attracted to the professoriate young people from higher social strata than had previously been the case, thus reducing the extent to which college and university teaching was a means of upward social mobility. It is also likely that those from more privileged backgrounds contributed to developing the occupation's professional trappings. Blau, *The Organization of Academic Work,* pp. 95–99, shows that elite colleges and universities exhibited class bias in the recruitment of their faculty.

21. Baldridge, et al, *Policy Making and Effective Leadership,* pp. 208–209, discuss these changes in the character of administrators. Also in these pages, they observe that the shift of the faculty, responding to student preferences, towards professional teachers of professional and vocational subjects will increase the segment of the faculty which has been the most politically quiescent in campus affairs.

22. The final report of the Carnegie Commission on Policy Studies in Higher Education, entitled *Three Thousand Futures: The Next 20 Years for Higher Education* (1980) states that "Students will be recruited more actively, admitted more readily, retained more assiduously, counseled more attentively, graded more considerately, financed more adequately, taught more conscientiously . . . The curriculum will be more tailored to their tastes . . . This may well become their Golden Age." Quoted in *The Chronicle of Higher Education* (January 28, 1980), p. 11.

23. Donald J. Campbell, "Ethnocentrism of Disciplines and the Fish Scale Model of Omniscience," in M. S. and C. W. Sherif (eds.), *Interdisciplinary Relations in the Social Sciences* (Chicago: Aldine, 1969), pp. 328–348, Carl R. Hausman, "Introduction: Disciplinarity or Interdisciplinarity?" in Kockelmans (ed.), *Interdisciplinarity and Higher Education,* pp. 1–10, and Tamara Swora and James Morrison, "Interdisciplinarity and Higher Education," *Liberal Education,* Vol. 60, #1 (April 1974), pp. 45–52, perceive interdisciplinary education in terms of coverage.

24. Philip Phenix, "The Use of the Disciplines as Curriculum Content," *Educational Forum,* Vol. 26, #3 (March 1962), pp. 273–280, clearly exposes these epistemological premises: "The structure of things is revealed, not invented . . . *given,* not chosen, and if man is to gain insight he must employ the right concepts and methods . . . [Therefore], disciplines are the only proper source of the curriculum." (p. 280, emphasis in original).

Drawing heavily from Freire and Habermas, Vincent C. Kavaloski, "Interdisciplinary Education and Humanistic Aspiration," in Kockelmans (ed.), *Interdisciplinarity and Higher Education,* pp. 224–243, is an excellent criticism of this position.

25. E.g., Laurence Veysey, "Stability and Experiment in the American Undergraduate Curriculum," in Kaysen (ed.), *Content and Context,* p. 61.

Hans O. Mauksch, "What Are the Obstacles to Improving Quality Teaching?" *Current Issues in Higher Education,* Vol. 2, No. 1 (September 3, 1980), pp. 49–56, makes an excellent case for reversing current practices and considering teaching as an essential type of professional development.

II. Disciplinary Professionalism: Second View

by

JEANNE HAHN

I shall not take issue with Weaver's broad argument on the nature of academic disciplines as "categories of knowledge fashioned by the interests of research professionalism," nor shall I take issue with his position that "the research orientation of academic professionalism has had the most deleterious effect on undergraduate education through its influence on the organization and content of the liberal arts curriculum." I shall, however, draw a different conclusion from these arguments. I disagree with Weaver's position that as changing power configurations within the university transform the nature of disciplinary teaching and attempt to meet the needs of a changing type of student, research-oriented disciplinary professionalism will wane in the undergraduate curriculum.

My argument is based on certain assumptions regarding a continuing era of limits and retrenchment in the larger economy and their reflection in changes in the internal landscape of higher education. If one focuses on the forces of this generalized economic crisis and the impact they are likely to have on the structure of higher education, one arrives at conclusions somewhat different than those of Weaver. However, like Weaver, I view higher education as a contested arena, in which a number of important contradictory trends are at work. The argument here is that the long-term trend likely to emerge from this contestation will be different from that posited in Weaver's essay.

I shall take the position that as the academic depression deepens—as the financial base of higher education erodes and as enrollments fall—the traditional mechanisms of disciplinary professionalism and departmental hegemony will reassert themselves. Tendencies in this direction can already be seen in the substantial number of innovative programs and "inner" colleges, produced by the education boom of the 1960s, that have closed or been absorbed by traditional departments over the past few years.[1] This trend is likely to accelerate during the 1980s. As the larger economy remains crisis-prone, students will be less inclined toward interdisciplinary and innovative curricula and will increasingly prefer disciplinary-based and professionally-oriented programs, programs that have some seemingly identifiable relation to the job market.

I will suggest that revolutions in the structure of higher education, most particularly in its substantive curriculum and teaching methodology, are more likely to occur in times of expansion and optimism than in times of contraction and retreat. I shall further attempt to show that there is a direct link between the present stagflation crisis in the economy and the retrenchment crisis in higher education, and that together they work to incline toward more traditional department-based, skill-oriented education. Finally, I will argue that this tendency has led (and will continue to lead) to the erosion or closure of innovative programs and to the reassertion of old patterns within established colleges. If I am correct, it is likely that "alternative" education institutions whose entire curriculum and educational philosophy are organized on other than departmental lines are more likely to survive the current trend that are inner colleges or experimental programs within the traditionally-organized college.

The economic boom period from the end of World War II to the late 1960s, with its attendant levels of relatively high productivity and relatively low levels of inflation and unemployment, was reflected in the structure and content of higher education. As in the rest of the economy, higher education experienced a period of expansion and increased state investment, both in the growth of institutions and in the training of ever larger numbers of new faculty to meet the demands of rising enrollments. Under the stimulus of an environment of economic prosperity and expansion higher education underwent a number of significant changes in the United States. Those changes resulted from increased enrollments from categories of entrants new to higher education (racial and ethnic minorities, women, working-class students) and, toward the end of the growth years, from the baby boom population. We saw a liberalization of the curriculum in order to meet the interests and demands of students previously excluded from higher education as well as those of students who, feeling the blush of economic prosperity, demanded more than the traditional department-bound professionally-oriented course format.

Colleges and universities, blessed with heretofore unprecedented levels of public and private sources of money, responded positively to the demands of many faculty and students for a broadened and liberalized curriculum and raised the expectations of those formerly excluded from higher education. Increasingly, this meant interdisciplinary and extradepartmental methods of study. In this environment of overall expansion and growth, these moves beyond disciplinary orthodoxy were not viewed as substantial threats to the power and influence of the traditional disciplines. This was also a period in which scientific research, technical knowledge, and the development of professional technicians and managers to fill a growing number of positions became increasingly significant. This surge toward professionalism and scientific/technical development—all well funded by the state—allowed the traditional disciplines not only to maintain, but to increase, their hegemony within the academy. These two movements could exist simultaneously as long as the prosperity continued, enrollments remained high, and funding plentiful.

In assessing the long-term implications, it is important to underscore the point that most of the curricular innovations came at the height of institutional growth and were thus instituted as add-ons rather than as structural reforms in the curriculum. Further, those programs developed outside the established departmental structure were rarely accorded departmental status and hence did not have the institutional power base to become significant long-term actors in the determination of academic policy. The add-on and non-departmentalized character of these innovations, taken together with the continued growth and further professionalization of the core of most of the disciplines, meant that the innovations posed little long-run threat to the professionally-organized and departmentally-administered dominance of the traditional disciplines. When the college-wide cutbacks began in the late 1970s, these programs found it difficult to maintain themselves.

A typical example of the fate of a large number of these innovative programs and the differential treatment accorded to those developed as add-ons without an institutional power base can be drawn from the experiences of the Centennial Education Program at the University of Nebraska (Lincoln) and the Goodrich Scholarship Program at the University of Nebraska (Omaha).[2] Centennial College was established in 1967 as an interdisciplinary living/learning cluster college and was closed at the end of the 1981 academic year. Centennial did not operate through the normal department chair-dean-provost chain of authority; it reported directly to the vice chancellor. As a college it had no faculty of its own, could not tenure faculty, and was increasingly staffed by non-tenured hires or those denied tenure in their departments. When University-wide budget cuts began in 1977, Centennial was hardest hit, despite high enrollments. With no vested interest in the maintenance of Centennial, all of the various deans at the University put it at the top of their recommended "cut" list. These cuts continued from 1977 until 1981 when the college was finally closed.

On the other side, the Goodrich Scholarship Program, established in 1972 to provide a two-year core curriculum and four years of scholarship support for economically disadvantaged students, has remained a vital part of the Nebraska curriculum. This program was, in effect, established as a department within the College of Public Administration and Community Service, a college headed by its own dean. In addition, its students received four-year scholarships and all the support services of the University, which further tied the Program to the university apparatus. Its faculty were tenured both in the Program and at the University, thus providing them a double security enjoyed at few colleges. When the 1977 budget cuts came, the Goodrich Program was little affected.

That the end of the long postwar boom in the early 1970s has had its effects on the structure of higher education is beyond debate. A major premise underlying my argument is that both the short- and the long-term prospects for disciplinary professionalization and alternative higher education are best understood when analyzed within the context of these long waves of prosperity and crisis.[3]

For my short-term argument, the most significant change in the internal landscape of higher education has been the deepening academic depression—in terms of the simultaneous fiscal and enrollment crises—and its relation to the systemic political, economic and social crisis faced by the entire society. The tendencies of the previous boom period, having established themselves as increasingly serious but not yet critical challenges to the orthodox disciplines, will give way to current political and economic realities, and the old structures will reassert themselves. However, having experienced some serious structural and substantive challenges in the organization and presentation of knowledge, and facing different structural arrangements in the larger society, the new academic landscape will not resemble the *status quo ante*. The reassertion of disciplinary dominance will be shaped by a convergence of student demands driven largely by market forces, by attempts to deal with the impact of the fiscal crisis, and by imperatives from the political and economic climate. At the same time, countertendencies exist which suggest a continuing struggle over the shape and content of the undergraduate curriculum.

As college enrollments continue to decline and departments compete for fewer students, the diversity that began to emerge in the 1960s and early 1970s is being increasingly squeezed out in a quest for internal unity. While making its cutbacks under the rubric of fiscal exigency, each discipline will likely attempt to reassert its methodological and professional hegemony by purifying its department of dissenting and methodologically unorthodox members and by restricting the scope of interdisciplinary teaching allowed within and between departments. This move will be legitimized by the "retrenchment" in higher education and the "back to basics" trends, both of which clearly threaten those programs and those faculty not protected by department structures and/or tenure.

Within the conventional college or university a large portion of the interdisciplinary and alternative curriculum is found either outside the departmental structure and/or taught by untenured and often part-time faculty. For example, in women's studies, one of the largest and most interdisciplinary areas of growth through the 1960s and early 1970s, half the teachers hold only part-time appointments.[4] In addition, unable to compete for budget allocations on the same footing as the established departments, the low funding of many women's studies programs forces them to hire the lowest cost teachers.[5] Interdisciplinary and extra-departmental programs and courses of this sort have also relied heavily upon untenured gypsy faculty, hired specifically to meet these needs and often on clearly-specified one- or two-year terminal contracts. These faculty find themselves in a doubly weak position: The programs into which they have been hired give them no bargaining power within the institution and little or no hope of tenured status; and they are called upon to teach in the most innovative and non-traditional areas of the curriculum while the reality of the academic job market is such that research, performance, and publication in an established and departmentally-recognized discipline are the primary means of advancement.[6] Those tenured faculty who do teach in these programs are most often department-based, released on the sufferance of their department chair and subject to recall. These faculty members' reward structures (sabbaticals, teaching assignments and schedules, salary recommendations and promotions, access to discretionary funds, etc.) continue through the department which is where they understandably feel compelled to place their primary institutional loyalty.

These circumstances have led to something of a caste division within higher education faculty, a division in which those with tenure, a departmental basis, professional status, and institutional power are increasingly divided from those who teach in the non-departmentalized, less institutionally powerful portions of the curriculum and who themselves are without the bargaining power that goes with tenure, professional security, and departmental support. Added to this caste division is the overall deterioration of faculty position, perhaps most clearly illustrated by the virtual collapse of the faculty labor market in all but a few fields. The Carnegie Commission indicates that the level of net faculty additions will remain at its current level—about zero—or below for much of the remainder of this century.[7] The increasing age of tenured faculty will further aggrevate the caste division, making it ever more difficult to introduce new programs and new innovations both inside and outside the departmental structure. The magnitude of this problem can be appreciated by considering tenure ratios which have risen from 50 percent in 1969 to 75 percent ten years later.[8]

While the above tendencies will work to reinforce the organization and dissemination of knowledge as defined by the traditional disciplines and administered through the departmental structure at the expense of innovative and interdisciplinary curricula, it should be fairly clear that in the long run they also work to undermine the power of the departments vis-a-vis the college administration and to increase the marginality of all faculty in the life of the college. As department chairpersons increasingly become administrators first and faculty members second and as the college governance system becomes more explicitly modeled after the methods of modern business management, all faculty lose a certain amount of control over the curriculum, to say nothing about other matters of traditional faculty prerogative. On this point Weaver and I are in agreement. My major disagreement regards the degree of significance Weaver attaches to the intra-institutional power struggle between disciplinary-oriented faculty and administrative control over the curriculum. I believe the struggle is wider and symptomatic of broader changes in the social system and that while there clearly has been and will continue to be a shift of internal political power from faculty to administration, departments will continue to monitor disciplinary orthodoxy and assert major control over the curriculum.

As the general economic situation worsens and as state expenditures are trimmed further, those programs and faculty considered frills to what in the post World War II period has increasingly become the task of postsecondary education—producing workers trained to meet the changing needs of the labor market[9]—will be eliminated in favor of a more "practical" curriculum. This trimming will also serve to protect departmentally-defined faculty jobs in a tight faculty labor market. In light of these economic and labor-related imperatives, the tendency in most departments and in the curricula they offer will be toward increasing specialization designed to produce professionals (in the four-year colleges) and technical workers (in the community colleges) for increasingly specific job opportunities. This, in turn, will mean that many of the struggles of the 1960s and early 1970s to transform departments and/or the college curriculum so as to speak to the needs of third world, women, and minority students will be lost as these special programs are dismantled and the faculty who taught in them are let go.[10]

An example of the impact of this financial crisis and the response of the college administration can be seen by a look at the $13.5 million reduction in the 1981–82 academic budget of the Michigan State University and at those academic programs most directly affected by the cuts.[11] While the 81–82 Michigan cuts are perhaps deeper than those in most states the cuts themselves exhibit an increasingly familiar pattern in higher education. Two special programs—Lyman Briggs, a residential college established in 1967 with a mandate to provide an integrated, "liberal" education for science students and the College of Urban Development—were eliminated entirely. James Madison College, a residential college with a curriculum oriented toward public affairs and originally targeted for elimination by the board of trustees, was severely trimmed. A fourth college, Nursing, was also slated for elimination; but strong opposition from legislators, professional associations, and other nursing schools resulted in its retention.

While eliminating and cutting non-departmentalized, nontraditional aspects of the curriculum, the budget

> "gave priority to traditional undergraduate and graduate curricula, to the university's land-grant mission, and to professional areas with the most student interest. The budgets of the three 'core' colleges—arts and letters, natural science, and social science—were cut by about 10 percent, and those for agriculture, business, communications, and engineering by between 5 and 8 percent."[12]

These sorts of reductions, and the power struggles that accompany them, are likely to spread to most state colleges and universities and to continue throughout the 1980s.

Institutions of higher education are in the process of retrenchment and of reassessment of their missions to meet changing political, economic, and social realities. Elimination of inner colleges and experimental and innovative interdisciplinary programs is part of this process. Directly affected will be the white, affluent student who, finding the range of extradepartmental and interdisciplinary options narrowed, will nevertheless in all probability remain in college. This is not, however, likely to be an option for many in the other large group of students affected by the innovations of the 1960s. While there is much concern and discussion over the prospect of declining enrollments throughout the remainder of the century due to the passage of the baby-boom generation through its college years, little attention has been given to the fact that sharply rising tuition, cutbacks in student loans and grants, increased student fees, and enrollment lids—all policy decisions based on financial considerations—also serve to reduce enrollment. In this case, it is enrollment of those least able to pay the higher tuitions, or to get by without loans or grants, which will be reduced. This will mean that those very people to whom much of the alternative curriculum of the late 60s and early 70s spoke, people of color, ethnic minorities, working class students, and women resuming interrupted educations, will be frozen out of a college education. For example, in Washington State the restrictive enrollment lids for the 1981–82 academic year fall much more heavily on the community colleges, which had been exceeding their contracted enrollments, than on the state's four-year colleges and universities. It should be clear who it is that these lids and their accompanying tuition hikes will most directly affect.[13]

This enforced decline in enrollment with its class-specific effect is not incompatible with changing employment opportunities in the labor market. Ernest Mandel's 1975 observation on the nature of the labor market will continue valid through the eighties to century's end: "What capital needs is not a large number of highly-qualified intellectual workers. It needs an increasing but limited quantity of intellectual producers equipped with specific qualifications and with specific tasks to fulfill in the process of production and circulation."[14] This changing job structure and the sort of worker it requires are not compatible with the innovative and interdisciplinary curricula with their stress on critical questioning, analytical ability, and the systematic investigation of broad questions. It is, however, compatible with the clearly specified and vocationally-oriented curriculum which is increasingly found in the four-year as well as the community college. As early as 1973 the Carnegie Commission in its *Final Report* recommended some restriction in access to four-year higher education and the simultaneous expansion of two-year community colleges. The argument was that these would meet market needs and not develop in students the critical faculties and "all roundedness" of the traditional curriculum.[15] So when Weaver argues that "colleges and universities will try to reallocate contracting resources to meet the interests of a changing type of student," it is a student whose "interests" are in very large part shaped by structural changes in the job market and by a narrowing range of employment opportunities which are increasingly demanding of specialized degrees.

Weaver suggests that new student-defined interests combined with a weakened faculty market position will lead to a further deterioration of faculty power vis-a-vis the administration and to a diminishment of the ability of disciplines to assert their professional orientation over the curriculum. While agreeing with this general tendency, I maintain that Weaver has not sufficiently explored the source of these new student interests.

Students' educational demands as well as the college curriculum have responded quite quickly to structural changes in the economy. The Carnegie Foundation for the Advancement of Teaching found that professional and vocational majors among undergraduates rose from 40 to 60 percent between 1969 and 1975,[16] and "by 1975, 95 percent of American undergraduates considered training and skills for an occupation to be either essential or fairly important goals for their college education."[17] The Council goes on to report:

> "When undergraduates were asked what was most essential for them to get out of a college education in 1969, learning to get along with people and formulating values and goals for their lives were ranked first and second. Seven years later, these desires were outranked by getting a detailed grasp of a special field and obtaining training and skills for an occupation. Three-quarters of freshmen report that they are attending college in order to get a better job.
>
> The single most obvious result of this emerging 'vocomania' is that students' enrollment patterns have changed. Among subject areas, the big gainers are business, the health professions, biology (the gateway to medical school), agriculture, and other technical fields. Nearly a quarter of all freshmen intend to major in business, which is at the top of the heap; this represents nearly a 50 percent increase relative to 1969. The big losers have been the least occupationally useful fields—education, the humanities, and several of the social sciences."[18]

In addition, the Council's data indicate that undergraduates are spending more time studying their majors—"between 1967 and 1974, the proportion of credits students were taking in their area of concentration increased from 44 to 58 percent"[19]—and less time on electives and general education credits. The Council suggests that without distribution requirements this situation would have been even more pronounced, "since 41 percent of college students feel current degree requirements restrict them from taking as many courses in their major as they would like."[20] Given developments in the overall economy, with its aggravated conditions of stagflation and an increasingly tight and specified job market for college graduates, it seems likely that this trend has increased since the Council's 1974 report and will continue throughout the remainder of the century.

The curriculum has accommodated this increased student interest in specialization, largely through departmental majors, without major student agitation (in contrast to the agitation accompanying the loosening of the curriculum in the 1960s). Again, the Carnegie Commission:

> "On the face of it, the poverty of undergraduate preparation, the race for jobs, the competitive atmosphere on campus, and the pressure for grades would seem to make college a dreadful experience for today's students. Not so. They are more satisfied with college than the students of the 1960s, who also were extremely satisfied. A majority of the undergraduates of the 1970s report being satisfied with college in general, with their majors, with their teaching, and even with the mechanics of grading.
>
> "The student of the 1970s is more traditional in academic values than the undergraduate of the last decade and is less interested in seeing things change. The demands of the 1960s for greater relevance, the abolition of grading requirements, and more attention to student emotional growth are less popular among students now. Fewer believe that less emphasis should be placed on specialized training in favor of a broad liberalized education or that teaching effectiveness rather than research should be the primary criterion for faculty promotion."[21]

As the undergraduate curriculum becomes more specialized and technical, as the segmentation of postsecondary education continues to develop a tracking system designed to reproduce the class structure and labor market needs, from elite professionals to vocationally-trained white collar and technical workers,[22] super/subordination in the classroom will likely increase. The transmission of knowledge in this fashion not only encourages students to fragment and compartmentalize their learning but it discourages them from thinking abstractly, analytically, and critically. In other words, it fails to equip students with the habits of mind necessary to act positively on large social issues, which are increasingly being seen to cut across all dimensions of social life. At the same time, the organization of the typical college classroom, the nature and transmission of knowledge within it, the testing and grading of students, and the tight labor market in which "desirable" jobs will be fewer and more difficult to obtain create a set of social relations among students reproductive of the larger society in which they will take their places. Competition for a scarce commodity—the few "good" grades which often become the currency, translated into a "spendable" GPA, necessary for the desirable job or the slot in the graduate or professional program—fosters individualism, lack of cooperation, hording of information, and, once the grades are distributed, invidious comparison of intellectual and even social worth.

My argument to this point leads to the conclusion that throughout the remainder of the century traditional academic departments will continue as the primary mechanism for organizing and administering knowledge within the academy. The thrust of the disciplines will continue to be increasingly directed toward more specialized and technical knowledge. The student experience will become more fragmented and dehumanized. This tendency seems clear to me. Yet it is not to say that those student and faculty initiatives of the late 1960s and early 1970s to break out of the confines of narrow specialization, to create learning situations that foster critical thinking, to establish courses and programs that call the conventional wisdom into question, have been extinguished. There are countertendencies that challenge and disrupt the new situation, and these countertendencies will continue to make the arena of higher education one of conflict and contestation. While the educational system plays a primary role in reproducing and extending those conditions necessary for continued capitalist accumulation and the attitudes and values necessary for continued capitalist hegemony, the university and professional disciplines which make up its academic core are not simply instruments of the imperatives of advanced capitalism. They retain a degree of relative autonomy that keeps open a sphere of critical discourse.

Furthermore, fundamental contradictions in the larger society, particularly the transformation of work which increasingly proletarianizes and bureaucratizes the sons and daughters of the middle class at the very time the college curriculum held out promise for greater self-determination, find their analogues as well as their points of opposition and protest in the university. Educational goals of autonomy, creativity, and self-definition, which have their counterparts in the larger ideology of liberalism, come increasingly into conflict with the conditions of work which are often repetitive, fragmented, and meaningless. Not only do the realities of the larger society thwart student aspirations for rewarding work and status but the realities of the changing curriculum and its administration increasingly prepare students for the acceptance of the new social reality.[23] Yet the emergence of new critical tendencies and social movements in the larger society in the 1970s—around feminism, gays, ecology, nuclear power and alternative energy systems—will continue to influence the academy, serving as lines of arguments against the compartmentalization and fragmentation of knowledge and providing alternative views of the conventional wisdom.

Thus the struggle both to obtain and to provide a liberating education continues in many colleges, although in muted and often somewhat precarious form. Many of the faculty who initiated and/or supported the changes of the 60s and 70s are still teaching and now have as their colleagues some of the radical students of that era. This group of faculty is largely responsible for the establishment of a marxist perspective and critical discourse as a strong presence in higher education, particularly in the liberal arts disciplines. While a number of these faculty have been victims of the closing of nontraditional programs, many others have established themselves within the traditional departments and there constitute strong voices against the current trend, particularly in their ability to address the failure of conventional methodologies, theories, and analyses and to propose a more integrated approach to understanding the past and addressing the current social reality.[24]

In short, the phenomena of the 1960s and early 1970s taken together with the developments of this period of contraction—the move to mass education, the integration of the formerly excluded into the colleges, the resistance to bureaucratized and alienating work relations, the tightening of the labor market, and the pressures imposed by the fiscal crisis—insure that higher education will remain a contested arena. While these tensions will continue to be felt, in varying degrees, in all institutions of higher learning, the tendency is clearly in the direction of a more traditional and increasingly specialized undergraduate curriculum, administered under the dominance of a revitalized departmental structure.

The developments discussed throughout this essay lead to the conclusion that those "alternative" educational institutions whose entire curriculum and educational philosophy are organized on other than departmental lines are more likely to survive the current trend than inner colleges or experimental programs within the traditionally-organized college. Of those alternative colleges established in the late 60s and early 70s, those organized on a nondepartmental basis—The Evergreen State College, Hampshire, Stockton State, Ramapo, and the University of Wisconsin at Green Bay—have been able to maintain their philosophical and organizational integrity, although not without some adjustments, particularly in the direction of a more rationalized and predictable curriculum. A detailed case study of how one of these colleges dealt with the new realities without undermining its philosophical base can be found in this volume: Byron Youtz's "The Evergreen State College: An Experiment Maturing."

The pressures toward disciplinary professionalism and departmental hegemony over the curriculum are absent at these colleges. But this does not mean that they can look forward to a trouble-free future, somehow immune from the historical factors affecting higher education. All but

Hampshire are public institutions, subject to state allocations and cuts within their respective state systems. They face the possible danger of closure by the state or a forced move to a traditional department-based curriculum. For reasons similar to those that make a nontraditional program insecure within a traditional college, the nontraditional state-supported college is in a weak position vis-a-vis the other colleges and universities in its system. In a case of extreme fiscal exigency, it is likely to be decided that the education it offers is marginal and/or extravagant to the main enterprise and thus expendable. I suggest, however, that short of a major fiscal crisis, as long as enrollments are maintained at a high level and the educational quality remains sound, these colleges will continue to exist. But, to agree with Weaver's final conclusion, existence is not sufficient: Alternative colleges must do more than remain "mere alternatives."

As the alternatives within the conventional college's undergraduate curriculum disappear or are transformed into increasingly specialized pre- or para-professional training, it becomes even more important that the non-traditional college provide a model of a truly alternative education, one that empowers individuals to act as informed, critical, purposeful, and responsible citizens in an uncertain world.

NOTES

1. For example, closure or substantial modification away from interdisciplinary or nontraditional programs has been the case at Goddard, Franconia, Thomas Jefferson College of the Grand Valley State Colleges, Prescott College, Johnson Center (Redlands), Strawberry College at UC Berkeley, Unit 1 of the University of Illinois, the Global Survival Program at University of Massachusetts, Amherst, Michigan State University's Lyman Briggs College and James Madison College, Hostos/CUNNY, and Centennial Education Program at University of Nebraska.

2. I am indebted to Barbara Leigh Smith for this example.

3. I am here following the argument of those who maintain that modern capitalist development is characterized by an overall pattern of long waves of two or three decades in duration. For example, see Eric Hobsbaum, "The Crisis of Capitalism in Historical Perspective;" VI *Socialist Revolution* (October–December 1976); David Gordon, "Up and Down the Long Roller Coaster;" in URPE, *United States Capitalism in Crisis*, New York: Union for Radical Political Economics, 1978; Ernest Mandel, *Long Waves of Capitalist Development*, (Cambridge, Cambridge University Press, 1980); and Thomas Weisskopf, "The Current Economic Crisis in Historical Perspective," LVII *Socialist Review* (May–June, 1981).

4. Emily Abel and Deborah Rosenfelt, "Women Part-Time Faculty," XVII *Radical Teacher* (November, 1980) page 61.

5. A graphic example of the high costs of this squeeze is in the closing in December 1979 of the Goddard-Cambridge Graduate Program in Social Change. Its Feminist Studies Section, perhaps its strongest and best known component, had been so undermined by tuition

increases, a reduced budget, and staff cuts that it elected to close the program rather than undergo the structural changes necessitated by the cuts. From "Notes for Educational Workers," XVII *Radical Teacher* (November, 1980) page 59.

6. This is the case not only at large state institutions, but at small liberal arts colleges as well. For a discussion of the situation at Oberlin College, see David Love, "Interdisciplinary Work at Oberlin," LXXVII *Oberlin Alumni Magazine* (Summer, 1981), pp 2–5.

7. Carnegie Council on Policy Studies in Higher Education, *Three Thousand Futures: The Next Twenty Years for Higher Education* (San Francisco: Jossey-Bass, 1980), page 80.

8. Ibid, page 82.

9. For a full treatment of this development and its relation to the rapid growth of an increasingly segmented system of postsecondary education corresponding to the segmentation and extension of the wage-labor system, see Sam Bowles and Herb Gintis, *Schooling in Capitalist America: Educational Reform and the Contradictions of Economic Life* (New York: Basic Books, 1976), pp. 201–203.

10. For some sense of the magnitude of problem, see footnote 1.

11. "Michigan State's Budget Cut $13.5 Million, 368, Many with Tenure, Face Loss of Jobs," XXII *The Chronicle of Higher Education* (April 13, 1981), pp 1, 8 & 9. The discussion in the following two paragraphs relies heavily on the *Chronicle* report.

12. Ibid, page 8.

13. Washington's enrollment figures for the academic year 1980–81 and the lids for 1981–82 are as follows:

College	80–81 FTE Enrollment	81–82 FTE Enrollment
University of Washington	31,210	31,000
Washington State University	17,266	16,682
Central Washington State University	5,895	5,900
Western Washington State University	9,120	9,100
Eastern Washington State University	6,575	6,800
The Evergreen State College	2,384	2,500
Community College System	97,000	92,000

This information was provided by Mike Bigelow, Budget Officer, The Evergreen State College.

14. Ernest Mandel, *Late Capitalism* (London: New Left Books, 1975) page 261.

15. Carnegie Commission on Higher Education, *Priorities for Action: Final Report* (New York: McGraw-Hill, 1973), page

16. ———. *Missions of the College Curriculum: A Contemporary Review with Suggestions* (San Francisco: Jossey-Bass, 1977), page 103.

17. ———. *A Summary of Reports and Recommendations* (San Francisco: Jossey-Bass, 1980) page 138. The heavy student investment in professional education can be seen from the following table:

18. Ibid, page 230.

19. Ibid

20. Ibid

21. Ibid, page 231.

22. This trend is perhaps most evident in the operation of the California College system with its clearly articulated three-tier structure. For further discussion of the class and labor-market related nature of this tiered system, see Burton R. Clark, *The Open Door College: A Case Study* (New York: McGraw-Hill, 1960); Jerome Karabel, "Community Colleges and Social Stratification," XXXXII Harvard Educational Review (November 1972), pp. 521–62; and XIV *Radical Teacher* (December 1979), Special California Issue.

23. For a more detailed discussion of the argument that the roots of the crisis of higher education exist not so much in the structure of higher education itself as in fundamental contradictions in the larger society, see Bowles and Gintis, pp. 215–219.

24. This development is not, however, without its ambiguity, particularly for marxist academics. The relative safety of the departmental rubric has led a number to restrict the scope of their work and to fragment broad questions in order to legitimate their presence within the disciplinary framework and hence to better secure their position within the University.

III. Disciplinary Professionalism—Response: to Weaver and Hahn

by

J. PETER EUBEN

Professor Weaver's essay makes three important points. First, it argues against the idea that higher education in general and nontraditional institutions in particular are passive victims of forces beyond their control. Though Reaganism may make this view tempting, it is self-fulfilling defeatism. Weaver rightly insists that we look to our internal possibilities and difficulties, and discuss what we can do internally rather than at those external forces that can only inhibit our capacity to act. If we accept his admonition we may escape vacillating between a defensiveness which implicitly accepts standards of judgment we explicitly repudiate, and a preciousness which makes us too uncritical of ourselves and too lax about generating appropriate criteria of excellence. In short, we need to recognize how much we are our own problem and how much we can do about it. Weaver's point here seems to me methodological as well as substantive. He suggests that the proper level of analysis should avoid both abstract structural critiques which become excuses for inaction in local situations, and those discrete analyses which ignore the connection between academic disciplines, professionalism and the organization of knowledge.

Secondly his essay makes a strong argument that academic disciplines are modes of organizing human knowledge analogous to the professions. Weaver is right in suggesting that such academic disciplines are simultaneously beneficial to the professions and detrimental to undergraduate education. Academic "disciplinarians," like professionals, try to enhance the prestige of what they do, enhance their control over who does it and monopolize the definition of what "it" is.

Thirdly the essay makes a good case that the idea of professional disciplines is more than contingently related to both the idea of education as transmission and a positivist epistemology. What Weaver points toward is the mutual implications between a theory of knowledge and communication on the one hand and the activity of teaching on the other. How one understands the world and knowledge about it—whether, for instance, knowledge is seen as available to daily consciousness or requires esoteric initiation, whether it is best presented in propositions or poetry—makes an enormous difference in how teachers understand their vocation and charge. Indeed the very idea of transmitting knowledge (as if one were transmitting a television signal) is the opposite of dialogue, where the teacher takes the kind of chances he or she demands of students. It makes a difference whether you regard students as children who have to grow up or potential citizens for whom learning about the world is a political and intellectual endeavor engaged in collectively by potential equals.

Despite these useful points I think Weaver's analysis incomplete for many of the reasons stated by Professor Hahn. She is right in insisting that we need a broader political and cultural perspective in order to assess how autonomous universities are and thus how important a discussion about academic disciplines may be in considering nontraditional education. Part of the reason Weaver exaggerates the autonomy of educational institutions is his being at Hampshire College, a private institution, relatively immune to continuous and direct political pressure and thus free to decide its own educational fate, and a school located in an area with long respect for liberal arts education that cannot be matched in the West. So my criticisms of his essay are really arguments from a different experience; the University of California at Santa Cruz, an institution hedged in by a local administrative maze, recalcitrant state-wide faculty committees, an intermittently supportive central administration and a sometimes hostile citizenry. I do not doubt that we benefit from our association with the University of California system and from the prestige of Berkeley. But we also have to fight hard and repeatedly for maintaining the distinctiveness of our educational mission. If my comments are sharper than Weaver's, it is because my reality is somewhat different.

My point then is that he exaggerates the autonomy of universities and therefore the importance of how academic disciplines are defined. Let me offer an analogy. In the 1960's there was extensive debate over whether America was a pluralistic society. One classic study—of New Haven by Robert Dahl—insisted that New Haven was pluralistic because different elites were dominant in different issue areas. Certainly the wealthy could not be said to play any consistently prominent role. I am not interested in refuting the conclusion so much as pointing out that *if* the wealthy were dominant in Hartford or Washington they would have no reason to be visibly active in New Haven. Having set the parameters of debate and policy at the national level they can safely leave local politics "pluralistic." The lower the stakes the greater the democracy. Similarly, if the dominant ideology of a country is liberal capitalism, and if those exploited by it accept it as a definition of reality, then capitalists have little need to overtly assert their power. Those who are ruled will rule themselves in the name of the ruling ideology.

Now I think something very much like this happened in American higher education. The definition of academic respectability—being tough minded, analytic, hard-headed—is an ideology that establishes standards for non-traditional institutions. And this ideology is established by elite institutions tied to government corporations and foundations. Thus insofar as these educational institutions define what it means to do intellectually respectable work, it is with the cooperation of institutions which have vested interests in maintaining the political and educational status quo. Needless to say these institutions and thus the ideology they foster, are derived from a research orientation rather than a concern for undergraduate teaching. And, needless to say, despite the inferior undergraduate education students may receive at them, they continue to be highly prestigious and desirable to many of our best young people. The conclusion is obvious—the outside sets the tone for the inside, and until we look at the outside we cannot understand what, or how important, what happens on the inside really is. Weaver may be right in his emphasis but we cannot know that until we do an analysis much like that suggested by Professor Hahn.

If I am right then we need to look at the way various educational institutions, departments, or groups within departments, use outside connections to enhance their power within particular universities on such issues as curricula, resources, and personnel. If these dominant groups or departments or institutions are the established paradigms of what academic disciplines and professionalism is, then all of us will be urged, tempted, or pushed, into imitating microbiologists, and economists rather than art historians or philosophers. We also need to distinguish between professional knowledge used for social control from those more benign or even critical academic disciplines, i.e., to distinguish medicine, law and managerial science from musicology, sociology or political theory.

These considerations lead me to differ with Professor Weaver's conclusions. What I see is the research orientation of our educational institutions being reinforced, not challenged. There will, I think, be an alliance between researchers and a new breed of managers whose anxiety to make the institution attractive and build its prestige will push them to imitate those institutions which foster a view of knowledge and teaching inimicable to what most of us are trying to do. More specifically, I think we will see: 1) a reassertion of professional hegemony and the further instrumentalization of the liberal arts; 2) a loss of power by departments to administrators, business managers, and public relations people trying to sell the institution; 3) continued loss of prestige and power by the humanities with dire consequences for interdisciplinary studies; 4) an increasingly precarious life for younger faculty (especially in the humanities), with resultant intellectual and political timidity and/or cynicism; and 5) the reassertion of technical-scientific-organization training at the expense of broadly humanistic education. If I am right, then the Trilateral Commission's call for technically oriented intellectuals to replace "value-oriented" intellectuals will be answered.

Much of my criticism is like that of Professor Hahn's; at least it is compatible with it. Let me then conclude with two issues not raised in either essay. First of all, it seems to me that the most important educational issue of all is how to democratize education and educate a democracy. That is the special relevance of alternative education in the 1980's. This requires—at the beginning and at the very least—a critique of professionalism and specialization and the inequalities they sustain. In this regard I disagree with Professor Weaver that the establishment of disciplinary professions in the late 19th century was "progressive." Indeed, I regard it as part of the consolidation of corporate capitalism, the fragmentation of intellect and everyday life, the defeat of insurgent democratic movements (such as populism) and the general concentration of political and economic power in a centralized bureaucratic state.

My second point derives from this. It seems to me that alternative education has a special obligation to be both radical and conservative. It needs to be both because the modern state promotes cultural homogenization *and* personal fragmentation. We must be radical in resisting the homogenization not only in what we teach, but in how we teach it, to whom and where. But we also need to be conservative and traditional.

We need, I think, to resist the blandishments of the here and now; and to nurture ideas, relationships and educational forms whose very persistence would be exemplary.

Being radical and conservative is perfectly consistent with the literal meanings of liberal and education. In Latin liberal (from liberalis and libertas) indicates doing and living in a way worthy of a free man or woman as opposed to a slave. To be educated "liberally" means being educated for public life. The Latin suggests that liberal education is opposed to one that is exclusively technical or professional, because being liberal implies being free of prejudice and therefore capable of a breadth of mind and vision denied those whose education remains narrowly technical. A liberal man or woman is one with the capacity and temperament to understand things as a whole, and the limits of professions and techniques in the whole of life. Concerned with the sweep of time and space, a liberal education is richly historical, theoretical and comparative. It seeks to deparochialize the world and so provide an expanded context for understanding the particular events and ideas of daily life.

Education (from the Latin educare) means to nourish or sustain, not only biological growth, but virtue, character, intelligence and the capacity for action. And like our word educe, educare suggests that this growth is a matter of eliciting or sustaining what a person already is or knows rather than transmitting "information" to a passive recipient. In these terms the aim of education is to make the latent manifest, to add dimension and complexity to what is rudimentary and simple, and to make real and palpable what previously existed merely as potential. To educate then is not to impart a skill, profession, or technique, as much as to develop character. And this requires mutuality and potential equality. It is such mutuality that keeps education from being abstract and impersonal and which confounds who is teacher and who is student sufficiently for both to be both.

I realize this vocabulary and these sentiments are old-fashioned and that in other contexts they have been abused for unattractive political ends. Still they are also a vocabulary with a rich radical and conservative potential.

If we do not come to define our aims in these ways and utilize this vocabulary, alternative education will cease being alternative and cease being education. Interdisciplinary studies will not cease but become unrecognizable, because of the homogenization process I mentioned above. For they will be organized around the dominant disciplines and conceptions of education—economics, business administration, engineering, etc. All of this contributes to a closing down envisaged by the sociologist Max Weber. In the concluding pages of his book on Protestantism and capitalism, Weber assays the future.

> "But victorious capitalism, since it rests on mechanical foundations, needs its support no longer. The rosy blush of its laughing heir, the Enlightenment, seems also to be irretrievably fading, and the idea of duty in one's calling prowls about in our lives like the ghost of dead religious beliefs. Where the fulfilment of the calling cannot directly be related to the highest spiritual and cultural values, or when, on the other hand, it need not be felt simply as economic compulsion, the individual generally abandons the attempt to justify it at all. In the field of its highest development, in the United States, the pursuit of wealth, stripped of its religious and ethical meaning, tends to become associated with purely mundane passions, which often actually give it the character of sport.
>
> No one knows who will live in this cage in the future, or whether at the end of this tremendous development entirely new prophets will arise, or there will be a great rebirth of old ideas and ideals, or, if neither, mechanized petrification, embellished with a sort of convulsive self-importance. For of the last stage of this cultural development, it might well be truly said: "Specialists without spirit, sensualists without heart; this nullity imagines that it has attained a level of civilization never before achieved."

PART TWO

Alternative Education at the College

Editors' Introduction to Part Two

The chapters in this section discuss alternative education at the college level. Santa Cruz, Evergreen and Southwest are state supported "new schools." Hampshire is a private institution. The two inner colleges discussed in this section—the Paracollege at St. Olaf's and Western College at Miami University are located in private and public institutions respectively. All were founded in the 1960's. All survive into the 1980's. They are not the institutions which they were at their founding, but most remain distinctively "alternative."

In his chapter on Evergreen, Byron Youtz suggests that colleges can be described in terms of their life cycles and developmental challenges. It is interesting to note how recurrent the themes are in the chapters describing the evolution of these colleges. Most were born in a period of heady experimentation, and rapid expansion in higher education. In many of these institutions enrollment projections were substantial and not to be realized as a large proportion of the projected college age population never materialized or was absorbed into the community college system in the various states.

With the exception of Western College and the Paracollege, the colleges in this section are somewhat unique in that they are free standing alternative institutions. Although some were more independent in their governance structure than others, as a group these colleges did not face the heavy internal struggle for survival that plagued many of the programs located within major research universities. To a much larger extent the alternatives at the college level had the opportunity to work out their own norms and values with respect to institutional reward systems, governance and academic structure and content.

Yet, the institutions also varied widely. Evergreen persists with its fundamental curricular innovations largely intact. But like Southwest and Santa Cruz, it has been under unrelenting legislative pressure to grow to the capacity of its physical plant, which will bring it to cost parity with its sister institutions. Southwest, too, in much earlier days found itself subject to the usual state standards and increasing centralization of authority. Perhaps a critical difference between Evergreen and many of the other institutions in this section is its later founding date which gave it the advantage of learning from the earlier "experiments." It is noteable how many Evergreen faculty came to Olympia via Old Westbury, Santa Cruz and similar institutions.

Newell's chapter on the Western College and the Paracollege provides an interesting discussion of the factors associated with success in interdisciplinary teaching at the "inner college." His contention that a clear definition of interdisciplinary study is important corresponds to Ingersoll's admonition about clarity in institutional mission. This lack of clarity clearly took its toll at Southwest according to Grubb.

Grubb's chapter describes the evolution of a college in the midst of a changing external climate. Founded in a period of relatively flexible institutional expectations, Southwest rapidly became embroiled in statewide requirements for more uniformity and control in higher education. Factions within the faculty vied for influence around the ambiguities in a system which had failed to build a structure to implement its espouced ideals.

Clark Kerr's 1980 preface to the Third Edition of his classic book, *The Uses of the University*, contends that the educational revolution of the 1960's has largely failed to affect the research university. He argues that much of this failure can be attributed to the nature of faculty.

> "Disaffected and disenchanted as they were with academic and political life—(they) would not let anything work well . . . Another reason is that the changes of the 1960's moved mostly in directions that faculty members by and large opposed . . . The attempted changes of the 1960's were oriented not toward the advancement of knowledge but toward improved environments."

And indeed, these "improved" environments cost the faculty dearly in research time.

The chapters by Holmquist, Nisonoff and Rakoff and Fairbanks speak directly to the role of faculty in the alternative colleges. They help us begin to answer questions about the influence of faculty attitudes, training and work styles had on the evolution of the alternative colleges. Were faculty cultures as unsuited to change as Kerr asserts? Did the alternative college carve out a different work style or simply impose additional demands upon existing work styles and expectations?

Holmquist, Nisonoff and Rakoff contend that alternative colleges have been particular victims of the trend toward "work acceleration" which has characterized work in America in general. They analyze the dilemmas surrounding the notion of the "ideal faculty member" at the alternative college—wholistic and cross disciplinary, interacting frequently with students, and part of a shared community of scholars. They contend that the multiple expectations which this model creates leads to the emergence of various individual and group "coping mechanisms.' These include allowing the rise of more centralized administrative structures, the development of a "cult of bitching," a decline in the community model, passive resistance, "going by the book," differential staffing, and learning to say no. All of these themes resonate throughout this volume in one way or another.

While Holmquist, Nisonoff and Rakoff argue that some of the sources of strain in the alternative college are structural and endemic to the American economy but exacerbated by the alternative college, Fairbanks thinks faculty are generally conservative and reject the daring and imaginative in academic curriculum. Like Thomas Kuhn, he argues that the training of most faculty influences their value systems in profound and lasting ways. Fairbanks argues that administrators are more frequently intrigued and interested in proposals for reform and that their interest in turn generates additional skepticism among faculty colleagues. Faculty, according to Fairbanks, do not think corporately and have no pressure on them to change. The two factors together explain their generally conservative response. Fairbanks thus sees the participatory norms of many of the alternative colleges of the 1960's as a potentially conservative factor. His argument has particular relevance for the cluster college, attempting to survive in an institution characterized by more conventional values.

IV. What Defines "Alternative Education" and What are its Prospects for the Future?

by

VIRGINIA INGERSOLL

Taken together, these case studies provide us with an initial characterization of alternative education. There seem to be eight dimensions that mark out the territory of alternative education. The first dimension is curriculum, with alternative institutions leaning more often than not toward an interdisciplinary approach. Second is the extent to which a student can individualize his or her education; the more "alternative" an institution, the more opportunities there are for individualization. Third, the cases suggest alternative education is characterized by the use of multiple pedagogical modes—more classroom experimentation. Fourth, alternative institutions tend to emphasize the importance of integrating classroom life with general student life. Fifth, in alternative institutions student participation in governance is encouraged. Sixth, grades are eschewed in favor of more qualitative evaluation systems. The seventh characteristic is the mode of faculty appointment, with a movement away from tenure. Eighth, a sense of social mission seems to pervade many alternative institutions.

One could make each of these eight dimensions into a bipolar scale. For instance, using the first—degree of interdisciplinarity—one could create a scale, the endpoints of which would be "totally departmentalized and disciplinary" and "fully interdisciplinary." The resulting series of eight scales provide an instrument for rating each of the institutions described in this volume and for arriving at a rough measure of "alternativeness." It is sobering to see that the more "alternative" institutions are also the most threatened. Institutions which deviate less from the norm of American higher education are experiencing fewest difficulties.

What makes an alternative institution not only work but thrive? Reflecting on these case studies leads me to propose three critical conditions for success. First, the institution must have a very clear idea of itself—a mission whose definition is both well understood and widely accepted within the institution. A number of the cases call to mind a very complicated self-definition which is neither accepted nor well articulated internally. This seemed not to be the case in the two programs Bill Newell describes, and these two programs were clearly less troubled. They contrast sharply with Von Blum's description of the DIGS program at Berkeley. The second critical condition for success is related to the first: an institution that is by design different from the educational norm must be able to articulate its differences both clearly and persuasively to a wider community, which usually has a larger investment in the norm than in the alternative. Since the community provides both resources and, ultimately, the student body, the alternative institution must make compelling arguments on its own behalf. Third, if alternative institutions are to continue receiving support, they must demonstrate that they fulfill a function which is positive in light of the community's changing needs. In other words, the successful institution is one that does not simply react to what is distasteful in the present, but that anticipates and recreates itself for the future.

Each of us harbors hopes and dreads for the decade ahead. Many would agree the decade promises conditions very different from those of its recent past. Consider, for instance, this modest list of challenges: 1) Despite a current abatement in price, we still face either energy shortages or increasingly costly energy. 2) There seems to be a return to traditional values, a swing toward social conservatism. 3) The Federal Reserve System notwithstanding, we could easily see a return to high inflation. 4) There are more single parent families and more women in the workforce, the full consequences of which we are just beginning to consider. 5) There will likely be less and less money available for education. 6) New communications and computer technology are creating social changes for the decades ahead. Some believe these will be as momentous as the changes wrought by the Industrial Revolution. 7) Home ownership has become increasingly difficult, and this creates different patterns of expectations and family relationships. 8) Tensions and the fear of nuclear confrontation are increasing.

This list is neither complete nor fully articulated. It is only a starting point. What are the likely consequences of these conditions? What are the outlines of the future into which higher education must move? What does such a future promise for alternative education?

The world that gave birth to many alternative institutions no longer exists. We must prepare for a new one, one that is already making itself felt, and one that needs fresh perspectives. These changing conditions provide us with an enormous opportunity in innovative education. They present us with a chance to really show what we can do and how valuable we are. In the challenging times ahead we will thrive to the extent that we are both very good and very aggressive in demonstrating our indispensability.

V. The University of California at Santa Cruz: Institutionalizing Eden in a Changing World

by

GEORGE VON DER MUHLL

Academic innovations appear doomed to a predictable trajectory. With much fanfare, a bold new venture in higher education is launched. Lovingly drafted prospectuses contrast the promise inherent in its pathbreaking instructional program with the deficiencies of "traditional" collegiate curricula. Intellectually adventurous faculty and students are invited to apply; foundations are approached for funds to sustain the undertaking in its early years. If well conceived, and fueled by further inputs of publicity and financial support, the experiment attracts many of the university world's best and brightest into its orbit. For perhaps a decade its precepts evoke wide discussion. Then, with an inevitability suggesting the operation of a gravitational law, the enterprise begins to sink slowly below the horizon of public consciousness, its innovatory impetus spent. Enrollments drop; the more academically mobile administrators and faculty move on. Those who remain are left to allocate the blame for the wreckage.

In its sixteen years of operation, the University of California campus at Santa Cruz has traversed this readily recognizable arc. Its recent decline into a marginally differentiated member of that system may therefore bear many aspects of a twice-told tale. It is a tale that bears retelling. For the Santa Cruz campus was not subject, through much of its history, to many of the forces most commonly associated with the demise of utopian experiments. It was in no simple sense the product of a single founder's inspiration. Its first chancellor displayed from his inauguration a political scientist's sophisticated attentiveness to the organizational incentives required to institutionalize his innovations. Backed by the treasury of a State-supported university system, its academic program did not depend on the transient enthusiasm of private donors for its survival. And perhaps no experimental pattern of instruction in recent decades addressed itself more directly and more self-consciously to a more widely perceived malaise in American university life. Those who retain an expansive faith in the margin for innovation in higher education have reason to look closely at this poignant case.

I. FLOWERING OF A VISION

Seldom have circumstances more favored the founding of an experimental campus than in the early 1960s. California in those affluent years was rapidly becoming the wealthiest, most populous state in the Union. In that fabulous kingdom by the sea, the most dazzling anticipations soon merged with reality. Optimistic forecasts proved underestimates in retrospect. And as economic productivity soared, so did the demand for higher education.

Already in 1957 a study by the State Department of Finance had projected the swelling of two of the University of California's six campuses to some 40,000 students apiece in little more than a decade unless new campuses were built. But public support for higher education had likewise reached previously unimagined heights. To most California voters, education seemed intimately connected with economic growth. In the heady atmosphere of the times, the case for expansion stated itself.

In October of that year, the Regents of the University of California announced their election of Clark Kerr as president of the system. They promptly authorized him to add three new campuses to the existing six. In short order, the necessary bonds secured approval. Yet merely providing new space for old patterns of instruction was hardly what the newly selected president had in mind. No one understood more clearly the emerging limits of mammoth "multiversities" than the man who coined the phrase.[1] Casual readers have sometimes assumed that Kerr endorsed the development he later described. Kerr did believe, to be sure, that large taxpayer-supported universities must serve many clienteles; but he had also taken note of the costs of surrendering uncritically to those pressures. Long before the Berkeley "free speech" movement burst like a thunderclap across the land, its former chancellor could observe at first hand the alienating impact on students of rigidly departmentalized campuses largely dominated by their organized research units and their graduate and professional schools.

Under Kerr's leadership, each of the three new University of California campuses would mark a departure from traditional patterns of university organization. Yet with marginal variations, the first two were expected to pursue instruction and research along familiar lines. These lines had already established the University of California as one of the nation's leading universities. They had also increasingly raised questions about the criteria used in that judgment. For the ninth campus, Kerr therefore reserved a more radical charter. On former ranch land of the Cowell Foundation above the aging seaside resort of Santa Cruz he hoped to bring into being a pilot plant to test the University's very capacity for self-renewal.

Kerr's operational program for institutional renewal had matured over many years. As a graduate student at Stanford, he had had numerous occasions to compare his undergraduate years at Swarthmore with those of his roommate from UCLA. They had concluded at that time that the ideal campus would combine the research facilities and egalitarian accessibility of a large public university with the student-centered intimacy of a Swarthmore. For nearly four decades that envisaged union of seeming incompatibilities had remained untested. But now, as president of the largest university in the United States, Kerr was in a position to offer his former roommate the chance to prove the practicability of their ideal. In July of 1961, he appointed Dean McHenry founding chancellor of the proposed University of California at Santa Cruz.

McHenry came well-prepared for the assignment. Without abandoning the utopian outlook of his earlier years, he had developed, while on the political science faculty of UCLA, a shrewd, clearsighted understanding of California politics.[2] Restoring unity to the "multiversity" was for him a congenial charge. He set about it with a combination of exploratory openness and practical assurance that quickly drew others in his train.[3]

Santa Cruz, he promised, would deliberately take on the challenge of countering the isolating, dehumanizing pressures of contemporary university life. Living and learning would be combined at modest cost in an enriching formula hitherto restricted to the most exclusive of private institutions. Undergraduates and graduates alike would be offered centering, self-exploratory, increasingly self-directed education of uncompromising quality in a sylvan setting unparalleled in the nation. Faculty members would be expected to work closely with students at all levels without distinction.

Others had made such claims before. But Santa Cruz would differ from other experimental ventures in one crucial respect. As a public institution, it could not limit its admissions to a carefully selected elite. On the contrary, McHenry insisted, the campus would fully accept its obligation to serve the taxpayers of one of the largest, most occupationally diverse, most ethnically heterogeneous of the States. It would therefore have to resolve the eternal tension between quality and quantity in education; and it would do so through its design. Santa Cruz would develop a series of small residential "Colleges" surrounding laboratories and a library appropriate to a full-scale university. Centering instruction in the Colleges would enable the campus to retain its intimate quality while accommodating first the thousands, and then the tens of thousands, of socially diverse but academically qualified high school graduates that a State university was charged with enrolling. Although systemwide plans called for Santa Cruz to accept in time as many students as the giant campuses at Berkeley and Los Angeles, it would continue (in the words of President Kerr) to "seem small as it grows larger." That feat was one other universities serving similar clienteles might well wish to study.

Such were the most immediately striking elements of the prospectus that Kerr and McHenry offered the California public. But around these elements radiated a penumbra of larger, less readily articulated concerns. The Santa Cruz campus was being founded at a time of confluence between rampant opportunity and growing unease in the academic world. Headlong expansion, proliferating specialties, successful performance in the market for foundation and governmental grants, limited institutional loyalty and an increasing search for recognition from prestigious external peer groups—these had become the hallmarks of dynamism in the American universities of the period. Mirrored in these preoccupations, still faint but ever more distinct, worried observers could discern the values of corporate capitalism. In the pursuit of such conceptions of excellence universities risked losing their integrity. Inevitably, the Santa Cruz experiment became invested with the anxieties and aspirations of an era. Here, it seemed, was a campus that sought alternatives to the impersonal, fiercely competitive pressures on which leading American universities had come to rely for extracting achievements from their students and faculty. Its proposed design raised hopes that, without retreating from the frontiers of scholarly research, a university could find the means to offset the centrifugal forces of grant-oriented professionalism that elsewhere were fractionating university campuses into isolated institutes. From this perspective, anchoring both faculty and students to the College system seemed not merely a means of facilitating contact between the two; even more, that anchoring might prove a structural precondition for maintaining the centrality of a liberal education in the pacesetting public institutions of the nation. Santa Cruz came conspicuously into being as a product of its times. Somehow, amid the flowery glades of the Coastal Range, it would also insulate itself against the predominant values of those times. By restoring old values to their proper primacy in the educational process, Santa Cruz would clear the way for the blossoming of the new.

Not surprisingly, this vision of a radical return to a Garden of Eden intrigued the educational world. It assured the Santa Cruz experiment a scrutiny reaching well beyond the borders of California. It forcefully posed questions as to a university's capacity to change an encompassing society without being changed in the process. And it fastened on the campus itself a restrictive legacy. Form could never, in this mission, be incidental to the ends served by the form. At Santa Cruz, form quickly became the end.

II. INSTITUTIONALIZING UTIOPIA

On one point the founders of the Santa Cruz campus were largely in agreement. Insofar as the limits of human imagination and resources permitted, the campus was to express an integrated utopian vision. Little that later struck its visitors was accidental. From its forest-circled parking lots to its program of interdisciplinary study, from the refusal to build a faculty club to the deliberate deemphasizing of competitive sports, its distinguishing features reflected a fundamental rethinking of the organizing principles of university life. Whether viewed as an ecological design, a set of administrative arrangements, a curriculum, or an expected form of faculty-student interaction, the distinctive patterns of Santa Cruz could be read as an ambitious, often novel, and highly self-conscious thesis concerning the proper goals of higher education. The soberest planning documents from its early years crackle with barely suppressed excitement at that mission. Repeatedly one encounters there a repudiation of the notion that Santa Cruz was to be merely the ninth campus (so many additional square feet of classroom space, so many beds, so many full-time equivalent faculty positions) within the settled system of the University of California.

The founders of Santa Cruz were not, of course, allowed free rein in designing their academic utiopia. Their campus was to be a unit of a State university; and over the previous century that university had evolved an imposing corpus of standards and procedures within a frame defined by the Constitution of California, the California Master Plan for Higher Education, the standing orders of the University of California's governing body of Regents, and the regulations of its Academic Senate. "We were handed the chalk and invited to write on the blackboard," its founding chancellor was later to remark, "but the slate was not unmarked."[4] Even before the campus had opened, Chancellor McHenry had found it expedient to allay Regental fears concerning the projected "country club" appearance of the campus through a pledge that the plans for Santa Cruz would be realized at no greater cost in public funds per student than at any other campus of the University. More intangibly, a taxpayer-supported university campus had to take into account prevailing public expectations regarding a public institution of higher learning. These were generally fluid in California in the tolerant early 'sixties, and mediated in any case through the University's Board of Regents; but they could not be presumed to be indefinitely elastic.

Nevertheless, these constraints remained quite loose. In an era of rapid growth and growing dissatisfaction with established patterns of education, a small campus could expect an ample initial margin for experiment. This margin was widened in the case of Santa Cruz by the shared vision and close working relationship of its chancellor and President Kerr. And the Santa Cruz campus possessed, in addition, the great advantage of virgin birth. It did not have to expand laterally or downward, absorbing and adjusting to the faculty and facilities of an existing institution, as was the case with all but one other of the more recently established University of California campuses; nor did its founders have to implement their reforms from within, as did Robert Hutchins at the University of Chicago or James Conant at Harvard. Santa Cruz was not one experimental college on a larger campus, but an entity unto itself. For most purposes, the existing University of California system acted not as a source of restriction but as a context of opportunity. Certainly it was in this spirit that the founders proceeded to draft their plans.

Despite careful examination of several possible prototypes, the planners found little to guide them in their search for a collegiate system appropriate to their mission.[5] Many felt an instinctive initial attraction to the College-centered education offered undergraduates at Oxford and Cambridge: Kerr himself had declared that a university could aim no higher than "to be as British as possible for the sake of the undergraduates."[6] On closer consideration, however, they could see that the radical separation of teaching and examining functions and the leisurely, empirical evolution of a curriculum out of faculty-intensive one-to-one tutorials for a selected clientele of students sharply limited the relevance of these models for a newly-founded State campus in California. Ivy League universities did not confront the problems of scale anticipated at Santa Cruz. In many cases, their undergraduate colleges had become overshadowed by their graduate schools. Nowhere, in fact, had planners faced so complex yet so ambitiously open-ended a mandate to provide an innovative form of education so quickly for so many students.

Lacking precedents, the task force created its own. Like many utopian planners, McHenry and the small group of faculty and career administrators he gathered around him appear to have felt the impulse to prescribe with unusual care in unusual detail the features that were to give their planned community its innovative characteristics. These impulses were held in tension, on the other hand, with McHenry's recognition, as a professional student of collective behavior, that the most lasting innovations often unfold organically from the daily choices of those who have been recruited to carry forward a common enterprise.[7] In any case, the very novelty of the undertaking, together with Regental pressure to open quickly, precluded decisions in advance in many important areas. The task force therefore came up with a mixture of highly specific prescription and deliberately open-ended delegation of future choice. McHenry and his planners gave particular attention to the structure of authority—who would participate in deciding what issues, with what supply of incentives to help make their preferences prevail. They also addressed themselves in depth to certain questions regarding the physical and social organization of the campus which, through prior definition, would symbolically communicate the value premises appropriate to future decisions. What the substantive content of many non-constitutional issues should be—even in so sensitive an area as that of which disciplines should be represented in what proportions on campus—they left to the future.

Amid the multitude of proposals and commitments appearing in early exchanges among the campus planners and between them and various outside agencies, a few indicate with particular clarity the innovatory pattern of education to be pursued at Santa Cruz:

1. With many parallel objectives in view, the campus was given an isolated pastoral setting recalling the ambience of a Cistercian monastery. Spectacularly located on a mountain slope above the Pacific, and encircled in the remaining three directions by many miles of dense forest, it visibly disengaged its members from the outer world, enclosing them in

the social network of the university community itself. The new campus was unique—perhaps in the world, certainly in the United States—in the degree to which nature was left to dominate artifice. Cows from the former Cowell Ranch continued to graze in the acres of rolling meadows separating the main entrance gate from the initially invisible college buildings. Deer—and sometimes a coyote—still emerged near the dormitories at dusk. Paths from the classrooms to the library were laid out to wind through dells providing a natural backdrop for performances of Shakespeare's *A Midsummer-Night's Dream*. Even the central administrative building was lost in the largely undisturbed redwood forest. To provide seating for campuswide assemblies and ceremonies, a Grecian amphitheater was hewed out of the depths of a limestone quarry, its dimensions adding further mythological intimations to the arcadian landscape. On every bridge, at every bend in the pathways, students were implicitly invited to dream new dreams, far from the busy haunts of man.[8]

2. Residential Colleges were adopted as the basic planning unit for the campus. Approximately fifty faculty and six hundred students were to be assigned to each College, and the majority of the students were to be housed and fed there as well. Classrooms and faculty offices were included in the cluster of College buildings in the hope of promoting a web of acquaintanceship among faculty and students. Each College was provided with a small administrative staff to manage the dormitories, maintain students' academic records, help organize their social life, and offer them advising and counseling assistance; and the Colleges as a whole were to be headed by faculty Provosts, whose broad but formally undefined responsibilities placed them one step below the chancellorial office in the administrative hierarchy.

3. Though in varying proportions, each College was to include faculty from every discipline represented on campus among its Fellows. All faculty, moreover, were to hold College appointments.[9] The rule of relative uniformity of disciplinary distribution was formally justified by the assumed need of each College to maintain a full complement of advisers for its entering undergraduates. Once several Colleges had opened, however, an important practical effect of this presupposition was to preclude the concentration of more than a small fraction of the faculty members of any one discipline in any single College.

4. The Provost and founding Fellows of each College were expected to develop a leading "theme" for the College that would give it a distinctive axis of orientation. Necessarily, this theme would be interdisciplinary in character. The chosen theme of the College was to be reflected in its version of the introductory core course the campus would require all

entering first-year students to take. It was also to affect the choice of such other courses as the Fellows might teach under College auspices. As undergraduates were expected to do most of their lower-division and some of their upper-division work in their Colleges,[10] the College theme would provide a basis for selecting students and faculty whose presumed commonality of interests should heighten academic intercourse.

5. Within the interdisciplinary environment sustained by the Colleges, the faculty were to evolve "a restricted curriculum, designed mainly to serve students' needs rather than reflect faculty interest."[11] This worthy goal was to be accomplished in several ways. It implied, to begin with, that faculty would pool their resources in large-scale collaborative efforts to provide students with a firm grounding in the core elements of a liberal education. Only later, when students had acquired a more informed base for making disciplinary and preprofessional commitments, would they be invited to choose among a carefully selected group of Upper Divison courses. "Non-proliferation" served as a watchword of early faculty committees on courses: there was a presumption against filling the campus catalog with advanced-level disciplinary courses that might signify a diversion of energy from meeting the core needs of the curriculum.[12] No faculty were to be exempt from teaching undergraduate courses. As a further check on fragmentation of faculty and student energy, the first Academic Plan included the provision that all courses were to be taught as "full courses" for five units of credit so that a student would normally carry no more than three courses in any one Academic Quarter.

6. All students, not merely the more demonstrably proficient, would be entitled—indeed, encouraged—to arrange courses of independent study, and even an independently designed major, with appropriate faculty, preferably within their College. Required comprehensive examinations or senior theses as the terminus of a major similarly pointed toward expectations of independent work on the part of each student. Considerations of cost ruled out reliance on one-to-one (or even group) tutorials as the primary mode of instruction. As at other universities, scheduled courses with final examinations or papers would form the basic building blocks of the curriculum. But early documents and statements anticipated that faculty-student interaction in the Colleges would lead to collaborative exploration of an individuated synthesis of knowledge.[13] "The pursuit of truth in the company of friends," the motto of Santa Cruz's first College, might readily have served for the campus as well.

Much simplified, with much omitted, these were the contours of the educational environment that Chancellor McHenry and his associates laid out in their blueprints for the campus. The leading strokes were bold enough; only time could show whether the finer lines of daily practice would eventually efface the original imprint. But no political scientist with McHenry's administrative experience would leave this development to chance. Patterns of human behavior, he had much reason to know, do not maintain themselves. His task force therefore planned the distribution of the political resources of the campus with care. It used them to motivate key actors to continue acting in accordance with the prescriptions of the founders' plan.

Some of the resources were merely facilitative. By creating the Colleges as the central units of the Academic Plan, the founders created agencies that could offer powerful inducements to obtain the loyalty of their faculties and students. Colleges were given broad authority to sponsor courses. They provided their faculties with office space and parking space, and harbored steno pools at which faculty received messages and mail and had their typing done. College Common Rooms were used for sherry hours, and College dining halls for weekly evenings of entertainment to which faculty and their spouses were regularly invited. Provosts were allotted various funds they could use to support collegiate academic programs and to hire short-term faculty to enrich the College offerings. They could parlay the name and organizational resources of the College to secure outside grants—in some cases exceeding a million dollars—with which to construct College libraries and recreation centers, erect fountains and art galleries, sponsor resident chamber orchestras, and extend the range of academic programs. Since even classrooms were located in the Colleges, many students and some faculty would find their lives centering within the College precincts for weeks at a time.

But the Colleges were also granted more direct methods of sustaining faculty loyalty to their programs.[14] They were to share with disciplinary groups the responsibility for initiating the recruitment of a candidate for the faculty. No faculty member could be hired without the approval of the College of which the candidate was to become a Fellow.[15] Before granting that approval, the Provost and the College faculty personnel committee were expected to inquire closely into the alignment of the candidate's academic interests with those of the College program. Thereafter, the Colleges would pay fifty per cent of the faculty member's salary; in exchange, they would expect each faculty member to teach at least one and generally two courses of interest to the College,[16] to undertake a share of student advising, to be available to qualified students wishing to pursue independent studies under College auspices, and to participate fully in the institutional life of the College. On the occasion of each personnel action, a faculty personnel committee of the College was required to submit a letter commenting on the Fellow's research accomplishments, and more specifically on his or her record of teaching and administrative services for the College, relations with students, and academic colleagueship. To this an independent letter from the College Provost would be appended. The extraordinary complexity of the University of California's personnel procedures precluded any firm statement as to the weight to be given these letters. That it was to be considerable was clear.

The founders of the campus saw plainly, however, that inducements to faculty to participate in developing experimental College-centered curricula would prove ineffectual if overbalanced by pressures emanating from sources that on other campuses had been blamed for exacting conformity to conventional patterns of education. They therefore deliberately set out to check, weaken, or at least retard the growth of such pressures.

Most cited among these agencies was the academic department; Santa Cruz would therefore have no departments. The Academic Plan acknowledged the inevitability—and even, to some limited extent, the desirability—of grouping faculty according to their specialties:

> . . . in many fields, distinction is unlikely to be achieved without a critical minimum of colleagues who associate frequently and who have access to appropriate facilities. . . . Contacts by discipline with colleagues in other institutions, and in learned societies . . . are desirable to place students, to find outlets for creative work, and to secure informed reactions to one's ideas and experiments.[17]

But this acknowledgment of professional concerns was to be institutionalized through creating three comprehensive "Divisions"—the Divisions of Humanities, Natural Sciences, and Social Sciences. Under the administration of three Vice-Chancellors (later Deans), the three Divisions received all non-collegiate instructional funds. They were to participate in recruiting regular ("ladder") faculty, to pay 50% of their salaries, and to provide the requisite complementary assessments of professional accomplishment in all personnel actions.[18] By no oversight whatever, no reference was made in the 1965 Academic Plan to the formation of any sub-divisional administrative structures. The only injunction was a negative one to the Colleges: "To encourage interdisciplinary cooperation and to minimize particularism, there will be no formal departmental organization within the colleges."[19]

Graduate and professional schools were the other preceived threat to the student-centered, interdisciplinary form of education the Colleges proposed to offer. Experience on other campuses suggested that these schools, whether by magnetic example or by active intervention, tended to exercise a pervasive influence on the undergraduate curriculum, converting it into a preparatory conduit for specialized advanced-level education while enticing professors into the hidden recesses of the laboratory, the library, the graduate seminar room, and the contractual grants office.[20] Those who most enjoyed such precincts, and who had made their professional reputation through sticking close to them, could be expected to have little sympathy for the experimental objectives of the collegiate curriculum envisaged for Santa Cruz. Graduate programs were therefore to be developed slowly and gingerly, leaving time for the Colleges to take firm root and to institutionalize the commitments required to prevent their faculties from reverting to patterns of behavior acquired on conventional campuses.

Two points stand out in this overview of the qualities the early planners hoped to institutionalize on their campus. The first is that their vision emerges most clearly in matters of procedure. With its careful allocation of administrative resources, its deliberate structuring of incentives, its checks and balances, its efforts to dissipate unwelcome pressures it could not altogether suppress, the plan strikingly resembles the cunning contrivances of eighteenth century constitutional inventors. Montesquieu and Madison would have found much to applaud in its ingenious alignment of forces. To be sure, there was much emphasis as well in the plan on communitarian values, on the humanizing virtues of intimacy and natural beauty, quite foreign to those thinkers. But in their abstractness, such aspirations sound common to any educational enterprise. The founders of Santa Cruz offered no new prescription for the integration of learning with labor, no new thoughts concerning the life of the mind and the life of the world. Their venture held the mind, then and now, not through its objectives but through its strategy for reaching them. It promised to stand apart from other anti-traditional undertakings through the institutional protection it would offer to innovative impulses.

This procedural profile is closely connected to a second general aspect of the plan. With all its idealism, despite its unmistakably generous and hopeful overtones, the founders' vision was an essentially negative vision. On one point only were they clear beyond controversy: Santa Cruz was not to become another Berkeley. Berkeley, despite the international reputation of its faculty and the prestige of its graduate schools, conspicuously concentrated on its campus all the forces that Santa Cruz wished to hold at bay. Its undergraduates disappeared from sight in long lines before central administrative buildings. They sat in lecture audiences of several hundreds in Berkeley's giant auditoriums. Powerfully entrenched departments and graduate faculties had captured its curriculum. Its younger instructors were held severely accountable to conventional professional standards devised by research-oriented senior professors; its increasingly anomic community became visible only at inflamatory rallies in Sproul Plaza. It was, in a few words, too big, too impersonal, too stratified, too rigid, too fragmented.

Such an image might be a caricature, and one laced with significant exceptions. Nevertheless, it was the image that gave the founders of Santa Cruz their mission. Such consistency as can be found among their goals derives from this negative identity. A small-college atmosphere was desirable because Berkeley's units were too large in scale. The curriculum at Santa Cruz would be interdisciplinary because Berkeley's was unequivocally disciplinary. It would give undergraduate studies central attention because Berkeley was too graduate-oriented; its return to a traditional "Liberal Arts" emphasis would be "innovatory" because Berkeley served too many external constituencies too uncritically. It would emphasize friendship and community in learning because Berkeley had pulverized its community through fiercely competitive pressures. In the early days, Santa Cruz saw little need for explicit scrutiny and defense of these values. The evils of Berkeley appeared self-evident. In the longer run, as the equilibrium of societal values shifted back again toward Berkeley, this dialectical relationship between the two campuses was to provide a rigidity of its own that threatened the very survival of the more vulnerable institution.

III. SYSTEM UNDER STRESS

In the fall of 1965, the faculty and students of the as yet half-constructed Cowell College assembled in trailers in an open meadow to inaugurate the first classes of the new university campus. Even while the paint and plaster was drying on the College's pergolas and belvederes, Santa Cruz was beginning to acquire an identity. On campus, as in the academic world at large, it was perceived and welcomed as an open-ended experiment. Faculty, students, and administrators throughout the country were soon applying for openings in the belief that the academic charter of Santa Cruz provided not so much a program as an invitation. This view likewise recurred in the faculty's Academic Senate, where all traditional practices appeared open to scrutiny and the most novel suggestions for improvement obtained at least a respectful hearing.[21] On other University of California campuses, stereotypical views of Santa Cruz developed quickly: life was agreeably undemanding there; personal values reigned supreme; teaching took precedence over research; the curriculum was anti-disciplinary, perhaps irresponsibly so; an academic counter-culture was rapidly becoming entrenched. Santa Cruz, for better or worse, was different.

For a while, the difference seemed for the better. Santa Cruz had little need to publicize its virtues; that work was done for it by others. National journals—and not only those devoted to education—found the combination of natural beauty and the novel collegiate system an irresistible attraction. One editor of a distinguished monthly even spent a term in residence and wrote a glowing account of his experience. With little difficulty, the administration obtained a Ford Foundation Venture Grant to deepen and extend the collegiate program. Internationally celebrated faculty from the leading universities in the country responded readily to the invitation to teach—or to found a new college—at Santa Cruz. Soon they—and an ambitious junior faculty—added further to the luster of the campus with an imposing collection of Guggenheim and Fulbright awards.

In their wake came a tide of students. Until well into the seventies, Santa Cruz was obliged to redirect the applications of four out of five qualified applicants to other campuses of the University.[22] Those it retained were from California's most academically promising students. For several years, among California educational institutions listed in the reports of the American Council of Education only the California Institute of Technology significantly outranked Santa Cruz in terms of the combined mathematical and verbal Scholastic Aptitude Test scores of its enrolled first-year students. Nationally, Santa Cruz was outscored in this respect by at most two dozen top-ranked private institutions. At the other end of the process, the better Santa Cruz students obtained admission in large numbers, often with handsome fellowships, to graduate schools at Harvard, Yale, Princeton, Stanford, and the University of Chicago. The rate of acceptance of pre-med students at medical schools ranked steadily among the highest in the country.

Internal developments gave substance to this favorable external image. The freshly-assembled Cowell faculty assumed responsibility for sections of a comprehensive three-quarter core course on Western Civilization. As new colleges opened each fall with themes of their own, their faculties followed Cowell's example. Stevenson's predominantly Social Science faculty found common ground with its Humanities contingent in core course on "Self and Society." Crown (the first predominantly Natural Sciences College) provided a bridge to the other Divisions with the theme of "Technology and Society." Merrill complemented the previously eurocentric orientation of the curriculum with its Third World program, while College V (now Porter College) provided a center for aesthetic philosophy and the Performing Arts.

Meanwhile, the College framework released an outpouring of creative courses designed by individual faculty members. Sometimes it permitted the flowering of a long-suppressed desire to teach outside one's professional field. A physicist turned his analytic powers to the study of Meso-American civilization, in which he had developed a deep avocational interest. An astronomer bore witness to a lifelong engagement with music through a successful course on Beethoven; an anthropologists's and an economist's discovery of a shared interest in architecture led to an analytic course on the structural properties of bodies and buildings. Sometimes, as in an historian's course on the social background of the 19th century Russian novel or in a psychologist's analysis of the paintings of Cezanne, instructors would apply the insights and explanations of their own disciplines to subjects conventionally treated under another heading. Alternatively, they might draw on texts from outside their disciplines to enrich the resources of their own, as when a political scientist used literature to illuminate the enduring dilemmas of public choice in the political arena. Collaborative ventures became common among College faculty who preferred to remain comfortably within their own discipline. A biologist, a psychologist, and a philosopher brought their distinctive disciplinary perspectives to bear on the phenomenon of death; an anthropologist, a linguist, and an instructor in American literature set out jointly to capture the elusive traits that define American civilization. More commonly, faculty met their obligations to their College through devising a general education course—a course for non-scientists in the history and philosophy of science, perhaps, or on the methodology and ethics of social research—of the kind that active, frontier-oriented scholars at other institutions have often proved personally reluctant to take the time to offer, even while acknowledging their place in a well-rounded liberal curriculum. Underlying these disparate endeavors was a common approach: a disengagement from the constricting pressures of the monographic tradition, a joyous affirmation of the capacity of the amateur to bring new life—and sometimes new insight—to old subjects.

Students responded to these examples with an efflorescence of independent studies and individually designed majors. Interdisciplinary and even transdivisional joint and double majors rose steadily from roughly 6% in the 1969–70 academic year to nearly 11% in 1973–74. Together with individual majors, they totalled precisely one-sixth of all degrees awarded in the latter year.[23] When Merrill College inaugurated a program of Field Studies, students quickly fanned out off-campus to undertake research projects of up to a year in such scattered locations as the nearby Salinas Valley, Bay area prisons and mental hospitals, the Bolivian *altiplano*, and the jungles of Sumatra.

Other initiatives in the early years reinforced the emerging subculture of the campus. Imaginative efforts were made at every level to promote congruence between its formal and informal aspects. Thus in rejecting high-pressure inter-campus competitive spectator sports, and emphasizing instead the acquisition of individual proficiency in such "lifetime" sports as scuba-diving and rock-climbing, the physical education office sought self-consciously to parallel the stress on individual tutorials in the Colleges. With administrative encouragement, academically overwhelmed students regained contact with more elemental challenges and rhythms through cultivating in the very midst of the campus an organic farm in which flowers and vegetables of exceptional quality were offered to all visitors. As more colleges were founded, emotionally integrative concerns began to displace more formally academic themes. Kresge College carried California's human potential movement to its logical conclusion in a university setting through using retreats, encounter groups, prolonged open-door office hours and Core Course seminars in humanistic psychology to promote affective bonding among faculty, students and staff. Under the forceful leadership of a charismatic black Provost, Oakes College undertook to provide a supportive community for "nontraditional" students from racial and ethnic minorities whose inadequate preparation and initial fears concerning the unfamiliar demands of university life had all too often impeded their effective entry into the academic mainstream. But by some margin the most widely noted development of this nature occurred almost casually one September afternoon when the newly-arrived Cowell College faculty responded favorably to a proposal from their founding Provost that they abolish the traditional letter grading system, with its misleading implication that all dimensions of a student's academic performance in a course could be logically compared with those of other students along a single scale. Shortly afterwards, the faculty adopted the practice of writing short narrative evaluations in which these dimensions would be separately assessed. To many subsequent instructors, and certainly to a near-consensual majority of Santa Cruz students, the narrative evaluation system soon came to seem the feature that most distinctively contributed to their sense that the campus cherished the individuality of each student.[24]

Santa Cruz was becoming an early monument to its own success. Intimations that construction of a City of God on earth was under way inspired student readers of the chronicles of old New England to entitle the campus newspaper "The City on a Hill Press." Within half a decade, nostalgia for the opening days reached flood tide in the form of reverent senior theses, memoirs, and public addresses. "Late" arrivals among the faculty—late by as little as one or two years—frequently found themselves patronized by the founding faculty of their College as unsubtly as were visiting faculty from such ossified institutions as Berkeley and UCLA. Meanwhile, Santa Cruz was being studied—and then restudied—by educators professionally concerned with academic innovation. So wide was the spectrum of possibilities being opened by the expanding campus that in one of the more prominent of these efforts two separate chapters were thought necessary to cover the emerging polar patterns of Cowell and Kresge Colleges.[25]

Then, at some unperceived hour in the early 'seventies, these heady developments crested. Almost imperceptibly at first, but soon noticeably, and then—toward the end of the decade—with a dismaying suddenness that attracted statewide journalistic attention, Santa Cruz lost its innovative momentum. This loss was both qualitative and quantitative. It could be measured in the diminution of new proposals, and in weakening faculty and budgetary support for the more experimental of the existing programs. It appeared in altered promotional criteria, and in the redefinition of mission to conform more closely to standards prevailing on other campuses within the system. In time, however, these trends began also to register as figures—figures that might merely signify that the campus had stopped growing, but that, in their implications for claims to State appropriations, inevitably chilled the expectations of the most ardent reformer. And this loss of momentum soon showed up in every aspect of life on campus: it affected not only the curriculum but also the pattern of physical construction, not only the number and kinds of students who came to campus but the character and calibre of the faculty who remained to teach them.

First to go were the College core courses. Spurred by the general rebelliousness of the Viet Nam years, students began to object in principle to required courses. An overcommitted, harassed faculty, now that the sheer novelty of collaborative amateurism had palled, were increasingly disposed to yield the point. Cowell abandoned its sophomore tier of core courses after three years, and its historic first-year course after six. Stevenson College progressively contracted its three-quarter course to a single required quarter; Crown abandoned all efforts of this nature following the departure of a crucial instructor for another campus. A small number of Merrill faculty members continued to offer an optional one-quarter version of the former three-quarter requirement amid mounting controversy over the appropriate geographical and political definition of the "Third World." College V resolved at the outset to forego a comprehensive year-long core course in favor of small single-quarter studio seminars in the performing arts; these were staffed by individual instructors without any particular efforts being made to generate a common experience through coordinated requirements, and soon disappeared as a mandatory element of the College program. The culmination of this trend occurred when College VIII, with limited residential facilities, expressly eschewed the core course approach, announcing that it intended to provide a home for the "neglected" upper-division transfer and graduate students.

Next the concept of a College "theme" came under attack. Stevenson College had been expected to inaugurate social studies on campus through its "Self and Society" program. By 1968, however, the senior Fellows in Literature had come to outnumber the social scientists. Soon the faculty was issuing formal statements to the effect that Stevenson should be considered henceforward a "general, liberal arts" College stressing "overall humanistic excellence" without any distinctive commitment to a particular mode of inquiry.

Other College faculties soon followed Stevenson's example. At Crown, structurally vulnerable from the outset through its dependence on a Natural Science faculty majority largely housed in and closely tied to the central laboratories, two successive Provosts stirred up intense controversy through their efforts to restore some degree of centrality to the College academic program. In due course the faculty resolved not only that Crown's core course and senior seminar programs should remain moribund but, for good measure, that no other courses should be taught under collegiate auspices by its "hard money" faculty. Kresge College had no substantive theme to give up; its much-publicized experiments in interpersonal dynamics had become a source of embarrassment, however, and were quietly contracted by a more conservative Provost. Faculty loyalists at Cowell, Merrill, and College V continued the struggle to maintain some semblance of a commitment to their Colleges' respective academic emphasis on Western Civilization, the Third World, and the (Performing) Arts. Particularly in the latter two Colleges, however, the primary instructional burden in the College programs were increasingly borne by "soft money" faculty. In an ironic turnabout, these temporary appointees came to have a greater stake in preserving the thematic identity of their Colleges than did the regular "ladder" faculty. And this paradoxical development accelerated in the early 'seventies as the Colleges, searching for roles to replace the one they had yielded as the academic home base for lower-division students, shifted their resources into uneconomically small and uncoordinated upper-division specialty courses and into such precariously financed upper-division ventures as the Cowell College major in "Arts and Crafts and Their History," Stevenson's "Modern Society and Social Thought" program, and the College V Aesthetic Studies Major.

These developments reflected an underlying tension in the original design of the Colleges. Requiring each College to harbor members of every discipline on campus while charging it with developing a definable theme assured that some Fellows would feel appreciably closer than others to whatever axis of orientation was chosen. The dilemma proved insoluble. Provosts could put pressure on those more removed from this axis—chemists in a "Third World" College—to reeducate themselves in line with collegiate objectives. Occasionally, such pressures might lead to a welcome expansion of capabilities; more often they would generate faculty irritation, insincere or incompetent teaching, and a strong disposition to withdraw from general participation in the life of the College. Alternatively, as at Stevenson, Colleges could relieve the stress by permitting their Fellows to follow their own bent in devising courses to be taught under College auspices, but at the price of blurring the curricular identity of the College. With no binding disciplinary or thematic thread, even the very best of such courses failed to cumulate into a coherent program, while the remainder became increasingly difficult to subject to commonly understood standards of academic merit. The self-indulgent idiosyncrasies apparent in certain College courses persuaded many sober scholars that the most egregious College courses were typical of College courses generally, discrediting the collegiate enterprise as a whole in their eyes. These problems compounded swiftly as faculty replacement shifted the ratio among disciplines within a College, as new extradisciplinary interests displaced those a candidate had strategically highlighted at the time of initial consideration by a College, or as faculty at all levels began once again to feel the pressures of long-term career calculations within their discipline.

The declining innovatory capacities of the Colleges might conceivably have been offset by growing momentum within the three academic Divisions that were their intended counterpart in the original campus plan. But the Divisions had long since lost such capabilities as they possessed to serve as magnetic fields of faculty energy. With more self-confident, far-sighted leadership than they received in the crucial opening years, they could possibly have been used as a framework within which to foster imaginative interdisciplinary combinations. Such leadership was not forthcoming. It would have entailed, in concert with the Divisional faculties, a fresh definition of the goals of university education, an uninhibited assessment in relation to those ends of the terms in which such education is currently compartmentalized, and an architectonic vision of the curricular possibilities the campus offered. It would also have required unwavering insistence, even in a period of rapid growth, on exploiting complementarities among neighboring disciplines in the recruitment process. The three Divisional Vice-Chancellors gave no indication during this period of any inclination to proceed along such lines. Ever mindful of the University of California tradition that authority over the curriculum rests with the faculty, they seemed content to allow faculty preference to shape defining choices.

Initiatives of this nature would probably have been doomed to failure in any case. From the outset, the Divisions suffered from a suspicion of artificiality. Divisions lacked the ecological base and social perquisites of the Colleges. They enjoyed no natural loyalties, being lines on organization charts embodied in small staff offices removed from the prime centers of research and teaching activity. Their faculties came to campus trained and certified in disciplinary, not Divisional, fields. Divisional appointments by title ("Professor of Social Sciences") were rare; and in a curious but significant omission, campus Academic Senate regulations made no provision until 1979 for Divisional sponsorship of courses. Divisional partitionings of knowledge, moreover, were not free from the charges of arbitrariness frequently levelled against the disciplines. The Humanities Division was deeply split between the standards of the traditional "letters" faculties and the orientations and needs of studio artists. "Social" historians, and instructors who approached literature as a cultural manifestation of society, tended to interact more intensively with social scientists than with their Humanities colleagues. Commonality of subject matter did more to determine the extradisciplinary ties of philosophers and linguists than did Divisional lines.[26] As each Division approached one hundred members, these slender ties attenuated further. By 1974, when incoming Chancellor Mark Christensen announced that he was changing the title of all future heads of the Divisions from "Vice-Chancellor" to "Dean," his action merely ratified a well-established expectation that such figures, whatever their title, would manage units essentially limited to processing personnel and budgetary requests.

As both the Colleges and the Divisions receded in importance, a superficially novel organizational entity emerged: the disciplinary Board of Studies. Departmentalization was, of course, precisely what the Santa

Cruz campus had been designed to head off. Insofar as the Colleges could not be expected to assume full and exclusive responsibility for curricular and personnel decisions, these functions had been left in the original campus plan to the three Divisions. Even the most idealistic among the founders foresaw, however, that as the campus expanded, some unit smaller than the Division would be needed to organize information relevant to the various personnel processes of the Division. In addition, some body—perhaps, the early planners thought, a rough equivalent to the various boards of examiners in England's two model collegiate universities—would be needed to establish the formal requirements for disciplinary majors and to administer the comprehensive examinations thought necessary to certify proficiency in these fields.[27] The inclusion in the opening class of 150 junior-level transfers from other campuses, most seeking to complete their degree requirements in a conventional field by the end of the following academic year, inescapably posed pressing questions concerning the future status of disciplinary studies on campus.

The central administration saw clearly where these pressures could lead. Departing from the practice on other campuses, it vested budgetary responsibility (and therefore the payment of one half of faculty salaries) in the Divisions. With self-conscious intent, it employed the title of "Convenor" for the Divisionally-appointed chairs of subcommittees called together from time to time from the various Colleges to transact disciplinary business, and resolutely denied the "Convenors'" pleas for special secretarial assistance. When obliged to request the convening of such groups, the Divisional Vice Chancellors proceeded with great caution. Thus when, early in the opening years, they called meetings of the Social Sciences and Humanities faculties to propose the creation of "Boards of Studies" in the several disciplines of the Divisions, they further proposed that membership on these "Boards" be limited to three to five appointed (and presumably senior) faculty, at least one of whom would be from an outside though related discipline. Moreover, they intimated that the functions of these Boards would largely consist in defining and maintaining formal standards for a degree.[28]

None of these precautions availed. Senior faculty were quick to point out that the proposed appointive power could be manipulated by the Chancellor to influence personnel recommendations and to breach the historic autonomy maintained by University of California faculty in curricular matters. Junior faculty were not disposed to turn over to a limited number of their senior colleagues the right to structure major requirements, initiate recruitment of additional faculty, and plan the graduate programs.[29] In December of 1965, the Academic Senate accepted the recommendation of its Special Committee on Boards of Studies that such Boards be established. Reflecting the objections that had previously been raised, however, it further endorsed the Committee's recommendation that the Boards automatically include as of right all Senate members in the discipline as well as a single "outside" member.[30] This move decisively increased the ratio of disciplinary to non-disciplinary members within the Boards.[31] It also converted the Boards into general-purpose action groups in the eyes of their members. Some junior faculty arrived on campus directly from disciplinary graduate-school programs; finding immediate inclusion in a familiar professional entity, unmediated by prior involvement in the life of the Colleges, they effectively (if unintentionally) added momentum to the disciplinary sub-divisions of the Divisions in relation both to the Colleges and to the Divisions themselves.[32]

The consequences were soon evident. A Senate motion to change the title of the Boards of Studies to "Departments" was overwhelmingly defeated in 1967. The Divisions maintained firm control over their budgets. But the Boards soon acquired most of the remaining accoutrements of conventional departments—among them, office space and a secretary for the "Convenor" (soon to be retitled "Chair"), full authority to sponsor courses acceptable to the Academic Senate's Committee on Courses, a virtually exclusive initiatory role in the recruitment of ladder faculty, and a major role in all subsequent personnel processes. By the early 1970s, five student enrollments in six were in courses taught under Board auspices; by 1978, the enrollment in College-sponsored courses had dropped below 10% of the campus undergraduate total. Apart from six College major programs, a small set of other interdisciplinary majors, and a scattering of individual majors devised by students under College sponsorship, the Boards administered all the routes to a major and the corresponding Comprehensive Examination or Senior Thesis it required. Several Boards had sponsored graduate programs on their own, although an interdisciplinary "History of Consciousness" program remained the most conspicuous—and most controversial—undertaking at that level. By 1975, few would take issue with the campus planning official who declared that "The Boards are where the action is."[33]

Thus were laid the conditions for a struggle that was to consume much of the energy and much of the emotion for most of the seventies on the Santa Cruz campus. Running like a fault line through every proposed initiative, polarizing and classifying colleagues, threatening interests and hardening stereotypes, was the issue how each decision would affect the delicate balance between College and Board. Bookkeeping issues displaced educational objectives in the contest for faculty time, for office space, for course sponsorship and credited majors. The question at hand might involve dollars and cents; it might take the form of an asserted right to consultation; it might have to do with the shadings in a choice of title. The assured constant was a rapid mobilization of concern in each instance around the implications of its resolution for this equilibrium.

Bitterest of all, predictably, were the disputes generated by personnel actions. These typically began with charges by the College that the Board had given it a thin file on a chosen candidate 24 hours before bringing the bewildered recruit for a hurried encounter en route to the Chancellor's office—charges that evoked increasingly contemptuous responses by the Board to the effect that the Colleges in any case judged candidates merely by their manifest social graces and their skill in feigning interest in the collegiate "theme." They ended five to seven years later amid allegations by the Board that College personnel committees and Provosts uncritically defended members of their social club even in tenure decisions, and lamentations in the College at the Board's confusion of quantity with quality, of the routinely documentable with the noble ideals on which the campus had been founded.[34] In between these crucial checkpoints, assistant (and even tenured associate) professors felt they were serving two masters, confronting demands of uncertain weight that were often incompatible and generally overwhelming in their cumulative effect.[35] Many faculty grew progressively more nervous over their physical and even professional isolation in a College from senior members in their discipline. And these concerns were often well founded; for the demands of the College could have injurious consequences for those assistant professors who, having failed to obtain tenure at Santa Cruz, subsequently discovered how low a value a conventional and increasingly glutted outside job market placed on evidence of gifted extradisciplinary teaching and imaginative contributions to institution-building in a dossier otherwise relatively bereft of publications.

Over time, the perceived pattern became simplified beyond reality. Colleges saw themselves as the sole remaining guardians of academic innovations on campus. The Boards of Studies, from a College point of view, had alarmingly enfeebled the innovatory possibilities of the campus by draining faculty time and energy from the Colleges into conventional channels. Board chairs replied with mounting weariness that the Colleges gave license to the faculty's most self-indulgent impulses while leaving the Boards the ungrateful task of maintaining a curriculum enabling students to make normal progress toward a degree. Students tended to endorse (often in highly rhetorical language) the College position; their actual choice of courses supported the Board's. Framed in these terms, the contest was one the Colleges could not win. Both Colleges and Boards might lose from it, however, since mutual distrust prevented Boards and Colleges from seriously considering recommendations that they collapse at least some of the numerous parallel committees their dual structure generated. The resulting administrative burden on faculty remained inordinate. And since virtually all "ladder" faculty were members of both Colleges and Boards, the perpetual contest between the two assured a progressively deepening institutional schizophrenia.

The debilitating effects of this conflict were not lost on the participants. But the faculty remained too divided to undertake coordinated reform themselves. Their single most vital organizational units—the Boards of Studies—were understaffed and beset by conflicting pressures. Board chairmanships rotated biennially among the more compliant (and too often junior) members. Yet Santa Cruz had now grown to the point at which no centrally administered remedies were readily available. Traditional faculty prerogatives in the University of California system markedly qualified administrative discretion in budgetary matters, severely limited it in personnel decisions, and excluded it altogether in the realm of the curriculum. By expanding the usual trilateral tension between departments, Academic Senate committees, and the chancellorial office to a hexagonal contest involving Divisional Deans, College Provosts, and College faculty committees, the campus had stretched the administrative process to its limits, diffusing accountability and stalemating every initiative. In a tangentially related but unfortunate coincidence, moreover, the Chancellor's office in Santa Cruz was in no position during the mid-'seventies to exercise such leadership in the crisis as might otherwise have been possible. Founding Chancellor McHenry retired in June of 1974. His amiable successor was deposed by a remarkably united faculty barely eighteen months later for insufficient administrative direction. President Saxon then appointed a University Vice President to preside benignly over the campus until his scheduled retirement in mid-1977, at which point the present Chancellor, a distinguished biologist largely unknown to the Santa Cruz faculty, was brought in from the California Institute of Technology to try his hand. For much of this period, questions of leadership necessarily displaced other items from the agenda of consideration without leading to policy conclusions. To disenchanted observers, the problem of Santa Cruz appeared not to be that its elaborately contrived system of checks and balances was failing to work. It was rather that this intricate clockwork, with its assurance of a fair hearing for all parties, was working too well.[36]

Meanwhile, a crisis of a different nature was gathering force. Suddenly and swiftly, Santa Cruz was running out of students. Until 1972, qualified applicants to the University of California had more difficulty obtaining admission to the Santa Cruz campus than to any other; three years later, recruiters for Santa Cruz were actively scouring the high schools, and the campus was accepting applications redirected from Berkeley and Davis. As the quantity of applications declined, so did their measurable quality. Nationwide test score averages were falling during these years, but those of the applicants Santa Cruz was obliged to accept fell faster—from mean verbal and math SAT scores (men only) of 611 and 647 in 1972 to 558 and 588 in 1975 respectively; from 67.9% reporting high school grade averages of "A-" and above in 1972 to 45.6% in 1975.[37] By 1975, too, the transfer students were beginning to outnumber first-year students among those newly admitted to the campus. Key administrators professed to welcome this development as a realization of the egalitarian ideals of the California Master Plan for Higher Education of 1960. In so doing they chose to ignore the implications for the distinctive collegiate programs of the campus of relying ever more heavily on constituencies with only a major in a discipline to complete.

Declining growth was perceived as a problem throughout the University of California system by the end of the 'seventies. But for Santa Cruz, it had especially ominous implications. During the halcyon budget years Chancellor McHenry had honored his pledge to keep the per-unit cost of his campus below that of any other in the system. He had done his work too well. Now, as Santa Cruz began to feel the pinch of overcrowded laboratories, overextended studios, Colleges of seven to eight hundred students designed for six hundred, and swimming pools and library facilities that remained on the drawing boards, it confronted a much more constricted financial climate. In this context, its declining admissions record and publicly visible weaknesses in its collegiate and leadership structures did not enhance its case. Yet rising student/faculty and student/facility ratios did not reveal the full extent of the problem. Santa Cruz had come into being at precisely the moment when expectations of wide-open growth had seemed most plausible. It had designed its collegiate system, organized its disciplines, and recruited its faculties on the supposition that it would be accommodating some twenty thousand students within twenty years. Campus administrators had regarded the planned opening of professional schools of engineering, business, and landscape architecture as essential to give "balance" to an exclusively Liberal Arts student body and to add to the standing of a largely undergraduate campus within the graduate-oriented University of California system. The projected contraction of student enrollments torpedoed these plans, leaving the campus with numerous truncated mini-departments and lopsided specializations alongside gaping holes in its curriculum. To fill these holes and round out the disciplinary and inter-disciplinary offerings in an orderly manner had now become impossible. In its concern to remain avant-garde the campus had neglected to tend its flanks.

From certain perspectives, advantages could be discerned in the enforced slow-down. It avoided a full test of the Kerr-McHenry thesis that might have been found wanting in the event. It gave the Colleges new life in their competition with potential graduate programs; it forced the Boards and Divisions to consider afresh the advantages of cooperation among ancillary fields in faculty hiring and course sponsorship; it relieved the pressure for proposed facilities that might not have been funded in any case. Undoubtedly, the slow-down helped preserve the beauty of the forest ecology. These blessings did not seem salient to anguished administrators and ambitious faculty, however. Santa Cruz was still a sufficiently American campus for many to feel that quantitative growth was a basic index of institutional vitality. And if not all of its members shared that view, high school counselors, potential applicants, State appropriations committees, and the central administrators of the University of California unquestionably did.

And now another statistical trend began to alarm the campus. Santa Cruz, which had always cherished the belief that above all campuses it gave first place to its students, had to face graphs that showed its rate of attrition among enrolled students to be the highest of the nine campuses—and highest by a large margin. Various explanations suggested themselves for this unwelcome trend. Most popular was the self-serving reflection that the utopian promise of Santa Cruz inevitably attracted a disproportionate number of unconventional, highly idealistic students—students who looked upon education not as an instrumental preliminary to a materially rewarding job but as a potentially transfiguring experience, and whose disappointment with any earthly institution was predictable. But Santa Cruz had broadcast its utopian appeal most strongly in the early days. The upward rate of attrition coincided with a rising proportion of students who had first chosen to attend conventional campuses before transferring to Santa Cruz—and it was among this group that the rate of attrition was highest.

One could also maintain the ultimately unprovable thesis that Santa Cruz had simply expanded beyond the small, fixed pool of California high school graduates for whom its programs was distinctively appealing, and that both its admissions and retention problems were attributable to this single fact. Less speculative were indications that the novel and poorly-understood narrative evaluation system was reinforcing popular suspicions of loose living among the redwoods. Journalists purveyed among receptive high school counselors and anxious parents the unfounded notion that it precluded academic failure, while Boards of Studies reported that they were losing their most ambitious students to Stanford and Berkeley because of an erroneous but unshakable conviction that a grade point average was needed to obtain admission to the most competitive graduate schools. As occupational concerns acquired more urgency in a decelerating economy, Santa Cruz's reputation as an experimental, exclusively liberal arts campus was proving a liability. And there was simply too much evidence, ranging from exit forms to survey data, that students other than the most secure and self-directed seemed to suffer from poorly coordinated advising, insufficient attention to their curricular needs during the years preceding selection of a major, and an uncertain relation between collegiate and disciplinary programs. But to make these observations was to call into question the central principles on which the campus had been founded. Merely to try to do better what Santa Cruz had always tried to do well would not suffice. Outside events were posing ever more squarely the question: could a campus founded to embody the most soaring aspirations of the 'sixties adapt to a prolonged projection of lowered expectations?

IV. REFORM AND REVOLUTION

Attempted reform, whatever its outcome, is instructive in either case. If successful, it may offer a validation of the diagnosis and strategy pursued by the reformers.[38] If unsuccessful, it indicates the weight and interrelationship of the variables with which they were obliged to contend. Either way, attempted reform highlights the perceptions of those who take action. It also illuminates the consequence of displacing certain variables of the system, revealing their critical range. So it was at Santa Cruz.

Amid mounting indications of system failure, the Santa Cruz campus attempted systemic reforms on two occasions within the past decade. The first attempt—the so-called "Reaggregation" movement—occurred under the auspices of the Santa Cruz Academic Senate's Budget and Planning Committee in 1974 during the first year in office of Santa Cruz's second chancellor, and indirectly contributed to his shortened tenure in that office. The second—this time styled "Campus Reorganization"—was initiated by its fourth chancellor in 1978 during his second year on campus and eventually became the responsibility of the three Divisional Deans in conjunction with several key Academic Senate committees and two *ad hoc* chancellorial bodies. "Reaggregation" had much effect on certain individuals, but little on the system. "Reorganization", on the contrary, threatened to affect the system so deeply in so many respects that many embittered faculty and students concluded the changes had destroyed precisely those qualities that made the campus distinctively appealing to them.

In the winter of 1974, for no reason directly attributable to a specific external event, several prominent faculty members began circulating mimeographed versions of their thoughts regarding the status of the Colleges at Santa Cruz. Other faculty responded in kind; by the end of the Quarter, an accumulation of proposals for reform had emerged. During the Spring Quarter, the Academic Senate's Budget and Academic Planning Committee addressed itself to the issue. At the unusually well-attended final Senate meeting of the academic year, the Committee presented a motion calling for a sweeping "reaggregation" of the faculty among the Colleges. After little discussion, and with one recorded dissent, the motion was carried.

In the report accompanying the motion, the Planning Committee offered an extended analysis of the malaise afflicting the College system.[39] Its thesis was that the membership of the Colleges had become incompatible with their missions. It suggested that a coordinated transfer of faculty members among the Colleges be implemented to concentrate faculty in critical masses more closely aligned with their professional interests. The central argument proceeded by two steps:

1. For the majority of the faculty in most Colleges, the College "theme" had become peripheral. Under the rule requiring representation from all disciplines in each College, many faculty had been placed from the outset in Colleges with curricular orientations far removed from their interests. Others had altered their professional interests over the years. Still others were in particular Colleges not because of any genuine affinity with the collegiate theme but because they were available in a certain year as the favored candidate of a Board of Studies at a time when that College had an opening. Rhetorically, the pattern of collegiate membership expressed an alleged commonality of interest; in actuality, it largely reflected the history of disciplinary hiring on campus.

2. Arguments for the current pattern were not convincing even at the

level of principle. The rule of full disciplinary representation had been justified by the alleged need to provide a full array of advising options for students at the College. Experience had shown the limits to interdisciplinary cross-pollination: an economist might well benefit academically fron interaction with an institutional anthropologist and a policy-oriented political scientist, but would derive only a very occasional serendipitous insight from having an office flanked by those of a potter and an instructor in French literature. The latter condition tended to reduce collegiate interchange to the level of mere sociability while enhancing professional isolation to a dangerous degree.

With these objectives in mind, the Planning Committee proceeded to construct and administer a questionnaire designed to elicit from faculty members a sociogram of their academic interests and the colleagues they had found most professionally supportive of their work. Using this data, the Committee grouped faculty names into tentative clusters that appeared least incongruent with the existing curricular orientations of the Colleges, and then initiated discussions with College Provosts and executive committees concerning the patterns these exercises had revealed. Soon, however, the Committee ran up against an elementary fact of human nature: academic roles were only one of many aspects in the lives of individual faculty members—and, in the intimate ecology of the Colleges, not necessarily the most salient aspect. Geography—and history—had already become destiny. In principle, College Provosts and faculties continued to support a policy they had endorsed the preceding May. In practice, they saw in Reaggregation an opportunity to pick off distinguished scholars and friends from other colleges while barring or extruding those they found personally objectionable.[10] Founding members of a College with deep roots in its institutions were not about to be "reaggregated" elsewhere because of mere professional incongruity with its themes. More psychically mobile faculty became frustrated at the endless formation and reformation of new coalitions. Many Colleges invented factitious mini-clusters in order to justify retaining or attracting a single favored faculty member. In vain the Budget and Academic Planning Committee insisted that the Colleges must commit themselves to predefined academic clusters, not merely to selected individuals within those clusters. The central administration, showing signs of the vacillation and unclarity of purpose that was eventually to lead to the deposition of Chancellor Christensen, offered little more than good will and privately expressed support to the enterprise. With no formal authority to enforce its proposed rules, the Senate committee retreated in disarray.

With the demise of Reaggregation into something resembling a fraternity rush, the Colleges let slip their major opportunity to regain the academic mementum they had lost to the Boards. By 1978, their condition approached catatonia. Except at Stevenson College, where a successful mandatory three-quarter sequence in the intellectual history of Western civilization had suddenly sprung to life, the College core courses were at most vestigial remnants in the form of optional single-quarter courses. Nothing had emerged to take their place as a form of predisciplinary education for undergraduates in their first two years: the catalog merely stated that undergraduates were obliged at some point to meet the campus breadth requirement through taking virtually any three courses in each of the three Divisions. College courses at the upper-division level contracted steadily in numbers while more and more resembling misleadingly labelled courses in a standard discipline. In only one area did Colleges show continuing vitality: their demands on faculty time for administrative purposes remained unstinting.

It was this situation that Robert Sinsheimer confronted in mid-1977 on assuming office as Santa Cruz's fourth Chancellor. Within a few months he had discerned how little support for its financial needs he could secure from other University of California campuses so long as his house remained in conspicuous disorder. His first response to a particularly ungenerous allocation of new faculty positions was a stiff letter of protest to President Saxon. His second was more original. In October of 1978, on the eve of his formal inauguration, he revealed to a hastily assembled gathering of Provosts, Deans, and Senate chairs a sweeping proposal for reorganizing the eight Colleges. Its central features cut the Gordian Knot: Colleges would henceforward be excluded from all personnel processes involving regular faculty, would cease to sponsor courses, and would be placed in a kind of administrative receivership under the three Divisional Deans, who would thereupon supervise a large-scale transfer of faculty among the Colleges to bring about greater coherence among interpenetrating disciplines.

Stunned by the boldness of the proposal, and reluctant to show conspicuous disunity before assembled University dignitaries at a precarious moment in the campus's history, the Academic Senate endorsed the plan a few days later in a display of virtual unanimity. It even added a phrase expressing appreciation for the Chancellor's "decisive leadership" in the hour of need. Soon various Senate and special chancellorial committees were at work on the detailed administrative implications of the plan. As these became more evident, the previous unanimity disintegrated rapidly into sharply polarized factions. Nevertheless, if often by narrow majorities, the broader elements of the proposal were approved intact.

Whatever the long-run implications for the power of the Colleges, the humanly exhausting and often inequitable dual-track personnel processes by now found few defenders. And to the rather general surprise of the campus, the Academic Senate's Curriculum Committee, together with a special chancellorial committee on the curriculum, was able to reassign all but one of several hundred College-sponsored courses to disciplinary Boards of Studies, to a small number of interdisciplinary Committees of Studies, or to the newly-empowered Divisions.[41]

Disciplinary reconcentration among the Colleges provided a stiffer challenge. For some months, campus reorganization threatened to founder on that rock.[42] This time, however, those responsible for supervising the transfer of faculty enjoyed firm backing from the chancellorial office. They also profited from deepening anxiety about the future of the campus and weary acceptance of the inevitability of change. By the end of the academic year the third, most controversial element of Campus Reorganization was largely executed. In six of the eight Colleges, at least three-quarters of the Fellows were members of the same Division as the Dean to whom the College Provost now formally reported. And as nearly half the faculty began unpacking books in new offices amid new neighbors in the early summer months of 1979, the campus seemed suddenly unrecognizable to many who had known it best.

James Q. Wilson has argued that organizations whose members are primarily attracted by its purported ideals will experience greater difficulty in adapting to changing circumstances than will those organizations that maintain their membership through supplying instrumental or social incentives.[43] To be sure, the faculty and staff would not long remain at Santa Cruz without paychecks, and most of its students are not indifferent to the value of their certificate of graduation in the outer world. Nor is sociability a minor factor on a campus dedicated to "the pursuit of truth in the company of friends." But Santa Cruz has always pulled the majority of its staff and students to the campus by visions larger than those just named. In that fact is to be found both its special attractiveness and the source of its most perilous restrictions.

V. RETROSPECT AND PROSPECT

As the University of California at Santa Cruz enters the 'eighties, it bears ever fewer marks of the hopes of the 'sixties. Gone are its days as a model for others to follow. For some years the campus has stabilized at less than a fourth of the 27,500 students it was projected to absorb by

1990. It shows no signs of expanding dramatically beyond that point. Its eight Colleges faithfully feed and house the majority of their students but no longer seek to reorient their minds. Its faculty now largely teach within their disciplines and expect to obtain their primary forms of institutional recognition through their achievements within these channels. The courses in its catalog do not differ greatly in subject matter and aggregate pattern from those of other universities of similar size. By default, its narrative evaluation system has come to attract a disproportionate degree of attention from students and the press as its principal sign of educational innovation. Even that institution, however, has entered a precarious passage from which it may not emerge intact.

Behind these formal similarities to other university campuses remain important differences. Santa Cruz retains its unparalleled natural setting which, while often spoken of in deprecatory tones as peripheral and even antithetical to a serious educational atmosphere, contributes to its members' sense of privilege at being able to live and work in a unique community. Though choice of College is no longer critical to students' formal curriculum, the Colleges have proven deeply rooted as a source of social identity and loyalty. Intracollegiate faculty interaction remains interdisciplinary in character, leading in many instances to College-based seminars and to the formation of Organized Research Units.[44] Santa Cruz has remained free of the corrupting influences of spectator-oriented athletics, and its faculty have continued to resist pressures to make the curriculum serve the vocational and avocational interests of various external constituencies in the State. As to the courses the faculty do teach, one has only to pay comparative visits to the textbook sections of campus bookstores in Berkeley and Stanford to appreciate the exceptional wealth and imaginative range of materials employed in the undergraduate curriculum of Santa Cruz.

These are qualities that make the tuition-free, publicly-supported campus of Santa Cruz one of the best bargains in liberal undergraduate education in the United States. But the founders of Santa Cruz had set their sights higher. For their object was not merely to provide a sensitive education of high quality for undergraduates and a scattering of graduate students. The more messianic among these planners had sought to institutionalize a disposition toward academic innovation that would make a decisive break with prevailing patterns of higher education elsewhere. Judged by their expectations, and by the academic goals their collegiate design was intended to serve, the Santa Cruz venture must be deemed a failure.[45]

What central thread runs through the record of retrenchment and reorganization this essay has recorded? Did this product of the reformist energy of the 'sixties experience a routinization of innovatory impulses? Did Santa Cruz suffer from loss of vision—and loss of nerve—by its leaders? Was that vision perhaps initially flawed and internally contradictory to begin with? Or were the prospects of utopian reconstruction on a single campus, however ingeniously designed and unstintingly supported, always limited by its external environment more severely than its founders were willing to acknowledge?

This essay has shown that any complete account of the fate of the Santa Cruz experiment must include elements from all four theses. "Burn-out"—a familiar problem of most high-stress contemporary organizations—was a prevalent affliction at Santa Cruz. It affected above all those founding faculty members who had repeatedly put aside their scholarly work to attend an institution-building meeting or chair a new program or stretch themselves beyond their prior disciplinary limits to take part in an interdisciplinary core course. But even those who retained their original enthusiasm and freshness of vision eventually found themselves adjusting to the growing pressures toward standardization accompanying sheer numerical expansion and greater complexity of the interdependent parts.

Certainly, too, there were failures of insight and firmness of purpose at the level of leadership. Failure to capitalize on even the limited potential of the academic Divisions was a case in point; collapse of the first reaggregation initiative was another. Beyond such choices, there were flaws in the original design as well. These have already been reviewed in connection with the pressures that led to reorganization. Yet perhaps the most consequentional of these flaws was not structural but philosophical. It was the failure to squarely face the ramifications of the faultline running between an Enlightenment view of "liberal" education as a clearing away of the institutional obstacles to a self-directed pursuit of individually-acquired academic interests, and a Rousseauist insistence that students must first be "liberated" from these accretions before they are qualified to take responsibility for their own education.[45] These views were thought compatible in the early days of Santa Cruz; in the event, they were not.

But of all the flaws of initial design and subsequent choice, the most damaging were those arising from failure to give sufficient weight to the problems of insulating a utopian campus from the outer world. Meadows could visually isolate the campus from a harmless seaside resort; they could not guard against the seeds of worldly ambition, of mundane occupational concerns, of deeply-ingrained cultural values that faculty, administrators, and even students carried in, often quite unknowingly, from their society. So long as faculty were trained in and hired from highly professional universities, so long as they respected the dominant canons of these institutions, so long as they retained ambition for scholarly accomplishment and recognition—so long, in fine, as Santa Cruz remained accountable to the values of the University of California, and beyond it, to the society that sustained that institution—these seeds would cling to them. When, not whether, these seeds would sprout was the only question. Among students, they might lie dormant a little longer. As the bright job prospects of the 'sixties became a mirage in the 'seventies, students, too, would discover in themselves a growing appreciation for the benefits of conventional disciplinary certification.

Santa Cruz was therefore faced by a fundamental choice. It could attempt to pit itself wholly against the world, accepting a leisurely rate of growth and limiting its recruitment to those who truly met collegiate needs. It could absorb new faculty into new collegiate colonies established by members of the mother College, and grant promotion for imaginative and dedicated College service and for various signs of intellectual distinction (including a modest amount of writing and research).[46] The consequence of this move would have been to reduce faculty to a form of feudal dependence on the unique environment and unique protections that Santa Cruz alone was prepared to offer. Alternatively, the campus could accept the inevitability of its linkage to the University of California (a research and graduate-oriented institution within the division of labor proposed in the California Master Plan for Higher Education). It could openly acknowledge that some of its faculty would choose or be obliged to exit into the external academic marketplace, and the probability that no amount of intensive on-campus socialization could ever wholly offset calculations appropriate to that world. It would then have to find some imaginative means of bringing about a reasonably good alignment between these calculations and the functional needs of its internal organs.

Given the use of external faculty peer review in promotional cases and the implications of continuing accountability to the University of California system as a whole, there never really was a choice. Those faculty who faced these implications, and who shaped their behavior accordingly, survived. Those who acted otherwise did not. But Santa Cruz as an institution could fudge the choice; and for many years it did so with considerable success. There could be much talk about the exciting prospects for a College-centered undergraduate curriculum, and then again about maintaining without compromise the standards of research appropriate to a large-scale public university with its laboratories and libraries. On the one hand, faculty could be urged to participate in interdisciplinary College core courses and to take undergraduate advising seriously. On the other, the campus could reserve both its practical awards and its public accolades for those who, regardless of whether they responded to these exhortations, had published an award-winning book or synthesized a new protein or obtained admission to a particularly exclusive scholarly honor society. But in the end, the contradiction resolved itself through a circularly reinforcing process. A high proportion of the faculty proved more interested in getting on with research and teaching in the discipline in which they had chosen to specialize than in continuing to share the burdens of the collegiate enterprise. And as this proportion survived in greater numbers than the more College-centered faculty, and came to predominate among the faculty as a whole, it began to insist that the reward system be brought more closely into line with that of other universities.

With these priorities clarified, the Santa Cruz campus has begun to reconstruct itself among motivationally consistent lines. Since Reorganization, most faculty in most of the Colleges are in but not of the Colleges. Spurred on by colleagues in allied disciplines, they tend to their research and publications, knowing that it is by these that they will be judged. Colleges organize a variety of social occasions for the faculty's benefit, and they provide (through their office space and steno pools) a physical locale for cultivating intra-Divisional interdisciplinary relationships. In return they request (without great expectation of a favorable response) assistance in College advising and participation in the College core courses. Those faculty members who do respond favorably do so without expecting significant professional recognition for their contributions. These conventions have worked inefficiently and inequitably, but at least without serious misunderstanding on the part of the participants.

Yet the Colleges, even under the conditions described, have stubbornly refused to die. Until late in the Reorganization process, the historic office of College Provost was cautiously referred to in working papers as that of the "Chief Executive Officer" of the College—a retitlement with deliberately bland and bureaucratic connotations. Since then, the three Divisional Deans have turned back to the Provosts the administration of the student-affairs dimensions of collegiate life; and the newly-revitalized Council of Provosts, now serving collectively in place of the former Vice-Chancellor for Student Affairs, has acquired for the first time an authority commensurate with the College mandate in this area. Pressed to justify the continued autonomy of their units, the Provosts have searched for roles for their Colleges that assist the campus's adaption to a changing educational climate. They have found such roles through changes that place students themselves—not educational theory and collegiate programs—at the forefront of consideration.

Thus the former part-time faculty College Academic Preceptors have been replaced in many colleges by professionally engaged staff members. College advising has been similarly strengthened on a professional basis. Each College has now capitalized on its greater intra-Divisional coherence to institute its own interdisciplinary core course in writing and critical thinking, and has made the course mandatory for all entering first-year students as part of a general drive to make the Colleges once again true academic communities for their increasingly poorly-prepared recruits. Meanwhile, in conjunction with the Senate Curriculum Committee and three newly-created faculty Divisional Curriculum Committtees, the Deans have now assumed a modest degree of leadership in defining and nurturing a small set of systematically selected courses deemed suitable for meeting the mandatory campus breadth requirements in the three Divisions. These seemingly disparate developments reflect an evolving understanding of a new and viable division of labor that leaves the Colleges performing the functions they are best equipped to perform—organizing the transition of high school students into the academic life of the university, and tending to their non-instructional needs thereafter—while elevating the interdisciplinary curricular role of the Divisions as a partial counterweight to the consolidated strength of the disciplinary Boards of Studies. By elaborating this emergent division of labor in terms that draw collaboratively rather than competitively on faculty energy, the Santa Cruz campus is groping its way toward a new game with old players but with new rules in which no one need be the loser.

The brightest blooms in the garden of the University of California's newest, most daringly-conceived campus have now faded; so much is generally conceded. The campus that once drew its negative identity from Berkeley, while planning to equal Berkeley in size, is now gratefully accepting an overflow of applicants from the Berkeley campus in order to maintain its enrollment at one-fifth that level.[48] For many, the experience has proved a humbling and a bitter one. Santa Cruz is an institution of excellence in many respects, but it is not the institution of which its founders dreamed. It has maintained a level of instruction that is often outstanding and has produced much research of high quality in a setting of beauty and intimacy, but it has not shown the way back to a Garden of Eden of academic amateurism and primeval community. Repeatedly, enrollment pressures and professional ambitions have served as catalysts for altering its most striking innovations to accommodate motivations oriented toward the encompassing society it had sought to challenge. The educational experiment at Santa Cruz has demonstrated once again that any large-scale institution in this world must be at least partly of it as well. In recognizing these constraints, and in converting them from obstacles to opportunities, lie such prospects for continuing innovation as an increasingly restrictive environment will permit.

NOTES TO SECTION ONE

1. See Kerr's Godkin Lectures, *The Uses of the University* (Cambridge: Harvard University Press, 1963).

2. McHenry's utopian propensities seemed in the fore in his active participation in novelist Upton Sinclair's unsuccessful 1934 election campaign for the governorship of California. Yet generally he showed an unblinking appreciation of the need for political support to execute his idealistic objectives. It was typical of him to have made a case for locating the proposed ninth campus of the University in the Almaden Valley near San Jose so as to have five potential advocates in the California Assembly instead of one. (Personal communication).

3. McHenry's own version of his role in the founding of the campus may be found in his article, "Academic Organizational Matrix at the University of California, Santa Cruz," in Dean McHenry (ed.), *Academic Departments* (San Francisco: Jossey-Bass Publishers, 1977).

NOTES TO SECTION TWO

4. McHenry, "Academic Matrix," p. 87.

5. During this preliminary planning phase, McHenry looked closely at Woodrow Wilson's proposed reforms for Princeton, the "house" system at Harvard and Yale, the cluster colleges of Claremont and the University of the Pacific, and the relationship of colleges to the university at Oxford and Cambridge. None seemed to match the initial vision underlying the venture at Santa Cruz—the "house" system because it lacked a strong academic mission, the cluster colleges because they were more a confederacy than a federation except for their administrative overhead, the Oxbridge arrangement because it relied for instruction on in-house tutorials and comprehensive university-level examinations to an extent inapplicable to American conditions. See McHenry, "Academic Matrix," pp. 88–101.

6. Kerr, *Uses of the University*, p. 18.

7. McHenry, "Academic Matrix," p. 107. The following characterization of McHenry's thinking draws heavily on his own account, particularly pp. 91–98 and 107–110.

8. Remarkably enough, the campus acquired its striking forest setting almost as an afterthought. The original ground plans were drafted on the assumption that, as on other California campuses, the buildings and parking lots would be located in open grasslands near the city limits to minimize initial clearing costs. Only as the architects began to appreciate the ecological potential of the forest zone abutting on the meadows did they come to consider the advantages of locating the campus in the redwood forest itself. The revised plan secured the assent of the initially skeptical Regents through being presented as a cost-effective means of reducing the landscape maintenance that would otherwise be required in California's dry climate.

9. As the astronomy faculty did not offer an undergraduate major, and as the primary base of operation for many of its members was some 50 miles away in Lick Observatory, a partial exception to the rule of College membership was made in their case. After the opening year, moreover, a substantial majority of natural scientists moved into offices next to their laboratories in the central laboratory buildings. However, they remained Fellows of specific Colleges and were expected to participate fully in the advising, instructional, administrative, and social life of their Colleges.

10. "Santa Cruz Campus Academic Plan, 1965–75," mimeo, p. 8.

11. "Academic Plan, 1965–75," p. 2.

12. This restriction was, of course, in the first year an almost inevitable consequence of opening a College with at most three or four faculty members in any one discipline. Its significance lies in the effort to maintain the principle even after the opening of several Colleges had brought in sufficient faculty in many fields to make feasible a relatively specialized division of labor.

13. McHenry, "Academic Matrix," pp. 89–90, summarizes these aspirations, which are also to be found scattered through the early campus brochures and catalogs.

14. Since students were in the majority of cases to be housed, fed, advised, instructed, and entertained in the College precincts, and (if Santa Cruz students from their first year onward, as typically envisaged in the academic plans) would enter the academic life of the campus through their College core courses and remain subject to College academic and social disciplinary procedures until they graduated in College-sponsored ceremonies, their identification with their College was correctly foreseen to be less problematic than that of the faculty. The chief exceptions to this generalization were transfer students who came to that campus with substantial advanced standing to complete a disciplinary major; for them, the Colleges from the outset were sometimes little more than a mailbox.

15. Regarding the issue of finding and recommending candidates for positions, the Academic Plan of 1965 stated that "Who takes the initiative and which recommendation to follow in case of disagreement will be determined by the Chancellor, advised by the appropriate committee of the Academic Senate" (pp. 15–16).

16. That faculty members would teach one course in five for the College (generally as part of a core course, with perhaps a second course at a more advanced level) evolved as a rule of thumb, with some variation among the Colleges. No ratio was written down as a universally binding rule. It seems clear, however, that the founders had expected a higher fraction of course time would be given to the College than was demanded in the event.

17. "Academic Plan, 1965–75," p. 15. Cited in *Academic Quality at Santa Cruz: Report of the Chancellor's Self-Study/Accreditation Commission* (Santa Cruz offset, 1975), p. 21. This report, an appraisal undertaken after a decade of operation, is by far the most comprehensive and systematic assessment of the campus to date. Karl Lamb, the political scientist who chaired the Commission, joined McHenry in 1962, three years before the opening of the first College, as one of the earliest faculty to participate in the preliminary planning.

18. McHenry credits the idea of "dual employment" of teaching staff with split salaries to a visit he paid to Cambridge University in the early 'sixties at a time of heightened interest there in integrating its excluded "university" teachers with the college system. ("Academic Matrix," p. 97). It was an idea that could be expected to recommend itself to a close professional student of the checks and balances of American constitutional government.

19. *Academic Plan*, 1965, p. 6. If anything, one can trace a progressive hardening of resistance to departmentalization in the founding documents. The 1962 provisional academic plan had held open the possibility of such formations in the remote future, even while providing a rationale for resisting such a development in the early years:

> The school or faculty might ultimately be further subdivided into campus-wide departments for convenience of administration. In the initial years, however, formation of departments will be deferred for policy and pedagogical reasons. Until the colleges are firmly rooted and the character of the undergraduate instructional function is established, it appears ill-advised to set up conventional departments. The early years should be a period of ferment and cross-pollinating among the disciplines. (UCSC, 1962, p. 9).

But by 1964, Clark Kerr and McHenry were inclined to hold departmentalization at bay "indefinitely, perhaps permanently". Cf. McHenry, "Academic Matrix," p. 100.

20. Joseph Tussman has argued, in *Experiment at Berkeley* (New York: Oxford University Press, 1969), that the conflict between the "college" and the "university" is endemic in American higher education, with undergraduates in their early years as the persistent victims. Tussman himself accepts as inevitable and appropriate that "university" interests

should dominate undergraduate curricular planning and teaching style after—but only after—the first two years. See *passim*, but esp. 104–106.

NOTES TO SECTION THREE

21. It is possible to overstate this early consensus. The founding Provost of the campus's second College returned to another institution after the College's first year of operation; the initial appointee to that position at the fourth College left even before the College had opened its doors to students. Several key administrative participants in defining the identity of the campus likewise moved on during the opening years. Santa Cruz, like many other innovative enterprises, continuously risked attracting both those whose bright hopes for radical change proved less widely shared than they had expected and those who discovered that the very real professional adaptations demanded of them at Santa Cruz were less congenial—and the rewards of more traditional institutions more important—than they had thought. On the whole, the latter reactions were the more prevalent.

22. The regulations governing qualifications for the University of California are complex, but essentially restrict admission to the top 12.5% of California high school graduates.

23. "Academic Quality at UCSC," pp. 68–71 and Tables II-6, II-7, and II-8. These tables show that by 1973–74, 102 of the 938 degrees awarded were interdisciplinary, including 38 trans-divisional majors, and an additional 54 were individually designed. "Double" majors at Santa Cruz were obtained by completing the full requirements for a major in each of two fields, "joint" majors by completing all but a few formal requirements of each major. Examples of "trans-divisional" degrees in the 1974 graduation list included "Mathematics and Economics," "Politics and Art," and "Psychology and Aesthetic Studies."

24. For statistical evidence of the preeminent importance attached by present and former students of Santa Cruz to the narrative evaluation system, and for supplemental anecdotal indications of the values they saw therein, see the results of the surveys conducted by the sociologist Mark Messer and recorded in "Academic Quality at Santa Cruz," pp. 9 and 57–60.

25. Gerald Grant and David Riesman, *Perpetual Dream: Reform and Experiment in the American College* (Chicago: University of Chicago Press, 1978). For systematic data on the impressively strong and much differentiated impact of collegiate membership on most students at Santa Cruz during its first decade, see the self study/accreditation report, *Academic Quality at UCSS*, pp. 44–56.

26. The logical outcome of these boundary problems occurred in 1978 when the Board of Environmental Studies—a conglomerate composed of field scientists and social planners—was given an ill-defined status as a kind of independent fourth Division without title.

27. McHenry, "Academic Matrix," p. 101.

28. McHenry, "Academic Matrix," p. 102; *Academic Quality at UCSC*, pp. 28–30.

29. *Academic Quality at UCSS*, pp. 29–30.

30. In the University of California system, all "ladder" faculty—i.e., those eligible for or enjoying tenure—are members of their campus Academic Senate unless placed on "acting" status pending completion of their Ph.D. Thus assistant professors are members of the Academic Senate even though tenure comes only with promotion to the associate level.

31. In fact, it so greatly undermined the power and legitimacy of the "outside" member of the Board that such appointments became otiose, and quietly faded away.

32. *Academic Quality at UCSC*, p. 33. Only Oakes College followed the original plan of recruiting a faculty cadre for each new College from the existing Colleges—a practice that might greatly have strengthened the socializing impact of newly forming Colleges.

33. Quoted in *Academic Quality at UCSC*, p. 33.

34. Inevitably, there were many important exceptions to this pattern. College personnel committees, hesitant to judge scholarship outside the committee members' disciplines, might wholly defer to the Board in certain cases, thereby lowering the prospects for confron-

tation but also lightening the weight of the College personnel letters. Lacking assured criteria for judgment, College committees might be more impressed by—and more insistently inclined to look for—the sheer number of articles a faculty member published, regardless of their redundancy or intrinsic merit; conversely, though more rarely, a College committee, stung by charges of club favoritism, might demand more in the way of recognized originality and distinguished achievement than a record of solid but routine scholarship that had satisfied a complacent Board. And there were many cases, both positive and negative, in which Board and College were able to reach substantial agreement. All modal generalizations of this nature have limits: were there none, the personnel conflicts on the Santa Cruz campus would soon have grown uncontainable.

35. It must be said that such sentiments not infrequently reflected a compound of ingenuously wishful thinking and suddenly activated self-interest. By the mid- 'seventies, the promotional record at Santa Cruz was becoming clear to those who were willing to see: faculty who compiled a respectable scholarly record and strongly supportive outside letters in relation to it were essentially invulnerable to charges of merely adequate teaching and modest contributions to instituion-building and curricular design, whereas those who put their energy into the latter activities chose a high-risk route that few survived. Hopefully cited instances to the contrary were usually drawn from the founding years of the campus.

36. In a formula precisely encapsulating the dilemma of the Santa Cruz campus, organizational theorist James Q. Wilson has contended that the rate of proposal of innovations in organizations is directly proportional to their structural diversity (i.e., to the complexity of their task structure and incentive systems) whereas the rate of adoption of proposed innovations is inversely proportional to an organization's structural diversity. See Wilson, "Innovation in Organization: Notes Toward a Theory," in James D. Thompson, ed. *Approaches to Organizational Design* (Pittsburgh: University of Pittsburg Press, 1966), pp. 193–218.

37. *Academic Quality at UCSC*, Table III-7, p. 88; McHenry, "Academic Matrix," pp. 113–114. One factor in the lower averages by 1975 was a more sustained and successful effort by the campus to recruit applicants through special action from among disadvantaged racial and ethnic minorities.

NOTES TO SECTION FOUR

38. Since actions in complex social settings often have unanticipated consequences, we cannot accept at face value the claims of successful reformers in this respect. The "successful" outcome may have occurred contrary to the initial intentions of at least some of the participants, or may reflect a disjunction at some point between their prescriptive analysis and their choices in concrete circumstances.

39. The report was prepared in May of 1974 by the present writer, at that time chair-designate of the Committee for the following academic year.

40. Formally speaking, individual faculty members had always been entitled to request a transfer to another College. To exercise this option, however, they were obliged to state in writing to the Chancellor that they were experiencing "personal hardship" in their College, and to offer substantiating detail. Chancellor McHenry's opposition to transference among Colleges, well known at the time, was subsequently reiterated in his "Academic Matrix," pp. 109–110. The point of Reaggregation in any case was not simply to enlarge a safety valve but rather to promote an orderly regrouping of whole clusters of faculty in light of a general curricular plan for the campus.

41. The one exception, the flourishing Stevenson Core Course, was itself initially assigned to the Division of Humanities. But after hearing vigorous protests from the Stevenson Provost, the present writer, as Chair of the Senate's curriculum committee, decided to keep a window open to an unknown future by devising a formula permitting Colleges to sponsor up to five courses, "introductory and interdisciplinary in character and required of all entering students, with a format designed to create an academic community within the

College." It is this formula that the Colleges were subsequently to use in reviving in modified form their various core courses. See below, page 39.

42. Reorganization was also threatened by a growing controversy over a logically unrelated but strategically and emotionally connected proposal to revise the grading system. Because certain medical and engineering schools insisted on basing admissions decisions on grade point averages, letter grades had been made available by special petition to students in advanced-level courses in the Natural Sciences since the opening of the campus. Over the years, a remarkably steady 8% of the students in such courses had exercised that right. Alarmed by rumors that falling enrollments might lead to closing the campus, impressed by indications that initial suspicions of the narrative evaluation system were contributing to that decline, convinced that collegiate reorganization would have little impact on admissions applications, and reassured by the nearly unanimous preference of students on campus for narrative evaluations without letter grades when not required by professional schools, the Academic Senate's Committee on Education policy proposed in the fall of 1978 that the right to petition for letter grades be extended to students in the other two Divisions as well. The proposal passed the Academic Senate but soon evoked a firestorm of opposition from students, who associated it with Reorganization as moves to save the campus by destroying it. Since students were more directly affected by the grading system than by the other elements of Reorganization, their voices were heard with special sympathy. In a subsequent mail ballot, Senate members defeated the measure by almost the same margin by which it had earlier passed. Two years later, under less heated circumstances, the Senate approved by mail ballot an essentially similar measure by a narrow vote of 111-108.

43. James Q. Wilson, *Political Organizations* (New York: Basic Books, 1973).

NOTES TO SECTION FIVE

44. For example, the so-called Comparative History Seminar—an informal assembly of social historians, sociologists economists, and political scientists from Merrill and Stevenson Colleges who met together (generally at least twice a month) to read and criticize a member's most recent paper—has now been given the status and funding of an Organized Research Unit and has recently sponsored a large-scale national conference on some contemporary theories of social change.

45. Clarity is essential regarding the point of reference from which the Santa Cruz undertaking has been judged a "failure." The failure to sustain the academic dimensions of the collegiate system does not necessarily mean that the campus has suffered a net loss of academic quality. It could—and has—been argued that reorganization has preserved the more attractive and defensible elements of Santa Cruz's hospitality to interdisciplinary teaching and intimate faculty-student collaboration while providing more impetus toward faculty professionalism and the creation of a sounder, more coherent curriculum. "Innovatory" was an adjective rather generously applied to campus activities in the early days. It covered many courses that were innovatory neither in pedagogy, content, nor in conceptual synthesis, and that might more properly have been described as conventional disciplinary courses taught under a collegiate label or specialty courses on familiar subjects taught by a faculty member trained in a different discipline. Many courses—e.g., the Core Courses at Cowell and Stevenson in Western Civilization—were "innovatory" only in the sense of returning to a tradition other campuses had abandoned. The ease with which the Committee on Educational Policy at the time of reorganization was able to find appropriate disciplinary sponsors for all but a small number of College courses says much about the character of such "innovations." It must be said, too, that the actual benefits of the curricular innovations were rarely established through experimental testing. Rhetorical claims generally substituted for systematic investigation of the impact of collegiate academic programs on choice of major, generation of independently designed majors, teaching of disciplinary courses, or subsequent faculty research and writing.

46. Without employing these specific historical references, Joseph Tussman is particularly clear on the conflict between these views. See his *Experiment*, pp. 27–42.

47. This point seems to have been grasped most fully by the founding Provost of Cowell College, who proposed half seriously, in consequence, in a memo circulated among the faculty a year before his retirement, that junior faculty be guaranteed tenure for good behavior and asked to involve themselves more wholeheartedly in College teaching and service than they currently felt free to do. Page Smith, memo to faculty, March 1972.

48. With the assistance of a newly vigorous Office of Admissions, Santa Cruz was able in 1981 to close its date of acceptance for applications several months before opening day of classes for the first time since 1973. It also registered a greater gain in applications from first-year students than any other of the University of California's nine campuses. But Santa Cruz's troubles are far from over in this respect. The early 'eighties mark the end of the great bulge the post-war baby boom placed in the demand curve for higher education; hereafter, Santa Cruz will have to compete with other campuses for a smaller, poorer, less well educated contingent of students composed increasingly of disadvantaged ethnic minorities who have characteristically preferred metropolitan campuses within easy commuting distance that offer more remedial and more vocationally oriented programs. The implications of this prospect for its liberal arts curriculum and narrative evaluation system are not encouraging.

VI. The Evergreen State College: An Experiment Maturing

by

BYRON L. YOUTZ

INTRODUCTION

The Evergreen State College is a survivor—one of the few major experiments in curricular innovation arising from the decade of the sixties which remains strong and growing at the beginning of the eighties. In the hope that some lessons can be drawn from this educational experience, I shall here provide a descriptive account of the founding, and evolution of the college over the past eleven years.

I think it important from the outset to admit that no one view of this institution's history and development will be either complete or free from bias. The choice of important factors and their analysis are dependent upon one's views of the larger society and the direction in which one sees that society moving. It is therefore both comforting and humbling to know that two fellow founders of the college will respond to the views expressed here.*

The innovations in both curricular design and college governance will be treated because they were developed together to be mutually supportive. Our current curricular and organizational structure will be described

*The critique, by Dr. Charles Teske, Member of the Faculty (Literature) and founding Academic Dean of Humanities and Arts, will appear throughout as annotative footnotes marked C.T.. The other, by Dr. Richard Jones, senior founding faculty and still Member of the Faculty (Psychology) appears as an appendix to this.

and analyzed for its strengths and weaknesses, again from my own perspectives, which may be strongly debated on this campus.

An effort will then be made to apply a theoretical structure, dealing with the growth and development of organizations, to the concrete experiences of Evergreen. The intent of this section will be to predict and seek insight into the developmental concerns, problems and crises which lie ahead of us in the hope that early recognition of likely problems will help with their solution.

Finally, I will give my own views of the directions this institution must take in the near and immediate future to continue our development and viability as an educational leader in the decade of the eighties.

AN ACCOUNT OF THE FOUNDING

The Evergreen State College is the first and only publicly funded, four-year institution of higher education founded in the State of Washington in the Twentieth Century. During the era of great expansion of the higher educational community all over the country, the State of Washington invested its growth efforts in the existing five state colleges and universities (U. of W.; W.S.U.; Eastern, Central and Western Washington State Colleges) and in the development of an extensive network of twenty-six community colleges.*

In 1965, a demographic study commissioned by state government concluded that Washington would require an additional 12,000 places in higher education by 1980, beyond what could be provided by the expansion plan then underway. Thus, in 1967, the Legislature authorized the founding of a new four-year state college in southwest Washington.*

Legislative intent seemed to contain three somewhat competing elements:

---

*This expansion—some might say overexpansion—of the Community College System is a factor which heavily affects many states' regional colleges, including Evergreen in the 1980's.

---

*Excessive optimism about growth in college attendance attended the founding of a number of new colleges including Evergreen, Santz Cruz, Grand Valley, and Southwest Minnesota. This legacy of not living up to enrollment projections would tarnish the colleges' public images for years.

1. To serve the needs of Southwest Washington where much of the demographic growth was expected. The authorization bill referred to "Southwest Washington State College" in language which paralelled the authorizations of the other three regional institutions (Western, Central, Eastern).
2. To provide services to state government and its employees. The selection of Olympia, the capitol city, as the site for the new college seemed to give us this special opportunity and obligation.
3. To develop an innovative structure that would not simply duplicate the existing academic resources of the state. The State Senator who headed the Temporary Advisory Council of Public Education (which recommended the new college in the first place) said at the first meeting of the newly-appointed Board of Trustees, "It was not the intent of the Legislature that this be just another four-year college; it is a unique opportunity to meet the needs of the students of today and the future because the planning will not be bound by any rigid structure of tradition as are the existing colleges, nor by any overall central authority, as is the case in many states."[1]

The original Board of Trustees seemed to give priority to the third and most clearly stated element of legislative intent in conducting its search for the founding president. Dr. Charles McCann, then Dean of the Faculty at Central Washington State College and an articulate spokesman for individualizing the college learning experience, was selected. The resulting commitment, to develop an alternative to the existing educational institutions in the state, was taken as a "mandate" by the early planners, to the exclusion of the other two elements of the founding intent. This commitment, while crucial to our subsequent development, has come back to haunt us on many occasions during the past eleven years.*

A second factor of our early history which continues to influence our development was the rivalry which developed over the location for the

*Historically, the mandate to fresh thinking given orally by Sandison and Governor Evans was not written into any official charter. Those of us representing the college early-on in budget justifications and public relations speeches soon learned not to say "we have been given the mandate" but "we have accepted the challenge" to be different. From the mid-seventies onward, however, we have had the twofold mandate, firmly legislated as part of the State Coordinating Council's long-range plan, to be the alternative campus for the whole state while providing essential services to Southwestern Washington. For most Evergreeners, I believe—or at least hope—that the emphasis in the later 1970's upon expanding our services to the region is not so much "changing with the time" as "taking care of unfinished business." It may not be too much to say that any lasting contribution we shall make to higher education in America will depend upon how inventively and usefully we reconcile the two sections of our mandate.

—C.T.

new college. Rather elaborate proposals and justifications were submitted for sites in the vicinity of Vancouver, Longview-Kelso, Olympia, South Tacoma, Port Angeles, Redmond, Arlington, and even Richland-Pasco. The loss of this contest, especially by the Vancouver and Longview-Kelso communities, was sorely regretted and is still a source of irritation for certain people; whereas, the winning of the contest was almost as traumatic and locally irritating for many of the old-time residents of the greater Olympia community.

The State of Washington was both generous and farsighted in providing funds for a planning year (1970–71). This enabled a group of 18 faculty, 3 Academic Deans and the Provost (under the watchful eye of the President) to work on curriculum design, governance structure, student admissions policies and faculty recruitment. This group represented a wide range of educational philosophies, pedagogical methods and academic dreams, from the highly organized Moral Curriculum of Alexander Meiklejohn[2] to the very individualized, personal development commitments of Carl Rogers. Fortunately, it also represented a considerable amount of experience with some of the other educational experiments of the sixties: New College of Florida, the General Program Experiment at San Jose, the Interdisciplinary Science Program at Oregon State, Prescott College, S.U.N.Y. at Old Westbury, and the national Outward Bound Program. The war stories of these veterans considerably tempered our wilder dreams.*

The competition between differing educational philosophies and methods was never resolved during the planning year. But some overarching principles did emerge which enabled us to get on with the work. President McCann had defined the new college largely in terms of a series of negatives: no grades, no departments, no faculty ranks, no requirements, no football teams, etc. But we soon learned that there were some positive consequences which emerged from each of the negatives and we were expected to follow them wherever they would lead: interdisciplinary studies, narrative evaluations, minimum red tape for both faculty and students, cooperative rather than competitive learning. The original three Deans were hired because each brought some experience

*I cannot emphasize too strongly how important it was to have in our planning year the wisdom of those who came to us from "earlier educational experiments" which either had failed or were wavering. Especially on the issue of governance, our first-year students might have been seduced from the difficult tasks of coordinated studies into the easier and superficially more exciting ways of educational-political argument. Our veterans saved us from those pit-falls. Indeed, it may not be all that wrong to maintain that we are still around because we were one of the *last* innovative colleges to open.

—C.T.

and some technique for implementing these principles: Mervyn Cadwallader because of his interdisciplinary General Studies Program at San Jose and Old Westbury (based upon the methods of Alexander Meiklejohn), Don Humphrey because of his interdisciplinary science programs at Oregon State and his strong interest in self-paced learning and Charles Teske because of his experience with the independent study learning mode at Oberlin College.

Much of the curriculum planning effort of the first year was devoted to detailed design of the strongest possible and most diverse set of Meiklejohn-like interdisciplinary programs we could conceive. We called them "Coordinated Studies".[3] The titles of our first year's programs, enlivened by the free imagination of the reader, will indicate our creativity: Human Development; Political Ecology; Space, Time and Form; Freedom, Causality and Chance; The Individual in America; Environmental Design; Contemporary American Minorities; Individual, Citizen and State; Man and Art; Communication and Intelligence; Human Behavior. Each of these programs was a team-taught, year long, full time (for both students and faculty) interdisciplinary study program involving four or five faculty and eighty to one hundred students.

The "Book Seminar" was the heart of the curriculum, original sources were used instead of textbooks, and the author was the teacher while the rest of us were "colearners". The weekly "Faculty Seminar" was (and remains still) the chief vehicle through which the faculty share their expertise and help their team-mates to become interdisciplinary teachers. The academic program was bound together by a "program covenant" which set forth the duties and the expectations of all parties and defined the basis upon which credit would be awarded. "Interdisciplinary Study", although never really defined, was the hub around which all else revolved: program planning, faculty hiring, catalog copy, etc. Still undefined, it continues (in multiple interpretations) to be the centerpiece of our curricular efforts.

The second, though somewhat minor component of our first year curriculum was the "Individual Learning Contract". This mode of study was generally called Independent Study, a phrase we chose to avoid because of the misunderstandings which had developed during the sixties (i.e. students heard the word *Independent,* faculty heard the word *Study,* and there was a mismatch of expectations from the beginning.) In our version, the student and the faculty member worked out a contract *in advance* which dealt with such details as the project definition, reading list, meeting schedule, final product of the study and the means by which it would be evaluated.

As the last two paragraphs indicate, we spent some time and effort in the development of our own jargon to avoid previous stereotypes and to express our philosophical principles. "Learning how to learn", that is, helping students to become independent of their teachers, was one of our principal educational goals. Rather than asking students to follow a set major or a list of institutional requirements, we asked students to "take charge of their own educations."

A key concept in all our planning was "flexibility". "Living with Ambiguity" became the norm at early Evergreen because we desperately wanted to avoid premature "hardening of the categories".

To avoid the decision-making squabbles of many of the earlier educational experiments, we developed a governance structure to serve for the first three years of our operation. A group was assembled in the spring of the planning year, the "Committee on Governance," composed of administrators, faculty, staff and some borrowed and future students. This group worked surprisingly well together and a document was produced which was only slightly modified at the end of the three-year initial period. Philosophically, the group recognized the delegated authority of the state and the need to give administrators not only responsibility but also decision-making authority. However, a collegial relationship was sought which would eradicate as many of the hierarchical barriers as possible. Hence, decisions were to be made by administrators who were "locatable and accountable", but only after consultation with those most affected. The "Disappearing Task Force", or DTF as it quickly came to be known, took the place of the more usual "standing committee" in providing the consultation. The planners had an abhorrance for the lethargy and inertia which they had experienced elsewhere with standing committees, to say nothing of the power (and hence the politics) which such committees vested in a few members of the academic community. The DTFs were to be randomly selected (as with a jury system), single problem or task oriented, and then dissolve. Only one standing committee was created and it was given no real power: "The Sounding Board", composed of five faculty, five staff, five administrators and fifteen students. It was primarily an information-sharing and issue-discussing group. An active appeals process was devised, starting with informal mediation and ending, when necessary, with an All-Campus Hearing Board. Much of this apparatus still remains intact and functional.

And so, after a truly breathless year, in September of 1971, we were *almost* ready to open with fifty-five faculty and just over one thousand students, eleven Coordinated Studies Programs (with 950 students enrolled), Individual Contracts (with some 70 students). I say "almost ready" because none of the buildings was quite complete! We opened the new college in churches, faculty homes, Legislative meeting rooms and forest campgrounds with the spirit of true pioneers. That spirit carried us through the first difficult year.*

EVOLUTION OF THE CURRICULUM

Over the course of the first year, three developments occurred, some by design and some by discovery, to diversify and enrich the curriculum. Our initial enthusiasm for Coordinated Studies ("If it's good for 100 students, it will be good for all 1,000 students".) was somewhat modified by the problems associated with specialized training for advanced students who were seeking careers. Because of the range of specialized interests it was impossible to associate 60–100 students in a single advanced Coordinated Study except in the most unusual of circumstances. Before the end of the first year the "Group Contract" had been invented and the first of these (Evergreen Environment) was offered in the Spring Quarter of 1972. This is a scheme in which a group of 20 (or 40) students and a faculty member (or two) agree to study a particular field or subject in depth, full time, for one or more quarters. The study can be either student or faculty initiated, and we have had many successful examples of each. We retain this format for most of our advanced work.

Also, during the first year, we developed our first Internship placements within the context of a Coordinated Studies program. This combining of the theoretical and the experiential was so attractive and successful that we also developed an internship program for the whole college, to be implemented through the Individual Contract mode. A Cooperative Education Office was established to develop placements, locate Field Supervisors and monitor the system in detail. Academic credit, however, is awarded by the *faculty* sponsor who has an obligation to provide related academic work, meet regularly with the student and prepare a final narrative evaluation for the transcript. This option has become one of the strong and effective parts of our continuing curriculum.

A third element, developed extensively during the first year, which still strongly influences our curriculum, was the use of a significant and real-world problem as the focus for either a Coordinated Study Program

---

*Nothing would seem to demonstrate so much the soundness of basic design of an organism than its ability to respond to crises. This was one of them: the need to open the instructional program of the college almost a month before we could take up residence on the campus. Had we committed ourselves to multiple courses, class-bells, and the rest of the educational traffic-management system which prevails at almost all undergraduate colleges, we should have been lost.

—C.T.

or a Group Contract. For example, the Environmental Design Program of that initial year, as one of its projects, took on the study of the probable impact of the new college on the rural, agrarian neighborhood in which it had been located. Preparation for this project required the students to do considerable theoretical study in economics, sociology, environmental biology, land use planning and community relations. By the middle of Winter Quarter, the groundwork had been laid and the problems defined sufficiently to bring local citizens and neighbors into the discussions. From this, a citizens' group, The Cooper Point Association, was formed; a professional Land Use Planner was hired by the Association to work with the students; a local zoning ordinance, The Cooper Point Plan, was devised and presented to the County Commissioners for extended debate and final approval. Many other excellent examples of the use of real-world projects as the centerpiece around which a study program is designed could be cited in programs such as, Applied Environmental Studies, Marine Inventory of Puget Sound, Energy Systems, etc.

To prevent premature rigidity in the curriculum, and to encourage a set of new and innovative proposals, a conscious decision was made that the first year's curriculum should self-destruct at the end of the year. Thus, the first Fall Quarter was only a few weeks old when the Deans began to accept proposals for the second year's curriculum. Every year, for the first five years, we operated in this frenetic manner, seldom repeating programs unless there was considerable student demand to do so.[4]

A first attempt at long-range curriculum planning, in the fall of 1972 (called the Lake Quinault Conference) attempted to address some of the difficulties encountered in our initial curriculum: there was no way to serve part-time students; foreign language, mathematics, dance and some other subjects did not lend themselves well to our "one thing at a time" study mode; skills development, especially reading and writing at the somewhat remedial level, were not being handled well; the artists among the faculty felt overshadowed and under-represented; the institutional commitment to education for minority students was strongly questioned.

The results of this conference, though minimal, were regarded with considerable suspicion and some hostility by various groups of students and faculty who wished to preserve the purity of the initial curriculum. In spite of the resistance, a part-time studies program was initiated through a group of courses (we called them "Modules") which were to be taught principally in the late afternoons or evenings and which would therefore be available to the Greater Olympia adult community. To allow our regular students access to these courses, we made it permissible for faculty to plan "three-quarter time" programs and allow students who wanted to take a course to do so. The courses were to be taught by regular faculty who were in the "Contract Pool" and could balance out their teaching loads by taking fewer Individual Contract students. We committed ourselves to more faculty hiring in the Arts and to the establishment of a Learning Resource Center for skills development. We reaffirmed our determination to serve minority students through the hiring of additional minority faculty and the inclusion of Third World concerns in all parts of the curriculum.

For Evergreen, the period 1972–1975 was one of expanding enrollments, curricular fluidity, trial and error, some risk-taking and some consolidation. But there were also danger signals on the horizon which we chose largely to ignore: enrollment troubles at two of our sister institutions,* faculty exhaustion (burnout) at our own, student complaints about the unpredictability of the curriculum and their powerlessness to influence curricular decisions. These concerns finally came to a crisis stage in the Fall of 1975 in a three-day Campus Forum during which the college motto, "Omnia Extares" was in effect: we "let it all hang out". The outcome of this close self-examination by the full campus community was the establishment of three Disappearing Task Forces: C.O.G. III to review our college governance structures, a Short-Range Curriculum DTF to prepare the following year's program, and a Long Range Curriculum DTF to recommend major improvements in our procedures and directions.

THE LONG RANGE CURRICULUM

The results of six months of intensive study by a task force composed of faculty, students and staff was an extensive report which proposed the curricular structure still in use today. Fundamentally, the report was a reaffirmation of faith in the importance of inter-disciplinary study, in our methods for delivering that type of study opportunity, in the central importance of helping students learn how to learn, and in the value of having students take charge of and plan their own curricular paths. In

*As a result of this, the Legislature decided in the spring of 1973 to put a ceiling on our enrollment and then to let us grow only to some 4,000 students rather than to the 12,000 student enrollment which had been predicted in the initial planning. In the long run, we shall probably be grateful that, however tardily, the Legislature recognized the errors which had been made in demographic projections and thus limited us to a more humane maximum size. The decision, however, did much to slow down the momentum we had built up on recruiting students, and it played hob with our plans for recruitment of a faculty capable of representing the range of experience we need.

—C.T.

order to provide some logic to the curriculum for ourselves and our students, we devised the structure of "Interdisciplinary Specialty Areas" for advanced work, "Basic Programs" for the interdivisional general studies offerings and "Annual Programs" for the frankly experimental programs designed by either faculty or students.

To provide predictability and continuity, we agreed to plan the curriculum two years in advance and to repeat successful programs as needed by the students. This also reduced the faculty burn-out problem by cutting down somewhat on the need for continuous new program design. We did, however, require that a faculty member rotate among programs so that no one teaches more than two years in the repeated programs. "Basic Programs" were a continuation of our regular Coordinated Studies mode, but we required that all programs, regardless of title, must emphasize skill development in writing, reading, the discussion of ideas, and serious use of the library. Academic advising toward useful curriculum choice and effective use of Evergreen's study opportunities was to occur here. Successful Basic Programs were to be repeated each year, but with enough faculty turnover to keep them from going stale. "Annual Programs" were to remain a substantial part of the whole curriculum and be the testing ground for new and innovative curricular ideas or for serving special but unusual needs of a group of students.

The advanced "Interdisciplinary Specialty Areas" were to provide a two year sequence of study which would take students well into upper division work on a repeatable and predictable basis. After one year of organizing experience, the titles of the Specialty Areas (as they still exist today) are: Environmental Studies, European and American Studies, Expressive Arts, Health and Human Development, Management and the Public Interest, Marine Sciences and Crafts, Northwest Native American Studies, Political Economy, and Scientific Knowledge and Inquiry. Each Specialty Area was to develop two-year sequences of offerings using our modes of study: Coordinated Studies, Group Contracts, Individual Contracts, Internships and (if necessary) a limited number of modular courses. The only prerequisite for entering any of these Specialty Areas is completion of satisfactory work in any of the Basic Programs (or its equivalent).*

*Some internal specialization was needed for efficient planning, the use of resources, and continuity. But having proliferated these growths, we must be vigilant and continually examine them to make sure that they are benign. At Evergreen, the most important debates about educational philosophy and policy do not take place among people but within people. It's not so much a matter of generalists vs. specialists in meetings. Rather it's a matter of arguing with ourselves. Departmental and divisional structures, particularly when they are connected with external rewards, have a way of inhibiting such argument, of stunting collegial citizenship.

—C.T.

To prevent these curricular units from becoming pseudo-departments, a number of precautions have been taken. First, these units have no budgetary base and no assigned faculty lines. Second, faculty are required to belong to at least two of these units for curriculum planning purposes and to teach in one unit for no more than three years in a row. Third, Convenors (rather than Chairmen) are selected by the Academic Deans for a two year period and given responsibility to call meetings, see to the completion of the curricular planning before catalog deadline, and advise the Deans on the needs of the Specialty Area. Finally, students are not required to stay within a single Specialty Area but can assemble their own majors from the entire curriculum if they prefer.

Under the leadership of the Provost and the Deans, several additional elements beyond the DTF recommendations were added during 1976–1977. The part-time studies program was greatly expanded by the addition of Adjunct Faculty hired solely for the purpose of teaching modular courses in subject areas which the regular faculty could not cover for one reason or another. In addition, our regular faculty planned and operated several half-time Coordinated Studies programs for working adults and for women re-entering college to complete long-delayed degrees. Further, we perfected an External Credit Program for the validation and crediting of experiential learning.

A major expansion was the opening of a satellite campus with a two-year, upper division coordinated studies sequence in Vancouver, Washington. For the first time, we began to take seriously our responsibilities to provide educational services to Southwest Washington. And we learned from these efforts that our instructional format was particularly well suited to adult learners.

This attention to Southwest Washington and to adult learners came none too soon. Academic Year 1976–1977 saw the peak enrollment of 2530 headcount, 2399 FTE students and then the enrollment began to drop. In the Spring of that same year, the State Legislature asked the state coordinating body for higher education, the Council for Postsecondary Education (CPE), to do an extensive "study and make recommendations on the curriculum and costs of The Evergreen State College. The study shall determine the actions needed to broaden the institution's clientele base by introducing traditional undergraduate and graduate course offerings and reduce the institution's total operating cost per FTE student to the average cost per FTE student of the other three state colleges (now regional universities)".[5]

Parenthetically, every year since 1970 there had been at least one bill introduced into the Legislative hopper to close Evergreen, turn it into state offices, or a police academy, or at least a southern branch of the

University of Washington. This time we were very concerned that the proposed study, with its desired outcome contained in the charge, would simply result in our becoming Southwest Washington State College for sure!

Since the first arrival of the planning faculty in 1970, the old time citizens of Olympia, encouraged massively by the local newspaper, were terribly nervous about Evergreen as "strange, hippy, radical, useless," etc. Other segments of the press throughout the state echoed the accusations of the local paper—and were always able to find a few examples of individual behavior among our alternative-minded students—to create an ongoing image problem for us. In spite of the generous help of many thoughtful and enlightened citizens, both locally and across the state—this initial image has been hard to correct and overcome. Among the educational community, both in public schools and even, to some extent, in higher education, the reputation developed (inaccurately) that we did mostly independent study, were very permissive, gave no grades, were not very demanding.* It was against this background that the Council for Postsecondary Education received its legislative commission.

The ensuing study was very thorough, included interviews and surveys of current and prospective students, alumni and their employers, faculty and staff and was done with the full cooperation of the college. The outcome was a constructively critical analysis and overall confirmation of the validity of our educational efforts, based upon the support and success of our 3000 alumni, the strong affirmative attitudes of our students and the quality and seriousness of our faculty. Two strong points emerged publically as a result of this study. Foremost was the dedication, diversity and academic strength of our faculty—the average college teaching experience was 12 years, much of it at very prestigious institutions: more than two-thirds hold Ph.D. degrees, and the others had equivalently valuable working experience; weekly contact hours with students averaged 18–19 every quarter; 16% of the faculty were of minority ethnic origins and 30% were women; most of the faculty were hired because they had more than

*Some of our colleagues have spoken of Evergreen as a creation of the late 1960's and early 1970's, responding to a climate favoring experiment, permissiveness, a "flower-children" syndrome among many potential students, concern with psychological development, and overt political radicalism. If the climate has changed, according to such reasoning, then we must change. I dispute such reasoning. Yes, we were able to try what we tried because of the openness to experiment. But the principles underlying coordinated studies, especially insofar as they can be traced back to Alexander Meikeljohn's ideas, are not those of permissiveness. Nor is the emphasis upon obligations in individual learning contracts. The planners of Evergreen, in effect, used an opportunity offered by the times to work toward sound and noble educational aims.

—C.T.

one specialty to bring to our interdisciplinary curriculum. Secondly, it was shown that Evergreen really offers the various things which many high school students say they want in selecting a college: graduates get jobs, teaching is the most important mission of the college, faculty expect students to work, students are committed to work, classes are small, faculty are accessible, graduates are admitted to graduate and professional schools. . . . all areas in which we believe ourselves very successful. But nobody among our potential student clienteles in our own state seemed to know it!

Twenty recommendations accompanied the CPE report, many of which had been discussed earlier on campus, to make Evergreen more attractive to a wider audience of students. The major recommendation was one of growth; from the 2200 FTE of 1977–1978 to about 4000 FTE by 1985. The 1979 Legislature committed itself to this plan and the fiscal support necessary to accomplish it. Among the recommendations was authorization to begin Masters Degree work, to provide more and better educational service to state government and state employees, to provide a wider variety of career options in the curriculum, and to recruit much more effectively in the high schools and community colleges of our region of the state.

Just as the CPE study was beginning, the college acquired a new president who was an expert in public affairs. Charles McCann, the founding president, decided to return to faculty life and was given a study leave to prepare for the task of teaching at Evergreen. The new president was Daniel J. Evans, retiring as Governor of the State after twelve years, in whose office in 1967 the organizational meeting of the Board of Trustees had been held! With characteristic vigor, President Evans set out to fulfill the demands placed upon us by the study, while still retaining those philosophical and structural features of the college which the study itself had proven to be successful.

CURRENT STATUS

Although there is some inevitable disagreement about the current state of the college and its curriculum, I will state for my part that we are still surprisingly faithful and true to our original ideals. We remain a bastion of interdisciplinary studies among U.S. colleges. We place a heavy emphasis on writing, reading and the discussion of ideas through the seminar experience. We ask students and faculty to devote *almost* full attention to one study at a time, though that study is enriched by the multifacets of the interdisciplinary approach to learning.

Because we reserve large blocks of time for such close work between students and faculty, we can write meaningful narrative evaluations (each for the other) instead of using the more trivial grading format. Because there are no set majors and no departmental requirements, students can set their own directions and create their own majors with whatever faculty advice they wish to seek. Through the Individual Contract mode, a student can dig deeply into a personally selected subject or activity. Through the Internship Program, a student can test a potential career and come away with the experience and the recommendations equivalent to a first job in that field. These are very close to our founding principles.

As is evident from these descriptions, we at Evergreen have not invented anything new. In that sense, we have not really ever been "experimental." We have simply taken a number of earlier experiments, some of them really quite old, and assembled them into a working system which is bound together with the rationale provided above.

We were all quite disappointed when Grant and Riesman's book, THE PERPETUAL DREAM, treated Evergreen only as a set of footnotes. Yet, they are correct in the assessment that Evergreen did not undertake a "telic reform." Instead, we were the beneficiaries of a number of such reforms. I am inclined to believe that it is the diversity of those reforms, which we have collected together and rationalized, that gives us our durability and attractiveness.*

Given all of this preamble, where then is the argument or concern over the current status of the college? Some faculty feel that we have become too career oriented, that we have lost our innovative spirit, that we no longer are committed to experimentation. It is indeed true that we have neglected our Annual Programs in the effort to launch the Specialty Areas, but we have noticed this and are taking steps to correct it. Many feel that we are slipping ever closer to departmentalism, although our

*"We are still surprisingly faithful and true to our original ideals" and "it is the diversity of those reforms, which we have collected together and rationalized, that gives us our durability and an attractiveness"—These strike me as Byron's most powerful statements about our present condition and the reasons for our vitality. Though there may be many tendencies to do the right thing for the wrong reason (e.g. extending services to more varied clienteles not because it is our duty and we believe in it but simply to show higher enrollment figures), I submit that our principles are still remarkably intact. We should stand and fight for them. What we should continually adjust to "the times" are our particular rationalizations, the interpretation of our principles to our audiences and to ourselves.

We have amassed a fund of experience here in the last ten years, and we should make use of it. An outside observer asked me if Evergreen was becoming "more traditional". My answer: "Yes. But to a surprising extent, they're our own traditions".

—C.T.

protective structures are still intact. Others feel that we have sold out to the public relations demands of the legislature and our continuing critics.

What are the actions we have taken in response to the CPE recommendations which generate these fears? We have defined more clearly for students a set of career pathways through our curriculum, and a large part of that curriculum continues to be quite predictable. Within that curriculum, we have defined and now offer a B.S. as well as a B.A. degree. We have improved the level and quality of student advising substantially. We have contracted with a nearby private college to provide teacher certification courses on our campus for our students at state tuition rates. We have opened our first masters level program, a Masters in Public Administration, with an emphasis on state and local government. We have taken our first cautious steps into inter-collegiate athletics through soccer, swimming, cross-country, tennis and sailing. As a result we are beginning to attract a more diverse and local group of students. Perhaps fortunately, the current economic problems of the state have slowed the pressure for the mandated rapid growth, giving us an opportunity to assimilate our new activities and student clienteles and to consider their effects on the quality of our educational efforts.

COLLEGE GOVERNANCE WITHOUT DEPARTMENTS, RANK OR TENURE

The development of Evergreen's system of college governance is an interesting story of its own, which has been told by President McCann.[6] Here, therefore, I will simply describe and critique our present scheme, reciting only enough history to provide a working rationale.

Decision Making

During the planning year, it was established by the first Committee on Governance that decisions would be made by administrators, commensurate with the responsibilities they had to carry as part of a state-supported system of higher education. A decision should be made at the level closest to those who will be affected, by an administrator who will be "locatable and accountable", only after advice and counsel has been sought through the mechanism of a fairly selected and representative Disappearing Task Force.

The problem-oriented and short-lived DTF was preferred over the more typical standing committee which often takes on a life and an inertia of its own. This became our form of participatory governance in the wake of the sixties experience. This general framework for decision making is still dominant today, although a few standing committees do now exist for those areas of decision-making that require consistency and continuity from year to year: Professional Leaves, Professional Travel, Faculty Hiring, Protection of the Visual Environment and of the Natural Environment on campus. The overall watchdog committee, variously called "The Sounding Board" or "The Evergreen Council", is still composed of five faculty, five staff, five administrators and fifteen students. Its principal functions are the debate of issues and the exchange of ideas, not the setting of policy. It reviews the appointment of all DTF's and receives copies of their reports for public information purposes.

Only since the Fall of 1978 has the faculty held regular monthly meetings. This move in the direction of traditon was necessitated by an increasing feeling of powerlessness on the part of the faculty, whether true or fancied was immaterial. Academic policy was established as the domain appropriate for faculty meeting action. Through this vehicle decisions were made on: implementation of the recommendations of the CPE study, whether or not to establish institution-wide requirements for graduation beyond the simple accumulation of credit (decided negatively), whether or not to change from a quarter to a semester system (negatively), the review and improvement of various special academic options (internships, credit for prior learning, upside down degree), etc..

The Non Tenure System

Evergreen's alternative to the traditional tenure system operates today almost unchanged from that presented by the planning faculty to the Board of Trustees in the spring of 1971. The system includes:

1. Three year contracts of appointment for *all* faculty, regardless of seniority.
2. A serious annual evaluation of the work of each faculty member by an Academic Dean, based upon a cumulative portfolio maintained by each faculty member and containing all previous evaluations *by* colleagues, students and previous academic deans, evaluations *of* colleagues, students and academic deans, and samples of the academic activities carried out in recent years.
3. An appeals process designed to be as neutral and fair to all parties as possible (each party in the grievance selects two representatives, those four select a fifth member, a due-process hearing is

> conducted and a decision rendered). In order to protect academic freedom, the real intent of the tenure system in the first place, we required of the Board of Trustees that the decision of the appeals process be *final* and not subject to overrule by their subsequent decision.[7]

During the second year of each three-year contract, the critical decision is made as to whether a new contract will be offered at the conclusion of the third year. If not, and provided clear warnings have been given the previous year, two options remain: either the third year of the current contract will be a terminal year, or a one-year reappraisal extension of the current contract can be given. During the extension year, very explicit directives for improvement must be accomplished (with proferred collegial assistance) or the fourth year will be terminal.

It is perhaps evident that the fundamental purpose of such a system is faculty development and the improvement of teaching by all of the faculty, no matter how senior. In spite of our idealistic intentions, it is inevitable that the final test of the process will be its ability to divest the institution of its unsuccessful teachers. On this score, the record is fair and improving. In the seven years during which terminations would have been possible (the first three-year appointments were awarded in the Fall of 1971), and not counting the simply voluntary resignations, 14 faculty have been either required to leave or have resigned after deciding that they could not fulfill the explicit improvements required of them. To show the even-handed application of the policy, 2 of that number were on the planning faculty and another 4 had served on the faculty for at least 6 years. In only one case has the full appeals board apparatus been called into effect, and that decision came down on the side of the institution. The real test of our system, of course, will be the case which is decided in favor of the terminated faculty member.

Academic Rank

At the outset of our curricular planning in 1970, it became clear that academic rank would be a serious impediment to the team teaching methods of Coordinated Studies. Members of a team could best work as co-equals so that the subject area expertise could pass from one member of the team to another as required by the study plan rather than by some seniority system. Often the designer and coordinator of a Study Program, who should therefore have temporary leadership authority, was a younger faculty member. And in teaching a Coordinated Study Program, all faculty learn from one another independent of seniority.

Thus, all faculty at Evergreen simply carry the title, "Member of the Faculty" (   ) with the parenthesis filled by the person's principal field of expertise.

Faculty advance annually along a graduated salary scale, provided that their annual evaluations are satisfactory and they are making normal progress toward re-appointment. The salary scale favors the younger faculty by providing them a larger dollar increase per step than the more experienced faculty. After twenty-nine years of experience, the salary scale plateaus at twice the normal starting level.

Critique

The decision-making process works quite well when we are making positive and forward-looking decisions. Students, faculty and staff have given innumerable hours each year to the DTF process and the great majority of the recommendations have become college policy. Nevertheless the workload of active participation seems to fall unevenly on certain persons among faculty and staff. We are reaching the limits of volunteerism and need to find a way to reward exceptional service in this, among other extra duties we ask of faculty and staff. The extremely egalitarian rank and salary system we have devised leaves little room to say "well done" in any substantive fashion. Some system of merit pay for outstanding service needs to be developed.

The decision making process does not work nearly so well in times of retrenchment. We have not had to face this problem very often, fortunately, but on the two occasions when cut-backs have been necessary (1973 and 1980) the results have not been encouraging. First, in order to avoid panic and endless debate at such times (which often demand very prompt action), administrators are reluctant to invoke the public mode of decision making which the DTF requires. Second, because the public mode is not invoked, all parties not consulted feel betrayed and assert that the decisions are arbitrary and capricious. In this upcoming period of fiscal stringency, we need to find a more satisfactory solution to this governance problem. Our system of academic governance without departments, through the Academic Deans, is working quite well. Last year, in its fifth year of operation in current form, the scheme was reviewed and reaffirmed by all parties directly concerned. The principal unresolved problem is the extreme workload which the Deans must carry, increasing steadily with faculty size and the burden of the annual evaluation of faculty.

We are feeling increasingly confident of our alternative to tenure in its present form. It is no longer subject to the early criticism the it was a system of "instant tenure" as we gain experience and some history of termination of unsuccessful faculty members. However, the system does have a troubling fragility in that it is entirely dependent upon the frank and honest appraisal of teaching quality by faculty colleagues and students. Perhaps any system which truly values and tries to appraise teaching quality is subject to this same fragility and criticism.

THE PROCESS OF MATURING

John Gardner has written, "Like people and plants, organizations have a life cycle. They have a green and supple youth, a time of flourishing strength, and a gnarled old age."[8] So starts an analysis by Lippitt and Schmidt, entitled "Crises in a Developing Organization".[9] The stages of organizational development proposed by them and displayed in Table I seem to provide a framework which will be helpful in analyzing where we have been as a developing college and what problems we must look forward to solving in the near future. I have tried to indicate in the fourth column the various stages of Evergreen's developmental history which seem to fit the categories of Lippitt and Schmidt. These assignments are admittedly subjective but, if correct, it would appear that we are approaching maturity (Step 5) and our next critical concern is to achieve adaptability along with uniqueness, to decide whether and how much to change to achieve this adaptability, to decide how to make full use of our (college's) unique abilities."[10] "Certain reactionary forces within (will) feel that there is more to be lost than was the case in creating the original organism."[11] "But such conservatism and a desire to avoid uncertainty lead to various kinds of harmful inhibitions. . . . Thus research and development—sometimes diversification are introduced in the hope of establishing relative security in an uncertain future."[12]

PROBLEMS IN SEARCH OF SOLUTIONS

There are at least four major problem areas facing Evergreen which must be addressed in order to ensure a stable maturity during its second decade. These can be characterized as:

(1) Growth and diversification
(2) Student retention
(3) Faculty and staff morale
and (4) Professional development opportunities

Table I

STAGES OF ORGANIZATIONAL DEVELOPMENT

Developmental Stage	Critical Concern	Key Issues	Stages in TESC Development	
Birth	To create a new organization	What to risk	1967–1972	Founding, Planning, Opening the first year of operation
	To survive as a viable system	What to sacrifice	1972–1976	Early Curriculum Planning and Governance evolution Defining the experiment Achieving the 5-year accreditation
Youth	To gain stability	How to organize	1976–1978	Long Range Curriculum COG III Changing the top administration
	To gain reputation and develop pride	How to review and evaluate	1978–1981	CPE Study Consolidate and strengthen curriculum Improve public relations and image ("Tell the Evergreen Story") Achieve 10-year accreditation
Maturity	To achieve uniqueness and adaptability	Whether and how to change	1981–?	How we can retain our uniqueness yet diversify and remain relevant to our times?
	To contribute to society	Whether and how to share	???????	

In many ways, these are the problems facing all of higher education today; but with Evergreen's unique structure and mission, the problems may demand unique solutions. We will be called upon for continuing invention, flexibility and adaptation; our problems will not be solved by conservatism, rigidity or by clinging to past methods and experiences.

Growth and Diversification

Legislative pressures to achieve economies of scale will continue to force us to increase enrollment from the current 2400 toward 3500–4000 FTE students. (At that level, it is predicted that our average cost per student will be similar to that of our sister institutions). With our current curriculum and methods, we seem to have a fairly natural niche on the national educational scene for some 2200–2500 students. Many of these are transfers who were dissatisfied elsewhere and wish to try our particular educational alternative. Others are older students returning to college after some years of absence. We have been slow in attracting younger students who choose Evergreen simply because of the success of our academic program and our graduates. We are particularly slow in attracting students from our own state and region.

This demand for growth is the most important single issue facing Evergreen. At least three factors are working directly against us: the predicted decline in the number of 18–25 year olds through the next decade, the deteriorating economic climate with higher tuitions and less financial aid, and our own conservative reluctance to change and modify our particular innovations. In 1980, the college administration undertook the development of a five-year growth plan at the request of the Board of Trustees. The intent of this plan is to utilize our current methods but to expand the range of our activities to a much wider and more diverse audience. Unfortunately, the plan received only desultory attention and interest from the faculty and a deteriorating state economy has at least slowed its implementation.

On campus, the plan is designed to strengthen the existing specialty areas at the undergraduate level, open one new graduate program every other year toward a maximum of four (the Master's in Public Administration was offered for the first time in the 1980–81 academic year), expand our part-time evening studies program in a coherent way so that working adults in the local area can succeed in achieving the Bachelor's Degree. Perhaps the least popular suggestion is the design of some specific career options by the addition of specialized faculty and programs at the senior-year level. The intent of these proposals is to attract to the College a more diverse student population in terms of career interests, age, race and life styles. We do not wish to dilute or divert our commitment to the liberal arts, but we do need to operate and expand in a conservative climate in which economic pressures have made students very career oriented and less interested in the liberal arts. Our particular mix of the liberal with the practical arts, of education with training, of classroom study illuminated by project research or internships, should be an especially strong and attractive magnet for students in these days—if we can tell our story clearly and simply.

Off-campus, the five-year plan calls for a considerable expansion of two year sequential programs at the upper division level, based on the successful model at Vancouver, Washington. This is a direct response to the predicted increase in population of the 25–40 year age group, many of whom hold two-year degrees in this state. To our pleasure, we have found that the Coordinated Studies model is very successful with adults reentering education. The mutually supportive cohort group which such a model provides quite naturally, is extremely effective in focussing attention on the learning process and away from the academic insecurities which many of these people feel. The growth plan calls for establishment of two branch campuses for adult students, the one in Vancouver and a similar one in Tacoma—the two main urban centers in Southwest Washington—each at a size of 250–300 students. It also proposes the development of similar smaller programs in three or four other towns in this region, perhaps operating on a two-year rotational basis. In spite of the enthusiasm of those faculty who have worked with adults in such programs, the majority of the faculty is very cool to the notion of becoming commuters. And yet, the distances are sufficiently large (up to 150 miles each way) that one cannot expect the adult students to commute. Clearly, some modification of our usual design is needed, perhaps making full use of our excellent media facilities, to provide the desired educational service to this new and expanding clientele.

Although the concepts of flexibility and curricular responsiveness to student needs were strong in the early conception and rhetoric of Evergreen, there is a noticeable tendency today to conserve and preserve what we have developed. There is a reluctance to move with the times, even within our philosophical framework, to meet the new needs of professionalism and career orientation. A new Long-Range Curriculum DTF will begin meeting this academic year to address these issues and to seek creative, Evergreen-style solutions.

Student Retention

Our record of student retention is not particularly enviable. It is comparable to our sister public institutions in this state and also similar to the retention figures found in other liberal arts colleges which place serious intellectual demands on their students. A number of things contribute to this problem for us. Among our transfer students, we tend to attract some who are looking for alternatives and may continue the search beyond our alternative. Another group of students, used to the traditional course structure, find our intensive focus on one study at a time to be too confining or restrictive. Still others seek to specialize in subject areas which we cannot yet offer at our size. We have no sororities, or fraternities, few social clubs and only a minimal intercollegiate athletic program, so the academic work is the principal activity on campus. Combined with the gray weather of our long winters, campus morale takes a noticeable slump every Winter Quarter, and Spring Quarter enrollment suffers significantly.

We have exerted considerable effort this past spring in data collection on the attrition/retention issues and will make this problem a major target of our creativity during the next academic year.

Faculty and Staff Morale

Since the earliest days of the college, we have placed unusual demands on the time and energy of our faculty and staff. To a considerable extent, the structure of our academic system will continue to require heavy contact hours of the faculty (19 per week is average) and much paperwork of the staff (narrative evaluations, annual catalog preparation, etc.). Added to this is the uncertainty caused by annual threats of closure, budget cuts by the state, and accompanying small reductions in staff by attrition or layoff. Anxieties and tensions can rise rather high at times, and have recently led to formation of our first collective bargaining unit (classified staff, primarily). Unfortunately, we have very few ways to say "thank you" by any substantive means. Classified staff salaries and salary increases are almost entirely established by the State Legislative and promotional opportunities are very limited because of our small size. The faculty have devised a very egalitarian salary scale, based upon years of relevant experience since the bachelor's degree, so that multiple steps on the scale are forbidden. We have about reached the end of volunteerism by both staff and faculty alike. Another DTF, to be formed in the Autumn, will be charged with the task of devising a system of faculty merit-pay-for-special-service, and perhaps of providing other recommendations for improvement of general morale on campus.

Professional Development

One of the most serious problems for a driven and hardworking staff and faculty, particularly in a teaching-centered institution, is maintaining contact with a profession and its advancement. Traditionally, a sabbatical program allows the faculty and certain staff to engage in professional study and updating, at least once every seventh year.

In the state of Washington, the Professional Leaves Program limits participation to only 4% of the faculty and professional staff per year—that is, about once every 20–25 years for each person! We are trying to supplement this austere program by developing faculty exchange opportunities with other colleges and universities in this country and abroad.

Several unique opportunities for faculty development exist at Evergreen because of our structure and policies. The faculty seminar is one of the most satisfactory devices for developing the interdisciplinary capabilities of the faculty. Shifting the teaching responsibilities within the curriculum every couple of years adds to the development of breadth. Organizing and teaching an advanced Group Contract in one's own field can provide the opportunity for an in-depth updating of one's expertise.

To share teaching techniques and methods of solving pedagogic problems, we hold a monthly all-faculty Teaching Strategies Session, organized around some special theme each time. Each Spring Quarter, we release one of our successful faculty from regular teaching duties to serve as consultant to any faculty colleagues who wish help in improving their teaching skills.

Certain members of the staff holding faculty rank (especially from the Library and the Computer Center) are rotated into the ranks of the teaching faculty for a quarter or two every three years. In exchange, a member of the teaching faculty rotates into the staff position to carry forward certain developmental tasks. For both parties, always volunteer, this provides breadth, new insight, and a break from the usual pressure and routine.

Although we have clearly given considerable attention to professional development, we continue to see it as a problem needing additional solutions. In our teaching context, the problem of staying current in one's own field of expertise is unusually large and particularly difficult to obtain, and our curricular structure makes it difficult to provide a reduced teaching load in order to encourage part-time research.

Conclusions

Our ability to respond creatively to these problems, and other only partially predictable challenges arising from the economic and demographic conditions of the time, will determine our future viability as an innovative institution of the 1980's. Continuing modification of curriculum and style may be necessary to serve the needs of a new generation of students and a new set of societal attitudes and problems. A continuing review of our fundamental educational principles may even be required to assure that we are serving those needs well.

The dangers, of course, are two-fold: Either we are so set in our ways that we cannot change at all, or we change so dramatically that we lose our sense of mission and become quite traditional. Either extreme would be disastrous.

My own prediction is that the educational pendulum, while now swinging strongly toward the conservative side, will begin its return motion before this decade is ended. As an institution, we are currently being forced to move in a conservative direction in order to survive; but, as the pendulum begins to return, we will be ahead of the motion and can again give leadership to the creative impulse in the higher education community. Thus, the experiment is by no means ended. The demands for flexibility and invention will be every bit as great in the decade ahead as in that just past.

NOTES

1. Gordon Sandison, Minutes of Organizational meeting of the Board of Trustees of the New Four Year College, August 30, 1967, College Archives, TESC.

2. *The Experimental College*, Alexander Meiklejohn, Harper and Bros. (1932).

3. For historical background, pedagogical philosophy, and additional organizational details see: *Experiment at Evergreen*, Richard M. Jones, Schenkman Publishing Co., Cambridge, Mass., 1981).

4. A considerable amount about Evergreen's early days appeared in the public-press. One of the best of these is *The Los Angeles Times*, Part II: Monday, April, 17, 1972 in an article by Education Editor William Trombley entitled, "College Takes New Approach—No Grades or Majors." Surprisingly little appears about Evergreen in the professional literature in higher education. Two exceptions are: *Change Magazine:* 4(4) 17–19, May 1972, Kenneth G. Gehart, Washington's Evergreen College (about our first year's curriculum) and *Alternative Higher Education:* 2(1) 41–46, Feb. 1977 "Trying Hard: Interdisciplinary Programs at TESC" by Dr. Mark Levensky, Member of the Faculty (Philosophy).

5. Council for Postsecondary Education, "The Evergreen Study" State of Washington, Olympia, WA February, 1979, p. 3.

6. "Academic Administration Without Departments at The Evergreen State College", C. J. McCann; chapter 8 of *Alternatives to the Academic Department*, ed. Dean McHenry, Jossey-Bass (San Francisco, 1977).

7. See TESC Faculty Handbook for further details.

8. "How to Prevent Organizational Dry Rot", John Gardner, *Harpers Magazine*, Oct. 1965, p. 30.

9. "Crises in a Developing Institution", G. Lippitt and W. Schmidt, *Harvard Business Review*, Nov.–Dec. 1967, pp. 102–112.

10. Ibid. pg. 103.

11. Ibid. pg. 104.

12. Ibid. pg. 109.

VII. Response to Youtz

by

RICHARD JONES

I read your paper last, Byron, having read the other conference papers as they came in during the summer. So, my reading of the paper had the special advantage of being informed by knowledge of certain contingencies which have bedeviled the growth of kindred ventures into alternative higher education. There are four:

1. The absence of autonomous political authority at the top, i.e. at the level of the boards of trustees. The ultimate failure of the University of California at Santa Cruz to sustain its alternative visions is a dramatic case in point. When the underenrollment crunch of the middle and late seventies spread to Santa Cruz, it was its constituent status as but one of California's many universities, subject to the central managerial authority of that vast system, that contributed largely to its having to survive by returning to traditional policies and practices.
2. Organization by department. This conference will hear of many examples of the virulence of departments in undermining imaginative innovations. Again, Santa Cruz is perhaps the most dramatic example, because the decision to departmentalize that institution was neither blind nor unqualified. The departments there were christened "boards of study," and were meant to generate a creative state of "dynamic tension" with the supposedly equally powerful constituent colleges. In ten years time, the boards of study became traditional departments and devoured the constituent colleges, in all but their residential functions.
3. Careerism. The temptations, especially among administrative leaders of alternative ventures, to advance their individual careers

by jumping from venture to venture; often leaving obscured visions, feelings of betrayal and various forms of institutional amnesia in their wake.

The almost comical musical chairs routine which plagued the Rocky Mountain Consortium nicely exemplifies the phenomenon. Closer to home, Evergreen's own 100% turnover in academic leadership in its first seven years would surely have eroded our commitments to innovation more than it did, had our founding president and two of our founding deans not chosen to take up regular faculty positions here, and had you not been willing to take the place of our first two provosts.

4. The inevitable dependence of fledgling alternative ventures on what you call "volunteerism," i.e., on the heroic investments of time, energy and anxiety on the parts of some faculty who somehow find it possible to accept virtue as its own, often exclusive, reward. The inevitable resulting burn-outs have readily led to rationalizations for returning to the easier old ways of teaching traditional courses. There is also the commonly known fact, following your analogy, that parents will make personal sacrifices for babies that they will not make for teenagers.

Against that background, drawn from the maturational experiences of a dozen or so of our sisters, I want now to highlight some of the major contributing factors in Evergreen's comparatively healthy childhood:

1. Our Board of Trustees is an autonomous governing body, accountable to no central managerial authority between it and the Governor who appoints it and the Legislature which approves the governor's appointments. Moreover, the particular trustees who saw us through our first year were among the most conservative, republican, successful business persons in the state.

They did not always understand what the planning faculty had planned, and did not always approve of what they did understand. But they did consistently support the plan in response to all forms of off-campus opposition. This or that legislator might call critical attention to this or that program title, or to faculty beards or to student dress (or undress) etc.; but when push came to shove on the several votes to close the college in its early years, the only politically significant eyeballs available for showdown confrontation were those of five white, conservative, republican, successful business persons—and their political clout. No more effective protective parenting could have been planned for such an improbable infant as we were; if, in fact, it was planned. In any event, in attempting to explain the health of Evergreen's childhood, the contributions of Herb Hadley, Hal Halvorsen, Al Saunders, Bink Schmidt and Janet Tourtelotte deserve more appreciation than they have received. Some political scientist may wish to assess the irony that may reside in that observation.

2. The planning faculty left no room for second thinking in its absolute eschewal of departments. True, the germ readily mutates, and we now have our specialty areas and specialty area convenors. But, in the five years since their appearance, these still have no stable means of reproduction, very little power and no budgets. Pretty good!
3. As to careerism, the planning faculty set an outrageous example: no tenure, no rank, no merit pay, no seniority perks. Not even the possibility of advancing individual careers within the college by repeating popular programs. Whatever the motives may have been which produced those founding decisions, and however over-reactive some of them may prove to be if programs of coordinated study should cease to constitute our center, they did create an institutional image that was unlikely to attract faculty who wished, even unconsciously, to exploit employment at Evergreen for personal advancement elsewhere.
4. Possibly as a result of numbers 2 and 3 above, our first two massive waves of new faculty (37 the first year and 35 the second) included a very large number of seasoned teachers who foresaw how much unpaid overtime they were signing on for, and who chose to sign on for it. The "volunteer" problem exists at Evergreen, and it will become worse, as you note. But part of Evergreen's comparative success, so far, is probably due to the truism that volunteers make better volunteers when they choose to be volunteers than when they are assigned that privilege.

By now, Byron, you must be getting antsy, waiting for me to drop another shoe, as I don't often sound so positive about Evergreen's maturation in your presence. But this is parlor, not kitchen, talk; so I hasten to say here that I agree with your major conclusions. Namely, that in retrospect, and on balance, we saved as much of our planning dreams as we could have saved; we compromised as little as we had to, in order to survive as a tax-supported alternative liberal arts college, given the peripatetic inter-generational dynamics of the 60's and 70's, and their social, political and economic manifestations . . . and, most especially, given our schizophrenic mandate to develop an alternative college which would be a model for the nation *and* also be a useful college for the citizens of Southwest Washington. Indeed, it may eventually even turn out that we succeeded in meeting this schizophrenic challenge by responding to it schizophrenically, i.e. by establishing a national reputation before we even paid attention to the needs of Southwest Washington.

But all of that is for historians to mull over. For the purposes at hand, I want to focus now on Evergreen's future, and what I see to be its most problematic next phase.

I don't foresee any major dangers to our continuing maturation from the four quarters listed above.

1. The authority of the Board of Trustees will continue to be autonomous, and in any future conflicts with the governor or legislature its political strength will be augmented by an increasing number of articulate alumni.
2. Careerism won't pose a danger for the stark reason that a market for advancement outside of Evergreen won't exist, at least not through the eighties.
3. You are probably right that sufficient checks were designed into the specialty areas to prevent them from being perverted into departments.
4. The pinch of our dependence on volunteers will become tighter as our best ones grow older, but there is at least the assurance that our present provost foresees this danger, and is looking for ways to assuage it.

So, I feel sanguine as to the staying power of those felicitous strengths which made for the health of our childhood.

The most problematic development we shall face as a maturing institution is the same as that which inevitably faces a maturing individual in our society after childhood: we are going to have an identity crisis. We already do. We cannot and should not try to avoid this identity crisis. Rather, we should try to live through it with all possible integrity of self-consciousness. What will this mean? It will mean learning how to conduct and represent the college *as it has actually become*. Never mind what it might have become, but didn't. Never mind what it might not have become, but did. (A teenaged individual and his parents had best unload similar memorial baggage.)

Also, never mind the oedipal projections of each incoming class of new students into the ink-blot of "the original Evergreen." And never mind some of the lingering regrets of some of the College's founders, who, like me at times, have been disappointed by some of the things the College has become, and by some of the things it has not become.

The question on which all of us—trustees, administration, faculty, staff, students and alumni—will be required by our identity crisis to reach a viable consensus is: *What kind of an alternative college has Evergreen, in palpable fact, become?* (My 13 year old son has not become the boy my imagination projected when he was two, either. But the son for whom my love must find a way for me to continue to father is the teenager that Andy has in fact, become.) I think the answers to what Evergreen has, in fact, become are pointedly there in your paper, Byron. We have become a college which offers two kinds of alternatives to traditional higher education. They are: (1) "collaborative, interdisciplinary teaching," and its counterpart, "cooperative rather than competitive learning." And (2) opportunities for students to "take charge of their education" and to "plan their own curricular paths." Those *are* the two essential components of our identity; in rhetoric, and, in deed. The challenge of living through our identity crisis in health will come in learning to represent the two different offerings differentially in both our public and private relations; and in learning to offer them discriminately, with skill, with candor and with authority. In growing these two identity components two growing pains have emerged which I do not believe are sufficiently articulate in our institutional self-consciousness. The first one is that while we can and do offer both alternatives well, we cannot (and should not try to) offer them simultaneously. This by self-evident definition. The room for confusion here is minimal when a student is pursuing an internship or an individual contract or a self-paced learning unit.

But when a student commits himself to a cooperative learning venture, whether in a program of coordinated study or in some of our group contracts, he must be actively disabused of the expectation that he can also "chart his own curricular path." At present, if a student wishes to join a program of coordinated study he has 100% latitude of choice as to which of the available programs to join. Having chosen a program, however, that latitude of choice is immediately reduced to zero; as such programs have been (or should have been) planned in advance by their faculty teams, down to the finest of details. I no longer offer this as a personal opinion; it is a widely experienced fact. We have not yet learned how to signal that fact of Evergreen life to all of our students; we should make this deficiency a top priority item in our faculty and governance meetings, soon.

The second problem is more serious. It is that the system of values which sustains collaborative teaching and cooperative learning is not only unfamiliar to almost any person schooled in America; it is countervalent to the system of values which *is* familiar to almost every person schooled in America. The average high school graduate may never have designed an individual learning contract, or done an internship or self-paced learning unit, but the individualistic values and habits of mind which govern those modes of instruction are familiar ones, being, for the most part, private enterprises. In a program of coordinated study, however, not only must the average high school graduate accommodate a novel instructional format; he must also accommodate a set of communal values and habits of mind for which he has been almost totally unprepared by previous school experience. Right now, for example, the most regular threat to the successful conclusion of a well-designed and well taught program of coordinated study at Evergreen are those increasing numbers of students who transfer out of the program at quarter breaks (often for the worthiest of selfish reasons, as our students go about "charting their own curricular paths") without even any consciousness of guilt over the broken commitment to the cooperative enterprise which they made to their fellow students. The most galling part of this problem is that few such students transfer out of programs from feelings of dissatisfaction with those programs: most simply think they see a greener Evergreen over some other curricular fence—and are often encouraged to do so by the College's own rhetoric concerning the values of self-determined curricula.

American schools encourage the keeping of commitments to self, to teachers and to subjects—almost never to classmates. Yet the keeping of this latter commitment (at least to the extent of it's being a conscious commitment) is essential to the success of a coordinated study program. Without it the cost to the program in morale, in continuity and in colleageality can assume deadly proportions. This problem cannot be solved at the levels of program design or program teaching, because the problem is caused by an undifferentiated college ethos. At present, while individualized and cooperative learning are given equal prominence in our rhetoric, the values of individualism are much more evident in our routine institutional habits. For example, our quarterly Academic Fairs, which often have the effects of encouraging solutions to individual problems while discouraging solutions to cooperative problems.

In respect, Byron, to both of these challenges to our identity development, your choice of the analogy of a maturing individual is apt. In personality theory we even have some refined concepts with which to discuss them. We speak, for example, of the needs for autonomy and for homonomy, i.e. for individual mastery and self determination and for belongingness and participation in ventures that are larger than self. Integration of these two sets of needs is not easily achieved in the individual's adolescent and early adult years. But achieved the integration must be if the individual is to enter his later years of responsible authority with a vigorous sense of identity. The same must be said of this college, I think.

The first step in the direction of successful integration in such matters is usually successful differentiation. And there, I think, is where we are presently stuck. We haven't yet learned to be sure when and how we are pulling for autonomy and when and how we are pulling for homonomy.

As a beginning to at least starting to raise our institutional consciousness on these issues, I suggest that we give some thought to this question: May our early adulthood be a good time in which to consider the desirability of re-structuring the college into two schools or two divisions or two what-have-you's? A School of Coordinated Study, and a School of Specialized Study. With faculty and students and deans distributing their time between the two, from time to time, as they wish. At the very least this would provide a structural reminder as to which of our two identity components a student, a faculty member or a dean is defining his or her efforts by at any given time. With everyone's experience thereby contributing to the integration demanded for the long-range developmental interests of the college. I have no investment in the idea as a solution to our identity crisis—only as a prod to some healthy kitchen talk, after the guests go home.

VIII. Interdisciplinary Curriculum Development in the 1970's: The Paracollege at St. Olaf and the Western College Program at Miami University

by

WILLIAM H. NEWELL

Introduction

This chapter identifies the factors affecting the development of interdisciplinary curricula in the early 1970's at the Paracollege of St. Olaf College and in the late 1970's at the Western College Program at Miami University.* I shall draw evidence from a detailed examination of these two cluster college[1] programs during their formative years—from initial conception to successful evaluation—when curriculum development was most in flux. I shall also assess the factors which will exert a major influence on interdisciplinary curriculum development in the 1980's in light of the anticipated context of lower enrollments and fiscal austerity.

Since there is no generally accepted definition of interdisciplinary studies available in the literature,[2] the ensuing discussion of interdisciplinary curriculum is based on two presumptions about the characteristics of interdisciplinary studies implicitly shared by most definitions. The first is that an interdisciplinary study builds on the disciplines. The second is

*I would like to acknowledge the assistance of Paul Fjelstad, Bobbi Helling, and William Narum in reconstructing the origins of the Paracollege, and the comments of Curtis Ellison, William Green, and George Stein on an earlier draft. Any errors are, of course, my own.

that it goes beyond the disciplines, involving some sort of synthesis or integration.

OVERVIEW OF THE PROGRAMS

The Paracollege

The Paracollege was founded in 1969 as a cluster college within St. Olaf College, a liberal arts college of 2,700 students located in Northfield, Minnesota and affiliated with the American Lutheran Church. At the initiative of the Dean of the College and after a year-long study by a subcommittee of the curriculum committee, a three-faculty "summer committee" drew up the detailed proposal[3] for the Paracollege. It was approved by the St. Olaf faculty. The committee members were selected for their commitment to innovative education. Together with two faculty drawn from outside St. Olaf, they served as the faculty of the Paracollege during its first year. The program grew by adding a new freshman class each year, and by increasing the size of the faculty as enrollment warranted. At first, majority-time faculty were hired through a national search, but then increasing numbers of part-time faculty were drawn from within St. Olaf. In almost all cases, the Paracollege faculty held joint appointments in disciplinary departments. Over twenty full- and part-time faculty were associated with the program by the end of its fifth year, along with more than 200 students.

The program was conceived as an experimental alternative for St. Olaf students, offering individualized studies through a combination of tutorials, examinations, syllabi, and interdisciplinary seminars,[4] as well as course work selected from St. Olaf College. Major requirements for graduation included satisfactory completion of the General Examination which covered the distribution requirements for general education, the Comprehensive Examination which covered the student's major and a Senior Project. Secondary requirements of all St. Olaf students such as physical education, religion, creative arts, and foreign languages were met through passing proficiency examinations. The Paracollege students also had a teaching requirement, such as leading a discussion group, and they had to attend a senior seminar. All graduation requirements were met through examinations unconnected to any specific courses, rather than through accumulation of course credits. The Paracollege was reviewed during its fifth year of operation and approved by the St. Olaf faculty and administration in 1973 following a ten-month review by a select committee.

The Western College Program

Western College (formerly Western College for Women) faced bankruptcy in 1973 after 120 years of operation. It was purchased by Miami University, a state-assisted and predominantly undergraduate university of 14,000 students located in the same town of Oxford, Ohio. Miami's president appointed a Planning Committee to review proposals for the use of the campus and buildings. The Committee recommended several alternatives.[5] Ultimately a residential, interdisciplinary college was approved by the faculty, administration, and Board of Trustees for a trial period of three to five years. An Interim Committee, much like the Summer Planning Committee of the Paracollege, was appointed by the president. The Committee developed a detailed proposal for the new program in the interim between the approval of the program and the selection of the new dean and faculty.[6] A dean and assistant dean were hired in the spring of 1974, the faculty selected by early summer, and the curriculum for the first year planned in midsummer. Students were recruited during Miami's summer orientation. By August of the same year the Western College Program had started operation with 150 freshmen and six full-time faculty. Like the Paracollege, Western grew by adding a new freshman class each year and faculty as enrollment and budgets allowed. Western had 12 full-time faculty serving 350 students by the fourth year of the program. Unlike the Paracollege, Western's faculty were all full time, with no official ties to disciplinary departments of Miami University. Most were hired through national searches. The program's status was that of a division with the University. It offered its own degree—the Bachelor of Philosophy of Interdisciplinary Studies—and set its own degree requirements.

Students took a core of required interdisciplinary courses in the humanities, social sciences, and natural sciences during the freshman and sophomore years. They lived in the Western residence halls during these years and participated in a community learning program designed to complement the formal curriculum. Students also took one or two electives each semester in other divisions of the University—often courses designed to prepare them for their upper-division concentration. Toward the end of their sophomore year, students drew up a learning contract with the assistance of their faculty advisor. The contract described and provided a rationale for their individualized concentrations, listing the courses they would take towards that concentration during their junior and senior years. The upper division featured the concentrations, junior seminars, senior projects, and senior workshops found in and partly modeled after the Paracollege. Students took one interdisciplinary seminar at Western each semester of their junior year with the rest of their course work in other divisions. During the senior year, they wrote a senior project through a year-long research seminar while completing course-work outside the division for their concentrations.

The Western College Program was reviewed in its fourth year by a special task force, which recommended to the President of the University that the program be continued. Following overwhelming votes of support from the faculty of the University and from the President, the Board of Trustees approved the program as a continuing division of Miami University in 1978.

CURRICULUM DEVELOPMENT

The Paracollege

The basic features of the program were fundamentally student-centered,[7] opposed to the traditional educational structures against which student activists had been rebelling in the late 60's. It was quite distinct, though, from the spate of reactive experiments in that it set clear-cut academic standards through the general and comprehensive examinations. The objective of the student-centered approach was to free students to study what, when, where, with whom, and how they wanted, by replacing traditional structures with ones designed to be supportive as well as freeing, such as tutorials and optional syllabi. Since advancement towards the degree was by examinations unconnected with specific courses, students were unaffected by course grades, permitting them to treat courses (and professors) as resources to be used for their own ends without concern for the structures of attendance, assignments, or examinations. In fact, the Paracollege system of examinations and proficiency tests freed students from courses altogether. If they really believed they would learn most from canoeing in the North Woods, then they were free to go, but they would have to pass the next examination to make progress towards the degree. The Paracollege reserved the right to determine the categories of knowledge and skill defining the degree, while it took on the obligation of providing sufficient educational resources for the students to attain that knowledge and skill in their own way. This student-centered approach turned out to conflict with the interdisciplinary aims of the program.

Surrounding the attack on the structure and the faculty-centered orientation of traditional higher education was a pervasive spirit of innovation and experimentation in the Paracollege. Some of the founding faculty perceived the Paracollege as only one of several desirable experiments; perhaps an umbrella for other experiments in later years if enrollment at St. Olaf continued to grow.[8]

The cluster college structure of the Paracollege was originally selected because it enabled St. Olaf to increase enrollment while maintaining a human scale learning environment where more "integration of college learning" could take place.[9] A sense of community was created by this small scale and by the prevailing spirit of innovation. This sense of community was consciously fostered by weekly community dinners, by joint student-faculty outings, and, generally, by interaction between students and faculty on a personal, first-name basis. Breaking down social as well as educational barriers was consistent with the individualized approach to learning which lay at the heart of the program. This ambience of innovation and community turned out to be the major source of support for interdisciplinary curriculum development in the Paracollege.

As the number of faculty grew during the first five years, its composition changed. The balance of majority-time and part-time appointments shifted, as did the balance of appointments from inside and outside St. Olaf. These changes had important consequences for interdisciplinary studies in the program. With one exception, faculty added to the founding members for the first two years of the program were all at least majority-time appointments from outside St. Olaf. One was full-time. Because these faculty came to St. Olaf for the Paracollege and their time was spent predominantly in the Paracollege, their commitment to the program was high. Most of these faculty held joint appointments in disciplinary departments, which meant that the departments had to approve their appointments; consequently, faculty with primarily interdisciplinary training were not hired. The summer committee had recommended that Paracollege faculty also be members of departments to avoid the estrangement between the cluster college and its parent institution that had developed at other experimental programs.[10] This rule also served to provide a home for faculty in other St. Olaf departments should the experiment fail.[11] The tension resulting from this dual allegiance led to neglect of disciplinary professional development, dilution of commitment to interdisciplinary studies, exhaustion and sometimes all three.

During the third year of the program, more faculty were drawn from the St. Olaf faculty on part-time appointments, partly to increase the number of disciplines represented and partly in response to administrative pressures to help resolve staffing complications in some departments. These faculty were still a small minority in the third year, but by the fifth year they formed a majority. While a few of these faculty became strong advocates of interdisciplinary studies, many retained their primary commitment to department and discipline. Consequently, the program began to experience some pressure for change, since under the prevailing spirit of egalitarianism part-time faculty had the same voice and vote as full-time faculty. Students were required to hold regular meetings with their tutors and were allowed to complete some degree requirements through passing courses. The ideological fervor of the program became somewhat diluted, and with it came a dilution of the commitment to integrative or interdisciplinary studies.

While "interdisciplinary" was used in the Paracollege promotional literature to describe course offerings and was frequently used by faculty in describing their upper-division seminars, the term most often used in the Paracollege was "integrative." Consensus was never reached, or even attempted if memory serves correctly, on the definition of either term; they were used interchangeably. The concept of integration at Paracollege meant applying disciplines to a common issue and then addressing the relationship among their insights, a conception consistent with the presumptions about interdisciplinary studies set forth earlier in this chapter.

It was not readily apparent how to develop a curriculum fitted to a student-centered program like the Paracollege. If students really were to decide for themselves what they would study, when, how, and with whom, then there would be no assurance that a course developed and offered by a faculty member would attract any students, or that those attracted would follow the syllabus. One might have been led to predict that the initial conception of the Paracollege would include the development of curriculum through student-initiated negotiations with faculty. While there was an element of this process in upper-division seminars and even more in academic tutorials, most lower-division courses were developed through a more traditional process. Students had considerable voice in the educational policies of the Paracollege, constituting half of the voting membership of most committees, but for the most part faculty retained control over what and how they would teach.

A tutorial system based on the Ox-bridge model was recommended by the summer committee as a natural component of a program of individualized education. The committee expected a substantial portion of the formal academic interaction between faculty and students to take place in that setting,[12] especially in the upper division. In practice, the most important function served by tutorials was the provision of faculty advice and support for students who entered the program without a clear idea of what they wished to study and why. It quickly became apparent that most freshmen cannot know what they want to study for their general education because they do not know what the various disciplines have to offer until they have been exposed to them. Thus, when the rhetoric of a student-centered education confronted the reality of ill-informed students, who were often bewildered by the very freedom they were seeking, faculty came to serve as counselors facilitating each student's search for meaning, challenge and identity through what came to be called advisorial tutorials.

While all faculty provided these tutorials, some faculty developed academic tutorials as well, similar to the Ox-bridge model. These tutorials made more use of faculty expertise while remaining faithful to the program's student-centered ethos. Topics were typically determined through negotiation between tutor and student. Such tutorials were rarely interdisciplinary, however, since faculty expertise was normally confined to one discipline.

The summer committee was aware that most students would come to the program out of highly structured learning environments. It felt the need to provide some transition to the unstructured education of the Paracollege. One required and graded freshman seminar was designated to provide the necessary bridge. The requirement of a course for graduation was a clear exception to the policy of advancement through examination, and the committee felt it was necessary to assure that the course be of the highest possible quality. Class size was restricted to twelve. Faculty were encouraged to make their individual seminar as stimulating as possible, and since no course in English composition was required, faculty were requested to assign frequent papers and to provide students with extensive feedback on their writing. The objective of high academic quality led faculty to offer topics that were firmly within their area of professional expertise, although the spirit of innovation encouraged them to approach the topic in an unconventional manner.

The freshman seminars were often excellent. The summer committee envisioned them as "always relevant to integration,"[13] and the college catalog occasionally claimed that they were interdisciplinary.[14] However, they seldom attempted to be interdisciplinary. The rhetoric of interdisciplinary studies, which reflected a genuine concern for a holistic approach to knowledge, ran up against the pragmatic consideration of student-faculty ratios which militated against the assignment of more than one faculty member to a small section. The system of joint appointments put pressure on new faculty to expand their expertise in their discipline in order to secure tenure and promotion, instead of undertaking serious preparation in related disciplines so that they might teach interdisciplinary courses. The Paracollege offered no counterbalancing incentives to faculty promoting their development of interdisciplinary expertise.

A new freshman course called Liberal Arts I was offered in the fall of 1974. It was added to the freshman seminar as a requirement for all freshmen. Although this course was a departure from the emphasis on unstructured education, it was an attempt to move the freshman curriculum closer to the ideal of interdisciplinary studies. Billed as a lecture series on the general theme "What is a Human Being?" the course was an imaginative array of eleven perceptions of human beings—from biocomputer to identity seeker to a self who celebrates—each of which was addressed by faculty from different disciplines. Discussion by faculty and students at the end of each lecture, debates among faculty in place of a lecture and informal evening discussions among students and participating faculty provided opportunities to contrast the approaches of different disciplines to the topic of the week. So little time was spent on any one topic that the full prespective of each discipline could not be developed in any detail. Nor was time devoted to pulling together coherently what was learned about each discipline by contrasting it systematically with other disciplines. The notion of interdisciplinary studies underlying the course emphasized "interrelationships among different [disciplinary] methodologies,"[15] one of several conceptions held by the faculty. Lack of consensus among the faculty on the meaning of interdisciplinary studies contributed, no doubt, to the decision not to include a final section on synthesis, even though the faculty organizing the course were committed to interdisciplinary education and recognized synthesis as a key element in the interdisciplinary process.

Freshmen and sophomores were particularly concerned with preparing for the General Examination, so the faculty offered courses containing background relevant to that examination. The four parts of the examination—humanities, social sciences, natural sciences, and integration—suggested a natural partitioning of the remaining lower-division curriculum. In keeping with the ambivalence of the faculty about integration—wishing it, while being unsure of how best to promote it—no syllabus was offered in this area. The most comprehensive efforts at interdisciplinary studies were undertaken in the social sciences.

In the second year of the program, the social science faculty put together a syllabus fully consonant with the ideology of individualized study. The first section listed provocative writings on a wide range of current issues. Next, three "short courses" were offered sequentially in psychology, sociology, and economics in order to provide students with an intensive and efficient introduction to the fundamentals of these disciplines. The basic concepts and theories of each discipline were covered in two weeks of daily lectures, supplemented by student-led preceptorials. A standard introductory text was assigned, and an examination comparable to the final examination in a traditional introductory course was provided on an optional basis to help students judge how much they had learned.

As soon as each short course was completed, the faculty member trained in that discipline would begin a seminar. Here the disciplinary material from the short course was applied to a current issue. While the syllabus referred to "interdisciplinary themes and issues of the seminars," the objective of applying concepts and theories from only one discipline worked against that goal. The syllabus also listed more advanced works in each discipline so that students might be guided to more sophisticated insight into the issues addressed by the social sciences. In short, this syllabus faithfully mirrored the original conception of the Paracollege. It offered an optional sequence of educational resources designed to support individualized learning and it favored interdisciplinary study while doing little to promote it.

Dissatisfied with the disciplinary nature of the previous year's syllabus, the social science faculty completely revised it for the third year of the program. The syllabus now had a broad focus. "Urban America: Problems and Prospects." The provocative readings at the beginning addressed a wide range of topics within this focus. The faculty then presented a course on the theme "Is the Good Life Possible in the American City?". Modules on health, crime, and so forth were addressed half the time by lectures from a disciplinary perspective. The rest of the class meetings typically featured two or more faculty contrasting their perspectives on an issue. These topics were well chosen so that faculty could demonstrate the power of their discipline to move beyond common sense discussion of issues. The frequent panels or presentation cum critique moved the course beyond a purely multidisciplinary[16] format, but the synthesis at the end was limited to a "legislative session" in the last week. Here students were encouraged to propose and defend answers to the problems discussesd from disciplinary perspectives during the semester.

Second semester, the social science syllabus started out with the short courses pioneered the previous year. Seminars followed which ranged from the disciplinary, such as "Electoral Politics," to a number of interdisciplinary themes. One faculty member's seminar on "Prejudice," for example, offered perspectives from psychology, social psychology, sociology, economics, legal studies, and philosophy. While the contributions of the disciplines to the central question were clear enough, the interrelations were merely alluded to in discussions. All in all, this year-long syllabus retained the commitment to individualized learning while moving significantly in the direction of interdisciplinary studies. Still, the course had as many multidisciplinary elements as it had interdisciplinary ones. The approach to interdisciplinary studies was still not systematic.

In an attempt to develop a genuinely interdisciplinary curriculum, the social science faculty again completely revised the syllabus the following year. The curriculum was in the hands of newer faculty, however, and some of the original emphasis on individualized learning was lost in the drive for interdisciplinary. The syllabus no longer began with provocative readings and it no longer concluded with more advanced readings to guide further study. In addition, the syllabus linked particular social science course offerings to particular sections of the General Examination.

The new syllabus, entitled "Social Science as a Discipline," focused on the theories of choice and decision-making in the behavioral sciences. It emphasized the common quantitative methodology underlying the social sciences and the common philosophical issues they raise, while pointing up their differences in underlying assumptions. A flowchart was developed which set out both the common method and the divergent world views and assumptions of the disciplines. Faculty took turns presenting a theory of choice from their discipline and showing how that theory could be applied to a question of interest to the discipline and then tested empirically in accordance with the flowchart. The other faculty then attempted to understand that theory from the perspective of their own disciplines, clarifying the assumptions and evaluating them in the process. Students learned something of how the various social sciences look at the world, their differences and similarities, as they both watched and participated in this analytical process. The syllabus argued for the need to apply an interdisciplinary social science approach to policy questions, but there was no attempt to apply the disciplines to a common topic. The interdisciplinary process of synthesis was still missing from the course.

Humanities syllabi were typically organized in terms of periods (e.g., The Ancient Mediterranean—Athens, Jerusalem, Rome) or movements (e.g., Romanticism). They were all largely multidisciplinary in format, with a series of lectures cum discussion from disciplinary perspectives with no attempt on the part of the faculty to reconcile or synthesize these perspectives. On the whole, the humanities offerings did not claim to be interdisciplinary. Students were expected to demonstrate integrative ability between the humanities and the other areas without any explicit models of integration, leaving unclear the interdisciplinary intentions of the humanities faculty.

Among the natural sciences, the mathematics courses proved most innovative. In addition to training in the discipline several crossdisciplinary[17] courses were offered. Here the theories or methods of various social sciences or humanities were expressed in the language of mathematics and examined for their consistency and power. These courses were especially effective at developing mathematical imagination, but they were more of an exercise in metadisciplinary than interdisciplinary thinking. There was no reciprocal contribution from the other discipline to mathematics.

Many of the offerings in the physical and biological sciences were innovative introductions to disciplines, or to their common scientific method. Occasionally a scientist would team-teach a seminar with a social scientist or a humanist, such as a seminar on science and ethics. The role of the scientist in such a course was typically to set the constraints within which the insights of the other discipline can operate. The element of synthesis was typically missing.

After completing the General Examination, students pursued such diverse individualized majors that it was impossible for the faculty to offer a coherent upper-division curriculum. Instead, faculty took the opportunity to offer seminars on their current professional interests. The extreme curricular flexibility and spirit of innovation made it possible for faculty to develop courses with each other as they discovered a common interest, pursuing the question from both their disciplinary perspectives until a common answer acceptable to both was developed. Here the rhetoric of interdisciplinary studies meant greater freedom for faculty as well as for students.

Completing the upper-division curriculum was the senior seminar. Students who had now developed some sophistication in their field came together on a weekly basis with a faculty member. They discussed a variety of issues from the perspective of their respective fields, and compared those intellectual frameworks, with an eye to achieving some consensus. In a relaxed setting, these students took time out from completing their senior projects to engage in some of the most interdisciplinary discussions in the program.

The Western College Program

The educational vision underlying the original formulation of the Western College program was holistic, within the curriculum, between the curriculum and the life of the student, and among the members of the community. The key elements designed to achieve this holistic goal were interdisciplinary courses, a residential learning program, and a required core curriculum. This educational mission was selected because it represented to the Planning Committee and the faculty of the University the best of the educational experiments of the 1960's. It was also a mission consistent with that of the parent university, and a program which retained much of the Western College spirit which it was replacing. This mission placed interdisciplinary studies at its center.

The curriculum was partitioned into three broad areas: humanities, social sciences, and natural sciences. Upper-division programs were established in American and Environmental Studies. These reflected the probable educational backgrounds of the faculty, the existing interdisciplinary programs at Miami, and the probable interests of students. A cluster college structure was chosen. Full-time faculty were hired and made eligible for tenure.[18] These decisions resulted from the take-over of a small private college by a relatively large public university. Miami feared it would be perceived as "gobbling up"[19] Western, and there was confusion over whether the Western faculty would be retained in the new program.[20]

The Dean, a veteran of the experimental college movement, was hired through a national search. He selected faculty for their commitment to interdisciplinary studies, the strength of their academic credentials by traditional criteria, and for their interest in innovative education. A commitment to a residential learning program was also considered desirable. Most of the selected faculty were young, with extremely strong academic credentials, generally from elite private liberal arts colleges. Half had no previous interdisciplinary graduate training or teaching experience; only one had taught in an experimental college setting. The faculty expanded from six to twelve during the formative years and proved remarkably stable, losing only one of its charter members and turning over only two in all. Their commitment to the program was unusually high, in part because they came for the program and were full-time in it, and in part because they only became eligible for tenure if the program was favorably evaluated.

The question of how closely the faculty must adhere to the original vision of the program came up early in the summer planning workshop before the opening of the program, and the Dean replied that the faculty was obligated to be loyal to the intentions of the original planning document, though not to the content of the courses it suggested.[21]

Even though there was consensus among the faculty and administration that the courses must all be interdisciplinary, there was no formal discussion of the meaning of interdisciplinary studies during the formative years of the program. When one finally did take place in the sixth year, the faculty split among those wishing to focus on the commonalities in the real world in order to see the world as more coherent; those wishing to focus on the commonalities of the disciplines by using systems theory or structuralism; and those wishing to apply several disciplines to a single topic and then integrate their findings. Still others didn't care, either out of a conviction that more than one approach was interdisciplinary, or out of lack of interest in the issue altogether. With such divergence of opinion among the faculty, it is understandable that in spite of the structural advantages of the Western program, many of its courses were not as interdisciplinary as they might have been.

The first-year freshman humanities course, The Creative Self in Modern Culture, was a study of what it means to be human and of how the concept of self is both expressed and determined by creative processes. A number of creative products were examined through their respective disciplines—architecture, music, literature, history anthropology, and film—for their contributions to the central question. Emphasis in the seminars was on the interrelations among these contributions. The course started with the assignment of a paper on "Who Am I?" Gradually, the course moved outward to the contemporary student culture, then to each student's family genealogy and then to the sense of self in various American subcultures. The teaching of writing was integral to all three core courses: frequent papers assigned and extensive faculty commentary on them reflected a program-wide concern with writing. The course met the aforementioned interdisciplinary presumptions, but the discussion of disciplines was more implied than explicit through their use in examining creative products.

Social Systems I, the freshman social science course, took the theme of education the first year. Like the Creative Self course, it asked students to reflect on their prior formal education. It introduced the sociological perspective through the use of structural analysis and the concept of socialization. This perspective was then contrasted with ones from economics (e.g., education as investment in human capital) and anthropology (e.g., structure as freeing). Winter quarter, students were asked whether economic, social, and political inequalities are the consequence of differences in educational background, and whether the extent and source of inequalities differed in the nineteenth century. In spring quarter the focus was on the actual learning process, contrasting operant conditioning and cognitive dissonance theories from psychology and social psychology. As in the Creative Self course, the emphasis in discussions was on contrasting the disciplinary world views, creating a coherent view of education and how it affects the student.

In contrast to the interdisciplinary team-taught social science courses in the Paracollege, both "hard" and "soft" methodologies were employed, and the focus was topical, not methodological. The core social systems faculty were aided by one of the housemaster/instructors, allowing numerous examples from life in the residence halls to be brought into the formal curriculum. The result was a course which was faithful to the educational mission of the program, both interdisciplinary and supportive of living-learning ties.

The freshman natural systems course was organized around a theme of energy. The first half year was devoted to physics (energy and matter). After a brief bridge of chemistry (energy in the chemical bond) the rest of the year was devoted to biology (energy in life). The course reflected a different conception of interdisciplinary studies than did the other two courses. The interconnectedness of the world, not the disciplines, was emphasized. The insights of each discipline were challenged by encounters between that discipline and the real world, not by other disciplines.

The format of the curriculum was varied through workshops in Creativity and Culture which emphasized active student participation in a variety of creative activities, and the use of the fourth hour each week in Social Systems to discuss the connection between the course material and the lives of the students. Further, all regular classes were halted for one week in the spring for a "curriculum fair," a potpourri of student-led workshops on everything from wildflowers to logical paradoxes, faculty-led ones on tennis and values-clarification, and workshops by half a dozen artists-in-residence teaching folkdancing, dulcimer-building, leatherworking, and the like. These activities broke down the roles of student and faculty and contributed to a sense of community much like that in the Paracollege.

The freshman courses underwent some transformation during the program's formative years. The Natural Systems course put increasing emphasis on scientists as human beings and on science as a creative activity. Historical scientific developments were also studied within a Kuhnian framework of scientific revolutions. In the spring, the scientists collaborated with the other cores on an integrative Darwin unit. These revisions all appear as responses to the prevailing ethos of holism by science faculty convinced of the need to present students with a solid disciplinary background of "real science" before undertaking interdisciplinary studies.

Social Systems tightened the organization of the education-focused course for one year, and then shifted to its present sequence which focuses on the individual in society in the first semester, on groups and institutions in the second semester and on societies and their interactions and evolution in the sophomore year. The individual in society course focuses on the rationality and the autonomy of individuals, retaining much of the subject matter of the older course, but organizing it abstractly instead of topically so that the contrasts between disciplinary world views and their underlying assumptions are more explicit. Dropping the focus on education also meant that more disciplinary concepts and theories could be introduced in an interdisciplinary context, better preparing students for upper-division disciplinary courses. The course concluded with an explicit synthesis (in which it was argued that people oscillate between the poles of rationality and irrationality and of autonomy and dependency) followed by an antithesis (in which examination of Balinese culture demonstrated that the entire question is culture-bound). The second semester course focused on the earlier issue of inequality, examining the inter-related topics of racism, poverty, and powerlessness.

The Creative Self course underwent a curious transformation, first to a self-consciously and explicitly interdisciplinary course focusing on various disciplinary approaches and how to relate them, and then to a strictly disciplinary approach introducing students to literature and philosophy first semester and to the fine arts and history second semester. This reversal reflected a growing belief among the humanists in the need to develop some appreciation of the disciplines before undertaking interdisciplinary studies and their desire to bring the course more in line with the perceived multidisciplinary approach to the other two courses. It probably also reflects the difficulties in persuading free-spirited faculty to cooperate to the extent necessary to develop a serious interdisciplinary course. Here, the failure of the faculty to discuss interdisciplinarity was partly responsible for an ironic movement away from interdisciplinary studies.

The first sophomore courses were offered in the second year of the program, and since all students now had some grounding in the disciplines, all the faculty were eager to offer relatively ambitious interdisciplinary courses. Following the recommendations of the Interim Committee,[22] the Creative Self faculty tried a different organizing principle each quarter: comparative cultures (literature, art, and film of South

Africa and the U.S.) in the fall; the spirit of an age (Victorian England through literature, history, architecture, drama, science, and politics) in the winter; and the development of an idea (utopia) in the spring. The focus of the sophomore Social Systems course on modernization meant that macro-level theory from the various social sciences was applied to such topics as the Industrial Revolution, the demographic transition, and urbanization, each viewed in historical context. A subtheme throughout the year was the interaction of nations and cultures, especially the conflict between traditional and modern.

The Natural Systems faculty examined world food and health problems from an ecological perspective in the fall and the role of fossil fuels in the energy crisis in the spring. All three cores combined for several weeks at the end of the year in a unit on the future.

The fourth year of the program the entire sophomore year was restructured to make it even more interdisciplinary by allowing faculty from different cores to teach together. A natural scientist and a social scientist team expanded the energy course in the spring to show the interrelations of economics and politics with the science and technology of the energy crisis. A humanist and scientist combined to teach a course on historical American attitudes towards the environment as they develop out of scientific and technical discoveries, evolve into public policy, and become portrayed in literature, art, and architecture. Another humanist and scientist revived the course on the spirit of an age. A humanist and social scientist offered a course on change agentry, designed to raise social consciousness and develop and apply strategies of change. Another pair examined modernization in the Western world as a process with roots in the ancient and medieval eras.

It should be clear that the lower-division curriculum formed a "core" in the sense that it was required of all students in the program, not because it formed a coherent, integrated package. While some vertical integration was developed within the areas, the holistic vision of the program was never successfully applied to coordinating the three courses.

Even though junior seminars were not team-developed or team-taught, most tended to be interdisciplinary since they reflected the current scholarly interests of the faculty, either interests building on interdisciplinary graduate work in the case of the humanists, or interdisciplinary research interests promoted or developed through two years of exclusively interdisciplinary teaching in the lower division for the natural and social scientists. Humanities courses dealt with the regional character of the American South (literature, history, architecture, and sociology), Jewish studies (literature, history, and sociology), the Harlem Renaissance (literature, music, history, and art), and landscape visions (literature, anthropology, art, and geography). The social sciences focused on research methods, such as team projects in quantitative local history and in field work. The natural science seminars varied from the interdisciplinary (food, public policy, agricultural innovation) to the disciplinary (environmental chemistry). In all cases, these seminars were designed to serve as an introduction to research and scholarship in the hopes of helping students to prepare for work on their senior projects.

Senior projects ran the gamut of student interests, and only a few were self-consciously interdisciplinary. Senior workshops provided some final sensitivity to interdisciplinary studies, however, as students with various disciplinary backgrounds critically evaluated the projects of their peers. The junior seminars and senior workshops also provided a link between the upperclassmen and the Western community.

SUMMARY AND IMPLICATIONS FOR THE 1980's

A number of factors affecting interdisciplinary curriculum development can be deduced from the experiences of the Paracollege and the Western College Program during the 1970's. These factors fall under the broad headings of structure and ideas and are not listed in any order of importance. While these factors are identified from an analysis of cluster college programs and meant to apply primarily to their prospects in the 1980's, several may be applicable to independent interdisciplinary institutions as well.

Structural Factors

1. The Educational Mission

While the formal statement of the educational mission of a program may include interdisciplinary studies as a goal, if the central educational vision does not include interdisciplinary studies or lead logically to them, they will tend to languish as scarce faculty time is drawn to higher priority tasks. The educational mission of the Paracollege included a genuine interest in interdisciplinary studies, but its guiding vision was of student-centered education, leading faculty to devote time to advisorial tutorials, for example, instead of interdisciplinary course preparation. Further, an antistructure bias underlay that student-centered vision, undercutting the development of an interdisciplinary curriculum. [Editors' Note: This tension is also noted in the Evergreen system by Jones.] Such a curriculum depends on the imposition of a systematic process onto intellectual inquiry. The Western program was favored with a mission which placed interdisciplinary studies at the center of its goals.

2. Faculty Appointments

Full-time appointments, which give the program control of the promotion and tenure process, are essential to faculty commitment to interdisciplinary studies. The faculty's willingness to take the professional risk of allotting time to learn other disciplines and to develop interdisciplinary scholarly or research interests also requires a full-time commitment. Further, those professional incentives must be used by the program to encourage such professional development activities. Otherwise, faculty may well redefine the educational mission of the program in a non-interdisciplinary way or simply fail to develop truly interdisciplinary courses. The Paracollege, with its system of joint and part-time appointments, suffered from a lack of faculty commitment to interdisciplinary studies. The Western program, in contrast, was blessed with a system of faculty appointments which promoted commitment to its interdisciplinary mission. The full-time appointments of the Western faculty created some estrangement from the rest of the University, but the faculty at Western were well respected by their disciplinary counterparts.

3. Faculty Assignments

Team-developed and team-taught courses greatly improve the prospects for achieving an interdisciplinary curriculum, because each faculty member must take seriously the insights of other disciplines and then come to grips with how those insights relate to those of her or his discipline. Team-teaching is not necessary if faculty are required to cover all course material in their sections of the course. Over time, this factor becomes less important as faculty are encouraged to develop some expertise in other disciplines. The Paracollege encouraged faculty to cooperate primarily in the development of area syllabi for the General Examination; the Western program required team-course development of all its faculty in all lower-division courses.

Ideas

1. Ambience of Innovation

Interdisciplinary courses are risky the first time they are offered. It takes practice to learn how to organize them so they appear coherent to the students. It also takes time for the faculty to learn the relevant literature in new disciplines. A spirit of innovation among both students and faculty and the willingness of administrators to accept occasional failure are essential in the early years. Both programs provided such an ambience; this factor largely accounts for what interdisciplinary curriculum was developed in the Paracollege.

2. Clear Definition of Interdisciplinary Studies

When one considers the structural advantages of the Western Program relative to the Paracollege, as well as its ambience of innovation, it may appear surprising that more of the Western courses were not interdisciplinary more of the time. The one factor working against the development of interdisciplinary curriculum in the Western program, as well as in the Paracollege, was the lack of a clear agreed-upon definition of interdisciplinary studies. Faculty must come to some explicit agreement about the meaning and nature of interdisciplinary studies so they can have a clear-cut interdisciplinary process in mind as they devise their courses.

The experience of both the Paracollege and Western shows that faculty willingness and administrative support are not enough to achieve fully interdisciplinary courses if faculty are unclear about what constitutes an interdisciplinary course. Faculty in some disciplines, especially perhaps in the natural sciences, need to be encouraged to view their discipline as only one interpretation of reality, one which can benefit through interaction with other disciplines.

As a first step towards achieving this goal, the following definition is offered. An interdisciplinary study can be defined[23] as an inquiry which critically draws upon more than one discipline and which attempts to integrate the resulting disciplinary insights. What is envisioned here is a process that starts with a question of sufficient breadth that it cannot be satisfactorily answered using only one discipline. The question is then reformulated more narrowly by each discipline so that the characteristic concepts, theories, and methods of that discipline may be brought to bear on the question. It is the set of disciplinary answers to these reformulated questions which must then be reconciled and integrated in order to provide an interdisciplinary answer to the original question. This definition is consistent with the presumptions set out at the beginning of the paper and with most uses of the term in the two programs; indeed, it grows out of attempts in both programs to devise interdisciplinary courses. What it offers is a process, an operational approach to the concept of interdisciplinarity, which clarifies how a course can be designed to meet that goal. If consensus can be reached on some such definition, the prospects look much better for the development of strong interdisciplinary courses.

The 1980's

The factors of structure and ideas drawn from the experiences of the Paracollege and the Western College Program are all compatible with the fiscal austerity and low enrollments expected in the 1980's. They are structural or attitudinal, not requiring additional resources. Thus, they are inexpensive. In fact, the relatively structured nature of interdisciplinary courses, which constituted a liability in the 1960's and early 1970's, may prove an asset in the 1980's.

The Western Program and the Paracollege were expensive because they insisted on small classes and close study-faculty contact, not because of anything inherent in the interdisciplinary nature of the curriculum. A program could offer team-developed multiple-section interdisciplinary courses where every faculty member teaches the same material in his or her own sections of 35 students. Such a program could provide students with an innovative interdisciplinary education at a *lower* cost than most other departments in the parent institution. In the absence of very large enrollments, such a plan would necessitate required courses to allow multiple-section courses. This development would have been unlikely in the 1960's or early 1970's, but quite feasible in the 1980's.

NOTES

1. Gaff defines a cluster college as ". . . a semi-autonomous school on the campus of a larger institution which shares, to a significant extent, facilities with the other schools." Jerry G. Gaff, *The Cluster College* (San Francisco: Jossey-Bass, 1970), p. 3.
2. Frequently cited works include L. Richard Meeth, "Interdisciplinary Studies: A Matter of Definition," *Change Report on Teaching*, 6 (August 1978), 10; William V. Mayville, "Interdisciplinarity: The Mutable Paradigm" (Washington, D.C.: ERIC, 1978); Centre for Educational Research and Innovation, *Interdisciplinarity: Problems of Teaching and Research in Universities* (Paris: OECD, 1972); and Joseph J. Kockelmans (ed.), *Interdisciplinarity and Higher Education* (University Park, Pennsylvania: Pennsylvania State University, 1979).
3. Paul Fjelstad, William Narum, and David Wee, "Report of the 1968 Summer Study Committee," September 1968, ms.
4. *The St. Olaf Bulletin*, April 1974, p. 95.
5. "Report of the Planning Team on the Western College of Miami University," *The Miamian* (Special Edition), 12 November 1973.
6. "Report of the Interim Committee on the Western College," March 15, 1973, ms.
7. See the discussion of "student-oriented curriculum" in Lewis R. Mayhew and Patrick J. Ford, *Changing the Curriculum* (San Francisco: Jossey-Bass, 1971), p. 3 passim.
8. In fact, Paracollege faculty subsequently developed proposals for a values-based program and for teaching mathematics to nonmajors. The former is described in Arthur W. Chickering et al., *Developing the College Curriculum* (Washington, D.C.: Council for the Advancement of Small Colleges, 1977), pp. 233–235.

9. Fjelstad, p. 2. See also pp. 1, 3, and 4.
10. Gaff, pp. 220, 225.
11. Fjelstad, p. 1.
12. Half of faculty time in the basic Paracollege curriculum, and a third of the total faculty load was projected for tutorials. See Fjelstad, p. 10.
13. Fjelstad, p. 14.
14. *Catalog*, p. 95.
15. "A summary report from the task force on Interdisciplinary Studies," prepared at the Paracollege Retreat at King's House, Buffalo, MN, February 24–25, 1973, ms.
16. Meeth, p. 10.
17. *Ibid*.
18. Larry J. Kennedy, *A Policy Analysis of a Merger in Higher Education: Miami University and the Western College (Oxford, Ohio: Miami University, 1975), p. 113*.
19. *Ibid*., p. 81.
20. *Ibid*., p. 84 passim.
21. "Notes from the General Meeting (7/28/74)," p. 2, ms.
22. "Report of the Interim Committee," appendix B, pp. 3 and 5, ms.
23. This definition is developed more fully in William Newell and William Green, "Defining and Teaching Interdisciplinary Studies," *Improving College and University Teaching* 30:1 (Winter, 1982), pp. 23–30.

IX. Comments on Newell

by

JOHN H. PERKINS

Many of the discussions of the alternative education movement in the 1960's were linked—in some unspecified way—to the New Frontier/Great Society of Presidents' Kennedy and Johnson and to the upheavals of the Civil Rights and Anti-Vietnam War Movements.

I don't want to raise any quarrel with the thesis that the social ferment of the 1960's was linked to the revival in educational styles. Certainly we all know faculty who chose to make their careers in the alternative colleges precisely because they were disaffected from the dominant powers and institutions in America; they found a congenial work place in the experimental institutions. From my own experience with students at Western and Evergreen, they, too, have sometimes selected alternative institutions out of a sense that they could find a comfortable home for their social and political values.

Two factors nevertheless concern me about the historical argument, and neither is addressed by Newell in any detail. First, if innovative institutions flowered because of the social and political ferment of the 1960's, what future do we have in the 1980's? Are we strong enough to weather the storm of conservative government? Will students reflect the values of the electorate and opt for traditional education? It's too early to tell yet, but I believe that for pragmatic reasons we must all be aware that we, too, must possibly make accommodation to the new conservatism. The trick will be to maintain the fundamental values that gave us our start but create a format that is attractive to students. Enrollment patterns at many of these institution, including Western, William James and Evergreen, point to a need for vigilance in this area. A brilliantly-conceived college to which no one comes is hardly a success. Perhaps it is not even brilliant.

My second area of discomfort with the historical thesis is that if the new colleges were responses to the larger social context, were they appropriate responses? The first major uprising of that decade of the 60's was for black liberation. Anti-war activity quickly followed and became intermingled with the civil rights issues. A sense of anti-corporate capitalism was ultimately added to the stew. Yet what can we say about our new colleges? Did they attract third world students? Sometimes, but never in the numbers committed whites hoped to see. Were the new curricula genuinely responsive to peace issues? Seldom explicitly and generally without self-consciousness. I doubt if world peace has been materially aided by the new colleges but maybe I'm wrong on this point. The new colleges never became explicitly anti-capitalist for reasons too detailed to outline here. We undoubtedly have housed our share of advocates for communitarian, anarchist or socialist economies, but I doubt if we have them in greater numbers than other colleges. In short, if our institutions were spawned by the spirit and conditions of the 1960's, we have not been great successes in terms of ameliorating the conditions that may have given us a start. Newell and others need to give greater attention to these matters in their analyses.

The other point I'd like to comment on is the content of the innovative colleges. The elusive term "interdisciplinary" always seems to emerge whenever one talks of alternative education. Surrounding the central core of interdisciplinary work are a host of ancillary notions such as independent study, experiential education, requirements for a degree or lack thereof, grades, tenure, faculty rank, publish or don't publish, student participation, and egalitarianism. While it is clear that a great divergence was found in Western, William James, and Paracollege in the ancillary factors, all agreed that interdisciplinary was central.

Should it be disturbing to us that the very core of what makes us innovative is simultaneously so difficult to define? Newell devotes a great deal of concern to this problem and concludes with an attempted definition.

I'll not use this platform to enter the fray on defining interdisciplinary studies. Rather, let me simply observe that the innovative colleges are not the only institutions of our society to go for interdisciplinary concepts. Agricultural experiment stations, industrial research labs, medical clinics, army and navy research programs, and others have each adopted an interdisciplinary approach in their work. Yet they are not at this conference nor would most of us consider them "innovative" institutions. Now to be sure, the institutions I have mentioned have quite different missions than we do as largely undergraduate colleges. My point here is that we run a risk by blandly assuming that "interdisciplinary" is equal to "innovative." Moreover, we must constantly keep in mind the target of our innovation. Personally I'm not attracted to innovation for its own sake. Innovation that could seriously address some of the contextual problems that helped spawn us would be interesting.

Finally, let me end with some comments on the conclusions of the paper: What are the structures necessary for the health and survival of the innovative colleges? Newell believes the college's mission must include interdisciplinary studies, faculty must have their reward structure in interdisciplinary studies, and that team-teaching is important to interdisciplinary studies. He also believes a proper ambience must be maintained and interdisciplinary be defined self-consciously. I believe Newell is correct insofar as he addresses the internal structure of alternative colleges.

Unfortunately Newell does not deal with interface problems of cluster colleges. Linking a small alternative school to a larger university is a difficult task worthy of serious attention.

What is more problematic are the external conditions faced by the colleges. We cannot control the external context, but we surely must pay attention to it. Do we?

The paper would benefit by a more explicit treatment of the larger social context surrounding higher education in the 1980's.

X. Innovative Politics in Defense of Innovative Education: A Case Study of a Faculty's Struggle for Survival

by

CHARLES GRUBB

BEGINNINGS

Opportunity and Entrepreneurship

Southwest Minnesota State College was authorized by the Minnesota Legislature in 1963. It opened in the fall of 1967 as a "Liberal Arts/Technical College." The Charter President of the institution, in an interview conducted in early 1973, described conditions in the mid-1960's as follows:

> . . . the legislature was very receptive at that period of time to providing funds for this college . . . a lot of other factors that came into play that allowed us to put the facilities together . . . the biggest problem . . . and also the biggest advantage we had in putting the institution together, came as a result of the instability that existed because of the turnover of people within the state college system, the department of administration, and the executive offices of the state. . . . And, as that is taking place, it does open up an opportunity for an aggressive institution to propose what it has in mind and to solicit support. . . .[1]

The Charter President has been described as an academic entrepreneur and he himself recognized that he played an entrepreneural role in the development of the institution. He was very successful in securing funds from the legislature. During the earliest years of the institution, the legislature made direct appropriations for the College. In the setting that he described, the Charter President maneuvered to provide the maximum fiscal support for development of the new college. He, and others in his administration, considered quantative growth—in enrollment, buildings, faculty and staff—as proof of success.

"EMPIRE BUILDERS" AND INTERNAL ENTREPRENEURSHIP

It is useful to distinguish two forms in which the entrepreneural ethos may be found in higher education. First, there is the old style entrepreneur whose spirit and style is represented by the Charter President. Opportunities to display and use this style are nowadays rare in an over-bureaucratized, over-rationalized higher education. Secondly, there is the exercise of the enterprising spirit within institutions in what is colloquially called "empire building."

The pattern of behavior denoted by the term "empire builder" is one way in which individuals may make a career in higher education. In the process of borrowing the term, I have used it to denote a social type which, in the Southwest case, at least, has two sub-categories. I shall refer to these sub-types as the Benefactor and the Departmental Aggrandizer. Both types of empire builders usually become department chairpeople or heads of divisions.

The Benefactor

One way to pursue an academic career is by participation in a patron-client system. Such systems are introduced into new institutions of higher learning by persons who arrive on the scene early and seek to reproduce a structure with which they are familiar and in which they have prospered. I use the term patron-client system to designate that situation in which a *Patron* or *Benefactor* plays a significant role in the internal politics of an organization, especially in decisions about the allocation of resources and opportunities, and his clients render loyalty and support in anticipation of continued or future rewards. Loyalty in such situations is not solely a matter of coldly calculated self-interest. Personal ties are frequently developed. Clearly, however, all parties to the relationship are in the process of more or less self-consciously promoting each other's careers. Melville Dalton has referred to similar systems of influence and loyalty as "vertical cliques."[2]

The Departmental Aggrandizer

A significant distinction between this pattern and the patron-client system is that support for the enterprising leader is based more upon the perceived convergence of individual interests, which are often temporary, than upon the loyalty and continuing relationships which characterize patron-client systems. Aggrandizers feel less obligation to advance the careers of those whom they lead in the interest of perpetuating a system of succession. At Southwest, aggrandizement as a form of leadership was most pronounced in the business area from about 1970–71 onward; and in the teacher education area from about 1970 on. In a growing institution devoted primarily to undergraduate education, this form of the enterprising spirit will find its primary outlet in recruiting as many students as possible for the department and in seeking to obtain additional teaching positions and additional space and funds to build programs. Career advancement for this type of leader consists either in going to larger or more prestigious institutions and repeating the process there, or in moving into the ranks of higher administration.

In many colleges and universities, coalitions, often temporary, between two or more such leaders, and their supporters, provide either the basis for working majorities on curricular and other decisions, or the basis for veto groups whose capacity to block action must be taken into account. The interest groups thus formed must be appeased before anything can be done.

IDEALISM AND ASSERTIONS OF UNIQUENESS

The Charter Dean,[3] a number of charter faculty members, many members of the charter class, and many additional faculty members who came in the first few years of the College attempted to make Southwest a distinctive institution. I have selected quotations from a document entitled "Recommended Emphases for the Academic Program" written in early winter of 1967, to illustrate the idealism of that period. This document was prepared by the Dean.

Southwest Minnesota State College will:

1. Narrow the gap between research and the classroom. . . .
2. Consider education as primarily a process within the student. . . .
3. Search for a new definition of "contact hours". . . .
4. Help students achieve an overview of their education.

   Develop interdisciplinary courses, utilize team teaching, provide instructional resource materials, permit flexible class assignments, give a senior seminar in each major area to help lead students to an overview that will relate their education to larger knowledge. . . .

5. Emphasize flexibility in curriculum.

   Allow majors in a single subject, a division, or in an area of concentration that might cross divisional lines. . . .

6. *Establish and work to preserve a college organization that is circular rather than hierarchical. . . .*

7. *Encourage faculty dialogues across [sic] interdisciplinary lines.*

   Handle intra-disciplinary conversations electronically and mix disciplines when assigning offices, so that one's immediate neighbor comes from another academic area. . . .[4]

Material sent to newly-appointed faculty members included the statement that there should not be "artificial status distinctions between students and faculty." This egalitarianism was also supposed to apply to the relations with support staff. Promotional materials and statements in the early catalogues emphasized the "openness" of the curriculum and the flexibility of the institution in general. The desirability of interdisciplinary orientations was emphasized and re-emphasized.[5]

This is an introductory description of the aims of academic affairs which appeared in early catalogues:

> The college of today can best serve its mission by 1) presenting clearly the central concepts of the liberal arts, and 2) relating these concepts to the values, experiences, feelings, and concerns of its students and to the way in which students learn. In this context, the key values of the past must establish their worth with today's students.This point of view in no way interferes with the College's commitment to establish a challenging program based upon rigorous demands.[6]

The two areas of the College which most embodied the emphasis on new forms of education were the Instructional Resources Center, and the interdisciplinary courses. The former was the President's special interest; the latter, the Dean's.

The division of Instructional Resources, which included the library, provided a Random Access Dial System in conjunction with the standard telephone network. This system, which could be dialed from any campus phone, and from private off-campus phones, had available 90 thirty-minute programs on tape, twenty-four hours a day. There was no limit to the number of individuals who could listen to any single program at one time.[7] Professors *and* students prepared programs for the system, and students frequently dialed these programs when blizzard conditions resulted in the cancellation of classes. Many faculty never used this system;

some misused it, and it was eventually dismantled because of its expense and because of reduced usage.

Two required interdisciplinary courses were developed. One was a three-quarter series called "Ideas in Flux"—the first quarter to be "taken simultaneously by all freshmen." The other was "Human Relations"—originally conceived as a means of helping students confront and work with the emotional dimensions of the learning process.[8] The "Ideas in Flux" course consisted of an examination of the questions: "What is Man?", "What is Reality?", and "Perennial Questions: Good and Evil," with one quarter to be devoted to each topic. The course was not to be the special property of any discipline.

At an early stage, however, the College became committed to a divisional-departmental structure. Significantly, this structure did not include a division or department of interdisciplinary studies. Interdisciplinary studies were coordinated through the Dean's office by an assistant who had a position in the education division. This was the result of competition for resources in a situation where almost no one, except the Dean, was planning for interdisciplinary studies.[9]

The Failure to Build a Structure to Implement the Ideals

The charter faculty and administration failed to implement the idea that the College should have an organization "that is circular rather than hierarchical." "Circular" is not a very specific descriptive term. Presumably, the Dean hoped that the institution would have a cooperative and egalitarian organization rather than a hierarchical one, but this point was missing in all formal publications describing either the aims of the academic program or the goals and practices of Southwest, although most of the other recommendations were incorporated verbatim. In a way, the failure in the early days to work systematically at developing any governance system is understandable. Interview data indicate that personal relationships were relatively egalitarian, though decision-making was not. All parties, administration, faculty, staff, and students felt themselves to be pioneers.

The College opened in the fall of 1967, amid a frantic surge of energy by carpenters and others to finish closing in the buildings and get the heating system in operation before winter came. Students who were to serve as Resident Assistants arrived early, the first of more than five hundred "pioneers." They swept construction debris out of their doorless rooms, and took showers at the homes of faculty members and in a nearby motel. There were forty-four faculty members. Two years later, there one hundred and ninety faculty members and twenty-two hundred students.

The Dean noted, in 1972, that it had been a serious error not to have an intensive introduction to the College for new faculty.[10]

ACADEMIC CITIZENSHIP

Because of a strongly-felt need for some organized body which included the whole teaching faculty, and because it was necessary to set up a grievance procedure for faculty members who were being terminated by the administration, the Faculty Forum was founded in the winter of 1969–70. Divisions and differences were at once apparent. The Social Science faculty adopted a critical stance almost from the beginning. Most of the Southwest faculty were relatively young, and many had participated in various battles with administrators on other campuses, an adversary relationship was almost inevitable. Despite a vague egalitarian idealism, there was no mechanism to involve most faculty members in overall policy planning of policy decisions. It was evident that a small group of "insiders" were involved in decision-making.

Everett Hughes has pointed out that one may have a career in an avocation as well as, or instead of, in a vocation.[11] The common avocation of many professors is academic politics and faculty governance. Persons who have such avocational careers in addition to their regular work may be referred to as "academic citizens." Such careers are especially available in new institutions as a result of the need to develop some governance system and put it in place.

If a "collegial model" of academic governance is to be produced or reproduced at a new institution, persons with the "academic citizen" orientation must be the ones most active in its development and maintenance. Benefactors and their clients will also play a significant role. Academic citizens willingly serve, at considerable personal and professional sacrifice, on committees directly concerned with the fundamental business of an institution. Such people are frequently recruited, or promoted by others, for administrative positions—in part because they are seen as "respected by the faculty" and not "just administrators." These faculty members, seem particularly committed to the ideal of faculty autonomy, and to the concept of a self-governing community of scholars. In issues involving governance, they seek to build coalitions or constituencies around particular issues or principles. Such faculty members are frequently committed to traditional disciplinary orientations as well as to traditional conceptions of academic governance. They regard themselves as watchdogs against administrative high-handedness.

The Activists

The faculty assembled at Southwest was relatively young. They were of diverse geographic and graduate school backgrounds. Most were attracted to Southwest because it was new, and for many, apart from newness, the fact that it was not a former teacher's college gave it superiority over the other colleges in the Minnesota system. One faculty member, whose attitude was not unusual, commented that it was exciting to come to a place that was trying to introduce something different, to provide an alternative to teachers' colleges in the state system.[12]

The faculty were committed to teaching, though a surprising number also did research. Faculty were definitely interested in better and more informal relationships with students, in marked contrast to the aloofness, formality, and even indifference which were so bitterly complained of in American higher education in the 1960's. Some, particularly those in the Social Sciences, had been campus activists or had in other ways been involved in the social movements of the 1960's. They hoped for an activist college and for the opportunity for politically relevant practice of their disciplines. Although they did not seek conflict between administration and faculty, they did not avoid it in a "naive" belief that a new college could be built on the basis of consensus.[13] These faculty members formed an important component of the group whose behavior pattern I have typified as "academic citizenship." They may be designated *the Activists*.

The Southwest Milieu

There was an atmosphere of intense excitement at Southwest from the early days on into the early 1970's. The Humanities and Arts area included a number of very gifted and creative individuals. Courses in Humanities, Social Science, and Teacher Education were offered which were "experimental" in the sense that everyone involved regarded them as a departure from conventional course offerings at other colleges and universities. It was considered important that the curriculum be kept open for such offerings.

Nevertheless, the formal innovations at the school were perhaps ultimately of less importance than the overall atmosphere of creativity and freedom. For example, in the spring quarter of 1970, art students turned the top floor of an as-yet-unfilled dormitory into studio space. Drop cloths were put down over the carpeting and individual dorm rooms with south windows became studios. Many students worked at night. Eventually, students began sleeping in "their studios" and the whole floor became a kind of artist's quarters, with very little supervision by faculty and little or no interference by custodial or student affairs staff. A charter class graduate recalls this period as the most creative and happy time of her four years at Southwest.[14]

Classes, particularly late afternoon or night classes, frequently met in students' rooms or apartments, dorm lounges, or faculty members' homes. In general, there was easiness, informality and personal warmth between faculty and students. There was almost a sense of family among the students, faculty, administration, and staff in the charter group. This spirit survived, in smaller groups, for some years. The "underground newspaper," founded in the spring of 1968, went through many incarnations under several names, but was renamed *The Family* in 1970 because, as one contributor put it, "we *were* a family by that time."[15]

EFFECTS OF STUDENT ACTIVISM

Any re-examination of efforts to establish alternative education in the late sixties and early seventies must take account of the effects of the war in Vietnam. Anti-war activism brought together students from different segments of the College and it tended to produce a general atmosphere of crisis. In the Social Sciences at least, considerable energy was expended that otherwise might have been devoted to analyzing the potentialities and problems of the developing institution. On the other hand, part of the intellectual excitement of the times came from the fact that growing numbers of people were in a position of explicit opposition to the government and, on campuses, were engaged in a critique of the legitimacy of all forms of hierarchical control.

Marches and rallies created a sense of solidarity among people from diverse segments of the Southwest community, and reinforced solidarity where it already existed. At the same time, this situation also sharpened tensions between activist and conservative faculty, and between students and activist faculty on the one hand, and the administration on the other.

The general spirit of distrust of authority had negative effects in that it made it difficult for a number of students and faculty members to trust anyone who appeared to be associated with "the establishment." This included the Dean, who was attempting, at times ineffectively, to provide academic leadership when most higher administrators were concerned with public image, building construction, and legislative relations.

Southwest was established as a new school in a town of not quite ten thousand. The town was, in some respects, quite conservative. The anti-war activities, and other expressions of divergence from "mainstream" values, disturbed many townspeople. This, in turn, evoked a response in a number of faculty members that can best be described as anxiety.

If the late 1960's and early 70's were a period of experimentation, innovation, and a search for alternatives, which was characterized by both activism and creativity, they were also years in which the bureaucratized management of public higher education was consolidated and made operational. The new College on the plains of southwestern Minnesota did not escape this trend. The impact of the trend was apparent by 1971, although its implications for Southwest were not yet clear to the campus community.

"EXTERNAL FORCES"

An End to Autonomy

In late April of 1971, as part of the self-study process required for accreditation, a consultant visited Southwest to advise the administration on "external relations." The area of concern was relations with the State College Board and particularly with the Office of the Chancellor.[16] The consultant's report summarizes the reorganization of the State College Board and the new orientation and growing power of the Chancellor's Office. Because it is a succinct summary of changing patterns of control, the consultant's report is quoted at length:

> During the initial years of the formation of the College and for the first year or so after it admitted students, the operation and guidance of the College was almost entirely within the control of the President and his staff:
>
> About three years ago, ________ was appointed Chancellor and immediately gave entirely new direction to that office. His staff has been enlarged perhaps six-fold and he has been given line responsibility by the State College Board for the operation of the state college system. This is well shown by an excerpt from a statement entitled "Operating Principles Governing the Administrative Relationship Between the Office of the Chancellor and the State Colleges." This statement was approved by the Chancellor's council, whose membership includes the presidents of the state colleges, on October 14, 1969. The excerpt is as follows:
>
> 1. The State College Board holds the Chancellor and his staff accountable for the successful functioning of the Minnesota State Colleges as a System of legally equal, unique, cooperating institutions of higher education.
> 2. The Board holds the President of each College and his staff accountable, through the Chancellor, for the successful operation of his College, including the offering of all educational and related programs and activities approved for the College.
>
> Many problems appear to have arisen in the implementation of this

> policy. The Chancellor has established Vice-Chancellors in five areas as well as a Director of Information Systems and a Director of Development Program Budget. The Vice-Chancellors have frequently operated in a somewhat autonomous manner, calling meetings of the College officers responsible in the respective areas of interest, and arriving at joint decisions concerning which the Presidents often have not had prior knowledge. Concern has been felt by some of the administrative staff and faculty at Southwest Minnesota State College that the decisions arrived at by the Finance and Budget Committee, for example, which is under the chairmanship of the Vice-Chancellor for Administration, . . . require actions on the part of a state college which may be inconsistent with its mission and purpose. They feel that such decisions might prevent the College from implementing in a proper manner at least a portion of its mission.[17]

The consultant also described the effects, in education, of the long-term trend toward rationalization of all the institutions of modern society. The completion of the bureaucratization of higher education is contemplated with something close to equanimity, and in the closing sentences of the report the officers of a new institution are told to adjust to the new reality.

Bureaucratic Functionalism

This trend toward increasing centralization of control in higher education made it impossible to maintain experimental and innovative education, in the absence of a sizeable surplus of funds and an ever-increasing number of students, at Southwest. The expansion of bureaucratic control and the imposition of bureaucratic procedures not only foreclosed options but caused a revolt that was far-reaching in its consequences.

Two classic commentators on bureaucracy, Max Weber and Peter Blau, note that bureaucracies are "institutionalized methods of organizing social conduct in the interest of administrative efficiency.[20] It is ironic, but not coincidental, that the successful establishment of bureaucratic control in American higher education took place during the period of a renewed debate in the United States over participation in academic governance and during an attempt by students and faculty to reconsider the goals and purposes of higher education.

Otto Feinstein has discussed the establishment of bureaucratic functionalism in higher education, pointing out that it is now the mechanism for decision-making and allocation of resources within state systems of higher education. As Feinstein points out, this clearly includes determination of values and selection of goals.[21] Decisions on all allocations in such a system are ultimately based on cost per credit hour of instruction and cost of space per square foot.

Feinstein has described the series of steps through which this new structure has been developed. He discusses

> the "evolution of a centralized accounting system based on the credit hour as the measure for educational cost and the square foot per student place cost for capital outlays. The credit hour achieved the status of a common language or code within the entire higher education system . . . The state higher education bureaucracy, the legislature, and the administration of the individual institutions wanted information in that language. Despite warnings from the originators of this language against its unqualified use in inter-institutional and inter-disciplinary comparisons, it became the language of comparisons . . . *warnings that such a calculus meant a redefinition of education and that the accounting system would eventually be considered* as the education process went unheeded. . . . Efficiency could now be measured, rationality was strengthened."[22]

Feinstein notes that now traditional concepts must, in many places, be defended in terms of credit hour production.[23]

> Unlike the previous steps, which were made possible by prosperity, [program budgeting] is occurring at a time of scarcity in higher education and has the power of a rationing system with the implied right to squeeze out inconsistencies and inefficiency. The transition from traditional to rational has taken place.[24]

This is the system that was applied to Southwest, beginning in about 1972. The changed context in which Southwest existed in the spring of 1972 may be summarized as follows: It had become increasingly clear, to administrators at least, since early 1971, that key legislators and the Chancellor and his staff were going to insist that Southwest conform to the formula budgeting which was used for the Minnesota State Colleges. It was also fairly apparent that total enrollments were not going to continue to increase and, in fact, would likely be smaller than the 3,100 students enrolled in 1971–72.

Southwest had been built for an eventual enrollment of around 4,500, and the charter administration had not conceived of the possibility that the institution's mission and unique character could be threatened by the combination of declining enrollment and the imposition of formula-based allocations.

Application of a credit hour funding formula, in this case a full-time student/teacher ratio of 19 to 1, effectively killed any hope of maintaining an experimental liberal arts/technical college at Southwest. It turned the internal politics of the school into a war between factions competing for students and funds.

The consolidation of line authority in the Chancellor's office gave the Chancellor the means to punish Southwest for its resistance to the application of these formulas. The plea that the institution was different, and new, was ultimately ineffective.

Perhaps the Chancellor saw himself as engaged in gaining control over an institution which had been too independent. He probably felt it necessary to demonstrate to the legislature and to other state colleges that the emerging bureaucracy was in control of the system over which it was supposed to preside.

ADMINISTRATIVE SUCCESSION

The Costs of Entrepreneurship

It was at about this time that the institution began to experience the negative aspects of the entrepreneural method of building a new college. Three aspects of this situation must be mentioned: 1) Southwest had been overbuilt. Projections of enrollments of 4,000 to 4,500 by the mid-1980's had been misleading. 2) The "bigger is better" ideology characteristic of entrepreneural ambition compounded this problem. The President once said that if he had had one more year of dealing directly with the legislature, he would have gotten a fieldhouse. He didn't get the fieldhouse, but his freewheeling tactics resulted in criticism by some state legislators. 3) Accumulated resentment and pressure came from other state colleges.[25] Faculty and administrators in other state colleges increasingly felt that the building of Southwest had deprived them of money and students. This resentment contributed to the increasing pressure that was brought to bear on Southwest to conform to the formula budgeting process.

Southwest was also going through the process of self-study in preparation for accreditation. Southwest was accredited in November, 1971. In retrospect, it appears that the resolution of some issues having to do with formula-based allocations were postponed by the Chancellor and the local administration until after accreditation. Indeed, it was only after accreditation that the larger problems of the institution received much attention from the faculty.

Local and External Problems as Parallel Processes

At the same time as the problems between Southwest and the state system continued to grow, the reaction of the people in the area to reports of continuing racial conflict also damaged the school. In 1970–71, there were more than sixty Black students at Southwest. The people of the surrounding area had had very little, if any, contact with Black people before the opening of the College. They did not know, in fact, that they were prejudiced. Some leading business people did not even realize the inappropriateness of the phrases "colored boys" and "colored girls" during the very period when Blacks were proudly asserting their identity as *black*, and even the youngest Black student, quite properly, read a traditionally racist meaning into terms like "boy" and "girl." On campus, there were numerous conflicts culminating in the burning of the temporary student center.

The reduction in federal funds for student financial aid—sometimes interpreted as the Nixon administration's punishment of higher education for opposing the war—probably also had its effect. Enrollment peaked in 1971–72 and thereafter began to decline. Enrollment decline and anticipated enrollment decline became the basis for a demand that Southwest reduce the size of its faculty.

In the spring of 1972, the Dean of Faculties—by that time the title had become Vice-President for Academic Affairs—left Southwest to accept the presidency of a private college in Pennsylvania. In the fall of 1972, the Charter President announced his resignation, to become effective on May 1st of 1973. An influential division chairman, who was a leading Benefactor, became Acting Vice-President, and the search for a new president began. The institution had been renamed *Southwest State University*.

The fear of racial conflict abated (mostly due to a sharp decline in Black enrollment). Anti-war demonstrations declined with the approaching end of U.S. involvement in Vietnam. But a new and more serious "negative factor" emerged as articles about Southwest began to appear in the *Minneapolis Tribune*. By 1974–75, there were reports questioning whether the school could or should continue to exist at all. There were continued declines in enrollment from 1973 until the fall of 1977.

REVELATIONS AND NEW FORMS OF STRUGGLE

Painful Reductions

In the spring of 1972, Southwest was far from compliance with the required 19 to 1 student-faculty ratio. Southwest was supposed to phase into this system after having been permitted a 14 to 1 staffing ratio as a new school. It was supposed to move to 17 to 1 and then to 19 to 1 by

1972–73. A "Bill of Particulars" was sent in the summer of 1971, by influential legislators, to the Board and the Chancellor demanding that Southwest be brought into compliance with the 19 to 1 ratio.

Many Southwest faculty members argued that the problem was that too many non-teachers were counted as faculty. They said that an across-the-board application of a 19 to 1 ratio was inappropriate, and that if every division of the College had to have such a ratio, it would wipe out whole programs; including some in technology which had very low enrollments.

The Fate of Interdisciplinary Studies

By 1972 interdisciplinary courses were under attack, and there was persistent criticism, usually indirect and muted, of those who enthusiastically undertook to teach them. More traditional faculty members questioned whether anyone could have enough knowledge to legitimately teach such courses.

In 1970 and again in 1971, the administration refused to make interdisciplinary appointments. Instead, appointments had to be in a specific department. There was no department of interdisciplinary studies. It seemed that there was little recognition and no reward for trying unusual or unconventional approaches. Much of this work was done on an overload basis, but faculty felt that the administration went no further than being mildly pleased that such approaches "fit the image." Whether or not this is entirely true, data from interviews show that generalist faculty members shared this perception. By 1973, there was, in the words of one survivor of this group, "a retreat into the departments."[26]

It was not easy to pursue a career as a generalist at Southwest. By the mid-1970's, a number of faculty most attuned to the interdisciplinary ideal were teaching numerous sections of standard introductory courses. This must have been an especially bitter experience for those people. Several of them resigned and left Southwest.

Threat to the Liberal Arts

The new President, who assumed office in early summer of 1973, immediately created a reorganization task force. Members of the task force were expected to produce or obtain statements on departmental goals. This was required by the state bureaucracy. The importance of this step and its implications were probably unrecognized by most faculty. Such recording of goals was the first local linkage to the process of centralizing programmatic review and establishing program budgeting.

By this time, however, the internal competition for students had begun. The word "relevance" was much used. In a situation where it appeared that further reductions in faculty position would be unavoidable, several programs (not yet termed "departments"), particularly those in business and technology, again and again justified their majors and even argued for transferring positions to their areas because of the greater "relevance" of these programs. Business, in particular, appealed in the strongest terms to the administration to go with the trend of the times. Later, the arguments over which programs should be retained at Southwest included frequent references to career education.

The increasing emphasis, nationally, on career education (at Southwest, often translated into the narrowest kind of vocationalism) has been nicely and critically summarized by Leon Botstein:

> In the sixties, when the young and colleges were perceived as centers of social if not radical criticism, parents, philanthropists, and federal agencies reacted. . . . The shift in student mood from 1970 to 1975 toward political inaction and quiescence has been especially visible in liberal arts colleges. Spurred by the excesses and failures of the earlier political initiatives, the economic reversals of the early 1970's, and the end of the Vietnam war, this shift has been actively accelerated by a systematic effort, including the career education movement, to bring institutions of higher learning into a closer fit with society. The ideal of the university as a seat of free, wide-ranging inquiry, or a searching criticism of culture and society, and as a place where idealism and the longing for a better world might be nurtured, seems to have vanished.
>
> In retrospect, the decade of the sixties was that ideal's finest hour, excesses notwithstanding. Ironically, the pursuit of that ideal remains at the heart of the presumed purpose of a liberal education: to inspire the young to ask the ultimate and basic questions about personal, intellectual and political life. The current suspicion, contempt, and rejection of liberal arts and the rush to career education and vocationalism in colleges and among the federal government and private philanthropy can easily be seen as a reaction to the sixties, an effort to move the young into established society without the experience of a serious reexamination.[27]

Certainly this rejection of liberal arts was evident among Southwest administrators. Certainly, too, in the atmosphere of those days, there were serious conflicts between liberal arts faculty and other segments of the faculty.

I think that, insofar as state level administrators had an overarching plan, it was to gain control of academic decision-making. I do not believe they had any academic visions or dreams for higher education. For them, such terms as relevance, participation and career education functioned mostly as ideological tools in the struggle to gain control. As Ida Hoos has suggested there is a "management syndrome" at all levels of educational planning.[28]

The identification of rationality with computerized bureaucratic decision-making[29] is the epitome of what Max Weber called formal (as opposed to substantive) rationality; it is not simply anti-intellectual, it threatens the limited independence that higher education still possesses. Within this framework, there is little or no place for self-government. Traditional academicians cause almost as much trouble as radical students. The rationalization process is one that adjusts the academy to the norms of the bureaucratic system.

At Southwest, faculty resistance to the emergence of managerial and technological control took many forms. Several activist faculty members decided that decentralized collective bargaining was the best means of resistance under the circumstances, and worked to achieve that goal. On January 25, 1973, forty faculty members applied for a local charter from the American Federation of Teachers. This group became the Minnesota Federation of Teachers Local 2399.

Counterforce to Bureaucracy

The MFT fought on several fronts at once. Its strategy may be summarized as follows:

1. to stop or delay implementation of management procedures and to use the state labor relations system for this purpose.
2. establish and maintain an independent system of legislative contact and influence through the state MFT, and to wage a political struggle in the legislature for a minimum staffing base at Southwest to prevent the gutting of whole programs and the loss of valuable faculty.
3. to fight for local bargaining units—which would preserve a great deal of campus autonomy as well as make difficult the operation of a systemwide bureaucracy devoted almost solely to "efficiency."
4. to unify the Southwest faculty, not just liberal arts faculty, in the process of waging this struggle.

The organizers of the MFT saw their union as a means of countering bureaucratic control in the system. One of those most active in founding the union commented on increasing bureaucratization in his resignation speech as Chairperson of the Faculty Assembly, and said explicitly that a major reason for the spread of collective bargaining in higher education was increasing centralization of control and the consolidation of bureaucratic systems.[30]

The leadership of the Union included people with experience in direct action protest and union organizing. These people were good at devising strategies to influence public officials. Close relationships were established with some legislators. Among these was the state representative from the local area, a graduate of Southwest, whose strongest support came from social science faculty and activist students on the one hand, and the less prosperous farmers on the other.

Among its other activities, the union local distributed reprints of articles and speeches which warned of increasing bureaucratization in higher education. These materials were well received by faculty, including those who supported an AAUP chapter and hoped to avoid affiliation with a trade union.

INTERNAL REORGANIZATION AND INTERNAL WAR

The Problem with Democracy

There had been a two-year de-facto moratorium on retrenchments but, in 1974–75, the issue was again how to conduct a faculty retrenchment. In the spring of 1975, on the last day of the school year, notices of termination were sent to five faculty members. These notices (in effect, one-year contracts) were sent to two tenured and three untenured faculty members. These were the first reductions in tenured teaching faculty. All of the positions eliminated were in the liberal arts. The notices were in violation of procedures required under the college constitution. Many faculty were especially angry, because it was clearly unnecessary to violate tenure in order to achieve the required reductions. Faculty members, mostly from MFT Local 2399, picketed graduation. Other faculty members, many not MFT members, walked out of Commencement when the President rose to preside over the ceremonies.

The administration's problem was that the governance system, with liberal arts faculty in key positions, was a center of resistance to efforts to obtain "programmatic flexibility". The administration had decided to promote career education and wished to de-emphasize liberal arts. Some members of the administration promoted the belief that the liberal arts and activist orientations of the faculty caused declining enrollments. The administration's strategy was to circumvent the university governance system and obtain greater administrative control over faculty units.

Although he had conducted a reorganization the previous year, the President and his new Vice-President for Academic Affairs carried out another reorganization. This reorganization was a blatant attack on the liberal arts faculty and seemed to many to be in violation of State College Board Rules and Regulations. Some thought it was in retaliation for the faculty's actions in the spring.

All but two of the division chairmen, then called "School Directors," were aware of the planned reorganization. The knowledge was concealed from the Directors of the Schools of Humanities and Social Sciences—who were known for their pro-faculty attitudes. These men were dismissed as administrators. The reorganization was undertaken without consulting faculty, and during the summer, a period when almost all faculty were off campus. The chairperson of the All-University Senate had not even received written notice when a news conference was held and the reorganization announced publicly.[31] When faculty returned, and as the nature of the reorganization became clear, there was—to use a phrase from the Watergate affair—"a firestorm of protest."

The reorganization was clearly an attack on the liberal arts. The reorganization combined the previous five schools into two, and allocated departments among these two new divisions, which were called "Colleges" and named *Alpha* and *Omega*. Alpha College was composed of "the various Business, Science, and [sic] Engineering and Technology departments; Hotel, Restaurant, and Institutional Management; Political Science; Economics; Speech; Literature and American Language; and Mathematics. Omega College . . . of the various departments in Education, Physical Education, Psychology, Sociology, History, Philosophy, Foreign Languages, Art, Music and Theatre.[32]

The most noticeable feature of this reorganization was that it split up the various departments in Humanities and those in Social Science, while attempting to co-opt the Science faculty by leaving it intact. This led many faculty members to characterize the reorganization as "cynical."

The announcement of the two persons selected to head the two Colleges evoked a very bitter response from both faculty and concerned liberal arts students. The head of "Omega College" had been Director of the School of Education. He was a former elementary school principal. His reputation among faculty in the arts and sciences did not lead them to think of him as a suitable administrator for academically respectable programs. The Chairman of the Science and Mathematics School, a successful operator of the Benefactor system, was made head of "Alpha College." Perhaps he had not anticipated the intensity of the faculty's fury over the secret reorganization and shabby treatment of the Directors of

Humanities and Social Sciences. He soon had a heart attack and took a year's leave of absence. The Director of the School of Business, a person who was perceived as combative, then became the head of "Alpha College." He was widely regarded as an empire builder, in the terms of this study an Aggrandizer, and a devoted enemy of liberal arts education.

The academic rationale for reorganization presented by the President and Academic Vice-President was not persuasive. Neither was the administrative rationale.

The long struggle to separate teaching faculty positions from administrative positions, and to reduce what was felt to be an overly large administrative complement, had led to a more aggressive stance by the faculty in the arts and sciences. The faculty felt that faculty reductions would be fewer if the institution got down to a smaller-sized administration. The reorganization increased the anger over this issue.

Defending the Liberal Arts

In September, 1975, faculty members met at the home of a Mathematics professor, and formed a Council on the Liberal Arts. Position papers from faculty groups began to appear, as did satirical leaflets and broadsides. It was a total political struggle that had the flavor of campus anti-war protests. Formal and informal protests were made by individual faculty members on behalf of various governance and union organizations. The State University bureaucracy responded that the reorganization was an administrative matter and a "management right."

The people of Marshall and the larger area of southwest Minnesota were, by this time, quite concerned about the situation at Southwest. The local paper printed many letters to the editor. Most were written by faculty members. Some of these letters emphasized the importance of the principles of collegiality and academic freedom. Other letters emphasized the importance of the University to the region. The Faculty Association held a series of public hearings on the reorganization.

The war *within* the faculty is difficult to describe in a succinct fashion. Perhaps one incident can serve to represent the general situation in which faculty members were divided against each other and "cannibalism" was encouraged. The following quotation is from a memo sent to all faculty in middle or late September of 1975:

> At a meeting between Dr. ______ (a department chairman and ______ (the head of one of the two "colleges"), the latter said that it was important for ("______ college") to develop a curriculum committee and work on staffing.

Dr. ______ indicated to Dr. ______ that one suggestion being considered would be to have each faculty member list five other faculty members he thought should be dismissed.

When Dr. ______ objected strenuously to this, Dr. ______ then said that perhaps each department should list those of its own members who could be dismissed, and add others from other departments if it wished. . . .[33]

Incidents such as this had the effect of unifying three major segments of the faculty: Science, Social Science, and Humanities and Arts. Some faculty from other segments of the University were also opposed to reorganization, and students formed a group in support of the liberal arts.

Resignation and Interregnum

In November of 1975, the President resigned. He said his resignation was based on principle, and said that a "small minority" of the faculty had made the situation impossible for him and had "degraded the scholarly tradition and academic values. . . ."[34]

The Chancellor's remarks on this occasion included the following statement:

> Anyone who sees Dr. ______'s resignation as an indication that a small faculty minority will run this University to their own benefit and to the exclusion of legislative and board policy, and regardless of the interests of the region, the majority of the faculty, and the students, will find they are mistaken.[35]

The Chancellor called for a study by the Higher Education Coordinating Commission to review the future of Southwest, and the future of "post secondary" education generally, in southwest Minnesota. One of the possibilities the Commission eventually considered was closing Southwest and replacing it with a junior college.

The final report favored the continued existence of Southwest, as a four-year institution. Throughout this process, considerable political influence was exercised by various groups and individuals in southwestern Minnesota. The Southwest Faculty, working through the newly-established stateside Union (the IFO-MEA), played a significant role in coordinating this effort.

Analysis of the Crisis

The elements of the situation which had produced the crisis may be summarized as follows:

1. Insistence upon applying bureaucratic funding formulas to Southwest in circumstances where such application seemed to endanger its continued existence in any form resembling its original one. This is *not* to say that some reductions in size of faculty and staff were not appropriate.
2. The existence of faculty rights in the governance system, which had to be abrogated in order to conform to directives from the legislature and the bureaucracy, thus angering faculty.
3. The fact that, under what was really a system of management control, at first disguised by the facade of governance, faculty were very reluctant to participate in any process that led to the termination of fellow teaching faculty.
4. A liberal arts faculty which had a high opinion of its abilities, high expectations for the future of Southwest, and a high proportion of members who had, in effect, committed their careers to the school.
5. A worsening job market for academicians nationally. This reinforced people's propensity to "fight it out" where they were.
6. Absence of wise leadership in the local administration. The administration underestimated both the abilities of faculty and their willingness to fight.
7. A growing hostility towards liberal arts.
8. An uncertain situation in the impending, but not yet accomplished, situation of collective bargaining; a situation in which some persons in the state educational bureaucracy saw the opportunity to bring Southwest to heel.

SECOND ADMINISTRATIVE SUCCESSION

Return to Entrepreneurship

The Vice-President for Academic Affairs served as Interim President during the HECC Study. In this interim period, attention again turned to relationships with the local area. Southwest needed to maintain and enlarge its constituency in rural southwestern Minnesota. The struggle for survival had taken energies that might otherwise have been devoted to establishing the institution's credibility in the region. During this period, some persons, including outside consultants hired by the administration, attempted to portray faculty members who were activists as "urban types," out of place in a rural area. In fact, some members of the faculty were from southwestern Minnesota and many others had grown up in rural areas. Some activists who were "urban" in background formed good relationships with people in local ethnic communities, and with the unionized or unionizing segments of the area's sizable non-farm labor force. Nevertheless, Southwest needed to turn its attention to elaborating and improving its relationship with the surrounding area. Rumors that the school would be closed had been harmful.

When the search for a new President began, many faculty members were encouraged when Minnesota's Commissioner of Agriculture applied for the job. The Commissioner had a Ph.D. in history, had taught for several years, and had a strong interest in farmer's movements. He had a neo-populist style when speaking to or about farmers, and well-known political connections. It seemed plausible that an individual with these characteristics would be less dependent upon the Chancellor and the bureaucracy.

The Activists, leaders of the opposition to reorganization and leaders in faculty union activities, helped inspire and organize a "grass-roots" movement to support the candidacy. Those who had been party to the reorganization quietly supported other candidates. It seems fair to say that the new Chancellor was not happy about having a strong President at Southwest, but the Commissioner of Agriculture became the third President of Southwest because, politically, it was too costly to reject him.

The new President promised a rural studies program at Southwest; one which was related to the school's creative liberal arts tradition and not simply a scaled-down version of land grant university programs. He said that such a program would be the first of its kind in the nation. He promoted Southwest with great vigor and enthusiasm. Southwest again came to resemble a joint enterprise rather than a battle ground. The President emphasized the superior quality of the faculty. No more was heard of Alpha and Omega. Under the present structure, broad areas such as social science and humanities are not split between two schools in an attempt to fragment their power and set close colleagues against each other. Although the University's enrollment is still about one thousand students fewer than it was in 1972, enrollment has increased substantially since the new administration took office in 1977. Enrollment is now approximately 2,100.

The faculty was able, through a series of negotiated understandings, to formulate a new set of requirements for general studies/rural studies representing about one-third of the total hours required for graduation. The total requirement is now larger than most students would like. Requirements have the familiar effect of distributing students (and FTE) so as to support existing departments and their upper division courses with large lower division enrollments.

The Continuing Problem of Bureaucracy

It must be noted that neither benign administration nor populist entrepreneurship solves the problem of centralized bureaucratic control within the State University System. The management system has intruded more and more into the day-to-day workings of University life. Such autonomy as Southwest has is quite fragile. It has not even been possible to secure approval from the State University Board and the HECC for an interdisciplinary major in Rural Studies. There is, however, a minor in Rural Studies. Centralization has now gone so far that even changes in requirements for concentrations within departments are supposed to be approved by the State University Board. In one case, a department has waited two years to have a minor approved. Feinstein's observation that the function of coordinating agencies is not really coordination but control certainly applies to Minnesota.

In Minnesota, union officers and negotiators seek ways to counter or reverse the growing centralization. The President of the IFO-MEA has called for the elimination of the Higher Education Coordinating Commission in the name of cost-cutting and decentralization. Apparently this proposal received some consideration at a recent session of the legislature, though no action was taken.

CONCLUSION

A Case Study of Southwest

The history of Southwest is, no doubt a unique one. The overall purpose of this paper has been to discuss the Southwest experience and to analyze the interaction of the forces which shaped that experience in order to better understand those forces.

Southwest was built by means of entrepreneurship. The Charter President sometimes referred to Southwest as a "joint enterprise." The pathological features of internal entrepreneurship made it difficult to build the institution as a joint or a collective enterprise. While the early growth of Southwest was due, in large part, to the enterprising zeal of the Charter President, the external pressures which seriously damaged the institution were partly the result of unrestrained entrepreneurship.

Many people were attracted to Southwest because they perceived an opportunity to pursue innovation and experiment in higher education. These goals were not clearly defined in the early period. The terms had different meanings to different segments of the Southwest faculty and administration. There was no firm alliance between the Dean, the Generalists, and other faculty members who had interdisciplinary or disciplinary interests that supported such goals. No organizational structure was established to further the realization of such goals.

In the absence of an academic structure which discouraged them, systems of internal politics developed which were antithetical to experimentation and innovation. Most of those who favored "something different and better" lacked a systematic plan for how to create it, and watched the opportunity for alternative education dissipate in the heat of controversy and conflict.

The positive aspects of entrepreneurship resulted in early institutional growth, excitement, and the sense of possibility; but the deficiencies of entrepreneurship and the growth of bureaucratic centralism, erected to restrain and ultimately replace entrepreneurship made it impossible to devise means of taking appropriate advantage of the opportunities which seemed to exist.

One way to build a structure which implements goals is to define the goals in such a way that they can be achieved almost mechanically. Few educational goals worth reaching can be achieved in this way. This study shows that bureaucratic centralism, applied to the educational enterprise at Southwest, tended to evoke and encourage the worst features of careerism.

The Nature of Patron-Client Systems

A Patron-Client system is, on the one hand, a system of patronage which serves to maintain a department or an area as a political bloc unlikely to oppose any system which leaves it somewhat alone and continues to provide it with resources. On the other hand, a Patron-Client system is also a means of providing sponsored upward mobility within an academic area and often into administration. Benefactors and their clients perpetuate the system as a means of pursuing disciplinary and administrative careers. For all these reasons, the system is adaptable to bureaucratized higher education. The members of such a system will oppose bureaucratization only when it becomes a threat to their system or when fundamental academic values are threatened. Such systems can usually co-exist with systems built on pure aggrandizement. In some settings, as at Southwest, members of the Patron-Client system will ultimately join with others in opposing the Aggrandizers.

Departmental Aggrandizement in a Small College Setting

When aggrandizement is pursued in a small college faced with declining enrollments, it is destructive of any possibility for community. Many people wanted to participate in some form of alternative higher education, in part, because they wanted to escape this kind of competition. If the ideals and goals of an institution are not clearly defined, Aggrandizers can, as they did at Southwest, use and pervert such terms as "relevance" and "experimental" to serve the purpose of empire building. Aggrandizers may be recruited for administration at a time when a centralized system is being imposed. They are not restrained by traditional values, as Benefactors may be, from imposing such a centralized system on others. They are not deterred by considerations of collegiality, or of traditional reciprocity. Their acquisition of administrative positions is the outcome of power seeking through ruthless competition and the recognition by others that these drives can be harnessed to serve the ends of larger systems. Aggrandizers, ultimately, care less about their disciplines and more about their careers.

The Achievements of Activism

Activists at Southwest made a career of fighting centralization of power. In the process they adopted some of the anti-system values that characterized the student movement of the 1960's and early 1970's. As was the case in that movement; activism tended to create, among the activists, a community of resistance. A community of resistance may be quite creative in developing strategies and may have wide influence.

In Minnesota, the innovative and militant politics pursued by the Southwest Activists has turned a former company union into a moderately aggressive representative for State University teachers. The present Statewide President of this organization is a Southwest Activist who has promoted the idea of decentralization when possible; and who seems to have had real influence in the selection of new members of the State University Board.

If, in spite of all that has happened, Southwest retains some limited freedom for innovation, this freedom is due to incessant and creative activism. In this context, the attempt of Southwest's current President to create a distinctive institutional character through a liberal arts approach to rural studies may well be a creative form of entrepreneuralism.[36]

Alternative Higher Education as a Collective Enterprise

Everett Hughes has suggested that all institutions are, in effect, enterprises[37] and hence need entrepreneurs. Ralph Blankenship has written that all organizations are ultimately constructed by their members as they are in the process of mutually negotiating their careers.[38] For any organization to be a joint or collective enterprise the members must be able to engage in this process of negotiating and renegotiating the conditions necessary for the pursuit of their interdependent careers. Perhaps, at Southwest, the combination of rural studies, liberal arts, and technical and business studies, provides a framework for such negotiations.

How can alternative higher education as a movement fulfill its ideals and find a means of serving the diverse aims and careers of its institutions and people? I suggest as a possibility the themes which, I hope, serve to unify this paper. *Innovative politics for debureaucratization may be joined with the continuing desire of many people to be free to pursue creative careers as individual enterprises.*

There appears to be a strong anti-bureaucratic sentiment in this country. For people to pursue personal careers as individual enterprises requires a considerable dismantling of bureaucratic structures. If alternative higher education can somehow serve these needs it should survive and prosper. Perhaps those devoted to alternatives in higher education should devote a significant part of their attention to reexamining models from alternative education for the purpose of devising cheaper and more humane alternatives to bureaucratic centralism. Perhaps alternative institutions, more fortunate in their history than Southwest, can serve higher education and society in general by seeking to propagate such models, and by seeking to train people in how to implement such decentralized systems.

There is a possible connection between these ideas and the increasing importance of so-called "non-traditional students" to higher education. "Non-traditional students" are usually students who are at mid-career, or who are seeking to change careers, or perhaps to begin careers later in life. At the least, they are seeking additional education to further their present careers. The challenge to higher education is how to serve these students without defaulting on its obligation to pass on and help people utilize the traditions of the liberal arts. Providing assistance in the effort to overcome obstacles to creative reflection and the building of human community is a legitimate aspect of liberal arts education; and is certainly associated with the history of alternative education. The pathologies of some forms of careerism and entrepreneurship are certainly examples of such obstacles. Traditional and non-traditional students may welcome as part of their education a searching examination of the concept of career and its meaning to the person.

If our students enter or reenter the overbureaucratized world of work in this society with some effective strategies for promoting decentralization and with a more reflective and informed stance towards their careers; we may have some hope of realizing two of the aims, found in somewhat incoherent form, in the visions of the late 1960's. Those aims are: to reduce hierarchical authority, and assist people in the pursuit of their lives as creative and adventurous enterprises.

ACKNOWLEDGEMENTS AND A NOTE ON SOURCES

This paper is part of a much larger work on which I have been engaged for some time. Some generalizations presented in this paper may require modification as additional data are accumulated and analyzed.

I have used interviews with charter faculty and administrators in the Southwest Minnesota History Center. In addition, I have had a number of personal interviews with faculty members; interviews with former students; and interviews with present and former members of the support staff, some of whom were present from the beginning. Interviews conducted by me were, for the most part, informal in nature. I have made use of internal documents of the University and the State University Board, from my files and the files of others who were kind enough to make them available to me. I have also used materials distributed by the Minnesota Higher Education Coordinating Commission, and newspaper accounts. I have relied, also, on my own observations at Southwest since I joined the faculty in the fall of 1970, and upon notes I made at various times since I have been at Southwest.

I have cited documentary and interview sources when direct quotation is used and otherwise have not always cited specific sources for statements of fact or summary statements of chronology.

I would like to thank the following people and organizations: Dave Nass and the Southwest Minnesota History Center staff; the Librarians at Southwest State University; Joe Amato; Maynard Brass (now deceased); Dorothy Frisvold; Jim Hayes; Bill Hunt; Penny Hunt; Marilyn Leach; Karl Obrecht; Rob Ross; Jerry and Cathy Stark; Teresa Treinen; Bob White; Posey White; and all the people who were willing to submit to interview, whether these were conducted by me or by faculty members connected with the Southwest Minnesota History Center.

NOTES

1. Interview with H.A.B. April 24, 1973, pp. 17–18. Southwest Minnesota History Center, Marshall, MN.
2. Melville Dalton, *Men Who Manage; Fusions of Feelings and Theory in Administration*, New York, John Wiley, 1959, pp. 57–65.
3. Interview with R.F. May 18, 1978, p. 29, Southwest Minnesota History Center, Marshall, MN.
4. "Recommended Emphases for the Academic Program" S.M.S.C. Document (Xerox) December, 1967, pp. 1–2.
5. *Southwest Minnesota State College Information Bulletin 1968–1969*, Marshall, MN., 1968, pp. 90–91.
6. *Ibid*. p. 32.
7. *Ibid*. p. 50.
8. Interview with M.S., May 31, 1972, pp. 8–10, Southwest Minnesota History Center, Marshall, MN.
9. This represents my summation of the situation. See: Interview with M.S., pp. 11–12.
10. *Ibid*. p. 23.
11. My use of the concept "Career," throughout this paper, is generally based upon the work of Hughes and his students. See: Everett C. Hughes, *Men and Their Work*, Glencoe, Ill. Free Press, 1958.
12. Author's Interview with R.W., May 19, 1981, Marshall, MN, p. 1.
13. *Ibid*. p. 3.
14. Author's notes on a conversation with G.J., March 28, 1981, Lacrosse, Wisconsin, p. 2.
15. Author's Interview with R.R. April, 1981.
16. Harold W. Oyster, "Report of a Visit to Southwest Minnesota State College, Marshall, Minnesota, April 19–20, 1971." In: *Southwest Minnesota State College: Self-Study for Educational Environment, Vol. II*., Marshall, MN., June, 1971. Appendix F, Section 5, p. 2.
17. *Ibid*. pp. 3–4.
18. *Ibid*. pp. 5–6.
19. T.C.R., Chairperson, Faculty Assembly, Memorandum: Resignation from Office," Undated, but December, 1975, p. 2.
20. Peter M. Blau, *Bureaucracy in Modern Society*, New York, Random House, 1956, p. 60.
21. Otto Feinstein, *Higher Education in the United States*, Lexington, Mass., D.C. Heath and Co., 1971, p. 1.
22. Otto Feinstein, "From Education for People to People for Education: The Rise of the Bureaucratic Planning System in Higher Education," *Journal of University Studies*, Spring, 1974, pp. 1–3.
23. *Ibid*. p. 3.
24. *Ibid*.
25. Author's Interview with H. J., May 18, 1981, p. 3. Also, interview with H.A.B., April 24, 1973, Southwest Minnesota History Center, Marshall, MN, p. 20. Here, as elsewhere, the Charter President showed considerable insight into the problems associated with his particular role. After his resignation (in effect a retirement) from Southwest, the Charter

President was engaged with others in various business enterprises in Southwestern Minnesota.

26. Author's interview with K.O., May 27, 1981, p. 5.

27. Leon Botstein, "College Could Be Worth It," *change*, December, 1976, p. 28.

28. Ida Hoos, "The Costs of Efficiency: Implications of Educational Technology," *Journal of Higher Education*, March/April, 1975, pp. 141–159.

29. Minnesota Higher Education Coordinating Commission, *Responding to Change: Report to the 1973 Minnesota Legislature*, St. Paul, 1973, p. 48. See also: Abstract of a paper presented by Desmond L. Cook, "An Overview of Management Science in Educational Research," a paper presented at the International Meeting of the Institute of Management Sciences, Cleveland, Ohio, September 11–13, 1968. Abstract taken from: A.A.S.A., *ERIC Abstracts: A Collection of Document Resumes on Program Budgeting and Cost Analyses*, Eugene, Oregon, 1969, p. 4.

30. T.C.R. Chairperson, Faculty Assembly, "Resignation from Office," December, 1975, p. 2.

31. J.T.R. Presentation to the Minnesota State University Board, August 20, 1975, p. 2.

32. President J.J., Letter to the Chairman of the Education Policies Committee, Minnesota State University Board, August 8, 1975, p. 5.

33. C.G., Memo to All Faculty, September, 1975.

34. *Independent*, Marshall, MN, November 5, 1975.

35. *Ibid*.

36. This president has become chancellor of the state university system.

37. See: Everett C. Hughes "The Ecological Aspect of Institutions," pp. 5–13 in *The Sociological Eye: Selected Papers*, Chicago, Aldine-Atherton, 1971. See also: "Going Concerns: The Study of American Institutions," pp. 52–64.

38. Ralph L. Blankenship, "Organizational Careers," *Sociological Quarterly*, Winter, 1973, pp. 88–98.

XI.

The Labor Process at Hampshire College

by

FRANK W. HOLMQUIST
LAURIE NISONOFF
ROBERT M. RAKOFF

I. INTRODUCTION*

Fundamental to the theory and practice of alternative higher education has been an ideal-type model of the committed faculty member. Rooted both in the tradition of the small liberal arts college and in the 1960's critique of the professionalized university, this model has envisioned teachers who would be wholistic and cross-disciplinary in their professional stances; who would foster students' independent learning through close, personal interaction; who would seek to define themselves as members of a teaching community in which the compartmentalization and competition of mainstream academic professionalism would be replaced by a shared dedication to the values of the institution as a community. Embodied in this model is a set of multiple expectations for faculty work which encompass classroom teaching (often collective and interdisciplinary), individualized tutorials, personalized narrative evaluations, academic and personal counseling, scholarly activity, institutional govern-

*Our thanks for concrete ideas and critical comment to colleagues Richard Alpert, Nancy Fitch, Joan Landes, Bernice Siegel, Robert von der Lippe, and Fred Weaver.

ance, supervision of extra-curricular activities, and, frequently, participation in the residential lives of students.

While those of us who teach in alternative colleges still believe strongly in the values which underlie these expectations, as well as in the importance (to us and our students) of the practical activities suggested above, it has become increasingly evident that the obvious satisfactions and benefits of this faculty model are sustained only at a significant cost. We find ourselves faced in our work lives both with the stimulating integrative experience imagined in theory, and with the reality of work intensification in the form of overwork, fragmentation of tasks, and speed-up, as well as loss of autonomy and the danger of long-term alienation from our institutions. Moreover, just at the time when such intensification reduces our capacity to engage in scholarly work within disciplinary frameworks, we are often faced with a partial return to traditional criteria of professional accomplishment in judging reappointment and promotion, as well as with stiff competition and reduced mobility in ever-tightening job markets. This noble revolution in the organization of faculty life and work seems to be devouring its own children.

As our colleagues at traditional institutions would quickly point out, however, we are not the only professional workers—and certainly not the only academics—faced with such dilemmas. Most recent literature[1] on the organization and experience of professional work suggests that even such traditionally autonomous professionals as doctors, lawyers, and architects are increasingly faced with a labor process in which overwork, fragmentation, speed-up, and loss of professional independence are prominent, particularly as that work becomes organized in hierarchical, bureaucratic fashion. The experience of faculty in most public colleges and universities certainly fits this pattern. But the fact that similar phenomena of work intensification should occur at small, experimental liberal arts colleges is an anomaly. These colleges, after all, are largely non-bureaucratic and non-hierarchical in their administrative structures, with faculty, singly and collectively, wielding significant authority. Moreover, in important respects, these colleges have rejected deliberately much of the specialization of disciplinary professional organization in favor of interdisciplinary programs in both teaching and research. And, of course, these colleges are devoted particularly to liberal, humanistic teaching, an art that defies the rationalization and intensification inherent in the bureaucratic organization of other professional work. Why, then, do so many of these characteristics of work intensification appear to be endemic, also, to the labor process in these colleges?

In this paper, we shall argue that an adequate explanation for this anomaly requires not only an analysis of the stresses and strains inherent in the design of alternative colleges, but also, and equally important, an understanding of the way in which these colleges and their faculties have mediated the larger structural rationalization of professional, academic work. In short, we seek to place an analysis of the labor process at alternative colleges within the context of a critical understanding of the changing structure and experience of professional work in capitalist political economies. Only within that larger context, we believe, can we begin to acquire a critical perspective on the nature of our own labor problems and on the strengths and weaknesses of alternative solutions to those problems.

The empirical focus of this analysis will be the labor process at our own institution, Hampshire College. The discussion will proceed as follows. First, we will briefly review the recent critical literature on educated or professional labor. Second, we will describe the nature of faculty work at Hampshire. Third, we will examine the nature of work intensification at Hampshire in some detail showing how attention to the major changes in the external, political economic environment of the 1970s can help us understand and explain the emerging contradictions in the objective structure of our work, in our subjective experience of that work, and in our individual and collective responses to it. Finally, we will assess the prospects of different strategies for overcoming work intensification while maintaining a distinctive, alternative blend of generalist and specialist, and will argue that only a strategy of collective faculty action can achieve a resolution that avoids the rationalization of bureaucratic organization and authority.

II. THE POLITICAL ECONOMY OF PROFESSIONAL LABOR

Professional people began to organize themselves into professional organizations—and to think of themselves as professionals—in large part to protect themselves from a competitive and uncontrollable marketplace. While there may well be some benign reasons for professional organization and some substantive content to professionals' claim to control of the content and circumstances of their work, it is abundantly clear that professional organizations have sought to establish monopoly control over entry into and practice within their respective fields. The means for achieving such control have become familiar: control over training, licensure, working conditions, discipline, wage or fee structures, and the like.

And in so doing, professionals (and would-be professionals) have relied upon a deep-rooted and persuasive ideology of professionalism—an ideology which above all, and regardless of substantive field, justifies such monopoly control and its attendant privileges in terms of professionals' special scientific knowledge and training. As Fred Weaver has argued,[2] the development of academic disciplines in the early decades of this century fits this model of the politics of professionalism quite well. Like doctors, lawyers, architects, nurses, and engineers, academic teachers and researchers have relied upon the ideology of professionalism and the organization of self-regulating professional associations in order to acquire and legitimize disciplinary control over hiring, firing, tenure, and curriculum. It seems clear that for academics, as for other professionals, the subjective satisfactions of thinking of oneself as a professional rather than as a worker complement the objective, material rewards that often come with monopoly control over work and ideas in one's chosen field.

These two urges, of course, are really two aspects of the same systematic response of educated workers to the changing context of labor in our time. The ideology of the professional may well hark back to the tradition of the independent craftsman, but the more important immediate referrent is the ordinary wage laborer of industrial and monopoly capitalism. By the time of the great rise of professionalism in the United States in the early twentieth century, the industrial working force had been largely transformed from its craft and hand-manufacture origins into a complex, rationalized social organism. The extension of the control of capital had brought with it both the powerlessness of the individual worker over the conditions and rewards of his or her work and the debasement of the labor process itself through intricate division of labor and the elaboration of bureaucratic, managerial control over shop floor and office. Faced with such proletarianization, the only response available to workers was the political one of collectively organizing to free themselves from the anarchy of "free" labor markets.

Consciously or not, the response of professionals to potentially threatening attacks on their autonomous work has been analogous. The collective attempts of professional organizations to create and maintain monopoly control over their working situations have constituted a similar political effort to avoid the loss of autonomy, power, and privilege which would result from unregulated subjection to a professional job market and from extra-professional control over the professional labor process. And, indeed, for decades this strategy seemed to be relatively successful in maintaining the traditional privileges and power of many professional groups over their own labor—that is, successful in preventing the "proletarianization" of professional labor.

Recent studies, however, suggest that this success is more apparent than real and that the claims of success in maintaining professional autonomy and privilege are large misinterpretations of the status and power of professional workers from within the ideological perspective of professionalism. Magali Sarfatti Larson,[3] in particular, has argued forcefully that as professional work increasingly is subsumed within bureaucratic organizations—whether in private corporations, state agencies, or research universities—such work is progressively "rationalized" in much the same way that manual work was proletarianized in an earlier era. In her review of recent trends in the organization of professional work, Larson identifies three major tendencies which have come to characterize the professional work process: (1) an increase in and rigidification of division of labor which has the effect of increasing the individual professional's dependence on the bureaucratic whole through the delegation of routinized tasks to lower level workers and, thus, diminishing his or her autonomy; (2) an intensification of work itself by increasing the absolute volume of work and, so, disrupting the traditional professional (or craft) work rhythm of accomplishment, inactivity, preparation, and accomplishment; and (3) the routinization of what were previously high level tasks and their assignment to management, its consultants, or its data processing machines.[4] These objective changes in the professional labor process represent, Larson argues, a kind of "de-skilling" that is analogous to the history of industrial work processes. Moreover, this professional transformation derives from analogous intentions and has similar effects—namely, the extension of managerial control over work, the workplace, and workers in the name of efficiency, productivity, and profit. In the face of such a profound transformation in the actual process of educated labor, claims of continuing professional control become mere ideological legitimations of only relative material and status differentials vis-a-vis nonprofessional labor.

Why has this happened? Why has the seemingly secure monopoly of professionals over their own working conditions been under attack? At the most general level, the rationalization of professional work merely reflects the bureaucratic centralization of production and employment that is characteristic of state capitalism; no less than self-employed craftspersons or mechanics, the self-employed and independent professional is an endangered species. This change in the locus and structure of professional work has been exacerbated in the last decade by progressive deterioration in the market for educated workers, a market in which both the supply of and the demand for such workers have been fundamentally changed. On the supply side, from the early 1970s on, we have witnessed a veritable glut of college-educated entrants into the labor force, a glut that extends as well to professionally trained people. The relatively autonomous, disciplinary-controlled graduate training departments reacted very slowly in the 1970s to the emerging over-supply of professional graduates. Even when they reacted by cutting back or redesigning graduate programs, the large cohort of professionals trained in the expansionist days of the 1960s remained to provide intense competition for a dwindling number of jobs and to close off career mobility for newer entrants into the professional labor force. This oversupply situation has produced the professional equivalent of a "reserve army" of unemployed and underemployed workers whose presence severely limits the traditional power and privilege of employed professionals in many fields.[5]

At the same time, the demand for professional workers (in professional capacities, at least) has declined. While this decline is, in part, a product of the more general economic recession of the 1970s, some specific components of the deteriorating market for educated workers can be identified. These include: a decline in government spending for research and development and for social services; a fall in school budgets, in response to declining school age populations and to urban fiscal crises; a specific and intense slowdown in the economic growth of "college intensive" industries; a fall in the proportion of private research and development spending that goes to basic research; and, finally, the continuing "crisis" in higher education itself as it reacts to the perceived excesses and experiments of the 1960s.[6] In concert with the conditions of oversupply, this weakened demand has exposed professional workers to the same economic vulnerability in a time of contraction and crisis that their non-professional counterparts have long faced. And the result for those who do manage to hold on to professional employment is the presence of those proletarianizing tendencies in the labor process outlined above.

In the face of these objective changes in the labor process and its political economic context, the traditional organization and ideology of professionalism have lost their force. Control over the conditions of training and career entry has been weakened by the extension of managerial prerogative in both graduate universities and employing institutions. Moreover, the managerial imperative to reduce costs and increase productivity has often led to their legitimizing the proto-professional pretensions of alternative groups of workers (e.g., social workers with B.A.'s only; legal and medical paraprofessionals) as a way of maintaining pressure on traditional professionals' diminishing autonomy over their own work. In this context, the ideology of professionalism no longer reflects genuine superiority in power, privilege, or autonomy, but only serves to rationalize their loss by legitimizing the remaining status differentials between professional and non-professional workers. In the short run, at least, both employers and professionals have their interests served in this process. Employers are able to retain the services and skills of highly educated workers and to do so at less cost in salaries (the cost of a symbolic title or a minor level of work autonomy is small) and with little potential disruption of institutional patterns of work and discipline. For their part, beleaguered professionals can still fall back on the subjective satisfactions of being deemed a professional by bosses and lower-level workers alike, much as manual workers find psychic satisfaction in the ideology of a free labor market unconstrained by class, racial, or sexual determinations. In both cases, ideology becomes a conservative force that reinforces the objective extension of rational control over workers and their work.

It is within this changing context that the labor process at alternative colleges has developed. These colleges have had to cope with the same sorts of economic transformations that have faced non-academic professionals, and they have done so in similar ways. Administrations have sought to rationalize the process of work in order to increase productivity and efficiency. Administrative offices have expanded to take on new educational functions; in the process, faculty control over the academic program and over their own work is threatened or compromised as pedagogical tasks become routinized and parcelled out to administrative functionaries. At the same time, the sheer volume of work—already onerous due to unrealistic, original expectations built into alternative college structures—has continued to increase. Like their non-academic counterparts, faculty at such colleges have had no clear or effective responses to these changes despite innumerable individual and group initiatives. Faced with overwork, they seek relief in administrative remedies. But faced with those remedies, they fear erosion of professional autonomy and of academic quality and experimentation. Faced with overwhelming demands on them as generalist-teachers, and perceiving few employment prospects, they fear the loss of professional and research competence. But whereas non-academic professionals might find some solace in their professional identities, these faculty members, committed to an alternative model of the generalist-cum-specialist teacher, have no such ideological refuge.

These contradictory aspects of the labor process at alternative colleges suggest that while the "proletarianization" of professional labor has affected these colleges, the impact has been subtle and unique. To assess just how this process has proceeded, we now turn to an examination of the labor process at one not untypical alternative college, Hampshire College.

III. THE NATURE AND STRUCTURE OF HAMPSHIRE COLLEGE

Hampshire College is a small, liberal arts college located in the hills of western Massachusetts, the creation in 1970 of its sister institutions within the Five College consortium (Smith, Mt. Holyoke, and Amherst Colleges, and the University of Massachusetts/Amherst). There are approximately 1200 students on campus during any semester, with several hundred more on leave in more or less structured off-campus settings. There is a permanent faculty of approximately 85 (F.T.E.) members, 40% of whom are women, situated within four divisions rather than traditional departments: Humanities and Arts, Language and Communication, Natural Science, and Social Science. The faculty are employed under a contract system, with a complex system for reappointment, but with no tenure. Because the College is quite new, and given recent competition for diminishing foundation and government support, its annual budget is 80 percent tuition dependent.[7]

Objectives of the Program

In many ways, the goals of the Hampshire educational system appear to be the same as those of other liberal arts institutions. The key difference is that:

> At Hampshire full development of one's potential is seen as requiring a high level of active decision-making on the part of the student. To cope well in a changing society dictates that the educated citizen understand the modes of conceptualization, explanation, and verification of knowledge. It is less useful to memorize a body of "facts" that may soon be obsolete than to "know how to know." In other words, it is more important to learn to *use* the intellect than to be able merely to *exercise* it. The Hampshire program emphasizes conceptual inquiry, or modes of inquiry: "how to learn, use, test, and revise ideas, concepts, theoretical constructs, propositions, and methodological principles in active inquiry."[8]

Each student progresses through the college with a personalized, unique program which focuses upon questions rather than a traditional disciplinary major. Officially, progress is measured by a series of examinations rather than by courses or credits. Each student must formulate ideas for these examinations and create a committee of faculty interested in supervising and evaluating them. Completion of six examinations is required: one "mode of inquiry" examination in each of the four Schools (Division I) usually taking the form of a research paper or studio project, a concentration examination (Division II) which typically includes the results of courses, research, and other activities over a three or four semester period; and an independent study project (Division III). While grades are not given in courses, faculty evaluate each student's performance in a written evaluation, and these supplement the extensive, personalized, narrative evaluations written for each of the six examinations. This means that much of the learning takes place in individualized settings as well as through the process of developing a program. Students select faculty to work with primarily on the basis of thematic questions, rather than disciplinary training, although disciplinary boundaries often correspond to the questions. Examination committees are often multi-disciplinary in composition,[9] and the need to respond to student-created demands often stretches faculty into areas that are outside their own focused expertise. Courses are viewed as tools, methods for acquiring the focus, interest, or information necessary to enable students to formulate or to complete examinations.

Multiple Faculty Roles

Fred Weaver perceptively notes that the formative documents of the college

> . . . underestimated the amount of faculty resourcefulness, patience, self-confidence and *time* required to negotiate and renegotiate each step of each student's academic program. The underestimation seems to have stemmed from a hydraulic conception of educational effort which suggested that more academic responsibility for students meant less for faculty. The enthusiasm of the faculty and students led, in the first three years of the college, to the creation of an academic program which is even more ambitious than that which was envisioned by the college planners.[10]

The reality of the multiple roles that the faculty must play within this system defied the less-work theory and created tensions for each faculty member even before recent changes within the larger political economy began to affect the College. There is an apocryphal story about the student who left orientation convinced that there were *three* sets of faculty at

Hampshire College: those who taught the courses, those who supervised examination work, and advisers. In fact, it's the same folks juggling many hats.

The primary task is advising and supporting students in the complex task of creating their own educational programs. Unlike traditional "major" advisers who may simply sign course slips for the semester and ensure the completion of a standardized curriculum with some distribution requirements, faculty advisers at Hampshire find that their responsibilities merely begin with course registration. They must listen patiently to help students articulate and focus their interests and then help match those interests with faculty, courses, and projects. Given people's natural reticence about giving and receiving advice, these relationships become more effective when they are long-standing and involve sharing on the part of the student and the faculty member. These relationships transcend office hours and office boundaries, and often follow the faculty into the swimming pool, the bathroom, and the home. The relationship is without clear boundaries, a particular problem for newer and/or younger faculty members.[11]

Another item the quotation from Weaver only touches upon is the intricacy of the negotiating and renegotiating of examination contracts. It may take several hours or several dozen hours spread over a week or over two years to encourage, and cajole, students in the process of refining and concretizing their examination plans. Many examinations necessitate the virtual equivalent of an independent study in a particular subject or in the appropriate methodology. There is no such thing as failure at Hampshire College. In other words, drafts of examination work are read, and extensively commented upon, and then returned with rewrites requested with the necessary supportive personal contact, in a manner that far exceeds the process of peer-review journals. At crucial moments in the semester, the faculty may be working over one hundred hours a week, reading and commenting upon portfolios and preparing for formal oral examinations, while continuing to teach classes and advise.

Despite all this individualized learning, the course is not dead at Hampshire. Most Hampshire faculty teach or co-teach four courses each year, and must teach during January Term at least once every three years. These courses are offered at all three Divisional levels to focus upon the respective goals of each level: mode of inquiry to understand a problem area for Division I; theoretical and empirical information of a broader nature for Division II; and integrative seminars that serve to place the individual student's Division III project within the context of a complex topic requiring the application of several disciplines.

One of the most time-consuming faculty roles involves writing discursive evaluations of students' course and examination work. Since these evaluations are a central source of diagnostic information to students and constitute the major elements of a Hampshire transcript, faculty try to remain conscientious about their quality, comprehensiveness, and timeliness. Inevitably, however, their completion gets delayed, and they become major sources of anxiety for faculty and important sources of strain among the faculty, administration, and students.

Traditional governance is another faculty role. Faculty are on committees which administer the Schools, appointment searches, the reappointment process, curriculum development, adjudication, community governance, and Five College programs upon which we are especially dependent. Each faculty member has at least one significant responsibility each year. The reappointment process is particularly time-consuming and requires that each faculty member up for reappointment write an extensive, introspective evaluation of his or her own work which also presents plans for the proposed new contract period. Other faculty selected by reappointment candidates write evaluations which are also incorporated in open files, and students, staff, and outside colleagues are also invited to contribute to the file. Then a committee of faculty and students within each School deliberates and recommends to the School. The School meets on each candidate. A committee of five faculty and two students meets for the entire month of January to deliberate over the cases of reappointment and promotion from each School. In a faculty of 85, twenty or more are evaluated each year under this process, with another quarter of the faculty serving on the five committees involved. Despite its obvious merits, this elaborate process demands an enormous, perhaps inordinate, commitment of faculty time and energy.

The original plan for the College proposed that faculty would not only participate as members of a School but would also be active participants in the planning and governance of one of the residential houses, including teaching special courses there. Faculty were to blend their personal lives with their daily participation in the houses, and this work, as well, was to be evaluated in the reappointment process. As will be noted below, however, house activities are now a marginal element in the work lives of all but a handful of faculty.

A final role is that of active scholar or artist. While Hampshire is, most decidedly, a "teaching" school, it has always been expected that faculty would be intellectually active, even if not in traditional, disciplinary forums. This expectation has received increasing faculty support, particularly since the overwhelming majority of the faculty have been trained in the nation's most distinguished research universities.[12] Scholarly output is high, despite the many other demands of the job, indicating both the intellectual stimulation of the College's environment and the impact of professional socialization prior to the choice of Hampshire. However, it is equally true that faculty report that "professional improvement" is the area that most suffers from insufficient time and attention.[13] As we will see below, this tension between professional, disciplinary activity and commitment to the demands of a generalist teaching model is an important component of the contradictions of Hampshire's labor process.

It is apparent that Hampshire faculty are confronted with an overwhelming array of job-related responsibilities. In fact, a study estimates that Hampshire faculty work approximately twice as many hours on college-related work as faculty at comparable institutions.[14] This results from the relatively high student-faculty ratio of 14.5:1[15] coupled with the multiplicity of roles which the faculty simultaneously perform. Moreover, it is potentially risky to establish a personal hierarchy of these tasks, as reappointment criteria assume substantial contributions in each area—the combination of the Oxford tutorial, the Harvard course system, and the vestiges of the New England town meeting form of governance.

IV. WORK INTENSIFICATION AT HAMPSHIRE COLLEGE

The original structure of the College established a series of contradictions in the faculty labor process that are analogous to the dilemmas faced by other professional workers. First, faculty were faced with two conflicting sets of work expectations. On the one hand, faculty were expected to operate as independent pedagogical agents in a system of education-by-contract, retaining a significant degree of autonomy in arranging their work. This promise of independence and autonomy surely has been a major attraction to faculty who have chosen to teach at Hampshire. On the other hand, we have seen that the educational structure requires faculty to fulfill multiple roles in their work. Responding to this expectation not only leads to the danger of overwork but also threatens to compromise the reality of individual faculty autonomy over the scope and rhythm of their work. This conflict appears to be analogous to the situation of professional workers more generally.

Second, this conflict between individual autonomy and educational structure is paralleled by the ideological duality built into the original faculty model, which expected faculty to be both generalist-teachers *and* specialist-researchers. Living up to both of these expectations magnifies faculty workload, creates constant anxiety about servicing students as well as professional needs adequately, and prompts faculty to search for ways to routinize and reduce at least some of the work they do. At the same time, the strength of subjective and shared identity is weakened: is one a teacher, a disciplinary specialist, both, or neither? This ideological confusion, too, is analogous to the weakening of professional ideology more generally, while the turn toward routinization and delegation of faculty work parallels the larger bureaucratization of professional labor.

These structural contradictions have, unfortunately, been exacerbated by the economic crises of the last decade which provided the context for the maturation of Hampshire. Recurring inflation, of course, has pushed the Hampshire administration to try to reduce the growth of basic expenses (including real wages, which have actually fallen) and promote greater efficiency and productivity in a labor-intensive enterprise. In both obvious and subtle ways, this has magnified the existing contradictions in Hampshire's labor process. Moreover, economic crisis has affected colleges like Hampshire in a special manner. First, rising tuition costs, along with a shrinking pool of potential applicants, have demanded greater attention to the problems of attracting and retaining students. Second, the deterioration in professional job markets and the consequent loss of mobility for faculty, has heightened the tensions inherent in the generalist-specialist model noted above. Together, these external pressures have exacerbated the built-in tendencies toward work intensification at Hampshire.

The Student Retention Problem

A consequence of the shrinking pool of college bound students, coupled with a student withdrawal rate of 40%, has been an administration led, and by and large faculty-supported, effort to retain students. The withdrawal rate is not abnormally high for schools with individualized study programs that often include off-campus work. But the withdrawal rate boosts the costs of beating the bushes for students. And, by the mid-1970s there appeared to be more parent complaints that students had little or nothing to show for a year or two of college—courses were not always completed and exams were stillborn while tuition costs rose.[16] As a result of these pressures, and an apparent decline in academic ability of the average student, the late 1970s saw considerable thought and effort put into ways to engage students productively early in their college careers and, since the majority of withdrawals occurred prior to filing a Division II contract, special attention has been paid to advising and to the Division I process.

In-house Hampshire studies pointed out that student "success" at Hampshire usually means having close ties to at least one faculty member who may be the adviser.[17] The renewed emphasis on advising meant trying to improve it qualitatively but also, and inevitably, subtle pressures developed to do more of it. Discussions were held in a variety of contexts in order to improve each faculty member's practice. As a result, advising performance has become a somewhat more significant, though decidedly secondary, factor in reappointment considerations. Because students appreciate good advising and faculty status among students can be enhanced in this manner, most faculty pay a good deal of attention to it. These pressures to deal with the retention problem have only added to the substantial advising burden already built into the system.

The second way to deal with the retention problem was to get students through the Division I process, by engaging them intellectually early on and thus cut down on "floundering." Again after considerable discussion involving faculty and administration it was decided to launch proseminars for entering students. These would be taught by an adviser to a class of his or her advisees and would be designed as a benchmark orientation to the Hampshire system as well as an early, diagnostic tool for entering students of perhaps lesser average ability than those in the early years of the College. The special attention to Division I courses marked a return to early Hampshire experience when a lack of advanced students prompted considerable creativity and attention to the design and execution of first and second year courses. Later on, as upper level Division II classes and Division III seminars proliferated, the Division I courses received less faculty attention and on occasion School deans had to go through complex persuasion and bargaining maneuvers to induce faculty to offer Division I courses. The renewed Division I emphasis, the apparent need to design more carefully class process as well as content, meant more work was required. This pressure was felt very unevenly by the faculty. Some ignored the effort and some had no need to change their emphases. But for many this solution for the retention problem required extra effort.

The Resurgent Classroom

The late 1970s also saw a growing faculty attention to classroom work in general although this greater emphasis was not felt uniformly across the

College, and its causes remain multiple and unclear. There was some student, and even indirect parent, pressure for more "orderly" learning through the classroom, but for many faculty the retention problem was simply interpreted to mean that the classroom was the most efficient way to stimulate students and facilitate their progress by examination; and while this meant imparting the skills for more independent exam work, it also involved fine-tuning classes, developing more cogent, focused, up-to-date lectures, and carefully designing frameworks for class discussion. There was also a greater concern for the content of the class—a feeling that ultimately only compelling ideas would elicit student imagination and interest.

Another subtle incentive for classroom emphasis came from the comparatively high Hampshire "export rate" of students to Five College institutions. While a high export rate is to be expected in a student-directed curriculum without departmental requirements for graduation that tend to keep a student on campus, the tendency for students to take a high portion of classes off-campus provoked anxieties among some faculty that the practice would eventually boomerang and other colleges would eventually refuse our export and their overload. At the same time, students appeared to be voting with their feet against Hampshire classes, especially when they took analogous classes elsewhere. Students sometimes complained that they preferred highly organized, well thought out, classes off-campus as opposed to somewhat less integrated and occasionally more chaotic classes at home. Partly to save face, some Hampshire faculty began to design more elegant, and occasionally lecture-prone, classes that inevitably required more time and effort.

Greater attention to the classroom may also be a product of recent recruitment of new Ph.D.'s who perceive the classroom, as opposed to exam work, as their definition of personal challenge and avenue of success. In this perspective, the classroom, and lectures in particular, are the ultimate demonstration of a teacher's "craft". Gradually this younger faculty element has brought classroom performance to a greater prominence as their numbers are felt in reappointment decisions.

The high percentage of co-taught courses at Hampshire also seems to put special emphasis on classroom performance and especially the "idea content" as opposed to the "process content" of teaching. Co-teachers expect to learn and be stimulated as much as students, and subtle competition among them for provocative ideas, arguments, and synthesis of materials may mean that co-teaching requires as much (or even more) work as solo teaching efforts.

Resurgent Research and Scholarship

While there have been pressures to improve and spend more time and effort on advising and Division I courses, as well as more subtle, though uneven, pressures to up-grade the classroom, somewhat greater emphasis for reappointment purposes has also been placed on scholarship and research which usually connotes publication and performance—the products of traditional professional life. Apart from the fact that some simply enjoy scholarly work and believe they have something to say, this deviation from what has been termed an antiprofessional ethos in the early stages of the College[18] has two roots. First, at the institutional level, the fear of a declining student pool created a perceived need to upgrade faculty credentials and make the College more attractive over the long run. Second, individual faculty, perceiving a declining market for their talents outside the College, began to pay more attention to their own marketability, particularly through the augmentation of existing standard professional credentials.

At the institutional level the scholarship emphasis is unevenly distributed through the four Schools of the College, and while the concern has seen peaks and valleys within each, the overall trend is clear. There has been no administrative edict charting this direction, nor is reappointment precluded without standard scholarly products. Instead, even in the early years of the College persuasive individuals on formal and informal occasions have quietly spoken for a scholarly concern or have supported the recruitment of faculty with strong scholarly potential, in order to maintain and continually up-grade the intellectual quality of the College, keep it lively, and help insure its survival. As some of the most "successful" faculty members, defined in Hampshire's own unique terms, are also seen to be productive scholars, and as their ranks expand, scholarship has increasingly become part and parcel of the definition of a good faculty member. And as the faculty market produces a surplus of rather spectacular talent recently out of graduate school, there is a subtle process of deflating the standing of faculty who may otherwise perform extremely well on other non-scholarly dimensions.

At the personal faculty level there is probably a greater desire to want to retain an active professional life than was present among faculty in the early years of the College. More recent disciplinary ties among younger faculty may be one factor. But more generally, as the faculty perceives a declining ability to be mobile outside Hampshire in academic or non-academic jobs, as job opportunities for employment in Hampshire-type institutions approach zero, as faculty perceive Hampshire's survival as something less than certain, and as they see exceptional talent behind them at reappointment time, faculty increasingly see professional credentials as their only safety net. As a result they try to pursue scholarly activity in Hampshire's otherwise extremely demanding work environment, which, in turn, raises the level of their frustration.

Experiencing Work Intensification

We have argued that an initially very demanding faculty work situation has been exacerbated by external changes in the form of declining student pools and collapsing faculty markets. The shifting external environment has created an intensified work process in the specific form of more attention to advising, first and second year Division I classes, a growing emphasis on classroom work in general, and the rise of scholarly criteria for reappointment. The faculty has experienced this intensified work process in several ways. First and foremost there is a feeling of chronic work overload to the extent that a recent survey of the faculty found 62 per cent saying that their role as an educator was compromised because of it.[19] An average work day or work week is hard to pin down and averages would mask an uneven experience, but for most there is a feeling of total immersion in work. Evening and/or early morning work is routine and weekends are hard to find. By Thursday many faculty members simply look bad—and sometimes act bad—due to progressive lack of sleep over the week.

Coupled with the feeling of chronic overload is a sense of fragmented work and constant and emotionally draining mental gear-shifting. The crowded schedule and constant role juggling makes it hard to find closure, to have a sense that one task is done and energy can now be devoted to another. Classes end but evaluations linger on and if possible, tend to be postponed to Christmas and summer vacations. Because the faculty knows that the exam system and classroom activity demand self-pacing by students that often plays havoc with deadlines, class papers and exam papers come in at any and all times with the former often signaling the need for a class evaluation months, or even years, after the fact. Exam papers are read, but due to time pressure the evaluations are usually written up much later requiring at least a partial re-reading to augment earlier notes—which is especially taxing when a Division II portfolio includes from four to eight or more papers. Office hours are long and crowded, the phone is active, governance work requires attention, recommendations are requested, colleagues are evaluated, classes need preparation and co-teaching requires coordination, exam meetings are scattered throughout the week, lunches are often the working variety, and the to and fro of communication with the professional world requires attention. Work feels like a constant interruption and nothing seems to be done right as brief amounts of time are devoted to multiple tasks. Sacrifices are made and the faculty believes that it comes primarily out of professional development and secondarily, advising.[20] Nancy Goddard's recent study also found the faculty feeling ". . . that they are spread too thin to do an adequate job of teaching."[21] Class preparation almost always requires work at home which is hard to schedule because of the multiple demands for a hands-on presence at the College. Richard Alpert sums up the nature of fragmentation and mental gear-shifting this way: "At different times with the same student the faculty member must be adviser, friend, registrar, advocate, counselor, task-master, or evaluator. Faculty must not only have a broad repertoire, but also must know which role to play with which students."[22]

The built-in and evolving pressures toward overwork, fragmentation, and excessive gear-shifting in the performance of multiple roles, makes it difficult to retain or deepen a specialization. Many faculty say they experience a drain on their expertise because there is little time to pursue a specialty; they feel most compromised here.[23] Because the demands of student contact and classroom work are very difficult to duck or put aside, very few faculty do significant research or writing during the school year, and one to three weeks of evaluation writing during Christmas holidays and the summer further diminishes the time available for scholarship.

The process of de-specialization is not directly analogous to the loss of skills involved in industrial proletarianization. Rather than assume a smaller routinized task as part of a total effort, the worker assumes many tasks; and rather than abandon existing skills the worker must multiply and intensify existing ones. The College's original design requiring faculty performance of several roles coupled with externally induced work intensification pressures means that the faculty pursue many tasks and demonstrate a variety of skills but at the risk of a corresponding loss of depth in any specialty.[24] Lack of time to do research and to write is further exacerbated by internally generated incentives to be a generalist rather than a specialist. This of course squares with the original design of the College and the personal goal of becoming generally educated by even the most professionally oriented of the faculty. But the problem comes when theory is put into practice in the current context. Responding to student suggested examination topics inevitably pulls the faculty member into new directions. But other pressures toward generalization rather than specialization also occur in the classroom. Faculty are formally allowed to teach virtually anything they wish and consequently could teach courses exclusively in and around a particular expertise. But very few do and many are pulled far afield because of the genuine excitement and enthusiasm of two or three colleagues who enjoy teaching together and want to plumb the depths of an old topic or open a new one together.

More subtle incentives and pressures are also at work. Because of the faculty contract system with its frequent reviews and diffuse and ambiguous criteria for reappointment, individual faculty survival at Hampshire depends a great deal on one's position in colleague social networks and even student networks. Thus, for reasons of reappointment it is advisable to co-teach with others in order to become a known and valued entity. It also means becoming a magnet for students—ideally to develop a small following who do exam work with you, take your courses, and ultimately applaud you at times of reappointment. In lieu of significant internal faculty power based on seniority or tenured status, new faculty members cannot attach themselves to one or two patrons in order to get assured protection and advancement. Good strategy implies that one should be a part of whatever interesting is happening—a key course with dynamic co-teachers who will also refer students to you, or perhaps a new "program" that may evolve unconsciously over the years, or appear suddenly over beer in a bar. And one should teach courses that draw students, not so much for the sake of enrollment, but in order to define one's expertise in a subject matter and encourage students to do related exam work. These pressures usually take the young and more vulnerable faculty members well beyond their original scholarly focus. In most cases the result is enormously stimulating and exciting for faculty and students, and it may lead to a new "teaching specialty" for the original teaching cohort and other faculty who may rotate in and out of the course over the years. But only in exceptional cases does the process lead to a new research specialty for any of the participants. And given the limits of time, old specialties may begin to atrophy producing considerable anxiety for the faculty member. Subsequent efforts to respecialize inevitably bring back the risks mentioned above and may create tensions among the faculty when one or two become overwhelmed by exam work in a particular field that is generated by many.[25]

The intensification of the current work process would, one might expect, prompt rampant faculty cynicism, disengagement from a positive emotional attachment to the College, and annual attempts to escape altogether. But by and large this does not happen. Instead we find, to a surprising degree, genuine attachment to the institution, its design,[26] colleagues, and students—in short a remarkable loyalty and commitment. This pattern is partially explained by the self-selection of many faculty who chose to come to Hampshire. Until recently, and now only in selected disciplines and specialties, most faculty could have gone elsewhere to institutions of comparable status. They chose to come, of course, for a variety of personal idiosyncratic reasons, but also because most wanted first, an environment congenial to good teaching; second, the chance to become generally educated beyond their specialties; and third, the opportunity to pursue their specialties—often initially seen by the new faculty member as the opportunity to "teach what you want."

But once at Hampshire, and especially in the second and third years, the contradictions among the initial three goals create anxieties which are usually resolved in favor of remaining. Gearing up for the first reappointment in the third year involves "psyching out" the place, trying to cover oneself on the multiple and ambiguous criteria for reappointment, and in the process fitting oneself to the Hampshire mold. New faculty members by choice, and by the incentives of the reappointment process, generally adapt with astounding speed and are occasionally among the most articulate supporters of the original College design. The informal strategies for reappointment are usually clearly perceived and in the process firm intellectual, and often social, friendships emerge, sometimes exhilarating co-teaching arrangements develop, compelling future plans are drawn, and intense and generally satisfying, if exhausting, contacts with students are made—all of which tends to bind the new faculty member to the institution and its people.

As time passes, these bonds to the institution, friends, and the locality often deepen while other factors come into play. Multiple roles and work intensification tend to run down the faculty member's "expertise capital," a progressively collapsing faculty market is perceived, individual scholarly credentials may be respectable but not exceptional, and more seniority means that the faculty member becomes more expensive for other financially-starved institutions to hire. In the face of these realities there is a tendency to become even more committed to the institution because, at least in darker moods, Hampshire appears to be the only thing between the faculty member and the abyss. One increasingly becomes a loyalist out of "necessity" rather than choice. In the process the faculty member is likely to exhibit greater concern for College-wide issues of institutional survival; and, of course, he or she is ripe for overwork as personal performance is more closely wedded to the problem of institutional durability.

V. RESPONSES TO WORK INTENSIFICATION

Individual Responses: Allowing the Rise of Central Administration

We have discussed the ways in which external trends of the 1970s have merged with Hampshire College structure to increase faculty workload and threaten faculty control over their own everyday labor process. We have also indicated what the result "felt like" from a faculty point of view. We now turn to the several faculty efforts to alleviate the effects of work intensification. These attempts will be discussed in terms of two broad categories—individual responses and group responses. We begin with *ad hoc* individual efforts.

Although faculty loyalty and commitment to the institution remain high there is a contradictory trend toward a centralization of power in the administration, a process which risks long term faculty alienation from the institution, but one in which faculty members have been complicit. Data on the comparative expansion of administrative and faculty personnel and remuneration indicate that the administration has recently expanded in numbers faster than the faculty and its consumption of college financial resources has increased at a slightly faster rate than those consumed by the faculty.[27] The administration's expanded numbers have also, according to some, signaled an accumulation of more power at the expense of the faculty. The all-faculty Academic Council gave way to an elected Senate which has, in turn, seemed to atrophy in recent years, thereby bestowing power on the administration by default.[28] In the early years of comparative budget largesse the budget was not a major faculty concern. However now, in a time of financial retrenchment, it is a matter of faculty anxiety but there is no indication of greater faculty involvement in the budgetary process nor is there significant faculty effort to gain entry to the process. In general the faculty retains a strong veto role but it has recently exerted less collective initiative than in the early years.

The precise degree of administrative power expansion, and the extent to which it has been at the expense of the faculty, cannot be resolved here. The important point is that the faculty has, on the whole, held a very ambiguous attitude toward the administration. On the one hand, the faculty has been complicit in bureaucratic expansion, often seeing it as a short term solution to faculty workload problems.[29] In the early, and somewhat chaotic, administrative environment of the College, some routinization was thought necessary for minimal predictability. Later, under the pressures of the everyday workload, and perceiving vague and ill-defined threats to the institution's existence, there was an element of the faculty, or a side to most faculty members, which increasingly saw the administration as a compatible support structure. In this view, the administration should take on, for example, some of the less consequential faculty administrative burdens and provide basic student services as well as deal with "difficult" students so the faculty will not be bothered by them. There is a tendency among an overworked faculty to give work to whomever will take it—especially work which does not appear directly related to the immediate educational mission. Most faculty are also sympathetic to the argument that the College needs to "come of age" and rationalize its procedures, particularly those related to the outside world. In order to secure long-term survival, it is implied that viable programs are necessary for alumni, parent, and general public relations as well as grantsmanship for the institution and the faculty. All of these trends, of course, parallel the routinization of tasks that is characteristic of the rationalization of professional work generally.

But while some faculty some of the time will acquiesce to apparent administrative solutions to the workload problem and problems of institutional viability, the faculty is very ambivalent toward the encroachment of administrative power. Many fear the possible consequences of work routinization and more elaborate division of labor that may enmesh them in new hierarchies. Some fear that rather than alleviate the workload, the administration expands it; that rather than support the faculty, the administration tends to summon it to help solve real or manufactured problems—or, at worst, to legitimize administrative decisions already taken. The faculty also fears it is losing potential faculty positions that could directly alleviate the workload. While the faculty appears to solve some of its workload problems by cutting back on time devoted to governance,[30] some faculty occasionally panic when they think they see an aggressive administration taking power unto themselves. It also appears that with tighter budgets, coupled with a maturing faculty with more curricular program ideas, the administration tends to become the arbiter of innovation.

We do not wish to exaggerate the loss of faculty power, although we see a trend in that direction in which the faculty has been complicit. It is likely that the Hampshire faculty remains exceptionally powerful in any comparative sense because of the latitude for faculty self-management built into the original design; because College trustees are new and assume the maintenance of an educational model of decentralized learning giving power to the faculty; and because the alumni are few, lack economic clout that could give them power in College affairs, and tend to support the Hampshire model of limited administration. Without strong trustee and alumni backing, the College administration cannot assume broad powers. The administration also lacks an alliance with the student body despite some financial incentives to do so.[31] Individual administrators generally lack systematic, long-term ties to individual students. Affective ties are also minimal because the administration applies rules that students tend to see as cluttering their landscape, proliferating paperwork, unnecessarily rigidifying the system, and not really facilitating their self-paced advance through the College.

Individual Responses: Decline of the "Community" Model

The need to find some relief from the pressures of the work process means that some faculty have actively distanced themselves from the governance system, while a similar withdrawal has taken place from broad-based campus community life, particularly that centered around the house system of student residence. The early model of the College and the early expectations of many faculty and students built in reaction to the impersonality of the "megaversity," were that work, community, and social life would be integrated and that much of it would occur in the houses. But this prospect began to fade early on and has now almost totally disappeared as faculty have successfully segregated the workplace from their private and family lives. The workload built into the design of the College, coupled with its progressively intensified character, found faculty trying to "escape" in order to get some distance from the place and have a social life where Hampshire affairs were never mentioned. When work and private life were more integrated the latter tended to be swallowed up by the former.

Individual Responses: Passive Resistance

A common faculty coping device for dealing with the workload problem is what we might call passive resistance to a large number of expectations. Broadly speaking, this means breaking rules and regulations and occasionally involves the conscious development of ignorance about them so one cannot be bothered by them. One form of passive resistance is delaying written evaluations of student work. Some faculty may be months or even years in arrears. This behavior is, for some, a form of protest but it is also an almost necessary means to gain some breathing space when the College is in session and an effort to find quiet space to do justice to student performance. An additional, analogous form of resistance is the scaling back of available office hours—regardless of student demand or official expectation—as a way of rationing time and energy.

Individual Responses: The Cult of Bitching

Another coping device is what we might call the cult of bitching. On the one hand there is something of an ethic that one should not protest too much because it is, after all, boring, and overwork is not "news" to anyone. And one should, through sheer intellectual brilliance, rise above it all and not, for example, have to spend long hours preparing lectures. As a result, some of the real pain of overwork is carefully hidden. But on the other hand, individual misery requires some company for the therapeutic assurance that one is neither crazy nor totally incompetent. As a result, the cult of bitching about overwork is thoroughly institutionalized in faculty culture and its ritual observation is carried out in a variety of encounters from occasional conversation between nodding acquaintances on sidewalks to long conversations between friends wallowing in collective self-pity.

Individual Responses: Learning to Say "No"

The most simple and natural way to obtain work relief is to say "no" to excessive demands from students to work with them on examinations and other projects. While most faculty do say "no" at times, and new faculty members are urged to say "no" for their self-protection, there are dangers and limits to its use. As we mentioned earlier, it is good reappointment strategy to be in demand by students which also affords one visibility to other faculty members on student examination committees. Also, student work not assumed by one faculty member inevitably is assumed by another which only adds to burdens borne by colleagues having similar interests and abilities. This form of work displacement risks creating tensions with colleagues, and particularly those with whom one normally works closely. On top of the calculated risks taken by saying "no" too often, most faculty members have difficulty escaping the institutional ideology, and ultimately the structural necessity, of servicing the students' chosen direction. In the back of the faculty mind is a small voice that asks, "What would happen if everyone said 'no'?"

Group Responses: Differential Staffing

Individual responses to work intensification have alleviated burdens to some degree and they have provided an *ad hoc* flexibility and measure of relief according to personal taste. But the feeling of work intensification is ever-present and, consequently, collective efforts have been tried. The differential staffing technique involves faculty member specialization in a particular role occasioned by Hampshire's structure, such as Division I examination work, courses, or governance. Thus, a kind of specialization creeps in the back door but it is quite different from normal professional specialization. This form of specialization cuts down on the feeling of fragmentation due to almost simultaneous performance of multiple roles and it allows some individuals to carve out a niche that is more comfortable for them. The device is used sparingly and unevenly across the four Schools of the College but where it occurs it is usually sanctioned by an understanding at the School level. However, given the multiple criteria applied at reappointment time, this device too has built in risks which limit its more extensive use; and it risks the development of status hierarchies among the faculty.

Group Responses: Going by the Book

Hampshire faculty have also sought work relief by the traditional tactic of "going by the book" or "working to rule"—i.e., interpreting and using rules in order to minimize required work. For example, on occasion faculty have chosen to enforce rigidly deadlines for the submission of examination proposals prior to the end of a semester; this can be an effective way of regulating the amount of student-initiated work without appearing to violate collegial or community norms. Another collective tactic for reducing the examination burden has been the informal imposition of quotas (based upon college-wide workload averages) by faculty in overlapping fields in demand by students. At least in the short run, this can be an effective slow-down method. As for reducing the burden of classroom teaching, with its constant demand for preparation and its associated supply of bureaucratic functions, faculty discovered early on that the College's official support for team-teaching provided an opportunity for direct work relief. It is not surprising that collective teaching (sometimes involving 4 or more faculty) has expanded throughout the College in recent years. Finally, faculty have sought to reduce the advising load by interpreting the expectations about adviser-advisee relations rather loosely. Where it was once expected that advanced Division II or III students could rely both on an academic superviser and on an independent adviser for support and guidance, it is now common for committee chairpersons to become the official advisers to the students with whom they are already working. This tactic satisfies official workload requirements but directly reduces the number of students making regular demands on any one faculty member.

Group Responses: Changing Formal Rules

Several notable attempts to change the formal rules through collective action in order to provide work relief might be briefly mentioned. First, over the years the faculty has pressed for and won a rather liberal leave and sabbatical policy. Second, the previous requirement of two faculty members on each Division I exam committee was changed to one faculty member plus a student. Third, the initial teaching requirement of five regular courses and one during January Term was changed to four plus one January Term course every three years. Fourth, there have been recent faculty-designed changes to the reappointment procedures partially justified in terms of easing constant reappointment anxiety, cutting down on the number of mutual references for colleague reappointment over the years, and generally reducing the emotionally taxing time that everyone devotes to reappointment considerations. The two major changes instituted a third contract period of ten years rather than the previous seven, and confined second contract deliberations largely to the School level unless substantial disagreement required extensive consideration at the College level.

Fifth, the School of Social Science proposed that students be allowed the option of substituting two successfully completed courses for the normal Division I examination process. Aside from a variety of pedagogical reasons for the move, the proposal appealed to many faculty because it would ease the burden of the individually negotiated contract process. The proposal was torpedoed, however, by an almost united student opposition as well as by considerable faculty opposition from other Schools.

Sixth, discussion of faculty unionization has come and gone over the years, and in 1977 the faculty were only a few votes shy of enough signatures to signal an NLRB election. This was the most significant attempt to date, and yet there was a certain lack of enthusiasm even among the leadership, while a kind of weary consensus was evidenced among most faculty who believed that it should be tried. Prospective gains were, however, couched almost exclusively in terms of salary and fringe benefits rather than matters affecting the work process. A variety of factors and attitudes contributed to the failed attempt: the inevitable reluctance to view oneself as "just a worker" thereby compromising residual community and professional consciousness; a perceived limited slack in the College budget allowing for only minimal income benefits; anxiety about the benefit of a national union affiliation; unease about potential struggles with non-unionized staff and with the student body,[32] and fears that the union would bring the faculty more meetings to attend and another role to play with the promise of only minimal potential gains in their wake.

VI. CONCLUSION

We opened this essay noting the evolution of professional labor with its characteristic work intensification, routinization, and growing division of labor. We have indicated why and how those characteristics, particularly work intensification, developed in small, alternative colleges like Hampshire. We pointed out why the changing political economy exacerbated declining student pools, collapsed faculty markets, and served to intensify a work process that was already more demanding than originally intended. The external changes prompted somewhat greater faculty attention to advising, lower-level classes, classroom teaching in general, and scholarship. Intensified work was, in turn, experienced as chronic overwork, fragmentation, constant mental gear-shifting, and professional despecialization. But rather than massive disaffection from the College in the face of these trends we found a surprising degree of faculty loyalty and commitment due to some combination of a conscious, positive, and continuing choice in favor of the Hampshire educational model, the socialization process associated with reappointment, and gradual professional despecialization and longer-term perception of personal immobility beyond Hampshire.

Over the years, the Hampshire faculty have asked themselves "What is to be done?" and have responded with a remarkable variety of individual strategies: complicity in the expanding rationalizing authority of the central administration for purposes of short-term work relief and long-term institutional survival; abandonment of the community model of intense faculty relationship to College and student life; passive resistance; a therapeutic "cult of bitching"; and selective use of "NO" as a short-term escape from excessive student demands. Collective efforts were also attempted: differential staffing; "work-to-rule" tactics and formal changes in the rules of the work process; and a still-born effort to unionize.

The faculty has pursued these means for work relief with mixed results. But few faculty would say the problem was behind them and most want to do something about it. In conclusion, we would like to offer some thoughts about what may happen in the future. We will assume, optimistically, that the relevant dynamics of the student pool, the faculty job market, and the general fiscal environment will not change significantly very soon.

Work intensification in the 1970s has laid the groundwork for a growing degree of faculty collective consciousness coming out of a structure that allowed little room for it. There are three broad models of faculty relationship to themselves and their surroundings—the community, professional, and union models—and while, for reasons we will point out, the first two are more or less out of the question, the third remains a conflicted possibility.

The community model of close faculty relationships to the campus and student life in general was an early casualty of the unexpected demands of the work process coupled with 1970s trends toward intensifying work. While an atomized student body remains strongly attracted to the community model, the "College family" proved too intense for the faculty and triggered their escape to non-College life whenever possible. At the same time, post-1960s graduate students recruited as faculty members were somewhat less attracted to the community model than were the founding faculty. Added to this trend is the changing family situation of many faculty and spouses which has increased their need for quiet, family time away from Hampshire's demands. However, with this demise of the community model, the way has been cleared for a greater degree of faculty collective consciousness—an attitude which was originally defined as a somewhat illegitimate, selfish interest in a "community" of "equals".

The professional model has not fared much better as a guide to faculty organization and ideology. An attack on this model was a premise of Hampshire's founding, and subsequent external changes in the 1970s (an oversupply of aspiring academics and a declining demand for them) have reinforced that attack. While some recently recruited faculty have tried to respecialize, or maintain specialized standing in the professional world for reasons of insuring personal mobility options and long-term institutional viability, only a small minority, if any, of the faculty would seriously suggest the professional model for Hampshire's future and students would oppose it *en masse*. Such a move would undermine Hampshire's *raison d'etre* and its fundamental asset in institutional competition for a declining student pool, and it fails to square with the conscious and continuing choice of most faculty to avoid the problems of narrow personal specialization, departmental exclusiveness, and distance from students that most believe compromise quality undergraduate education.

The collapse of the community model and the lack of broad support for the professional model, leaves room for the unionization model or some variant of it. Work intensification and concomitant faculty perceptions of an oppressive workload, coupled with a progressive clearing of the ideological terrain of alternatives makes the unionization option attractive although it presently is a vision without a program. Agreement over the desirability of higher income and more fringe benefits is not hard to find, of course, but the multiple work roles, fragmented work process, uneven work pressures experienced between individuals and schools, and semi-autonomous school "cultures" have encouraged precious little historical faculty agreement over what to do about the work process.

We believe that the latent consciousness of collective faculty interest may best be realized through the organization of a hybrid "professional union" seeking to preserve and extend the faculty-based self-management model built into the College. It would identify the faculty's shared interests not (or not primarily) in opposition to the College administration, but rather in concert with the students. It is they who have the most to lose from faculty over-work. And it is in the name of their quality education—defined in terms of Hampshire's threatened ideal of specialist-cum-generalist pedagogy—that such an effort has the most promise.

A professional union of faculty seeking to maintain a healthy and innovative teaching environment would have many positive benefits. It would provide a non-antagonistic forum for all-faculty discussion of daily work and long-term goals—a forum that does not now exist. In particular, the pedagogical intent and implications of the existing program and possible revisions, and the nature of our working conditions, could be addressed. It would assist in overcoming lingering faculty suspicion of unionization, whether based on professional self-image or on family and class background. It would afford the faculty a legitimate basis for participation in long-term planning for the College, a task increasingly monopolized by administrative staff. Most importantly, it would provide a vehicle for collectively managing overwork—with neither bureaucratic centralization nor disciplinary over-specialization. A union, for example, could press effectively for a reallocation of resources (including targetted fund-raising) toward the hiring of additional faculty, thus reducing directly the burdensome student-faculty ratio to a more realistic figure. A union could also promote the expansion of existing, *ad hoc* collective responses to overwork, and do so with fewer problems of power and authority than could the administration.

We offer these thoughts about unionization ever mindful of the limits of such proposals (including the self-defeating prospect of more meetings and further bureaucratization). As we have argued throughout, the intensification of work at places like Hampshire has partly been a response to more fundamental transformations in the political economy of labor in American capitalism, transformations that are likely to continue unabated. If these external trends of the 1970s made it more difficult for faculty to deal effectively with labor process issues, it is likely that only external changes will allow fundamental relief. But understanding the structural and ideological roots of our particular condition, we need not be slaves to or victims of seemingly unstoppable forces. If the "experiment" at places like Hampshire is to survive during continuing economic crisis, the absolutely central role of faculty in that experiment cannot be sacrificed to imagined administrative or fiscal necessity. And only faculty themselves, acting together, have the potential for preventing their own, and the College's, disintegration.

NOTES

1. See, in particular, Harry Braverman, *Labor and Monopoly Capital* (New York: Monthly Review Press, 1974); Dan Clawson, *Bureaucracy and the Labor Process* (New York: Monthly Review Press, 1980); Rosalyn Baxandall et al., *Technology, The Labor Process, and the Working Class* (New York: Monthly Review Press, 1976); Magali Sarfatti Larson, *The Rise of Professionalism* (Berkeley: University of California Press, 1977); Magali Sarfatti Larson, "Proletarianization and Educated Labor," *Theory and Society*, 9 (1980) pp. 131–175; John and Barbara Ehrenreich, "The Professional-Managerial Class," *Radical America*, XI, 2 (March–April 1977) pp. 7–31; Pat Walker, ed., *Between Labor and Capital* (Boston: South End Press, 1979).

2. Frederick Stirton Weaver, "Academic Disciplines and Undergraduate Liberal Arts Education," *Liberal Education* 67, no. 2 (Summer 1981) pp. 151–165.

3. Larson, "Proletarianization and Educated Labor."

4. *Ibid*., pp. 163–164.

5. Additional discussion and evidence of this phenomenon can be found in Emily Abel, "Teachers and Students on the Slow Track: Inequality in Higher Education," *Socialist Review*, no. 60 v. 11, no. 6 (Nov.–Dec. 1981) pp. 57–75.

6. Larson, "Proletarianization and Educated Labor," p. 158.

7. Hampshire was planned to be a tuition-dependent college. See Franklin Patterson and Charles R. Longsworth, *The Making of a College* (Cambridge: M.I.T. Press, 1966), pp. 233–244.

8. Nancy Thornton Goddard, *Progress by Examination* (Amherst, MA: Hampshire College, 1981), p. 2. The internal quotation is from Patterson and Longsworth, *The Making of a College*, p. xiv.

9. Frederick Stirton Weaver, *Interdisciplinary Learning and Teaching at Hampshire College* (Amherst, MA: Hampshire College, 1980), pp. 13–19.

10. *Ibid*., p. 26.

11. Alpert ascribes this problem of ever-expanding student/client demands to the prepaid, rather than fee-for-service, nature of Hampshire faculty. Moreover, we are, he argues, "general practitioners" rather than specialists. Richard M. Alpert, "Professionalism and Educational Reform: The Case of Hampshire College," *Journal of Higher Education*, 51, 5, (1980) pp. 497–518. High, and perhaps growing, student demands upon faculty may have something to do with a probable decline of overall student body ability as applicant pools have diminished. See Joel S. Meister's essay comparing his experience teaching at Hampshire and nearby Amherst College "A Sociologist Looks at Two Schools—The Amherst and Hampshire Experiences," *Change* 14:2 (March 1982) pp. 26–34.

12. Weaver, *Interdisciplinary Learning and Teaching*, pp. 26–27.
13. Survey data kindly supplied by Professor Nancy Goddard.
14. Goddard, *Progress by Examination*, p. 47.
15. "This figure may seem workable, but it is misleading. New faculty are not assigned advisees during their first semester at Hampshire. Sabbatical leave replacements (temporary, short-term faculty) do not know the system well and are not assigned advisees, nor are other short-term faculty. The resulting advising ratio ranges from 18 to 21:1. Even this ratio is further skewed by the multiple ways a professor often works with a student, usually one on one. Hampshire's ratio of 14.5:1 is higher than that at most comparable colleges (Marlboro, 8:1; Amherst, 10:1; Smith, 9.8:1; Mt. Holyoke, 11:1)." *Ibid.*, p. 46. The current official 15.4:1 ratio is an improvement over the original 16:1 ratio. The improvement occurred in the mid-1970s when a declining applicant pool brought a slightly lower student enrollment while faculty, and some administrators, successfully argued for keeping faculty numbers constant.
16. College data indicate, however, that tuition costs have not risen as fast as the cost of living index.
17. Goddard, *Progress by Examination*, p. 24, and Garry Dearden and Malcolm Parlett, *Ways and Byways Through Hampshire* (Amherst, MA: Hampshire College, 1980) pp. 13–14.
18. Alpert, "Professionalism and Educational Reform," p. 505.
19. Goddard, *Progress by Examination*, p. 44. The survey yielded a 51 percent faculty response rate.
20. *Ibid*.
21. *Ibid*.
22. Alpert, "Professionalism and Educational Reform," p. 507.
23. Goddard, *Progress by Examination*, p. 44.
24. Larson sees this as a general result of work intensification in college teaching; Larson, "Proletarianization and Educated Labor," p. 168.
25. Generalizing tendencies coupled with work intensification may also provide incentives for a certain kind of scholarship. Given the limited time available for research and writing, coupled with an evolving general education for faculty through co-teaching and the exam process, there may be a tendency for faculty to opt for interpretive and theoretical writing as opposed to detailed empirical work.
26. Goddard, *Progress by Examination*, p. 3. Goddard reports that 90.6 percent of the faculty responding to her survey say they are strongly committed to the Hampshire system.
27. Data from the College's "People Budget" show that from 1975–76 to 1979–80 Administration FTEs increased 17.7 percent, while instructional FTEs increased only 6.6 percent and non-instructional staff FTEs remained unchanged. During the same period, the percentage of total personnel expenses going to instruction has remained constant, while the percentage going to administrative and student services has increased. Among the major beneficiaries are the central offices of admissions, development, and student affairs.
28. Causes of the Senate's apparent decline are not clear but might include the preferred attention by some of the most vigorous faculty members to school (the level of greatest personal political significance) rather than College-level governance, indirect control of the agenda by the administration and consequent trivialization of Senate business, and a feeling that faculty time and attention paid to this level of governance has few payoffs.
29. *Cf.*, Larson, "Proletarianization and Educated Labor," p. 162.
30. Goddard, *Progress by Examination*, p. 44.
31. Both have an interest in limiting faculty wage increases. Although no conscious administration—student alliance has emerged, tuition increases have been slightly under the rise of the cost of living index, while the real wages of faculty have declined.
32. The staff unionization attempt was vigorously opposed by the administration of a previous president.

REFERENCES

Abel, Emily. "Teachers and Students on the Slow Track: Inequality in Higher Education," *Socialist Review*, no. 60 v. 11, no. 6 (Nov.– Dec. 1981) pp. 57–75.
Alpert, Richard M. "Professionalism and Educational Reform: The Case of Hampshire College." *Journal of Higher Education* 51 (1980), pp. 497–518.
Baxandall, Rosalyn, et al. *Technology, The Labor Process, and the Working Class*. New York: Monthly Review Press, 1976.
Braverman, Harry. *Labor and Monopoly Capital*. New York: Monthly Review Press, 1974.
Clawson, Dan. *Bureaucracy and the Labor Process*. New York: Monthly Review Press, 1980.
Dearden, Garry, and Parlett, Malcolm. *Ways and Byways Through Hampshire*. Amherst, MA: Hampshire College, 1980.
Ehrenreich, John and Barbara. "The Professional-Managerial Class." *Radical America* XI, 2 (March–April 1977) pp. 7–31.
Goddard, Nancy Thornton. *Progress by Examination*. Amherst, MA: Hampshire College, 1981.
Larson, Magali Sarfatti. "Proletarianization and Educated Labor." *Theory and Society* 9, (1980) pp. 131–175.
———. *The Rise of Professionalism*. Berkeley: University of California Press, 1977.
Meister, Joel S. "A Sociologist Looks at Two Schools—The Amherst and Hampshire Experiences." *Change*, 14:2 (March 1982) pp. 26–34.
Patterson, Franklin, and Longsworth, Charles R. *The Making of a College*. Cambridge: M.I.T. Press, 1966.
Walker, Pat, ed. *Between Labor and Capital*. Boston: South End Press, 1979.
Weaver, Frederick Stirton. "Academic Disciplines and Undergraduate Liberal Arts Education." *Liberal Education*, 67, 2 (Summer 1981) pp. 151–165.
———. *Interdisciplinary Learning and Teaching at Hampshire College*. Amherst, MA: Hampshire College, 1980.

XII. Venturing in Academe

by

JONATHAN FAIRBANKS

Faculty often reject the daring and imaginative in academic curriculum on the assumption that all cases of the unconventional are strange and unsound. This is partly because of the special role faculty have in preserving the integrity of academic curriculum. Experimental courses are difficult to evaluate whereas the standard course meeting thrice weekly for a semester, with a heavy reading list, and frequent call upon the library's reserve desk, bolstered by substantial research papers and memory-straining examinations is relatively easy to assess, if indeed it occurs to anyone that it needs assessment.

Faculty also tend to be pedagogically conservative because their graduate training did not encourage them to be innovative. Quite the reverse; for most of us, our graduate training was a stiff, often oppressive apprenticeship. We were not encouraged to think imaginatively or pursue whimsy. By the time most of us clutched the doctoral sheepskin we had been thoroughly disciplined. Thus we exited from ivy walls and entered a new set of ivy walls to pass along our discipline as we learned it.

My perspective on college faculty derives largely from my experience over the past eight years at two institutions (SUNY and Skidmore College) where I conceived and administered two programs that created academic controversy. The first program (the Wilderness Workshop) telescoped into the next (the Adirondack Institute). The latter offered credit courses in six liberal arts disciplines, using the outdoors as the place of instruction. Since an understanding of the nature of this type of program is crucial to what follows in this chapter, I will illustrate our pedagogy by describing one of the English courses we offered.

Students were required to read ten volumes of literature in a course entitled, "Wilderness in American Literature." The reading tended to be classic (Thoreau, London, Faulkner, Hemingway, Jeffers, and Roethke). All reading was done independently by the students before they arrived in the Adirondacks for the ten-day instructional period in the field. Upon arrival, the students were given a preliminary examination on the reading. The testing was rather exact in order to determine the extent and quality of the reading. If a student failed this exam, he generally failed the course because it was, after all, an English course and there seemed little justification in awarding credit to a student who had not done the reading.

In addition, students were required to keep a daily journal during the ten days in the field, participate in evening seminars around the fire, and write a final exam, synthesizing one's readings with the wilderness experience. Groups consisted of 12 students and two staff, one of whom was an academic.

The rationale for the course was that direct experience with the wilderness would offer insight into wilderness literature. Consequently, most of the instruction occurred by exposing the students to as many facets of the wilderness as feasible. The curriculum involved a night walk, extensive bushwhacking, river fording, a 24-hour solo, and a bivouac on a peak—standard activities borrowed from the Outward Bound curriculum and modified somewhat by the propensities of the particular instructor. There was an attempt to attune the student to the wilderness—by taking him straight across beaver ponds, through the thickest spruce, jamming up waterfalls, navigating by the sun and stars. Erudite discussion followed experience; people grew close and community developed. In my welcoming speeches, I indicated that the student would have three encounters: with one's self, with others, and with nature. The benefits of this kind of program are well known generally, but not particularly appreciated by academics. Faculty generally concentrate on scholarship and view ancillary benefits as peripheral.

The English course I have described above was designed and controlled to protect the sanctity of academic credit. If students took the course for a lark, they failed it. Our academic instructors were well credentialed; the literature was above reproach. The brevity of ten days of instruction was compensated by the careful unraveling of the curriculum, the continuous exposure to the wilderness, and the intensification of time. Time carries different freight depending on how it is loaded. Academically, we appeared to have been successful, and garnered several substantial endorsements.

But all of this made little difference to most faculty. The course was suspect because it varied from the norm; it eschewed laboratories, libraries, and classrooms; it was a bird my colleagues could not identify and therefore was of questionable value. Many judged it adversely without ever discussing the details of the course with me. Most faculty who inspected our program approached it with a bias that prevailed in the end.

My ideal of a professor is one who approaches all subjects with an open mind, displays a careful and impartial intellect in making judgments, and refers only to evidence. A scholar's judgments are, ideally, controlled by knowledge. He is respected because he is envisioned as the model of intellectual discretion and careful judgment. We like to think of the scholar as the informed speaker as opposed to the irresponsible individual who says whatever he thinks with little respect for facts.

But if these were my expectations, I was often disappointed. And the reasons for this arise primarily from the type of individual who enters the profession and the type of training he receives. In 1977, I decided to try to expand the Wilderness Workshop into an institute at an independent college or university where I would be unencumbered by the red tape of a state university system. I sent a four-page prospectus to a number of colleges which yielded interviews at 20 institutions. The prospectus proposed using the wilderness English course I had established at SUNY as a model for other disciplines. During my interviews I observed a pattern. The administrators (deans and presidents) were intrigued and interested, partly because the proposed institute would enhance the image of the college and might help recruit students. In other words, quite aside from the educational merits of the program, they considered it in terms of how it might help the institution as a whole.

Faculty, on the other hand, were wary. I was regarded as an outsider who was peddling something and violating territory—someone who had an alternative mode of education which brought their own traditional method into question. My methodology was too radically different from what they knew. Besides, many of them confided, why introduce a radically new method of instruction if the standard methods (their own) were already working successfully? These appear to be good questions. However, the very questions created a polarity where none existed. The right questions to ask would have been: 1) Exactly what is your curriculum? 2) Does your program work? And if so, how do you know that it does? 3) What is its place alongside traditional curriculum?

For the faculty my presence quickly became a power issue. If the proposed program takes root here, what happens to our stake? The faculty invariably decided it was better and safer to say no, and do it with the usual excuse of "his proposal is not academically rigorous enough to justify credit." Professors are the ultimate arbiters of academic credit, and as long as they control credit, they can use that power to discourage change.

It would have been easier for me to have introduced the course from within—in fact, I did that at SUNY—but it is not as easy as one would think. I succeeded in my innovations at SUNY by scampering around the ends, never by plowing straight into the line. I worked quietly through the chairman and launched the first course without ever presenting the syllabus to the English Department. If I had followed due process I might not have succeeded—just as one does not get a job by applying to a personnel department. Faculty are rigorous guardians of academic credit to the degree that they function as obstructionists. They meet and discuss and modify proposals endlessly as if they sat on the Supreme Court. They take forever because they can afford to take forever. Their strength is in deliberation; their weakness is in action. In short, the great problem with faculty in respect to change is that 1) they do not think corporately and 2) there is no pressure on them to produce change. Placing an academic proposal before faculty is much like pushing it into a long dark tunnel. It will be months, perhaps years before that proposal reaches the other end—if it does not languish in the meantime. And if it does emerge, it is likely to have a very different shape.

There is another reason faculty inhibit change. Although I have said they do not think corporately, on curriculum matters they function corporately; thus they present the worst of both worlds. By not thinking corporately, they do not move with any particular speed toward creative change for the sake of their corporation (i.e., the college). But faculty are a democratic lot and so insist on all the processes of democracy. For instance if a professor wishes to propose an unorthodox course, it must pass through a legion of committees. Thus many new ideas are never launched because of the enervation the new idea faces as it staggers through a noble democracy which is really a burdensome bureaucracy. The academic senate puts creative ideas through a scrutiny that often requires the creator of the idea to prove his innocence, as it were, as he attempts to diverge from the status quo. Why should one bother? Why become a focus of controversy? Why even start the process if it will take a year or two to pass—if it does?

How to overcome this impasse? By reducing faculty power. Give the dean the power to allow a professor to try something new. Let us assume the dean is ideal: open minded yet of sound judgment. He or she is intelligent and secure enough to recognize promise and shrewd enough to winnow out the flaky from the sound. Let us also leave some power to our colleagues, for someone must review the success of a new course in order to insure academic integrity. So a small, high quality review committee (perhaps three members) should review the new course after it has been tried in order to determine the degree of success. The committee would then send its advisory report to the dean who would in turn consult with the course professor. The course would then be adjusted, continued as it was, or discontinued. Again, to avoid campus politics as much as possible, the dean would be empowered to make this decision. Bright ideas come from individuals, not from committees.

An example of excess faculty power comes to mind: During my attempt to establish an institute, a prestigious college in New York State expressed interest to the extent that my proposal received approval from the president, the dean, and the faculty academic affairs committee. The English Department was relatively small and ruled by three tenured professors, all of whom disagreed with my pedagogy. By refusing to approve the English course, they effectively barred the Institute. Their power seemed inordinant in this situation. One of the professors remarked that he felt he need know nothing of bears in order to teach Faulkner's "The Bear," and that my attempt to introduce real, furry bears into the curriculum would in no way enhance the reading of the story. I, for my part, felt he could indeed teach the story successfully without any particular knowledge of real bears. A story can be read and taught in many ways. I saw myself as allowing him his way but the privilege was not reciprocated. I was seen as violating established practice. Yet all who innovate violate established practice.

Consequently, faculty generally function as preservationists rather than an innovators, and tend to take a defensive position when confronted with change. The sort of individual who is drawn to the academic tradition partly explains this mentality. We tend to be egotistical, solitary, self-seeking, contentious, and verbal. We are cowed during our probationary periods as assistant professors, then often become insufferably arrogant, righteous and unaccountable once we have received tenure. Our loyalties are first to ourselves, second to our discipline, third to our academic grouping, and only last and rather vaguely to our institution. We are forever in an adversary relationship with the administration who are seen as Machiavellian, intent on depriving us of our rights and resources. These, of course, are our worst characteristics, but they are characteristics most of us, alas, recognize in our colleagues if not ourselves.

Professional resistance to change also reflects one's training, and can be seen analagously in other professions where, for instance, there is an inordinant reaction among M.D.'s toward chiropractic and acupuncture. The resistance is largely a reflection of American medical training rather than the official explanation that chiropractors, for instance, are misinformed, uneducated and dangerous. There may be instances of these charges but why eradicate the good with the bad? Training obviously has benefits where a student is taught to do something well. But training is also an indoctrination where in absorbing a certain tradition we come to set it above other methods which vary from our own. We come to believe what we are taught—whether it is a catechism or the Yale doctoral program in deconstruction of literary texts.

Academics fight for their doctrine as if it were a case of survival, and attempt to dominate if not destroy alternate schools of thought. If these schools persist, we refer to them condescendingly. We are like Christian sects, convinced that our sect reflects the True Word and all others are but faint, often errant facsimiles. When I studied analytic philosophy at Cornell, existentialism was not included in our courses because the analytic philosophers did not recognize existentialism. When I studied English at Northwestern for my M.A., I was told to symbol hunt in Blake's "Milton" even though I had little interest in symbols and might as well have been picking up eggs in a hen house. When I attempted to introduce biographical material about Thoreau into a reading of *Walden*, I was told that I was violating the principles of New Criticism, the prevailing doctrine at the time. And, I remember a geology class 25 years ago at Cornell where the professor gently ridiculed theorists who believed in continental drift. My conclusion from these experiences is that the possessors of knowledge are but temporary stewards, and most academic thinking tends to be conformist and dogmatic. Consequently, innovation must often break in from the outside and revamp.

A professor's training reflects a successive narrowing from the broad sweep of the B.A. to the rather more concentrated M.A. to the rigorous confines of the Ph.D., culminated by an elaborate dissertation on an obscure topic. This training does not encourage breadth of mind; rather it endorses extensive knowledge about limited subjects. It tightens us up; it narrows us; it specializes us. The MLA job list announcements cry out: "We need a specialist in late 19th century American literature." Whether you wish to be a specialist or not, you better become one.

Moreover, graduate training fragments the student. Matters of the mind become paramount; questions of the spirit are pushed aside as if they were beneath us; questions of the body are put aside altogether, left offhandedly to physical educators. The wilderness literature course I instructed deliberately engaged the whole person: mind, body, and spirit. The course's particular success arose from bringing all dimensions of an individual into play simultaneously. The student did not feel sated in one respect and starved in another. But my colleagues asked, "What's a nice literature course like you doing out in the woods?" They saw the blend not as enriching but as polluting—the purity of the academic enterprise was being compromised.

All this in spite of my pains at providing a substantial reading list, conventional testing methods, and enforced standards. It did not matter how well I executed the course; what disturbed my colleagues was *how* I was doing it. They concentrated on process rather than on results. This is not because my critics were perverse; it was because the course violated their sense of priopriety. What I was doing was not seemly. One Skidmore English professor sniffed, "I don't feel comfortable with the length of the instruction period," as if he were feeling clammy from too much rain. My colleagues enjoyed none of Thoreau's expansiveness: "Wherever I sat, there I might live, and the landscape radiated from me accordingly." Indeed, Thoreau remarked on another occasion, "Scholars have for the most part a diseased way of looking at the world." While some of my critics were simply pedestrian, others were yearning to do something creative but were hampered by the baggage of their doctoral pasts.

Training is after all training. There is a reward/punishment scheme which encourages obedience. When you enter the august company of doctoral candidates, your course professors do not say to you: Become all that you may. They impose themselves and their curriculum upon you so as to produce a reputable scholar. Some of us no doubt need such a shaping. I, for one, did, so I am carping against the very forces that gave me sufficient training to be a competent professor. There is a gain, but there is a loss. The gain is in our becoming proficient as scholars; the loss is in the confinements of indoctrination.

Beyond these considerations, change is doubtful in the 1980s because the industry of higher education is in a prolonged depression and so the cautious and conservative voices will dominate. Once we ride out the 80s, there may be a flush of new ideas in the 90s if the good times return. Our national economy will remain uncertain through the decade and hard times encourage the sterile vocationalism we see in the determined faces setting off for law school. Philosophy is seen as useless, a mere ornament. Chairmen search for faculty who are specialists; colleges seek administrators who are managers; industry seeks technical graduates. The world is quickly becoming programmed and it is all electronic.

Shall I close with no ray of hope, no possibilities for the creative spirit? Quite honestly I do not feel these are very creative times—at least in higher education. But for those who must be creative, as an old warrior I can give some advice. And this is exactly what one must become: a warrior. Indeed, not merely a warrior, but a general.

First ascertain the terrain. What is your landscape? Which way does the water run? In other words, analyze as precisely as you can where power lies within your institution. Next, consider who your proposed change will benefit, and analyze just why it will benefit these parties. Eventually when you approach these parties for support you will emphasize your innovation in those terms, just as an advertising man markets his Pepsi. Third, consider those individuals or factions likely to be your adversaries either by acts of commission or omission. Consider how to disarm them or steal around them. Be likeable. Then mount your campaign, subtly, ingeniously, delicately, insuring always that you are in control, that nothing unforeseen rears its ugly head. Soon all those who have a vested interest in your enterprise will become advocates of your innovation. If you assume all of your allies will help you along lines of their own self-interest, you will seldom miscalculate. A simple example will suffice. When I was having difficulties at SUNY with my immediate supervisor, the Director of Continuing Education, I approached the Dean of Graduate Studies who I knew was concerned about faltering graduate enrollment and suggested we add graduate courses to the Wilderness Workshop. He responded enthusiastically to this proposal. As Dean of Graduate Studies, he also supervised the Director of Continuing Education, and soon I was working closely with the Dean on establishing Workshop graduate courses, and my problems with Continuing Education dissipated.

The lesson is simple and stark. An innovator must be a skilled politician. In the late 60s and early 70s idealism and rhetoric were often enough to carry the day. Now, one must employ strategy and slip through the lines. Avoid due process wherever you can; it will only stall and perhaps quash you. Once your course is established, then reroute through due process to receive its blessing. (Seldom will a committee refuse to endorse a course that is functioning and successful.) Present your proposal as crucial to the survival of the college. Become friends with the administrators, and they will exert necessary leverage where needed on your behalf. Be prepared to be controversial and suffer from being different, and react to criticism graciously. Remember envy is often disguised admiration. Neutralize the enemy; protect your flanks. Remember warriors, even generals, sometimes die. Those who seek change become ready targets, but our culture only goes forward with the energy and vision of those who dare to go first.

PART THREE

Innovation in Very Large Universities

Editors' Introduction

The four chapters in this section describe a number of educational experiments in the context of the large research university. All of these experiments represented efforts to improve the quality of undergraduate education. Taken as a group these chapters raise serious questions about the ability of large universities to sustain educational alternatives.

Are there some features of the large university which are productive of educational experimentation? What is the capacity of the large university to nurture and sustain educational alternatives? What factors appear associated with their success or failure? Is there, as George Von der Muhll has previously suggested in his discussion of Santa Cruz, a "predictable trajectory of doom" for educational innovation? How do the conditions of the 1980's differ from those under which these educational alternatives were originally conceived?

Von Blum's chapter on his experiences with interdisciplinary programs at the University of California—Los Angeles, and University of California-Berkeley provides an excellent historical overview of some of the roots of the alternative college movement in the 1960's and early 1970's, and the historical, political, financial, and psychological differences between that period and the present. Von Blum points out that even in the best of circumstances educational alternatives will have a marginal existence in large universities simply because their priorities lie elsewhere. Nevertheless, there are certain persistent themes throughout these four chapters which convey a sense of the conditions which favor continuation.

For instance, Von Blum's more recent experience with interdisciplinary programs which bridge the professions implies an ongoing though changing role for interdisciplinary programs in the 1980's. Similarly, comments on hypothetical "Wednesday College" suggest a model for times in which students are more oriented towards careers and the professions. Knapp's proposal for combining the liberal and practical arts provides a possible rich agenda for the 1980's.

Hill's discussion of the Federated Learning Communities (FLC) at SUNY Stony Brook is important because this program has served as a generative model for similar programs at other institutions. The Federated Learning Community represents a fairly low cost educational alternative which builds upon the existing curricular and organizational structure of the traditional university.

The Goodrich program at the University of Nebraska-Omaha exemplifies a successful approach to serving traditionally by-passed students. Gillespie and Secret describe this program in some detail in terms of its underlying assumptions, its curricular approach, and its supportive services. This program has had substantial success in serving Omaha's low income, minority population. It represents an important model for providing educational opportunities to nontraditional students. The author's comments about admissions criteria and the importance of comprehensive services are particularly apt as the United States moves into the 1980's, a period in which well over half of the public school population will be nonwhite in many parts of the United States.

XIII. Marginality, Survival or Prosperity: Interdisciplinary Education in Large Research Universities—Berkeley and U.C.L.A.

by

PAUL VON BLUM

> Almost any proposal for major innovation in the universities today runs head on into the opposition of powerful vested interests. And the problem is compounded by the fact that all of us who have grown up in the academic world are skilled in identifying our vested interests with the Good, the True, and the Beautiful, so that an attack on them is by definition subversive.
>
> Nowhere can the operation of vested interests be more clearly seen than in the functioning of university departments. The average department holds on like grim death to its piece of intellectual terrain. It teaches its neophytes a jealous devotion to the boundaries of the field. It assesses the significance of intellectual questions by the extent to which they can be answered without going outside the sacred territory. Such vested interests effectively block most efforts to reform undergraduate education.
>
> —John Gardner
> No Easy Victories

John Gardner's depressing observations about the prospects for serious institutional change and educational reform were written in the mid-1960's, a time of enormous political ferment and educational experimentation in American colleges and universities. Since that time, there have been many impressive efforts at curricular change in American institutions of higher learning. Several schools have established and supported outstanding educational alternatives to the standard disciplinary fare,[1] while a few institutions such as Hampshire College and Evergreen State have totally eliminated traditional educational structures in favor of a total commitment to interdisciplinary education. The spirit and turmoil of the 60's doubtless have had some beneficial effects upon the course and direction of contemporary higher education. Many of today's innovations that seek more integrative approaches to knowledge and that explore the political, social, and ethical implications of academic work would never have been initiated without the agitation of the 60's and early 70's. At the same time, Gardner's gloomy remarks about the problems and prospects of academic change are still disturbingly relevant to most large, prestigious universities where research and graduate training are the dominant priorities.

The research-oriented multiversity has played an increasingly powerful role in American higher education since World War II.[2] The proliferation of extramural funding from government agencies, foundations, and corporations has had profound consequences for universities. It has strengthened research priorities and has contributed to the decline of undergraduate general education. It has also reinforced the hegemony of departments within the multiversity.

While many academics were delighted with a system that provided professional status and pecuniary rewards for narrow and often trivial research production, others realized that these priorities could result in widespread student dissatisfaction. Even before the events of the 1960's, they saw that universities were becoming increasingly blind to some major educational deficiencies.

President Clark Kerr of the University of California, for example, identified many of these educational problems in his book written revealingly only a few years before the student eruptions at Berkeley and elsewhere:

> [T]here are some problems still to be fully faced; and they are problems of consequence.
>
> One is the improvement of undergraduate instruction in the university. It will require the solution of many sub-problems: how to give adequate recognition to the teaching skill as well as to the research performance of the faculty; how to create a curriculum that serves the needs of the student as well as the research interests of the teacher; how to prepare the generalist as well as the specialist in an age of specialization. . . ; how to treat the individual student as a unique human being in the mass student body; . . . how to establish a range of contact between faculty and students broader

than the one-way route across the lectern or through the television screen; how to raise educational policy again to the forefront of faculty concerns.[3]

Events would shortly reveal that Dr. Kerr's concerns were largely theoretical and rhetorical. In the autumn of 1964, the Berkeley campus of the University of California exploded into a series of massive student protests unprecedented in the history of American higher education. The Free Speech Movement began initially as a response to a stupid and unconstitutional regulation that prohibited political advocacy at the entrance to the university. As the confrontation intensified, other fundamental issues affecting the character and quality of university life emerged as prominent features of the conflict on campus. In due course, many of these educational and political issues spread throughout the country and throughout much of the Western world.

At Berkeley, thousands of students began to focus on the educational inadequacies of modern university life. They questioned the impersonal character of teaching and campus administration, institutional complicity with the military, CIA, and other governmental agencies, exploitation of graduate students, unfair patterns of university governance, and indeed, the whole concept of the "multiversity." As important as any other issue was the comparatively low priority of undergraduate education at the University of California (and by implication at other large and prestigious institutions). Closely related was the growing consciousness that knowledge was being presented in absurdly fragmented packages and that the organization of learning into minute disciplines worked powerfully against the goal of a genuinely liberal education.

The FSM was the major catalyst for a more general national consideration of these complex and troubling problems. In the ensuing decade, there were hundreds of student demonstrations about a wide range of political, social, and educational issues. Racism and the growing escalation of the war in Vietnam, of course, were central to these conflicts. Still, the focal point of much of the activity was the movement for educational innovation and reform. The post-FSM era saw countless proposals for educational change and interdisciplinary alternatives to academic orthodoxy at large research universities. The era also generated scores of official commissions, investigations, and committees as well as a massive barrage of public rhetoric about the subject of improving higher education.

Some of this activity was instrumental in effecting serious change. The record in major research institutions, however, has been far more modest. Undergraduate education remains a relatively low priority while departmental domination in shaping institutional policies continues to be the norm. In many schools, the educational problems identified during the 60's remain unsolved; many, indeed, have been exacerbated during the past decade. All too often the results have been little more than the establishment of a few token programs and projects. Sadly, many of these are designed more to provide public relations gloss than to improve serious educational problems. In many universities since the 60's and early 70s', interdisciplinary programs have been created, permitted to endure for a few years, then phased out and replaced by new programs. Often the entire process is repeated. Meanwhile, little of permanent value remains, while hundreds of committed interdisciplinary teachers suffer additional insecurity in a depressing academic job market.

The University of California is an interesting case in which this phenomenon has occurred. As an institution, it epitomizes the enormous range of problems faced by academic innovators, especially those who seek to create and institutionalize interdisciplinary entities. For many years its international reputation has been predicated on the quality of its faculty's research and on its excellence as a center for graduate and professional training. In the years following the Free Speech Movement at Berkeley (and similar if somewhat less publicized eruptions at many of the other campuses), the entire institution came under severe attack by many students, some faculty, and certain members of the State Legislature and Board of Regents for failing to address its pressing educational problems. Critics argued persuasively that its research prestige, based as it was on narrow disciplinary accomplishments, often defeated the objective of a more integrative education for undergraduates.

In response to such pressures, University officials generated some actual curricular change as well as the usual commissions and reports. Many of the critics, however, maintained that most of these changes were mere window dressing, particularly at Berkeley. Two scholars who investigated this situation at Berkeley as part of a broader inquiry into the politics of educational innovation concurred:

> Berkeley is perhaps the prototype among American universities, of frenetic activity, grandiose planning, dramatic pronouncements, and virtually no change.[4]

A decade later, the University of California continues to be an excellent source and focus for an examination of the severe problems and limited prospects for interdisciplinary innovation at large and prestigious research universities. The multifaceted activities of the University of California have a powerful influence in scholarship and education throughout the entire world. The possibilities for serious educational reform in this institution therefore have significance far beyond the boundaries of its nine individual campuses. Clearly, of course, there are important differences among large research universities. Local conditions are always crucial and the presence or absence of faculty members and administrators with educational vision and strong leadership capabilities is a major variable in the long-term success of interdisciplinary innovations. The fortuities of time and place cannot be overemphasized.

Nevertheless, a careful assessment of both the broader barriers and opportunities within the University of California can have implications for similar institutions throughout the country. A useful approach to such an assessment involves an investigation into three currently existing interdisciplinary programs at Berkeley and UCLA, the two most powerful units within the University of California system. All three programs have been deemed educationally outstanding in repeated student evaluations. The Berkeley program, however, has been politically beleaguered and has been constantly faced with threats to its existence. The UCLA programs, conversely, appear to enjoy, at least for the present, some impressive institutional stability.

Using the Berkeley Division of Interdisciplinary and General Studies[6] and the UCLA Program in Medicine, Law and Human Values and the UCLA Freshman/Sophomore Professional School Seminar Program as comparative examples, it is possible to identify and analyze some major historical, political, financial, and psychological differences between the educational ferment of the 1960's and early 1970's and the present. The analysis of the three University of California cases can be used to draw more general conclusions about the prospects for interdisciplinary education in the essentially conservative world of research universities.

The division of Interdisciplinary and General Studies (DIGS) was created in the wake of the Free Speech Movement. It was one of the results of the numerous reports on improving undergraduate education at Berkeley arising out of the turmoil of the era. Although it continues to survive in a diluted and marginal fashion, it is a clear and dramatic example of a quality educational program that could never receive full institutional support. Created originally by the College of Letters and Science in 1969, its original charge was to be a place for courses that could not find a home in any one department and for field majors in humanities, natural science, and social science. In its first years it underwent numerous transformations. There were several changes among the junior faculty and in due course the natural science field major was eliminated. Shortly thereafter, the original emphasis on classical knowledge was reduced and a relatively stable group of faculty members emerged.

Almost from its inception, the social science field major established itself as the dominant unit within the broader Division of Interdisciplinary and General Studies. Its faculty and its particular educational programs soon became the focus of significant controversy at Berkeley. Operating with no more than four or five instructors, the major attracted over 300 students, each of whom devised an individual program combining core courses in social science theory and methodology, historical courses from the ancient and modern eras, and a personal area of concentration that cut across traditional disciplinary lines. With careful and detailed assistance from faculty advisors, students combined courses in the program itself with offerings from throughout the College of Letters and Science.

DIGS social science students were drawn from a wide diversity of backgrounds. Despite the widespread impression among the faculty that DIGS constituted a ghetto for marginal students seeking an easy degree,[7] the level of student performance was high, even by Berkeley standards. Indeed, a significant percentage of DIGS students entered the program precisely because they wanted the challenge of taking personal responsibility for the course and direction of their own educations. Furthermore, a large percentage of social science majors subsequently entered graduate and professional school, where many compiled exceptional records.

From the start, DIGS was perceived as encouraging academic superficiality and contributing to a general decline of intellectual standards. It is worth mentioning here that such accusations by orthodox academics have been frequent in the recent American history of educational experimentation. It is also worth noting that while the allegations against nontraditional colleagues have sometimes been true, they are often the defensive response of the members of a guild, mindful of their own interests and fearful of change and disorder. At Berkeley, the accusations against DIGS were omnipresent. They were expressed in public and even more often in the private conversations in dining rooms, office corridors, and social gatherings that, despite official denials, have enormous consequences for academic policy in all colleges and universities. Without doubt, DIGS had a "bad press" on the Berkeley campus and only a handful of prestigious regular faculty members spoke publicly or privately in its defense. Subsequent analysis reveals that a convergence of historical, political, and psychological realities made this condition virtually inevitable.

Notwithstanding, closer scrutiny of the program in a series of official inquiries and reviews indicated the existence of an enormous gap between the public image and the educational reality. Faculty review committees determined that DIGS was responsible for some outstanding educational contributions at Berkeley. The specific comments of one of the review committees are particularly revealing both about the gap itself and about the broader character of academic life in major American research universities:

> [T]hanks to the devoted service, fine teaching, and superb advising of its Chairman, faculty, and staff, it can now proudly make the claim that it has survived. And it has done something more than survived; it has established its credentials as a serious academic enterprise . . . DIGS has been the prey of rumors of its immediate demise, and even if the reports of its ill health have been erronious and ill-founded, the suspicion continues to exist the DIGS is not long for this academic world.[8]

The committee concluded by offering a variety of recommendations that would, if implemented, have strengthened this form of interdisciplinary education at Berkeley. The report affirmed vigorously that DIGS had earned a place as a permanent part of the continuing undergraduate program on the Berkeley campus. It argued that the program should not be perceived as a pious extra by faculty members who were totally immersed in their departments. It urged the university to support the program as part of a serious commitment to educational pluralism. Most important, it recommended the allocation of modest permanent resources in order to ensure programmatic stability and continuity:

> A university as great and varied as this should have a place for a small number of ladder appointments devoted to DIGS. . .[9]

DIGS faculty and students were understandably elated when their report was presented. For the first time, there was optimism that the program would survive and that its faculty would receive some formal institutional support for its educational accomplishments. These hopes were quickly dashed. In spite of its academic successes and its increasing reputation beyond the Berkeley campus for its interdisciplinary innovations, the program remained in serious political trouble.

The College of Letters and Science declined to provide any permanent resources, a major blow to the highly vulnerable junior faculty in the program. Regardless of their teaching and other academic achievements, neither tenure nor any other form of recognition was made available.

Repeated attempts to convince the administration to implement the recommendations of the review committee proved fruitless. The controversy soon broadened and the atmosphere became tense and unpleasant. Political lines were drawn, with militant students, organized parents, and sympathetic Regents and State Legislators on one side and a resistant administration spearheaded by a strong and hostile Dean on the other.

The sustained political activities of DIGS supporters probably served to preserve its existence if not its essence. At present, its faculty are all part-time appointees who must be reappointed yearly. Its enrollment has declined and reports suggest that the character and quality of its students have changed in negative ways.

While it is tempting—especially for participants who expanded time and emotional energy in constructing and defending the Division of Interdisciplinary and General Studies—to bemoan the fate of a valuable interdisciplinary program, it is more important to explore the underlying reasons for its difficulties at Berkeley. The results of such analysis can reveal much about the recent history of higher education and can be useful to educational innovators and reformers who wish to avoid similar problems in comparable universities.

The major factors in the precarious marginality of DIGS are historical, political, psychological, and institutional. These variables transcend the important but local vicissitudes of power on the Berkeley campus. The failure of DIGS to establish a permanent institutional foothold is a function of its perceived association with 60's radicalism; its use of confrontation tactics; its threatening implications for the emotions of orthodox scholars; its status as a degree-granting unit relying on its own faculty; and the widespread indifference of prestigious research universities in the 60's and early 70's towards enrollment and student satisfaction.

From the beginning, the Division of Interdisciplinary and General Studies was tainted by an association with the political ferment at Berkeley and elsewhere during the 1960's. Ironically, its actual educational activities were surprisingly conservative, with a strong emphasis on historical background, a modest integration of traditional academic fields, and a heavy focus on written and oral communication. Its premises were not unlike those propounded by Robert Hutchins, and its courses used Plato even more than Marx. Nevertheless, the program would never have been created had Berkeley not erupted a few years earlier.

It is important to emphasize that an extremely large percentage of faculty members at Berkeley and elsewhere found the events of the 60's to be traumatic. Accustomed to the tranquility of the scholarly calling, these men and women saw those events as an attack on academic order and thus as a frontal assault on their most intimate personal values. For many, the 60's were nothing short of a major life crisis.

Many Berkeley opponents of the DIGS innovations were unable to separate educational experimentation from the broader political radicalism. The emotional consequences of many years of building occupations, tear gas, street fighting, mass arrests, and extreme polarization of opinion were enormous. Antagonists of DIGS often saw it in the same mold as those who would burn buildings and destroy academic life. While this attitude was uncritical and often astonishingly simplistic, it had immense significance for the creation of a hostile campus attitude toward academic experimentation in general. This phenomenon, of course, was hardly confined to the University of California at Berkeley.

The specific Berkeley situation was exacerbated because most of the DIGS social science instructors had themselves been graduate student supporters and participants in major campus protests such as the FSM. Some continued their commitments to broader social change, even though this was far from their daily concerns as interdisciplinary university teachers. Furthermore, the DIGS controversies themselves, while never violent, were frequently characterized by forceful and articulate student advocacy. Clearly, any form of student protest reminded people of earlier violent demonstrations. In a basic way, therefore, all such advocacy on behalf of DIGS was doomed to failure because of the powerfully negative effects of the entire turbulent decade.

Psychological factors in general are immensely important in assessing the problems and prospects of academic innovation. At prestigious research universities, many faculty members appear unusually defensive about their academic specializations and research. They often seem threatened by educational activities that depart from their own training and disciplinary outlook. Underlying John Gardner's pessimistic prognosis for educational change are some hard truths about the attitudes and emotions of departmentally-bound professors. These personality variables played a powerful role at Berkeley and continue to have enormous political significance throughout higher education.

Intellectual synthesis and interdisciplinary education apparently are disconcerting enterprises to large numbers of research-oriented academics. Human beings in general view anything different and unorthodox with suspicion. The identities of many university professors revolve heavily around their academic specializations. Like most professional people, they acquire a strong emotional interest in their work. Similarly, they develop strategies, often unconsciously, to rationalize their basic activities. A concomitant effect is the development of defensive attitudes towards those whose educational and scholarly outlooks proceed on different assumptions.

The implications of these natural processes are sometimes striking. At large research universities, status and professional recognition depend on expertise and publication in specific academic fields. In practice, this means production in relatively narrow sub-areas of knowledge. Scholars already trained as graduate students in a culture of extreme specialization adapt easily to this norm. Such powerful specialization is quickly internalized, with significant emotional consequences. For many academics, greater academic breadth is outside their ken, and therefore subject to *a priori* rejection.

The occasional harsh verbal attacks by traditional scholars on interdisciplinary colleagues are reflections of these emotional consequences. These attacks sometimes mask feelings of personal inadequacy. Allegations of complicity in reducing academic standards may indeed be attempts to convince themselves of the value of their own intellectual contributions. While psychological variables cannot explain the totality of faculty hostility to interdisciplinary education, their importance should not be ignored.

One other dimension of this scheme of explanation is worth elaboration. In major research universities, faculty members are selected among persons who are often more comfortable in the library or laboratory than they are in personal interactions—especially with undergraduate students. At Berkeley and similar institutions, large numbers of students often report difficulties in communicating with such professors, particularly if the subject matter transcends specific course content. The major and overriding strength of the DIGS social science program was its student-centered perspective. Formal evaluations of the program repeatedly noted that students felt extremely comfortable in talking with DIGS faculty. This close student-faculty relationship clearly evoked hostility among members of the traditional faculty. A harsh but obvious explanation is that some persons resented a form of personal education of which they were apparently incapable.

A variety of institutional factors also contributed to the beleagured status of DIGS at Berkeley. An examination of these factors is useful in determining some significant historical differences between the 60's and early 70's and the present. One important variable was that during much of the DIGS controversies, a relatively stable enrollment base existed. This reality, in turn, had a powerful influence on general campus attitudes, including those about educational innovations. Specifically, this meant that university officials were confident that they would always have substantial numbers of students. Thus, they were confident of a relatively secure funding base. There was—and is—a strong foundation for such attitudes. Regardless of demographic changes in the nation as a whole, Berkeley always receives applications from many thousands of college-age men and women. The very prestige of the Berkeley name encouraged officials to believe that they could avoid the catastrophic implications of declining enrollment for higher education generally.

Such attitudes inevitably influence campus policies and priorities. At Berkeley during the 60's and much of the 70's, there was little concern about retaining students. Similarly, there was no systematic institutional commitment to ensure student satisfaction with the quality of undergraduate education. Confident that dissatisfied students could and would be replaced by other students, the university showed general indifference in this realm. The consequences for DIGS were powerful and negative. Arguments about a cost-effective program generating widespread student satisfaction fell on deaf ears. Conversly, the dissatisfaction of DIGS students in response to official hostility to the program had little impact under the circumstances. The view was that Berkeley would always attract first-rate students and that the unhappiness of a few hundred students in a marginal program could be easily ignored or absorbed with minimal trauma.

Another significant institutional factor ensuring the marginality of the DIGS social science field major was its degree-granting status. Students completing the major were awarded the B.A. in social science. Although DIGS students might otherwise have selected majors in such traditional disciplines as political science, history, sociology, economics, and psychology if the field major had not existed, there is no evidence to suggest that they eroded enrollment figures in these departments in any material sense. Once again, the existence of a degree-granting interdisciplinary interloper seemed to have immense emotional significance for orthodox academics at Berkeley.

That DIGS could award bachelors degrees from the University of California apparently seemed, in the minds of many, to confer an unacceptable status and legitimacy to the program. In addition, it seemed to place it in direct competition with traditional departments, an image it sought unsuccessfully to avoid. It is significant to note too that the program has never had a graduate component and therefore no specific mandate to conduct research. Its responsibility instead was nothing more—and nothing less—than the improvement of undergraduate education. In a research university like Berkeley, only educational activity closely associated with research is perceived as fully respectable. The existence of a uniquely undergraduate program offering Berkeley degrees, therefore, was untenable to many faculty members and administrators.

A closely related factor underlying the precariousness of DIGS was its almost exclusive reliance on its own faculty. Most of its courses and almost all of its advising were done by men and women with no formal connections or affiliations with regular social science departments on campus. This further exacerbated the estrangement of DIGS from the mainstream of academic life. Unfortunately, however, recruitment of regular faculty into DIGS was almost impossible. Since rewards and prestige were derived through research within specific disciplines, there was little incentive for faculty members to participate in a politically suspect interdisciplinary program.

At Berkeley, it was often said that interdisciplinary efforts needed to be rooted in specific academic disciplines. Indeed, opponents of innovation turned this into an almost ritual refrain. Although the content of this refrain was questionable, its political implications were clear. More participation from sympathetic senior members of regular departments would have strengthened DIGS' case on the Berkeley campus. The severe imbalance of research versus educational priorities and the strong disincentives against association with all such programs combined to eliminate that potential.

The climate for interdisciplinary experimentation at the Los Angeles campus of the University of California is an interesting contrast to the Berkeley experience. While UCLA shares the research orientation of its Berkeley counterpart, certain interdisciplinary innovations have been able to survive and, in a limited sense, even prosper. Noticeably absent in the recent past has been the overriding institutional hostility encountered by DIGS. It is useful to examine why such differences exist and to assess their significance for educational change more generally in comparable institutions.

A major specific variable at the moment is that there are persons with greater educational vision in positions of leadership at UCLA. Partly this is fortuitious; partly it is itself a function of some significant historical, demographic, and psychological differences between the mid-1960's and the present. These differences have combined to make UCLA a more hospitable setting for certain kinds of carefully constructed educational alternatives.

Two UCLA examples give rise to some cautious optimism in this domain. The UCLA Program in Medicine, Law, and Human Values and the Freshman/Sophomore Professional School Seminar Program are limited enterprises that have been well regarded on campus for approximately five years. Both programs operate out of the same office and many of the same personnel play important roles in both. The first program was designed in order to engage the attention of members of the professions, professional school students, undergraduates, and the general public in legal and ethical issues in health care. The major objective is to inquire into the underlying issues of value found in such controversial topics as abortion, genetic screening and counseling, DNA research, the use of placebos, euthanasia, informed consent, and many related problems. The program seeks to identify the perspectives of the major actors in these controversies—doctors, nurses, lawyers, ethicists, the clergy, and so forth. An important goal is to analyze and illuminate the conflicting values and positions and to promote a context for responsible value clarification and decision making in both individual cases and broader public policy areas.

These ends are accomplished through a variety of mechanisms, all of which necessarily cut across the traditional disciplines of contemporary academic life. In addition to public forums, conferences, research projects, and bioethics seminars in the schools of Medicine and Law, program faculty teach a variety of undergraduate courses existing outside of the regular campus departments. The major feature of the undergraduate program is a core course entitled "Medicine, Law and Society." The program also offers several seminars for small groups of students who have completed the core course. Invited faculty from professional schools and Letters and Science as well as program faculty have offered courses on such topics as Constitutional Issues in Health Care; Ethical Issues in Human Experimentation; The Language of Suicide in Literature; Law, Ethics, and the Mental Health System, and many others.

The program is highly respected at UCLA and elsewhere for its academic stature and accomplishments. Program personnel are regularly invited to regional and national conferences and to serve in various consultant and advisory capacities. Educationally, Medicine, Law and Human Values courses are consistently rated highly, with many students reporting that the courses have permanently altered their understanding of the intimate relationships between scientific and human values and of the complexities entering into decision-making in medicine and health care.

The other UCLA innovation, the Freshman/Sophomore Professional School Seminar Program, is more specifically directed to improvement in undergraduate education. It is a small, high quality effort designed to meet a variety of instructional needs particularly of lower division students. Drawing on the resources of UCLA's 11 professional schools, faculty members offer seminars that provide the opportunity to learn about the nature of professional work and about the relationships between scholarship, basic research, social problems, and legal and ethical standards of professional life. Seminars are designed to enable students from all fields to understand more fully how professionals' values affect society and the economy. Enrollment in the seminars is generally limited to 15 students in order to provide the opportunity for close contact with faculty and fellow students—an urgent necessity on an enormous campus of 30,000 students.

The courses themselves are not small-scale or diluted versions of professional education and training. Neither are they intended to be vocational or pre-professional in nature. Rather, they are broad, interdisciplinary efforts that deal with social, political or ethical implications of various features of professional practice. Faculty members combine intellectual breadth and theory with their experiences as practitioners and professional educators.

During the past five years, the program has offered courses such as the Ethics, Art and Science of Medicine; Law, Literature, and Politics; Interpersonal Violence in America Today; Information, Computers and Society: The Social Impact of Computerization; Social Change and Social Welfare; Engineering: Its Role and Function in Society; and numerous other topics that cross professional and disciplinary boundaries. The seminars are taken by students on an elective basis. There is no set of core offerings. Instead, topics vary from term to term and year to year. Some faculty members teach regularly in the program while others offer courses on a one-time only basis. The program as a whole is thus a shifting series of interdisciplinary courses oriented to some general thematic concerns.

Like the Program in Medicine, Law, and Human Values, this effort is well regarded at UCLA. In formal faculty evaluations, the Freshman-/Sophomore Professional School Seminar Program has been favorably reviewed. Students show unusual enthusiasm for both the quality of instruction and for the breadth and diversity of the seminar topics. Furthermore, program faculty, professional school deans, and some influential administrators have expressed considerable satisfaction about this innovative educational arrangement.

Although neither UCLA program is fully and permanently institutionalized, the prospects for long-term survival in some form are good. This is of course a striking contrast to the example of DIGS at Berkeley. There are several reasons for these different conditions at the two most powerful and prestigious campuses of the University of California.

Both UCLA programs operate without many of the burdens and constraints faced by DIGS. Perhaps above all, the UCLA efforts have no connection whatever with the political disorder of the 1960's. They were not created in response to political pressures emanating from the events of that era. That the Program in Medicine, Law, and Human Values and the Freshman/Sophomore Professional School Seminar Program are not even remotely perceived as associated with 60's agitation makes it much easier to survive among numerous academics for whom the entire 60's were deeply traumatic. The irony is that perceived separation from the specific historical conditions that made such educational experimentation possible is a dominant variable in the institutional standing of given innovations.

An additional advantage for the Program in Medicine, Law, and Human Values is that an entire field of bioethics has emerged during the 1970's,[10] adding further legitimacy to the various public and campus features of the program. The proliferation of academically rigorous enterprises in this area engenders a more receptive environment for specific programs on individual campuses. Once again, there is virtually no association between the field of medical ethics and the violent disorders that dominated university life only a few years before.

Finally, few of the personnel involved in either UCLA program are identified in any major sense with 60's activism. And since neither program has had to engage in a campus struggle for survival, there has been no rancorous activity or student-based confrontations that could evoke the fears generated by the earlier militancy. One other distinction is significant in this domain. While UCLA had its share of civil disorder, it was rarely as shattering as that of its sister campus in Berkeley. The consequence is that while deeply ingrained fears and memories of the 60's exist at UCLA, they are not quite as traumatic as they are at Berkeley.

Although both UCLA educational programs have the advantage of no direct association with political and social radicalism, they must still operate in a psychological context similar to that of Berkeley and comparable research institutions. The same types of narrowly based researchers are selected to join the UCLA faculty. Research priorities dominate the campus, as they do throughout the entire University of California system. Despite the presence of some historical and institutional variables more encouraging to educational innovation, interdisciplinary activity still carries a heavier burden of proof than more orthodox academic enterprises. It still evokes suspicion among traditional academics, if somewhat less openly than before, certainly in the more private councils of daily academic life. This condition is likely to persist as long as the patterns of graduate instruction and faculty selection remain the same. John Gardner's distressing observations, once again, are rooted in the basic fabric of contemporary academic existence.

Certain fiscal and demographic realities, either not present or not properly comprehended a decade ago, now operate to keep some of the underlying psychological factors in modest check. The effect is to encourage the survival of various interdisciplinary innovations at UCLA. It is well known that financial conditions have changed drastically since the prosperity of the 1950's and 1960's. Even at prestigious universities, there is considerable anxiety about the decline of various funding sources. Reduced support has generated severe cutbacks in campus programs and projects. It has also generated considerable concern about student enrollment and retention, major variables in future competition for scarce and declining resources.

For all its international stature and recognition, UCLA still labors somewhat in the shadow of Berkeley. This awkward self-image imposes some limits to its generally vigorous self-confidence. An intriguing consequence is that it appears to be far more concerned about its capacity to attract students in the future and to retain these students, many of whom are likely to come from diverse cultural and ethnic backgrounds and to have some serious academic deficiencies at the time of matriculation. Indeed, UCLA officials seem acutely aware of demographic realities affecting higher education now and in the future.[11] Enrollment and retention are thus far more important than they were even a few years ago, because nothing less than institutional survival in the first rank is at stake.

This new consciousness has significant implications for both traditional and innovative educational programs. The basic irony is that bad times may promote a more favorable climate for educational efforts generally. The desire to retain students elevates the importance of student satisfaction. When students express approval and enthusiasm for specific academic programs, they cannot be as easily dismissed or ignored as they had earlier been, even during the era of militant agitation. Greater institutional attention to students works to the advantage of regular and interdisciplinary units that evoke positive student response.

At UCLA, both the Program in Medicine, Law and Human Values and the Freshman/Sophomore Professional School Seminar Program do well in this context. Both draw impressive numbers of students given the limited character of their offerings and the limited structure of a seminar format. More important, they have an enviable and impressive level of consumer satisfaction, a factor that should be advantageous in future determinations about resource allocation and programmatic survival.

The crisis in enrollment and the resultant concern about retaining students has had some beneficial consequences for large research universities throughout the United States. It has forced them to realize that they have educational as well as research responsibilities and that research too will deteriorate on a declining base of enrollment. The present crisis in higher education has been valuable in forcing universities to pay more attention to bridging the serious gap between instructional rhetoric and reality. External political, demographic, and economic pressures have therefore ironically been more important than the earlier agitation in propelling research-oriented universities in progressive directions. It is wise, however, to realize that movement in this direction is often grudging, and that good results may occur in the absence of good motives.

The two UCLA programs also operate without some specific disadvantages faced by the DIGS social science major at Berkeley. Neither UCLA effort offers degrees. Their instructional contributions consist entirely of optional, elective courses for students who typically major in traditional disciplines. Neither the Program in Medicine, Law and Human Values, nor the Freshman/Sophomore Professional School Seminar Program draws students away from established departments. Equally important, neither is even remotely perceived as a competitive element on campus.

The psychological and political ramifications of this arrangement are as positive at UCLA as the opposite situation has been at Berkeley. The UCLA programs are both in fact and in popular perception an adjunct to the primary educational operations on campus. In large research universities, an adjunct relationship is far more acceptable. It is less threatening to orthodox academics and easier to support by sympathetic administrators. The political and emotional advantages are underscored even further when program personnel themselves proclaim their adjunct role in public and in the decision-making councils of academic life.

A closely related institutional factor lending political support to both programs at UCLA is that they make extensive use of faculty members from traditional schools and departments. This appears to be a determinative variable in the power realities confronting academics seeking to initiate and sustain interdisciplinary educational programs. The conditions at UCLA provide some advantages in this area that have never existed for DIGS at Berkeley. For example, participation by regular faculty in Medicine, Law, and Human Values provides unusual opportunities for entry into an emerging, exciting field of inquiry. Significantly, the domain of bioethics lends itself well to research and publication possibilities.

There is thus a strong incentive for involvement of regular faculty along lines that reinforce traditional values and priorities in a research institution.

In the Professional School Seminar Program, there is much less opportunity for personal research. Nevertheless, participation in the program has been seen by contributing faculty as a refreshing contrast to their traditional work with professional school students. Furthermore, since some of the most exceptional UCLA undergraduates enroll in these seminars, the teaching experience promises and delivers considerable personal gratification.

Educationally and epistemologically, it should make little difference whether faculty members in interdisciplinary programs are drawn from regular academic units or whether they are persons for whom integrative education is a full time responsibility. What should matter is their competence and rigor. Politically, however, it makes a crucial difference in conservative research universities. It is apparently the only way to establish connections with other campus constituencies and to achieve a basis of support through well-placed protagonists in established departments.

The comparative examples of DIGS at Berkeley and the Program in Medicine, Law and Human Values and the Freshman/Sophomore Professional School Seminar Program at UCLA provide powerful insights into the problems and prospects for interdisciplinary innovations at the Universtiy of California and comparable American institutions. What the comparison suggests most strongly is that academic quality and educational excellence are far from adequate in ensuring the survival of such educational programs. In its essence, the large research university is an awkward and generally inhospitable place for undergraduate interdisciplinary experiments. The reason simply is that priorities lie elsewhere. It is possible in America to establish a Hampshire College or an Evergreen State, and thus create an environment totally conducive to the interdisciplinary investigation. It is even possible to establish specific interdisciplinary programs in many research universities throughout the country. At places like Berkeley and UCLA, however, it is possible to initiate and sustain such programs only at the periphery of the dominant operations. The blunt reality is that to a greater or lesser extent, interdisciplinary education will remain a marginal concern at the most prestigious large institutions.

Marginality, however, has many dimensions, some favorable, and some catastrophic. It can mean different things in different places, as the Berkeley and UCLA examples reveal. It can range from precarious existence and debilitating struggles to quiet and largely unbothered survival.

Certainly, the comparative California examples provide some valuable lessons on how to achieve the kind of positive marginality that best ensures the avoidance of serious institutional conflict.

There are several strategies that can be employed to effect survival or even modest prosperity within a marginal framework. Above all, it is essential to maintain the highest standards of academic quality. This is a prerequisite to any kind of survival and, in any case, a poor or mediocre interdisciplinary program has no business surviving. Moreover, if interdisciplinary educational programs are to endure nationally in significant ways, it is equally essential for their quality to match or exceed that of more orthodox educational efforts. Moreover, a commitment to the highest standards is strategically desirable because it generates the kind of student satisfaction that is valuable in an era of enrollment and retention consciousness.

Beyond that, it is important to separate these programs from the agitation and turmoil of the 1960's. Even though this era was instrumental in creating the conditions for educational change, its widespread perception as a tragic interlude in the life of American higher education has powerful political consequences. This disagreeable reality must be carefully considered in constructing rhetorical and institutional strategies within prestigious research universities.

The lessons of Berkeley and UCLA also suggest that more secure marginality is facilitated when steps are taken to make interdisciplinary programs complementary rather than competitive. The major variables in accomplishing this objective consist of making extensive use of traditional faculty and, perhaps somewhat less important, refraining from offering university degrees. Low visibility and repeated assurances of modest ambition are additional expedients in the psychological and political context of major research universities. Finally, it is useful to reassure traditional faculty and administrators that research priorities are properly dominant and that interdisciplinary education is merely a small part of a pluralistic whole.

These strategies clearly elevate the probabilities that some innovations can survive and even flourish in large research settings. There is a question, however, that should not be avoided: Is it worth it?

In one sense, there are only deeply personal answers to this question. Those who have spent considerable time and effort in working for educatonal change in large universities know well that the personal costs can be high. It is not easy to determine whether limited results and marginal status justify the personal price. There is immense frustration in constantly explaining and justifying interdisciplinary education to university officials and review committees whose perspectives are narrow and deparmentally based. This frustration is compounded when the identical process must be repeated with new officials and new committees.

It is equally disconcerting to exist in an institutional setting as a second-class citizen. It is no secret to note that powerful status hierarchies prevail in America's prestigious research universities. Academics choosing to do interdisciplinary educational work often evoke attitudes ranging from extreme contempt and hostility to patronizing amusement. All too often, their efforts are dismissed on the ground that they are only pursued in order to compensate for research inadequacies.

To compound this unpleasantness, it is often tactically advantageous to reinforce the marginality of interdisciplinary education through calculated and repeated verbal assurances of modest ambition, adjunct status, and research dominance. Constant pandering to political authority is unhealthy and debilitating. Once again, the determination of whether such cost is acceptable is intensely personal.

For interdisciplinary educators sympathetic to the social and political ferment of the 60's and early 70's, it is especially distasteful to maintain silence or even disavow such sympathy in favor of political expediency. Regrettably, a still dominant view in major universities is that the 60's were a fashionable, irrational, and irresponsible aberration now best forgotten. Many academics involved in interdisciplinary enterprises see that period instead as a series of profound events in recent U.S. history. They find it emotionally distressing and intellectually illegitimate to disassociate their present educational activities from the moral sources of their professional commitments.

Even "successfully" established marginal programs can generate frustrations for interdisciplinary teachers. Programs that offer little more than a series of elective interdisciplinary courses can scarcely provide the satisfactions available from more comprehensive educational programs. These latter efforts encourage greater opportunities for sustained contact with students. They promote more advising, more intensive intellectual collaboration, more possibilities for social interaction, and, indeed, more reciprocal commitments from student populations. Such pervasive involvement in the educational lives of students is almost intrinsically impossible in limited, adjunct enterprises that merely supplement traditional educational activities in large universities. To eschew, for political or other reasons, the establishment of degree-granting interdisciplinary entities means also to eschew the fullest range of professional fulfillment.

A strong burn-out factor exists among interdisciplinary academics seeking institutional recognition and legitimacy in prestigious research universities. There is no paucity of embittered, emotionally scarred men and women who have abandoned their commitments to educational change as a result of corrosive institutional struggles. Academic strife is as petty and vicious as any other strife in employment relationships—and perhaps even more so. To have been victimized by academic brutality can have tragic consequences for personal and family as well as professional life. The answer to the question of whether it is worth it is of necessity ambiguous. Those who undertake the responsibility of reforming research universities should have strong personalities, thick skins, a high tolerance for frustration, a good sense of humor, a reliable personal support network, and an abiding belief in the tragic life as exemplified in the figure of Sisyphus.

Fifty years ago, the Spanish philosopher Jośe Ortega y Gasset delivered a remarkable series of lectures at the University of Madrid on the proper role and structure of higher education. He combined trenchant criticism of existing priorities with a passionate call for reform. His brilliant critique of narrowness and intellectual fragmentation anticipated the similar indictment of more than a generation later. Responding to the pervasive trivialization of knowledge and of learning, Ortega urged a renewal of an older, yet more progressive tradition of intellectual life:

> From all quarters the need presses upon us for a new integration of knowledge, which today lies in pieces scattered over the world. But the labor of this undertaking is enormous . . .[12]

His proposal to accomplish this objective was the creation of a radical mode of university organization:

> Personally, I should make a Faculty of Culture the nucleus of the university and of the whole higher learning . . . The need to create sound synthesis and systemization of knowledge, to be taught in the 'Faculty of Culture', will call out a kind of scientific genius which hitherto has existed only as an aberration: The genius for integration. Of necessity, this means specialization, as all creative effort inevitably does; but this time, the man will be specializing in the construction of the whole . . . Men endowed with this genius come nearer being good professors than those submerged in their research. One of the evils . . . has been the awarding of professorships in keeping with the mania of the times, to research workers who . . . regard their teaching as time stolen away from their work in the laboratory or the archives.[13]

This noble ideal remains almost hopelessly utopian. Ortega's interdisciplinary Faculty of Culture will scarcely replace the existing arrangements at Harvard or Yale, or Michigan or Wisconsin, or Berkeley or UCLA. But the extent to which his broader ideals can be implemented through a steady infusion of integrative programs into the curricula of these influential institutions will have much to say about the direction of higher education and of society for the remainder of the 20th century and beyond.

NOTES

1. See William V. Mayville, *Interdisciplinarity: The Mutable Paradigm* (Washington: American Association for Higher Education, 1978) for a useful guide to existing programs in the United States.
2. The best description of (and apology for) this model is Clark Kerr's *The Uses of the University*, written in 1963.
3. Clark Kerr, *The Uses of the University* (Cambridge: Harvard University Press, 1963), pp. 118–119.
4. Joseph Fashing and Steven Deutsch, *Academics in Retreat*, (Albuquerque: University of New Mexico Press, 1971), p. 33.
5. Some participants in these programs prefer to use "multidisciplinary" or "transdiscipl-nary." Debates on the proper terminology have been conducted for many years among academics seeking to transcend traditional disciplinary education and scholarship. For some, such debates are crucial epistemological problems. For others, such debates are frustrating and fruitless. This issue, however, is beyond the scope of the present paper.
6. This unit is now known as the Division of Special Programs, a change imposed during the height of the campus controversy surrounding its struggles for institutional permanence. The earlier designation will be used in the present text.
7. The impression was investigated and dismissed in an official evaluation of the program. See the Report of the Committee on Academic Program in DIGS Field Majors in Humanities and Social Science, University of California, Berkeley, June 3, 1975, p. 3.
8. Report presented to the Executive Committee of the College of Letters and Science by the Advisory Committee to the Chairman of DIGS, University of California, Berkeley, 1976, p. 1.
9. *Ibid*., p. 3.
10. For a comprehensive directory of programs and courses in this field, see the *EVIST Resource Directory*, published by the Office of Science Education of the American Association for the Advancement of Science, 1978.
11. This awareness is reflected effectively in *The Report of the Chancellor's Conference on Undergraduate Education in the 1980's*, prepared by the Office of Undergraduate Affairs, University of California, Los Angeles.
12. José Ortega y Gasset, *Mission of the University* (New York: Norton, 1966), p. 79.
13. *Ibid*., pp. 75–81.

XIV. Embracing and Transcending the World of Work: An Image for the 1980's*

by

ROBERT KNAPP

In considering the future of interdisciplinary education, it is as important to take stock of possible institutional forms it can take as to work on the general need and rationale for interdisciplinary work. Other papers in this collection point out how deeply imbedded the standard disciplines are in colleges and universities, and how powerful an influence they can therefore exert in sustaining the present dispensation. If interdisciplinary work must always be offered in a setting dominated by disciplinary schedules, budgets, and hiring/firing criteria, it will always be at a disadvantage, no matter how abstractly right it is. On the other hand, the creativity and initiative that interdisciplinary approaches have set free in intellectual life may also transform institutions if such approaches are brought to bear on them.

My goal is to encourage a look at other forms of organization at the college level by presenting one image of a thoroughly non-disciplinary format. It is very hypothetical and very coarsely sketched, but I think it illustrates some of what needs to be done by any successful non-disciplinary approach to education over the next few years and some of

*Knapp's vision of Wednesday College which embraces the world of work provides an interesting role for alternative education in the career dominated 1980's. The student remains at the center of this vision, firmly embedded in the contemporary social and economic context, but the idealism and enduring features of a more classical education are continued. Like Von Blum, Knapp sees opportunity for innovation in a professional context.

the issues any such program will have to confront. What it lacks in completeness I hope it will make up in drama.

Let us begin by questioning the very, very old distinction between liberal and pre-professional education. It goes back at least as far as the Greeks, and persists through most of Western culture. It is thriving right now. Education for practical matters—for economic production, for healing, for everyday life of all sorts—has been conceived quite separately from education in transcendant matters—the good, the true, the beautiful, the nature of God, first and last things, or whatever phrasing suits a particular time and place. The Greeks believed this; so did St. Augustine, the Renaissance, and 19th century American liberal arts colleges as they trained ministers; so do most educators today. For contemporary American society, however, for this secular, officially egalitarian, business-centered society, it may well be that the best education, both for living in this society and for transcending it, will come from finding the great questions we need to study in its very fabric and from developing the ability to think broadly, critically, carefully, and independently about these questions by working with the materials which this society itself presents. From this general conviction grows my image.

THE IMAGE: WEDNESDAY COLLEGE

Wednesday College is a unit of the University of Kansifornia, a large state university with a typical table of organization. Kansifornia has divisions, departments, and professional schools. The only untypical thing about it is Wednesday College, but Wednesday itself enjoys divisional status because it has paid careful attention to Jeanne Hahn and Fred Weaver's lessons, elsewhere in this collection, on the essentials of institutional position. As a division, Wednesday College has the right to recommend for tenure and promotion, a healthy slice of the university's instructional budget (complete with discretionary funds and reasonable staff support), and the beginnings of an earmarked endowment. What is startling about this is that Wednesday College is entirely devoted to undergraduate teaching. Its faculty carry no graduate students nor do they engage in graduate research. It owes this unusual combination of undergraduate orientation and organization security to its success in attracting both student applications and the vocal support of Kansifornia's business and professional community. This success in turn flows from its success in implementing and publicizing a curriculum which is keynoted by these words of Paul Goodman's which are emblazoned over the entrance to Wednesday's building, recently reclaimed from the contracting department of business studies:

> "Curriculum is always given; it is the sciences, mores, and institutions of our civilization."

Wednesday's embodiment of these words was at first considered a curiosity, but has drawn increasing attention (and controversy) as the college has grown and succeeded. It is very simple to describe. Each student takes all work in a given year from the offerings of a single one of Wednesday's six departments. During the four years of bachelor's work, he or she must spend two years, one basic and one advanced, in one department and one year in each of two others. The six departments are as follows. (Read them slowly.): Agriculture, War and Peace Studies, Management and Labor Studies, Architecture, Medicine, Household and Neighborhood Studies. All teaching in the college falls under one of these departments. Each department offers a structured array of basic and advanced courses which together cover the sciences, mores and institutions of its area, including its historical roots, ethical questions, environmental impacts, spiritual dimensions, and key techniques—including writing and logic. The character of teaching is generally conventional but has two or three subtle features. Despite the titles of the departments, teaching is not primarily pre-professional or pre-occupational, though much of relevance to careers is transmitted. The intent and the content of the courses, individually and taken as a whole, is to take each area as an object of study—to characterize its workings and to explain and understand them profoundly. Take Management and Labor as an example. I don't have a complete course catalog written up, but after a few comments you can probably fill it in for yourself. Management and Labor require students to demonstrate competent typing, but would dispense with other aspects of office procedure in favor of discussing the significance of the typewriter in business communications and in networks of influence. It might contrast American practice with Japan, where the only typewriters which can deal with the language are so slow, bulky and expensive that businesses rarely if ever use them. Letters and reports are written by hand or done orally, with effects on efficiency and decision-making that are well worth debate. Leaving that bit of technology aside, one could discuss staff support as a phenomenon over the history of the west with its varying levels of responsibility, varying chances for advancement, and varying links to social classes and position. The Management-/Labor area could naturally tackle many other questions: loyalty; the question of status versus contract and the nature of leadership; the role of Puritanism in capitalist development; the question of slavery; the Holocaust. In my dreams I even have a vision of teaching accounting as a branch of epistemology—a sort of applied way of knowing about the world.

This rough sketch is an image, but its imagined success is based on factors that are real enough. Its internal organization reflects its educational goals; its goals give it a niche in the larger society. Wednesday College embraces the world outside the academy, instead of fending it off as a transitory and imperfect embodiment of eternal forms. It is in that world the College will encounter the good, the true, and the beautiful. This stance gives the College access to support from businessmen, professionals, and other non-academics by accepting their activities as worthy of study, while it secures the College against simple co-option by focussing academic study on transcendent things.

Even more important, studying the immediate world makes contact with the experience of undergraduates, and so can hope to affect them in ways that more remote studies cannot. This is parallel, in some ways, to that early 60's rallying cry, "Relevance!" which quickly acquired a bad name on grounds of shallowness. The accusation rang true about much of the cosmetic curriculum-shuffling of that time, but therefore to shun relevance and return to a canon of time-honored "basics" is to misunderstand students in basic ways. Though the present-day experience of most students is incoherent, it is exceedingly rich and vivid. It gives them high anxieties but also high excitement. It is vivid enough, in fact, for standard liberal arts materials to seem pallid in comparison, no matter how important they may ultimately be. Correspondingly, many teachers of liberal arts are cold to student concerns. Take employment anxiety. Some of us are scornful, some of us gripe about it, some are paternalistic ("You'll thank me later for making you stay, spend time on art history.") Even the sympathetic feel in an adversary position to their students, who they fear will do almost anything to guarantee a job. Indeed, some students fit this image, and a useful role in the system is played by the institutions that cater to it. On the whole, however, I think this notion misrepresents what many students are interested in. They have a paradoxical combination of anxiety and idealism. They are worried, as who is not, about whether they will make their way in the world, whether they will stay alive, pay the rent, support or participate in families, and whether they can do work or lead lives that are respected by those around them. At the same time, though, students retain the hope for wider and better things, for fuller lives, for the whole litany of things which we faculty all have hoped for in our time and continue to pursue in our better moments. It is a terrible mistake to shut down this idealism in the course of allaying pragmatic anxieties. This is the familiar stand against "careerism". It is an equal mistake to ignore these anxieties: any such approach will seem suited only to moments of leisure or luxury, not to the "real" business of the world. Students are better served if one provides them with the promise and possibility of getting into the job market without narrowing them into highly specific, technical, and transitory curricula. The best example of employment-oriented curricula are found in two-year community colleges. They have many virtues, but I simply don't believe that they have the kind of vibrancy, the sense of fulfillment and satisfaction on the part of students, that one would expect if being reassured about job anxieties was the main thing that students were after. There is a grim, utilitarian aspect about much community college teaching even when in its own specific terms it is being done well.

Wednesday College's departments grow naturally out of this willingness to take the world seriously. Agriculture, medicine, war and peace, and the rest are great fields of work around which lives and social institutions have organized themselves. (Of course one could choose others than the ones I've mentioned.) None are closed or tamed: they have an ineradicable depth, because they grapple with enduring, centrally human problems. As such, they bring to the surface all the great questions of the liberal arts, inescapably and with greater subtlety than when approached outside their worldly embodiment. If you read the great Greeks without reference to problems in the real world you will end up with a thinner understanding of questions of meaning, goodness, and the source of truth than if you couple your contact with the Greeks with a close study of things that have a vibrancy and completeness all their own.

Switching from rationale to structure, one sees that organization by fields of application provides the Wednesday College faculty with some much-needed points of reference. I imagine their faculty to be well-trained holders of disciplinary degrees. Among them are historians, physicists, psychologists, and philosophers, who were hired by their departments because they are both passionate and insightful about their respective fields of application—a historian about agriculture, a sociologist about medicine, and so on. To conduct themselves as colleagues, they need standards of quality, reality checks and ways of delimiting their scope of inquiry. The applied fields can suggest all of these, since each field is an on-going enterprise with an evolving but always powerful self-definition. Doctors, for example, have strong views about what constitutes good medicine. At the same time the faculty members disciplinary backgrounds suggest quite distinct standards and self-definitions, which set the faculty apart from the profession or group they study. This dual perspective, even if experienced as a tension, keeps the Wednesday College faculty from lapsing into purely disciplinary or purely professional patterns without casting them totally adrift.

Another principle which sustains the College's mediatory position is primary loyalty to understanding. The College does not aim primarily to do things or to get anyone to do things (except its students): it aims to understand things that are being done in the world outside the academy. This is a natural stance for academics to take, a defensible one in the sense of the functional separation between the activities of the academy and those of the world of work, and one which deals with the question of whether the university which embraces agriculture, medicine, architecture, and so forth becomes a captive of its society and narrows its vision merely to what exists and to the particular ideologies and power structures of a given time. Loyalty to understanding, with all the probing and analysis it entails naturally puts one in a critical stance. To understand, one must look beyond the particular embodiments that one is confronted with. Placing understanding ahead of acting is not a matter of all or none. Many Wednesday College students will no doubt go on to work in their major field, and their studies must prepare them for useful roles. Faculty may well develop advisory, research, or direct employment relations with their department's field: if this failed to occur, the claim of understanding the field would be shaky, indeed. These forms of involvement must, however, remain secondary. The College is neither trade school nor extension service, and evaluates its success in an academic, not a professional perspective.

If anyone does start a Wednesday College, the sailing will not be smooth. Can such a college retain the imagined intellectual independence from the existing professions? Can even this form of organization stand against the self-regarding, self-reinforcing guild mentality that afflicts the conventional disciplines? The professions, after all, have strong internal cultures of their own, attuned to an existing pattern of relations with the academic world based on much more specific, job-related, technical curricula than what I have sketched. Especially in the early years, the college might find itself trapped between the world and the academy of derision. Some maneuvering room is offered by the expansion of government planning and regulatory activity, which calls on a difference range of abilities from traditional practice, and further, quite different room by the appearance of "alternative" professional roles in many fields. For example, the energy field was once dominated by civil, mechanical, and electrical engineers of well-defined training and professional orientation. A host of converging influences have now brought economics, social psychology, the pure sciences, and other disciplines into the picture, have broadened and vastly complicated the issues, and have created niches for solar designers, community activists, and dozens of non-engineering equipment and advisory businesses. Traditional engineers are still in the center of the action, but the scope for lively, hard-headed liberal/professional programs a la Wednesday College have broadened enormously.

From the student standpoint, there is an important question whether organizing study around work-related fields would be narrowing in the end. Conceivably, such study would be too closely linked to students' career choices for them to succeed in standing outside it. My personal experience in energy studies supports the Wednesday College thesis—applications foster breadth (if you let them). Some such distribution requirements as I have suggested would also promote breadth, but the issue is real and can only be resolved in practice.

Academics may find this college deficient in intellectual activity for its own sake. Where is cosmology? The arts? Medieval history? The interdisciplinary departments would draw together surprising combinations, so that any of these might well find a place. However, since the college selects its curriculum mainly to pursue understanding of its six fields, there is certainly no guarantee that the usual range of "pure" fields would be represented. Whether this is undesirable is, again, a real issue.

Other difficulties can be suggested. Against them I return to the original theme. Colleges and universities face a rising flood of fiscal and enrollment problems. Some may hope to escape the waters by clinging to their roof tops, but sooner or later most institutions will need to start swimming. They may not change their names to Wednesday, they may pick other fields than my six, but I suggest that one way to achieve a vibrant liberal arts program in this era is to adopt the foregoing principles: embrace the world; use the depth of its problems to motivate and enrich the understanding of abstract questions; as academics, aim primarily to understand and explain, not to act. This blend of involvement and transcendence is a powerful way to attract and reach students, by addressing both their anxieties and their persistant idealism.

XV. The Goodrich Program at the University of Nebraska-Omaha: A Non-Traditional Approach to Non-Traditional Students

by

DIANE GILLESPIE AND PHILIP SECRET

INTRODUCTION

The University of Nebraska at Omaha (UNO) can be best described as an urban university. The City of Omaha, in which UNO is fairly centrally located, has a current population of 314,255; the minority population is comprised of approximately 37,864 Black Americans, 7,319 persons of Spanish (Latin) origin, and 7,319 Native Americans.[1] Most UNO students are residents of Omaha or surrounding towns, and all students commute since there are no dormitories on the seventy-three acre campus. UNO, which has an open admission policy, had 15,492 students enrolled during Fall semester 1981; 8,232 were part-time and 7,260 full-time. The average age of UNO students is 25. More than seventy-five per cent of UNO's students work; approximately forty-two per cent work full-time. In July 1968, UNO was designated as one of the three education institutions within the University of Nebraska educational system.

The Goodrich Scholarship Program was instituted at the University of Nebraska at Omaha in 1972 to provide effective educational opportunities to low-income students. An appropriation from the Nebraska State Legislature to the University of Nebraska at Omaha provided funds for "a program to get more economically-deprived young people in, and through the University of Nebraska at Omaha." Named after the Senator who introduced the legislation, the Program gives direct assistance to low-income students in the form of tuition waivers, a special academic program of general education and supportive services. In addition to tuition waivers, the Program pays for all the textbooks used in its general education courses and assists students who depend on public transportation.

Like other programs created for non-traditional students[2] in institutions of higher education during the late 1960s and early 1970s, the Goodrich Program was designed to give students who had traditionally been denied access to higher education the skills and tools to gain a strong foothold in academia. In *Accent on Learning* (1976), Patricia K. Cross summarizes the various approaches institutions of higher education have taken to provide educational opportunities to non-traditional students. The *access* model opened the door to educational opportunity through providing non-traditional students financial assistance. The *remedial* model addressed the concern that access alone was insufficient in retaining non-traditional students who often entered college ill-prepared academically; and so, in this model, basic skills courses and study skills programs were designed to help students gain the academic skills and background necessary to succeed in college. These two models assumed non-traditional students should be brought into accord with traditional values of higher education. The *pluralistic* model, which Cross identifies as the most recent and desirable model for meeting the needs of non-traditional students, assumes traditional educational values and standards are not appropriate for all students; the emphasis of this model is that institutions must change instructional strategies and curriculum to meet the needs of non-traditional students. Although the Goodrich Program certainly has characteristics that parallel all these approaches to non-traditional students, it does not readily fit into any one of these models. In combination, the various educational strategies and interventions make it a fairly unique approach to the education of non-traditional students.

Certainly the Goodrich Program has evolved in response to the particular needs of its students, the university in which it is housed, and the community at large. Nevertheless, the success of the Program has implications for all involved with programs which serve non-traditional students, and particularly economically disadvantaged ones. We shall present three features of the Program which might be of relevance and importance to others working with non-traditional students in higher educational institutions. Specifically, we shall argue that the role of the

Goodrich faculty, the academically rigorous sequence of Goodrich courses, and selection of Goodrich students have important implications for programs serving non-traditional students. Before turning to these features, we will provide information about the structure and operation of the Program and present some evidence of its success.

A DESCRIPTION OF THE GOODRICH PROGRAM

The Program currently has 253 students, seven faculty members, a study skills specialist, a coordinator for student personnel, two office personnel, four graduate assistants, four student tutors and a Chairperson. Housed in the College of Public Affairs and Community Service, the Program functions administratively like a department; however, the Program does not offer a major. Each year the Program recruits, selects and admits approximately 65 students into the Program. These students are free to major in any department throughout the university. During their freshman and sophomore years, all Goodrich students are required to take a total of twenty-four semester hours of Goodrich courses in the Humanities and Social Sciences; most of these courses count toward fulfilling divisional requirements for their majors. Goodrich Program faculty members who teach the Program's courses hold courtesy appointments in correlative departments within the University; however, their main affiliation is with the Goodrich Program.

Since its inception, the Goodrich Program has assumed the following: 1) deprived students should not be restricted to remedial programs and 2) if given close personal contact with faculty and remedial help where necessary, these students can successfully pursue an academically rigorous course of study. According to Hubert Locke, the administrator who originally conceptualized the Program, this philosophy is based:

> 1) on the assumption that low-income students have the same capacity for academic achievement as that of middle- or upper-income students admitted to the university through regular processes; 2) on research findings (e.g., the Coleman study) which indicate that *teacher expectation* is the most critical single factor in the achievement or failure of low-income students; and 3) on the premise that an innovative, intellectually stimulating teaching-learning atmosphere can be created which will motivate low-income students to excel academically, complete degree programs, and prepare for meaningful vocations.

Coupled with these assumptions is the Program's strong commitment to cultural diversity—a commitment that is actively promoted in the composition of its faculty, staff, student body and curriculum offerings. In essence, the Program assumes the ability on the part of low-income students to succeed and excel academically, if exposed from the start of their college careers to rigorous intellectual stimulation, complemented by multicultural sensitivity and the necessary support services which enable them to have confidence in themselves and their ability to succeed.

The Program does not create educational experiences that in any way shift or alter the *predominant* educational goals of the university at large; on the other hand, it does not assume that the "usual course of study" best facilitates retention of the non-traditional student. The Program's resources are not directed to *all* economically disadvantaged students expressing interest in college. Goodrich's faculty and staff believe that given certain indicators of academic potential, detected, to a large extent, through non-traditional criteria, the Program can intervene to prevent the high attrition rate characteristic of low-income students. As a result of this philosophy, the Program has a student body which is economically homogeneous, but racially and academically diverse.

Generally, then, the Program can be described as an agency which intervenes between "non-traditional" students and a "traditional" institution. Financial assistance constitutes the baseline intervention. Beyond that, the Program offers academic courses and supportive services. The following chart illustrates the sequence of Goodrich courses and identifies the support services available to students throughout their undergraduate years:

The nature of the Program's educational component can be illustrated best by a brief description of Goodrich courses. As outlined in the preceding chart, the sequence consists of courses in English composition and Critical Reasoning in the first semester of the freshman year; a humanities course focusing on contemporary American culture in the second semester of the freshman year; and a two-semester sequence of courses in the social sciences in the sophomore year. These required courses constitute six credit hours per semester during the student's freshman and sophomore years. In the first half of the Fall semester, all incoming freshmen also take a one-hour, non-credit course called Communication Laboratory.

The English and philosophy courses required of first semester freshmen are designed to develop students' writing and reasoning skills. Some students who have already demonstrated a proficiency in writing are exempt from the English composition requirement; however, all students are required to take Philosophy 121: Critical Reasoning, a course de-

CHART OF THE GOODRICH PROGRAMS OVER 4 YEARS OF COLLEGE

Year	Semester					*Goodrich Support Services*
First Year	Fall Semester	Goodrich sections of English Composition English 111	Goodrich sections of Critical Reasoning Philosophy 121	Goodrich Communication Lab 1 hr/week Fall Semester only	6–9 hours in courses outside the Goodrich Program	*Study Skills Center
	Spring Semester	Perspectives on American Culture; a 6 hour course in the Humanities offered by the Goodrich staff			6–9 hours in courses outside the Goodrich Program	*Writing Lab
Second Year	Fall Semester	Research Techniques and Urban problems I; a 6 hour course in the Social Sciences offered by the Goodrich staff			6–9 hours in courses outside the Goodrich Program	*Job Counselling *Personal Counselling
	Spring Semester	Research Techniques and Urban Problems II; a 6 hour course in the Social Sciences offered by the Goodrich staff			6–9 hours in courses outside the Goodrich Program	*Goodrich Student Organization *Tutoring
Third Year	Fall & Spring	12–15 hours in courses outside the Goodrich Program		Non-credit activities with Goodrich advisor for juniors		
Fourth Year	Fall & Spring	12–15 hours in courses outside the Goodrich Program		Non-credit activities with Goodrich advisor for seniors		

signed to teach students how to analyze and criticize arguments and theories, as they are typically presented in textbooks, articles, lectures and speeches.[3]

The requirement for the second semester of the freshman year is a six credit hour humanities course entitled "Perspectives on American Culture." This course explores contemporary American society and some of the major ideologies which have shaped it from a multicultural perspective. Materials used include films, novels, short stories, essays, and presentations of paintings and music. The purpose of the course is threefold: to enable students to understand how ideas are presented through these various media, to help them gain a perspective on the culture in which they live and to appreciate artistic contributions made by different ethnic groups in American society.

The course "Research Techniques and Urban Problems" is required for sophomore students in the Program. It is a two semester course (6 credit hours for each semester) that attempts to synthesize the knowledge and perspectives of various social sciences with the hope of providing students a better understanding of how public policy decisions are made in our society, what their consequences are and what options for change exist for them and their society.

The first semester of the course focuses on such topics as the individual in the social context, the importance of groups in influencing behavior, and general theories of policy analysis and examines various urban problems and public policy alternatives. An important component of the first semester is the module devoted to an examination of the political, social and economic roles of minorities (Blacks, Chicanos, and Native Americans) in America. In order to become effective public policy change agents, students need to have an understanding of how to obtain and interpret information; thus faculty introduce students to a variety of social research techniques. At the end of the semester, students participate in a research project in which they apply the research tools they have learned.

The second semester of the course is divided into a series of eight week public policy modules. Each student is required to take two modules. Modules have included such topics as: (1) The City and the Person, (2) A Survey of Social Science Issues in the Native American Experience, (3) Women and Politics/Women and the Law and (4) Social Science and the Supreme Court: An Introduction to the Role of the Court as a Public Policy Maker.

The humanities and social science classes are held three days a week throughout the semester and last one hour and fifty minutes. During the entire freshman year, one hour a week is set aside for small group tutorials in which five to six students and a faculty member or graduate student have an opportunity to interact on a more intimate basis. During the sophomore year, small group tutorial sessions are convened when necessary.

No Goodrich courses are required during the students' junior and senior years. Students still receive financial aid and can avail themselves of all support services offered by the Program. Juniors and seniors are all assigned to Goodrich faculty and staff members who meet with them periodically.

In addition to the academic component, the Goodrich Scholarship Program has established counseling services for its students. Recent literature about cross-cultural counseling indicates economically disadvantaged students, particularly minority students, do not avail themselves of traditional counseling services (Sue, 1977). Since students may have misconceptions or simply lack information about counseling and its benefits (Schauble et al., 1979), the Goodrich Program has structured in a counseling component which provides activities that bring the students into contact with counselors. A Communication Lab, taught by the Program's counselor, involves all freshman students who meet weekly in small groups during the first semester. In this setting, students explore their own educational goals more fully. Other activities offered by the counselors include individual and group counseling, academic planning, career exploration, and workshops on various topics of personal interest to Goodrich students. Closely tied to counseling services are the Program's tutorial services.

The Writing Lab and Study Skills Center focuses on writing, reading, vocabulary, spelling and the various study skills needed to succeed in college. During the regular school semester, students may set up one-time or continuing appointments in the Writing Lab, or they may come to the Lab without an appointment. Each tutoring session, scheduled to last one hour, provides an opportunity for the student to work on a specific individual skill problem. Additionally, the Lab provides tutoring in various academic subjects. Some small group sessions are planned to assist students in developing study skills, such as taking notes during lectures, reading textbooks, and taking exams. During the summer, the Writing Lab/Study Skills Center staff offers a non-credit, preparatory study skills course to incoming freshmen. In this course, students not only learn how to take lecture notes and study textbooks but also work on improving their writing, reading, vocabulary and spelling skills.

In summary, financial assistance, a sequence of academic courses and supportive services constitute the Program's major efforts to retain the non-traditional student. The Goodrich Program has undergone two reviews—one internal, one external. These reviews have been favorable and indicate that such a three-pronged approach has yielded positive results. These reviews suggest two separate and important impacts that the Program has had on its students. First, the Program has graduated 40% of the students it accepted between 1972 and 1977. Table 1 sumarizes enrollment and graduation figures for these years. Although data for exact attrition comparisons of Goodrich students and University of Nebraska at Omaha students at large are not available, the available attrition data does allow us to make some meaningful comparisons for the 1974–1976 years.[4] Table 2 summarizes the attrition rate for Goodrich freshmen and UNO freshmen for the years 1974, 1975 and 1976 respectively and collectively. For each of these years the Program's attrition rate is about equal to that of the larger university; over the years, the attrition rate for the Program is three percent less than the corresponding rate for the university at large.

Table 1

ENROLLMENT/GRADUATION STATUS FOR GOODRICH STUDENTS (as Projected to May 1982)

Year	Number Enrolled	Number Graduated	Number Enrolled in Spring term 1981–1982	Number Not Enrolled in Spring term 1981–1982
1972–73	98[1]	39	1	58
1973–74	74	32	1	41
1974–75	49	21	1	27
1975–76	70	27	0	43
1976–77	58	20	2	36
[a]Subtotal	349 (100%)	139 (40%)	5 (1%)	205 (59%)

[a]Reflects five-year enrollment period. Goodrich Program provides tuition for five years.

[1]The larger number of students admitted in the first year (1972–73) occurred because *all* scholarship monies were awarded to freshmen only. As they moved through their sophomore, junior and senior years, the number of freshmen admitted had to be decreased accordingly.

Table 2

PROGRAM AND UNO ATTRITION RATES BY YEAR

Year	Program Attrition	UNO Attrition
1974	55% (49)*	59% (2794)
1975	61% (70)	62% (2988)
1976	62% (58)	54% (2456)
1974–1976	59% (177)	62% (8238)

*The numbers in parentheses indicate total freshman enrollment.

Given the fact that the Program by and large serves a non-traditional student population, one could plausibly hypothesize that its attrition rate would be higher than that for the larger university. The available data suggest that the Program intervenes in the students' educational experiences in such a manner that one of the outcomes is a student retention rate that compares favorably with that of the larger university, the Program's non-traditional student body notwithstanding.

Other evidence about the Program indicates that it positively affects Goodrich students' attitudes. In an evaluation study of the Program, Francis (1977) administered an alienation questionnaire to all Goodrich students and to a selected sample of non-Goodrich students. Of the twenty-four items on the questionnaire, Goodrich and non-Goodrich students differed significantly ($p \leq .05$) on seven.[5] He concluded, "A distinct picture emerges of Goodrich students as less alienated and with more of a sense of control and confidence" (p. 18). Finally, an initial review of the results of a study of Goodrich graduates (Stephenson, in progress) indicated that an overwhelming majority of Goodrich graduates rated their experiences in the Program as satisfying. The results of these studies suggest that the Program is making a very positive educational impact on its non-traditional student body.

We have provided a general description of the Goodrich Program and given evidence of its success. While replication of all facets of the Program may not be feasible at other institutions, certain of its features have important implications for those who work with non-traditional students; specifically, the role of the faculty in the Program, the curriculum and its education function and the selection process. The supportive services in the Program, it should be noted, constitute an essential factor in its success; however, since most programs for non-traditional students offer counseling and tutoring, we have chosen to focus on those features of the Program which may not be characteristic of other programs.

SPECIAL FEATURES OF THE GOODRICH PROGRAM

Faculty

From its inception, the Goodrich Program has emphasized the importance of a faculty who actively participate in the education of Goodrich students. Faculty play a key role in the total operation of the Program. In addition to supporting and advising the Chairperson in the overall development, planning and evaluation of the Program, they take part in the recruitment, selection, orientation, and supervision of Goodrich students. Historically, the faculty have worked together in two teaching teams—one in humanities and one in social sciences. These teams develop and teach the general education courses in the Program. Since the Program's philosophy assumes that low-income students can pursue a rigorous course of study, faculty hold high expectations of students and design courses in ways which will challenge their students academically.

The faculty teach courses in which all Goodrich freshman and sophomore students are enrolled, so a natural source for faculty-student interaction emerges in the classroom. Such contact results in a familiarity between faculty and student that extends far beyond that in the traditional classroom setting. Faculty know which students are absent from class and which ones are struggling academically. The Goodrich faculty member uses this information to take action and intervene, if appropriate. This familiarity between faculty and students becomes invaluable in retaining students in school.

According to the results of a study of Goodrich graduates (Stephenson, in progress), Goodrich students do find a difference between their interaction with Goodrich faculty and other faculty on campus. The following table indicates Goodrich graduates' satisfaction with their interaction with Goodrich and non-Goodrich faculty during their freshman and sophomore years:

Table 3

RELATIVE SATISFACTION OF GOODRICH GRADUATES WITH FACULTY INTERACTION DURING THEIR FRESHMAN AND SOPHOMORE YEARS

Faculty/Student Interaction		Very Satisfied
With Goodrich Humanities Faculty	(78)*	57.7%
With Goodrich Social Sciences Faculty	(82)	52.4%
With Non-Goodrich Faculty	(82)	14.6%

*The numbers in parentheses indicate total number of respondents.

These results suggest that a majority of students find, during the first two years of college, that the Goodrich faculty become involved with them in ways more satisfactory than non-Goodrich faculty. Such close interaction allows for faculty attention to students' course work, their problems and their general progress in college.

Another factor that promotes faculty-student interaction lies in the team teaching approach. The Goodrich teaching teams are diversified in terms of race, age, sex, temperament, style, academic viewpoint and area of expertise. Thus, throughout their first few years of college, students are exposed to a number of different role models, all of whom are committed to the students' educational growth. Such diversity becomes instrumental in meeting the educational needs of a varied student body, especially in light of recent psychological research on observational learning. Bandura's social learning theory (1977) maintains that contrary to traditional psychological assumptions about learning, "The capacity to learn by observation enables people to acquire large, integrated patterns of behavior without having to form them gradually by tedious trial and error" (p. 12). Relevant to the teaching approach of the Program are Bandura's research findings which indicate what variables maximize the affects of observational learning through modeling. One is the provision of a diversity of models. "If people of widely differing characteristics can succeed, then observers have a reasonable basis for increasing their own sense of self-efficacy" (p. 82). Another variable is similiarity of the observer to the model; the more similar the characteristics of observer and model, the more likely the observer will identify with the model.

The Program attempts to maximize observational learning by providing a diverse teaching team, members of which model various academic behaviors, attitudes, approaches, and skills. The Program also respects the fact that its student body is culturally, racially, and sexually diverse; provision of faculty models similar to the student body composition enhances learning as well. Although such diversity among faculty exists, the faculty have identified (Francis, 1977) four characteristics critical for becoming and being effective with Goodrich students: a command of teaching techniques appropriate for non-traditional students, a feeling of responsibility for student success, interpersonal communication skills and experience with minority and disadvantaged students.

There are several implications of the Goodrich Program's use of faculty for other programs dealing with non-traditional students. Although counselors and tutors serve as absolutely essential resources for retaining the non-traditional student, provision of these resources alone may not be sufficient. A group of faculty members, directly involved in educating non-traditional students and committed to excellence in teaching, may be the determining factor in retaining such students. Additionally, the Program's faculty assume students can perform academically; they do not expect deficiencies in or lower-quality work from their students. Given weekly contact, the faculty can more naturally establish contact with a student and observe the student's academic performance over time. The most important result of faculty-student interaction is that the faculty member can usually identify when a student experiences difficulty and intervene so that the student neither drops out nor flunks out. Thus the faculty become more than teachers; they become advocates for the students and facilitators of their personal and academic growth.

The Goodrich faculty, then, hold fairly traditional expectations of their students; their involvement and interaction with the students, however, go beyond the traditional models. In general, this same approach characterizes the Program's curricular offerings. On the one hand, the courses are academically demanding. Throughout the sequence of Goodrich courses, students read only college-level material, take all types of examinations, make oral presentations, write themes and research papers and participate in class discussions. On the other hand, the content of the courses and teaching methods employed differ from traditional general education courses. Goodrich faculty often adopt teaching methods which encourage active learning. Apart from conducting fairly frequent group discussions, faculty have utilized various simulations in the classroom, assigned students to work on group projects and involved students and/or visiting lecturers in various panels. The multicultural emphasis in all the courses provides the opportunity for students to explore academic materials from various viewpoints. Faculty, then, attempt to create an atmosphere conducive to participatory learning.

Curriculum

While the close interaction between faculty and students make intervention with individual students possible, Goodrich courses provide an opportunity for the students to form a supportive community in which they establish relationships with others who have similar educational goals. At a predominantly white institution such as the University of Nebraska at Omaha, such a supportive community becomes extremely important for the retention of minority students. Generally, courses encourage discussions of contemporary issues from a multicultural perspective and promote cross-cultural communication. As stated in the report (1977) of an Ad Hoc Committee which evaluated the Program:

> The General education courses are designed to introduce students to a comprehensive exploration of the problems and issues of contemporary American society and to develop in students the requisite skills for undertaking an independent, rigorous, critical analysis of those problems and issues. (p. 13)

It is important to note, however, that tutoring services supplement the course work.

For those working with non-traditional students in other institutions, the most relevant aspects of the Program's educational component may not be the specific content of the courses (as that changes from year to year) or its multicultural emphasis (as that has been widely recognized as important). What may be unique in the Program's approach is the provision of rigorous academic course work rather than, as is often the case, mere provision of only remedial courses or tutoring services. That the Program's courses challenge students academically was confirmed in the Ad Hoc Committee's report (1977):

> Goodrich Program courses, in some areas, appear more demanding than courses these students might have chosen to fulfill requirements for a degree in the College of Arts and Sciences. Examinations clearly show students are held responsible for the ideas presented by the many outside resource people brought in to supplement the courses. (p. 14)

In his evaluation report, Francis (1977) concluded, "[The Goodrich curriculum] meets the highest standards of academic quality and yet is so designed as to be relevant to the student's social concerns" (p. 65).

The experience of the Goodrich Program has been that given an academic challenge, low-income students can perform well, if not above average. The average of Goodrich students' grade point averages in Goodrich courses during the Spring semesters of 1978 and 1980 were randomly selected to serve as an example. The average grades achieved by Goodrich freshmen in the Humanities course during 1978 and 1980 Spring semesters were 3.18 (on a 4.0 scale) and 2.68 respectively; in the Social Sciences the average sophomore grades were 2.95 and 2.45 respectively. Table 4 compares these figures with the average of the grades these students achieved in non-Goodrich courses:

Table 4

GRADE POINT AVERAGES OF GOODRICH STUDENTS

Student Classification	Humanities	Social Sciences	Non-Goodrich Courses
	Spring Semester 1978		
Freshmen (N = 60)	3.18		2.58
Sophomores (N = 45)		2.95	2.37
	Spring Semester 1980		
Freshmen (N = 58)	2.68		2.37
Sophomores (N = 68)		2.45	2.04

For comparison, during the Spring semester 1978, the mean grade for all 100 level courses at UNO (N = 17, 273) was 2.45 and for all 200 level courses 2.68. These figures indicate that Goodrich students performed on par with their cohort groups in their non-Goodrich courses but above average in Goodrich courses.

The fact that students achieved higher grades in Goodrich courses (as compared to non-Goodrich courses) is evidence, we believe, of how the Program's strategies interface to form an effective educational delivery system. First, the curriculum is designed to be rigorous, and faculty expect students to perform well academically; and second, the faculty intereact extensively with students in a supportive manner. Table 3 indicates that a majority of Goodrich students were *very* satisfied with their interaction with Goodrich faculty in their freshman and sophomore years. It is our belief that such a high level of satisfaction operated to help students obtain higher grades in Goodrich courses. Moreover, we believe that the level of faculty/student interaction, the demanding course work and faculty accountability were positive factors which helped these students to perform at satisfying levels in non-Goodrich courses. The overall academic performance of Goodrich students becomes more relevant when their ACT scores are considered. Our analysis of association between GPA and ACT, based on available data from the 1976 Goodrich class suggests that the combination of strategies, discussed above, made an important impact on the GPA's of students who, based on low ACT scores, were not expected to do well. Table 5 summarizes our findings. As indicated, seventy-one percent of those students with low ACT scores obtained grades in the medium range; forty-two percent of those who had medium ACT scores, scored in the high GPA range.

The Program's responsibility to its students lies in its provision of well-conceived courses, supportive services, and available faculty. Moreover, in the teaching of the courses faculty strongly encourage student responsibility for their academic work. A tutorial group, consisting of approximately five freshmen students, meets weekly with a faculty member to discuss materials from the large classes. In the sophomore classes, graduate assistants and/or faculty meet with small groups of students when necessary. As the Ad Hoc Committee report (1977) noted about these tutorial sessions, "It is difficult to hide unpreparedness in a small class where students *must* become involved" (p. 14). In small group sessions, faculty can routinely seek evidence of a student's progress. Without such monitoring, the non-traditional student may fall behind and ultimately disappear from school.

The experience of the Program's faculty in delivering more challenging components of the curriculum strongly suggests that teacher expectations dramatically affect student performance. This would directly support Rosenthal and Jacobson's (1968) findings that when teachers of disadvantaged students were led to believe some of their students could improve, by the end of the year those students' IQ scores were dramatically higher. Indeed, many of the students in the Program have been victimized, in various degrees, by negative stereotypes; many low-income students have been labelled, at some point in their education, academically "deficient." We believe, along with Cross (1976), that a very large proportion of the students we admit "*can* learn traditional subject matter, given appropriate time and treatment" (p. 41). Thus, the curriculum and expectations of the faculty do not demean the student's intellectual capabilities. We believe that this respect enables our more non-traditional students to perform on par with non-traditional students.

The totality of the Goodrich experience does not meet the personal and academic needs of all low-income students. As the Program has developed, we have identified the students we can best serve; and so, over the years, the selection process has become more and more refined. This process and the rationale behind it have important implications for other programs designed for non-traditional students. It is to this feature of the Program that we now turn.

Selection Process

The Goodrich Program has been an experiment in higher education which is based on the premise that the traditional indicators of college success are not, in and of themselves, the only factors which are accurate predictors of college success. The Program conceded that standardized aptitude tests such as SAT and ACT and high school grade point averages may be good predictors of college success at extreme ends. That is, a student who obtained an extremely high composite score on the ACT or who earned an extremely high accumulative GPA during his or her high school studies would in all probability be successful in college. On the other hand, it was conceded that a student who scored extremely low on these measures would in all probability have difficulties in college. However, the philosophy of the Program is that it can help many students to succeed in college even though traditional predictors would not support this claim.

The Program identified a number of major prerequisites that these students should possess. The two most important of these were intrinsic motivation and determination. The selection process reflects the importance of these factors.

No student is eligible for a Goodrich Scholarship who cannot demonstrate financial need. The need is determined by the university financial aids office in the same manner that such need is determined for all students who are in quest of tax-based financial assistance.

In selecting among its eligible candidates, the Program considers a number of factors other than past academic performance. An eligible student may receive from zero to five points based on his or her financial status. Subsequently, the selection process includes the following elements of consideration. An eligible candidate may receive a score between zero and twenty-one points for his or her high school academic record. This score is awarded after an objective examination of the candidate's class standing, SAT/ACT scores and cumulative GPA. Each candidate also receives a score between zero and twenty points based on his or her writing sample. These samples are graded by the Program's English instructors who independently grade the samples and subsequently agree on a final score.

Each candidate is interviewed by a team of three persons selected from the Goodrich faculty and staff. Each interviewer rates the candidate between zero and four points on the following five items:

1. Ability to establish and work for goals
2. Ability to respond to problems or difficult situations
3. The candidates' perceptions of their academic strengths
4. Personal commitment to education
5. Future orientation

Each candidate is then assigned a total score for each of the above items. This score is determined by taking the average rating of the interviewers. In addition to the foregoing, four other criteria are used in the selection process. Each candidate is assigned a score from zero to ten points based on an average of the interviewer's grading of the candidate's motivation and multicultural experiences. Each candidate receives a score based on his or her letters of recommendation. These form letters of recommendation are scored by the faculty. Finally, each candidate receives an affirmative action score between zero and twenty points. This score reflects a point scale based on sex and race.

In the final analysis each Program candidate receives an overall score and candidates are subsequently ranked according to their respective scores. The Program then awards its allocated scholarships to those candidates who have received the highest scores.

Clearly, the Program's criteria for selecting candidates are not based solely on traditional indicators of past academic performance such as ACT/SAT scores and GPA. To shed some light on the Program's assumption that these traditional indicators may not be accurate predictors of college success, we randomly selected one year of the Goodrich Program to do a seminal examination of whether ACT/SAT scores are good predictors of college success and attrition rate. Missing data decreased a sample size of 50 students to only 31. Hence, cell size causes us to look at our findings with some skepticism. Yet, the results are interesting and suggestive for further research.

Table 5 summarizes our findings with respect to associations between composite ACT[6] scores and cumulative GPA[7] after two years of college. The Table shows that there is a statistically significant association between these two variables. It is important to note, however, that only 29 percent of those students who scored in the defined low range on the ACT had low grade point averages after their fourth semester of college. Seventy-one percent of the students in this range were able to earn cumulative GPA's of 2.0 or above on a 0-4.0 scale. Moreover, 42 percent of the students who scored in the defined medium range on the ACT test were able to earn high cumulative GPA's.

Table 6 presents our correlation findings with respect to ACT and Attrition.[8] Although we assumed that those students who were more academically prepared for college, in terms of ACT/SAT scores, would be more likely to return to college after their first year than those who were less prepared, our correlations do not substantiate this hypothesis. The

Table 5

GOODRICH STUDENTS' GPA BY ACT—1976

	ACT		
	Low	Medium	High
GPA	%	%	%
Low	29	0	20
Medium	71	58	60
High	0	42	20
Tau b[1]			.3*

[1]A positive tau b correlation indicates a positive association between ACT and GPA.
*Significant ≤ .05.
N = 31

Table 6

GOODRICH STUDENTS' ATTRITION BY ACT—1976

	ACT		
	Low	Medium	High
Attrition			
Yes	26	25	20
No	74	75	80
Tau b[1]			.04

[1]A positive tau b correlation indicates a positive association between ACT and attrition.
N = 31

data here suggest that there is no substantive or statistically significant association between ACT and the likelihood that one will return to college.

Moreover, when we assigned points to the variable "return to college," our analysis suggests that ACT score range is not a good predictor of whether or not one will drop out of college. Those in the low, medium and high ACT range were about equally likely to return to college.[9] Thus, it would appear that there is evidence to support the Program's assumption that ACT scores are not necessarily accurate predictors of college success.

CONCLUSION

The Goodrich Program represents a concerted effort on the part of the University of Nebraska at Omaha and the Nebraska State Legislature to increase educational opportunities for economically disadvantaged students, students who might otherwise be denied access to a college education. Because of racism and/or socioeconomic deprivation, low-income students often enter college with inadequate academic preparation. In their educational experiences, low income students can become alienated from an educational system which historically has served the needs of and reflected the values of the upper and upper-middle classes (cf: Katz, 1975; Lazerson, 1971; Tyack, 1974; Weinberg, 1977 for historical analyses of American education institutions and their relation to class structure). The Goodrich Program recognizes both the inadequate academic preparation of many low-income students *and* the alienation they may feel from educational institutions in general.

The Program believes that placing low-income students in remedial courses alone further fuels the students' feelings of alienation from the educational process. Rather, the Program contends that the educational experiences provided low-income students must be enriched and challenging enough so that the student becomes involved intellectually. Moreover, the Program maintains that given enriched educational experiences and a supportive environment, the low-income student will be able to remedy whatever academic deficiencies he or she may have. Thus the Program provides tutoring and counseling; but these services, ideally, supplement the Program's main thrust—its academic curriculum.

In addition to the educational philosophy that undergirds the academic curriculum of the Program, we have discussed two other features of the Program which, taken in combination with the academic component, may make the Program's approach to the education of the non-traditional student unique. First, Goodrich faculty hold high expectations of Goodrich students academically, but go beyond the traditional role of the college teacher through interacting with their students in such a way that problems which might otherwise lead to a student's dropping out are detected and, when possible, solved. The interaction between faculty and students (as well as between student and student) produce a supportive, academic community; and this support, we have found, sustains the students in their non-Goodrich courses where instructors and students may not readily become acquainted.

Finally, the Program has recognized that the educational experiences it provides students will not necessarily meet the needs of all low-income students. The Program, for example, encourages social interaction which some students may not desire. Traditional predictors of college success, such as ACT scores or high school grades, receive less emphasis than do other, more non-traditional ones. The Program determines motivation and academic potential, for example, by looking at students' past accomplishments (not necessarily academic), their future educational and career goals and their desire to participate in a multicultural educational setting.

In conclusion, many of the educational strategies implemented by the Goodrich Program parallel those of other programs for economically disadvantaged students at other institutions of higher education. From their survey of academic programs for disadvantaged students, for example, Mares and Levine (1975) concluded that "higher education programs for disadvantaged students tend to depend on traditional academic approaches, but at the same time they put great stress on responding to pupils' needs for personal understanding and encouragement" (p. 176). Several contributors in *New Directions for Higher Education: Increasing Basic Skills by Developmental Studies* (Roueche, 1977) suggest instructional strategies directly applicable to the educational needs of many Goodrich students and utilized by the Goodrich faculty (cf: Spann, pp.

23–40; B`. Mink, pp. 51–64; O.G. Mink, pp. 77–92). In many respects, then, the Goodrich Program is similar to other programs for economically disadvantaged students in higher education; however, we believe the combination of features of the Program which we have described constitute a non-traditional approach to the non-traditional student.

NOTES

1. *Census of Population and Housing: Summary Characteristics for Governmental Units and Standard Metropolitan Statistical Areas—Nebraska*. U.S. Department of Commerce, Bureau of the Census. PHC 80-3-29. (Washington: Government Printing Office, September 1982), Table No. 1, p. 12.

2. The term "non-traditional student" as used in the paper refers to students who are not the traditionally average college students in terms of sex, age, or socioeconomic status. Our Program has not only served proportionately more females, older persons, and persons from low socioeconomic status and backgrounds but has also sought to serve public assistance recipients, those incarcerated and on educational release and those who may not possess various traditional indicators of college success such as above-average test scores and high school grade point averages.

3. During the last two years, freshman students have had the option of taking an autobiographical writing course in place of Critical Reasoning. Although this course has been offered on an experimental basis, student and faculty reactions to the course have been very positive; the course will likely become a permanent part of the curriculum.

4. The comparative figures for the total university for the years 1974, 1975, and 1976 were compiled from three sources: (1) Raw Attrition of Fall 1974 full-time freshmen. First Annual Report. The University of Nebraska at Omaha Office of Institutional Research. December 15, 1977. (2) The Second Annual Report, November 27, 1978 and (3) The Third Annual Report, April 10, 1980. In making these comparisons, it should be noted that, first, the University's figures include attrition *only through* the junior year and ours include attrition through the senior year. Second, the Program's figures have been continuously updated, while the University's have not; however, the number of Goodrich students graduating during subsequent years has been small. This comparison, then, is only an approximate one, based on the data available.

5. Those seven items showed that:
   1. Non-Goodrich students feel more strongly that it is wishful thinking to believe one can really influence what happens in the University.
   2. Non-Goodrich students feel less an integral part of the University Community.
   3. Non-Goodrich students feel more that things have become so complicated within the University that they really do not understand just what is going on.
   4. Non-Goodrich students feel more that they don't have as many friends as they would like at the University.
   5. Non-Goodrich students feel more helpless in the face of what is happening within the University.
   6. Non-Goodrich students feel more that the forces affecting them within the University are so complex and confusing that they find it difficult to make effective decisions.
   7. Non-Goodrich students feel more that their experience at the University has been devoid of meaningful relationships.

6. An ACT score of 1 through 15, 16 through 24, and 25 through 30 were defined as low, medium and high respectively.

7. GPA scores of 0 through 1.99, 2 through 3.50, and 3.6 through 4.0 were defined as low, medium and high respectively.

8. Attrition here refers to students who did not return to college after their first year.

9. This analysis of variance is not reported in a Table. The respective averages for the three ACT groups (see reference number 1, Supra) were 1.74, 1.75 and 1.80.

REFERENCES

Ad Hoc Committee to Evaluate the Goodrich Program, *Final Report*, 1977.

Bandura, A. *Social learning theory*. Englewood Cliffs, N.J.: Prentice-Hall, Inc., 1977.

Cross, K. *Accent on learning*. San Francisco: Jossey-Bass, Inc., 1976.

Francis, B. J. *The Goodrich Scholarship Program: An evaluation*, 1977.

Katz, M. B. *Class, bureaucracy, and schools*, expanded edition. New York: Praeger Publishers, Inc., 1975.

Lazerson, M. *Origins of the urban school: Public education in Massachusetts 1870–1915*. Cambridge: Harvard University Press, 1971.

Mares, K. R. & Levine, D. N. Survey of academic programs for disadvantaged students in higher education. *Research in Higher Education*, 1975, *3*, 169–176.

Roueche, J. E. (Ed.) *Increasing basic skills by developmental studies: New directions for higher education*. San Francisco: Jossey-Bass, 1977.

Schauble, P. G.; Parker, W. M.; Probert, B. S.; & Altmaier, E. M. Taking counseling to minority students: The classroom as delivery vehicle. *Personnel and Guidance Journal*, 1979, *26*, 176–180.

Stephenson, W. A follow-up study of Goodrich graduates, in progress.

Sue, D. W. Counseling the culturally different: A conceptual analysis. *Personnel and Guidance Journal*, 1977, *24*, 422–425.

Tyack, D. B. *The one best system*. Cambridge: Harvard University Press, 1974.

Weinberg, M. *A chance to learn: The history of race and education in the United States*. Cambridge: Harvard University Press, 1977.

XVI. Inter-Generational Communities: Partnerships in Discovery

by

PATRICK J. HILL

I.

The breakdown of inter-generational community is among the more pervasive phenomena of unravelling Western society. The phenomenon manifests itself in many ways, including decreasing family size, widespread child-abuse, changing social priorities reflective of the "greying" of America, grossly ineffectual public education, the disregard of the long-term consequences of our actions on the planet, a general collapsing of institutional authority and a disturbingly more isolated and alienated youth subculture. The first indications of these trends were understandably misinterpreted, spoken of in the early sixties and seventies as "the generation gap" and later (less benignly) as "the conflict of generations." The conflict was most intense in higher education, the institution which above all others might claim to be the one in which the generations are communicating about the significance of the past and the future. And in retrospect, it is not surprising that the authors of a comprehensive institutional "Self-Study" of the period, undertaken at the Stony Brook campus of the State University of New York, entitled *The Eclipse of Academic Community*. What we were witnessing was the indeterminate loss of the sense that the generations were willing partners in an academic enterprise of mutually acknowledged and mutually respected importance.[1]

The aforementioned Self-Study and a major grant from the Fund for the Improvement of Post-Secondary Education (FIPSE) led to the creation in 1976 of the Federated Learning Communities (FLC) at Stony Brook, a cluster of curricular innovations designed to revitalize undergraduate education in large universities.[2]

The major reform efforts of the sixties were animated in large measure by concern for a cluster of five values: freedom, diversity, relevance, participation and wholeness. The efforts embodied a profound dissatisfaction with the unresponsive, authoritarian, monolithic, exclusionary and fragmented character of our major institutions. FLC is also concerned with these central democratic values, but it has been animated by a second cluster of values as well: by the communal value of shared experience, upon which the rationale for democracy rests; and by the value of specialized expertise, upon which much of the rationale for the University rests.[3] One researcher of the early sixties concluded that "students and faculty are two societies occupying the same territory."[4] Paul Goodman, by contrast, regarded that conclusion as a "catastrophic anthropological error,"[5] a failure to see that students' subculture is merely a reaction to their exclusion from the real business of adult society. The two views aptly frame a central question: to what extent do students and faculty have a common understanding of the nature and value of the academic enterprise?

Some have declared that the diverse expectations of students and faculty are irreconcilable. If one believed this, then one would seek means to confine higher education's efforts to situations of matched expectations, e.g., cutting back the number of people who attend college, or finding different students whose expectations are more in accord with the faculty's. Such a decision, one that American society seems in fact to be making, would be viewed by some as a courageous acknowledgment of the mistaken over-extension of higher education. Others, closer in spirit to Dewey and Goodman, would look upon such a decision as a) an unimaginative acceptance of the sacredness of present structures in higher education; and b) more devastatingly, as an endorsement of the "two societies" analysis of the generations. We would be saying in effect that the skills and knowledge necessary to understand the emerging world a) are already perfectly developed by the disciplinary experts in the University and b) only a small number of young people have the intelligence and disposition to master those skills and thence to participate in the decision-making of the society.

To reject this exclusionary alternative is to affirm a commitment to academically-based inter-generational communities. That commitment is significant: it says that despite our differences we are still members of a single society, that we have business together, maybe we are even concerned about each other's welfare. However, the commitment is not only ethically rudimentary but dangerously misleading, a function of the emotional connotations and incredible ambiguity of the term "community." The inclusionary commitment in question might be compatible with the faculty's regarding the students' set of expectations as altogether immature and thus in need of correction; or with the students regarding the faculty's set of expectations as arbitrary and outdated impositions of the powerful which must be circumvented. In short, the commitment to inter-generational community, although fundamentally necessary, tells us next to nothing about the nature of faculty-student relationships and offers us no insight for revitalizing the institution. We need more specific directions.

We can sense that direction by defining academic community with specific reference to the problems it must address and the parameters within which it must operate. What we are seeking are new structures of association readily intelligible structures of association which engage the intellectual and personal energies of students and faculty in common and shared enterprises, which confirm and work to realize the worthwhile expectations of students and faculty, which effectively challenge the unconstructive and devitalizing practices of students and faculty. Not incidentally, these new communities must operate in a context which can be counted on for many years to be reinforcing of centrifugal and privatizing pressures.

These general characteristics of the desired academic structures might be restated in the Deweyan terms of a "simplified," "balanced," and "purified" learning environment. The environment must be simplified, or as we would now say "mediated," in the sense that its features are at first "fairly fundamental," and readily intelligible to the uninitiated. The environment must be balanced, in that it contains a sufficient variety of elements to challenge the students to go beyond their personal and intellectual starting points. And the environment must be purified in the sense that the unworthy features "are insofar as is possible eliminated."[6] We are looking, in other words, for a learning environment which is a challenging microcosm of the University's potential, its ideal potential as the focus of inter-generational communities.

II.

A cluster of five interacting structures constitute FLC's learning environment: federated courses, a new kind of course called a Program Seminar, new kinds of teachers called Master Learners and Mumford Fellows, an inadequately named "Core Course," and interdisciplinary independent study projects. Three or four of the structures have been employed elsewhere—e.g., in Evergreen's Coordinated Studies Programs or Minnesota's Cross-Disciplinary Program or SUNY Binghamton's Integrated Semester Program or UCLA's Lower Division Program or Madison's Integrated Liberal Studies Program, but at least two of the structures and the entire cluster are, we believe, unique to Stony Brook.

1. Federation

The academic and social foundation of the FLC program is a federation of six or nine thematically related but disciplinarily diverse courses into two or three consecutive and cumulative integrated semesters. The themes are urgent contemporary issue, e.g., "Technology, Values and Society" or "World Hunger" or "Social and Ethical Issues in the Life Sciences." The courses are already existing disciplinary courses from the immense Stony Brook curriculum. For example, the program on "World Hunger" was created from the following departmental courses: "Contemporary Moral Problems," "The Ecology of Feast and Famine," "The Economics of Developing Countries," "The History of Latin America Through Film," "The Psychology of Eating and Drinking," and "Politics of Developing Areas." The programs are offered as academic minors, advertised as complementary to the majors of the participating departments, and spoken of as opportunities to expand horizons and to give focus and depth to one's career choice.[7]

Federation is the simplest of FLC's structural innovations, but relative to the eclipse of academic community, it is the most important. Other innovations have attracted more attention, for reasons of more obvious novelty, but federation of the sort described here is the necessary condition for the creation of vital academic communities. Many important consequences seem to flow solely from the federation. Hence, I need to explain in some detail this first structure of FLC, taking up three distinguishable elements within the federation: the focus on contemporary issues, the interdisciplinary or holistic context created by the federation, and the use of already existing courses.

A. *Focus on Contemporary Issues*

(1) *The emphasis on contemporary issues bridges generational gaps.* Students can understand much more readily what academic inquiry is about when it is so focused, especially in holistic and interdisciplinary contexts like FLC. Presumably, this was what we meant by "relevance" in the sixties.

The focus on contemporary issues should not be understood as if it excluded or even depreciated the study of history. The foci of FLC programs have always been such as to highlight the importance of studying the history of the problem.[8]

(2) The contemporary issues in question are in varying degrees, the very kind which Marshall McLuhan had in mind: urgent, open-ended questions for which the experts do not have answers. We are not talking about merely interesting contemporary themes—like "The Influence of Joyce on Contemporary Writers & Film Makers"—but urgent issues that are engulfing us, e.g., genetic engineering, Three-Mile Island and its implications, the poisoning of our food and water, the Women's Movement, the computer revolution or the reassessment of human potential.

(3) *FLC chooses only those contemporary issues which cannot be adequately addressed within the framework of a single discipline or division of the University*. While the structures of FLC might prove useful in a less inclusive context, one of our fundamental concerns is to render the University intelligible. Hence, almost all FLC programs have drawn courses from the three traditional divisions of the University, thus creating the desired microcosm of the University's resources. After FLC's guided introduction to those resources, students should be able to construct their own federated program.

B. *The Interdisciplinary Context*

(1) The federation creates the possibility of *shared experience between faculty and students*. Each of the faculty understands the problem under consideration primarily in terms of one discipline, broad though that might be. The students approach the problem in the light of several disciplines. Gradually, the faculty come to look upon the students as intellectually interesting, perhaps even as junior colleagues.

(2) In a real community, the members know what each is doing and how that activity relates to one's own and to the whole enterprise. This awareness on the part of the federated faculty, vital to its participation as learners in the community, is developed in a weekly *Faculty Seminar* which precedes by one semester the offering of the federated courses and through the circulation of detailed notes on each course. While still preserving the integrity of its own courses, the faculty is thus enabled to refer the material and perspectives of one course to others that the students are taking. In effect, each FLC program operates as a comparatively autonomous educational unit.

(3) *The federation of disciplinary courses to address a contemporary issue decreases the perceived arbitrariness of the University's enterprise and provides a manageable whole in relation to which the parts make*

sense. While FLC students do not develop even undergraduate-level expertise in all the disciplines federated into a program, they intuitively understand major aspects of what disciplines are and how they relate to each other.

(4) For the most part, *the federated courses complement each other*. Occasionally, they come into more or less direct conflict, as when someone from literature suggests that a colleague's apparent approval of a Monsanto pamphlet on the role of chemicals in our lives. In the presence of conflicting authority figures, students then perceive two important things: they cannot wholly rely on the judgment of the experts; and the disciplines, however complementary at some times, do not fit neatly back together like the pieces of a jig-saw puzzle.

(5) *The problem-focused federation offers a horizontal coherence that complements the vertical coherence of the departments*. At the outset, the courses have a thematic coherence which is supplemented as the students' own interest in sub-themes of the program generates connections between courses that none of the professors has seen. Some FLC professors regard this kind of horizontal and personal focus as more valuable and reliable than normal patterns of departmental preparation.[9]

C. *Already Existing Courses*.

The use of already existing courses, something that surprises many visitors to FLC, deserves more than passing consideration. We had the capacity, given the FIPSE grant, to generate entirely new courses. We rejected that course of action for the following reasons:

(1) A jettisoning of already existing courses would be altogether inconsistent with the diagnosis of the institution's ills in terms of atomization rather than specialization.

(2) Specially created courses and programs often court institutional marginality and create a refuge for their students.[10]

(3) Using already existing courses does not imply a total acceptance of the courses as they are. We *start* with already existing courses. Some of those courses, for good or ill, remain exactly as they are. Others get transformed beyond recognition.[11]

(4) The use of already existing courses has important implications for student involvement. The federated courses are of the same kind, if not identical with, courses the students might have taken anyway to satisfy distribution requirements or some requirements of their majors. Thus, students need not feel, as they often did in the sixties, that participation in an educational experiment places them out of the mainstream and wastes time with respect to what many regard as far more important

businesses, viz., fulfilling the requirements of one's major and thus preparing for a career.

2. The Program Seminar

The second of FLC's cluster of structural innovations is the variously-titled "Program Seminar" or "Meta-Seminar" or "Learning Seminar." Built atop the three federated courses of each semester, and led by the Master Learner and Mumford Fellow, the Seminar is most simply described as a discussion-session with three courses, rather than one, as its academic base.

Registration in the Seminar is limited to 35 students per section, with multiple sections as needed. These students are enrolled as a subset of the total enrollment in the federated courses. The organizational relationship of the federated courses to the Program Seminar is illustrated in the diagram on the following page.

The students gradually assume responsibility for the conduct of the Seminar. That responsibility includes choice of topic, designation of relevant material from the federated courses, opening presentations and facilitation of discussion. An uncommon amount of assistance is provided prior to a session as well as extensive evaluative feedback afterwards. Throughout the Seminar, more individualized intellectual activity occurs in journals, multi-staged papers, lengthy term papers and action-oriented projects. Master Learners and Mumford Fellows provide extensive feedback to the students, pressing them to gain optimal benefit from the federated courses and providing assistance as each defines his/her interests within the theme of the program. These individual products feed back into more public activities of the Seminar. Students thus participate in, indeed they are co-determiners of their curriculum.

Seminar activities vary greatly, a function of different features in the federated courses and diverse student interests and difficulties. A few examples may be worth more than the abstract statement of goals and operating mechanisms:

(1) In one FLC program, students responded incredulously to the engineer's claim that technology had never solved a major human problem without seriously offsetting side-effects. Puzzled students considered seemingly obvious counter-examples, e.g., eyeglasses, only to have them shot down by other students. Professors in philosophy and history were consulted in class and outside, and eventually the question was brought to the Program Seminar where several sub-groups of students were asked to

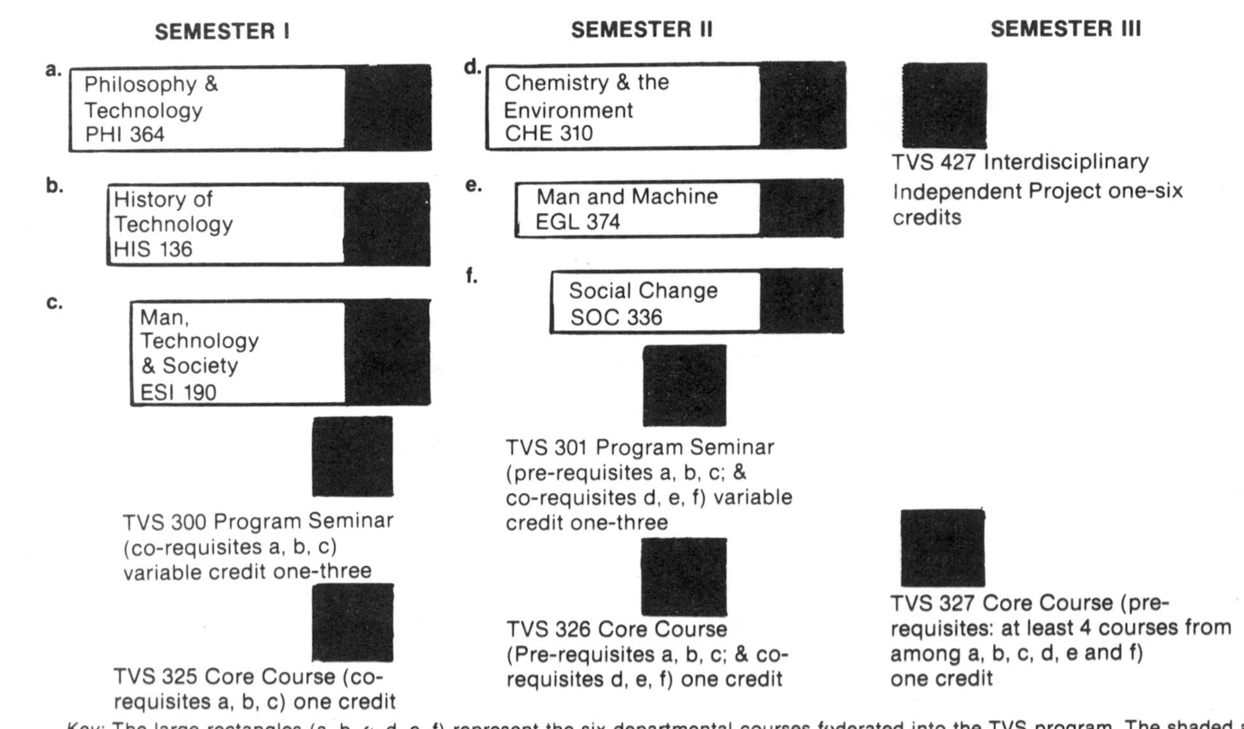

Key: The large rectangles (a, b, c, d, e, f) represent the six departmental courses federated into the TVS program. The shaded areas represent TVS students. In the large courses, both TVS students and the general student population are enrolled. The smaller squares represent the unique components of the TVS program: the Program Seminar taught by the Master Learner, the team-taught Core Course, and the Independent Project.

agree on the best examples from history which confirmed the engineer's claim and the strongest counter-examples. In the plenary session, the group assessed the examples and began to discuss (at the philosopher's suggestion) the concept of "solution" which underlies the claim.

(2) Professors in the program on "World Hunger" were employing different concepts of exploitation: an ecological one based on the carrying capacity of the land, an economic one based on the amount of return necessary to encourage re-investment, and a philosophical one based on the non-instrumental nature of the human being. The three concepts were compared in the Seminar, the results reported to the professors, and a modification was made of the final examination in economics to invite different perspectives on the subject matter.

(3) Students in a particular FLC program were evaluating the contribution of one federated course in polar ways, a function of the disciplinary prejudices of some students and of the unusual teaching style of the professor. A debate was set up in the Seminar, pitting three students (including the Mumford Fellow) who most appreciated the course, against three who deemed it worthless. The rest of the students mediated, pressing the debaters to be open to what the others were saying. Valuable insights were gained, among them a greater awareness of the kind of student who would have difficulty with courses of this sort and of what might be done to help them.

(4) Without being coaxed to do so, students frequently are on the lookout for more effective means to become involved with course material. The FLC program on "Social and Ethical Issues in the Life Sciences" elevated field trips to a central role in this enterprise. Participation in a highly emotional debate on abortion in a nearby school district and witnessing a commitment hearing at a psychiatric hospital became "real world" bases for reflecting in the Seminar on the material and perspectives of the federated courses.

The Program Seminar functions as a reliable cybernetic mechanism for the program. Many reactions to the courses which might never surface or be taken seriously elsewhere are discussed and evaluated in the Seminar. Students are aware that the Master Learner is monitoring teaching effectiveness, so they themselves are inclined to let fewer things pass without comment. Additionally, the comparative context of the Seminar's activities usually involves explicit and implicit evaluations of the material of the federated courses. Students might never tell one of the faculty that they think her course misconceives the nature of ethical decision-making, but that can emerge in the Program Seminar as it becomes obvious that the students do not take the professor's approach seriously. In the Seminar, the Master Learner and the Mumford Fellow are concerned to know why. The explanation may be an intellectual one or it may be an emotional one—e.g., a feeling that the professor just doesn't care about students. The response will be listened to; and if it is justified and widespread, an appropriate means will be found to communicate the information to the professor. The potential for improving the teaching at the institution is enormous. The impact on FLC students, however, is almost independent of a response to their reactions; they know that they are being listened to, they know that their feelings will not be dismissed *a priori* as irrelevant, and they learn in time (partly through exposure to the sharply diverse reactions to any style of teaching) that effective teaching is more difficult than they first supposed.

The idea for the Seminar originated in the awareness that shared residence could not be relied upon as a basis for vital academic community among the students. Opening up reflective spaces in the curriculum for students with common academic experience allows genuine academic community to flourish. The community can justify itself in purely academic terms—e.g., by the work of its students and its graduates. Along with those developments, however, must be noted the striking impact of the community on the personal lives of its members and on their commitment to the institution. Only a brief word about this extra-academic impact is possible here. For many students the Seminar is their first experience of any sort of community. For the vast majority, it is an engaging and exhilarating experience; they receive both encouraging support and challenging feedback for their fledgling ideas; they learn to provide that to others; they test different self-conceptions in a relatively safe environment; they learn about the difficulties of communicating in a diverse environment; they learn to take the needs of a group into account; and they feel the warmth and conviviality of sharing a wealth of good and bad academic experiences with friends. All of this in a context where they are beginning to think of themselves as persons with intellects and with valuable contributions to make to a troubled society. For the vast majority, it is a valuable and maturing experience.[12]

3. Master Learners and Mumford Fellows

The third of FLC's structural innovations is a new kind of teacher, the Master Learners and Mumford Fellows. Regular members of the faculty or advanced graduate students, these persons are "masters" in two senses: they have mastered one discipline to a degree which has earned the respect of their colleagues; and they are sufficiently accomplished as teachers to have earned the respect of both students and colleagues. As "learners" they undertake full-time study of a contemporary issue in which they have prior interest but no prior expertise. The Master Learner and Mumford Fellow (henceforth referred to as ML/MF) do everything the undergraduates do: they take all the federated courses, they write the exams and term papers, and they are graded. While working in FLC, the ML/MF's only teaching assignment is in the Program Seminar.

The ML/MF's are essentially builders of academic community. They strive to actualize the intergenerational community made possible by the structures of FLC. Full analysis of these complex, ambiguous and multi-faceted roles is beyond the scope of this essay; just six dimensions will have to suffice.[13]

A. ML/MF's serve as *role models* for the students, embodying all the ideals of the University: love of learning, the benefits of reflection and of critical thinking, the process of disciplinary inquiry, empirical orientation, openness, and the joys of discovery, to name but a few. Taken-for-granted aspects of the ML/MF's life, e.g., relating course materials to a television program or to a course of the previous semester or to personal problems, frequently open a student's eyes to the meaning of the reflective life.

B. The ML/MF's are *mediators or interpreters*. They interpret the expectations and behavior of faculty and students to each other, pressing each party to transcend initial caricatures and to respond to what is worthwhile in the other's expectations.

C. The ML/MF's are *integrators*. They communicate regularly with the federated faculty, calling attention to agreements, disagreements, connections and lacunae. In written reports and in the Faculty Seminar, they grope for a common language and for a common understanding of the issues that divide the faculty.

D. ML/MF's *provide feedback to the federated faculty* regarding the (in)effectiveness of their teaching. Such feedback is more differentiated (with respect to types of students), more empirically-based, more individualized, more long-range, more credible, more comparative and more extensive than a teacher is likely to receive in all of her career.

E. The ML/MF's are *midwives*. Comparably barren in the area of the programs' thematic focus as was Socrates, they are not able to transmit scores of heavily researched ideas. Like Socrates again, they are aware of their ignorance and in search of insight. One of their primary obligations is to assist in the development and evaluation of the students' own ideas. In case the image of midwifery is not clear: the ML/MF's are providing students the support and guidance to utilize freedom intelligently in a pluralistic setting.

F. The ML/MF's are *facilitators*. In the Program Seminar they maximize the intellectual potential of the community by improving the listening and presentational skills of the students, by identifying resources and opportunities for learning, and by placing students with similar or complementary interests in touch with each other.

4. The Core Course

The fourth of FLC's structural innovations is the inappropriately titled "Core Course." The print-out from the Registrar lists all the federated faculty as the teachers of this course. It would be more accurate to list all the participants—both faculty and students—as co-teachers and co-learners in the course.

Nowhere in FLC are the intergenerational partnerships more visible than in the Core Course. *The most striking feature of the Core Course is its meeting schedule*. The course is divided into three one-credit segments, usually meets once a month and is spread out over three semesters. This unusual structure, somewhat dictated by the discovery-oriented character of FLC themes, supports the academic and programmatic goals of the Core Course.

At the outset of the Core Course, the faculty have responsibility for the Core Course meetings. Their goals are three-fold:

A. To illumine by sustained interdisciplinary inquiry the central themes, and issues of the program;

B. To exhibit the nature and relationship of the federated disciplines; and

C. To model how persons skilled in one discipline integrate the sometimes complementary and sometimes conflicting perspectives of other disciplines and ideologies.

Topics of Core Course meetings must be broad enough to require multidisciplinary analysis. They must also be contemporary in the sense that students will recognize the importance of the issues. The faculty of the "Cities, Utopias & Environments" program, for example, examined shopping malls and each drew up a list of the questions most important for understanding the phenomenon. Discussions focused on the economic function of the mall as a major employer of the region, its socio-psychological function as a meeting place for the suburban young and its aesthetic and ecological impact upon the wider environment.

The Core Course meetings usually open with a panel presentation, followed by small-group discussions, and then a plenary summation. Two faculty members lead each discussion group, drawing upon the students' greater familiarity with the material of the federated courses to illumine the issue under discussion. When appropriate, the faculty leaders will contribute their own expertise or draw upon the often superior expertise of students in fields far from their own. Ideally speaking, the nature of the questions and of the discussions is such that the diversity of perspectives is experienced by all as an invaluable resource.

As the Core Course proceeds through its multi-semester life-span, an important change takes place. Gradually, students with special contributions to make become part of the opening panels, and eventually the entire opening presentation is made by the students. Not quite literally, faculty and students exchange roles. Symbolically, the exchange (which all participants know of in advance) fore signifies a changed relationship between the generations and underscores the academic meaning of the partnership. Pedagogically, the exchange has two important functions: it requires that the students project and then assume a non-passive role; and secondly, it focuses the efforts of faculty and students on a competency-outcome which is useful throughout the program (but especially in the Seminar): after a year in FLC, students should be able to put together a coherent presentation which draws on the perspectives of the federated disciplines to illumine a contemporary issue. But the exchange has more than symbolic and pedagogical justification. Ideally speaking, the exchange is justified as well in terms of merit: the younger partners in the inquiry have been studying (say) world hunger virtually full-time for over a year in the light of at least six disciplines. Most of the federated faculty, even with the best of efforts, will remain confined in the perspective of one or two disciplines. The students, like the ML/MF themselves, should have acquired a range of information and insights that is superior in an interdisciplinary context to that of the federated faculty. Hence it is altogether appropriate toward the end of a program that faculty and students should exchange roles. Lest the exchange remain merely symbolic, a simple criterion of success is employed: the federated faculty should be stimulated by and learning from the presentations of at least the good students in ways that the faculty themselves will judge to be interesting and valuable.[11]

5. The last in the cluster of FLC's curricular structures is the *Interdisciplinary Independent Study Projects*. Although important features of the FLC curriculum, they require but passing mention, since they are the least novel and the least complex of FLC's structures. Following completion of roughly 18 credits in an FLC program, students may construct a

project with two of the federated faculty. The length and intensity of the projects vary greatly and may involve an off-campus "field" dimension when appropriate. Many students will choose the professor in their major field to facilitate transferring the credits to the requirements of their majors.

III.

The organization of this essay around the five curricular structures has ignored crucial extra-curricular dimensions of community-building, e.g., block-scheduling and the creation of public meeting places. The exposition has also isolated the academic dimension from the holistic environment of FLC. To provide a sense of the interaction of the academic, the social, the personal and the generally extra-curricular, we would need an exposition focused on the daily and weekly experience of the FLC student. Since space limitations preclude such an exposition, two brief examples must suffice as images of the FLC experience:

1. An attempt to acquire an FLC lounge for use between classes succeeded after two years and 31 memoranda, but a request that the lounge be repainted seemed to be triggering another two-year battle. The students decided to paint the lounge themselves. Some faculty donated the paint, the equipment, moral support and a bit of muscle. Sandwiches and refreshments were brought in to keep the effort going all day long. As the students painted and ran down the ladders for cokes, they talked about their courses and about the sociobiology debate which they had recently encountered. They talked of other things, of course; but easily and naturally their common academic experience kept bobbing up in their interactions. In the opinion of my colleague, Lynne Mitchnick, this story captures the essence of FLC.

2. The second example is almost a left-handed compliment to the engaging nature of the FLC socio-academic environment. Susan, a non-FLC student in a philosophy class, burst into tears when she saw the take-home examination. "I'll never be able to do this," she cried. Linda, an FLC student, tried to comfort her by promising to help. "But you can't help me," Susan said, "you're not a philosophy major and you hate this course." "It doesn't matter," replied Linda. "I'm in FLC and you can't help learning the stuff even if you don't want to."

FLC is by no means a total success, neither with respect to the huge social problems which energized reformers of the sixties nor with respect to the much smaller slice of problems which it addresses. Regarding the former, the decision to work within the framework of already existing courses and personnel places severe limitations on what might be done. To take just one example, there are far too few women and minorities and Third World citizens on the faculty to create a truly diverse set of perspectives. And with regard to the latter: while we may have been impatient to have expected otherwise, FLC is only now beginning to refine its awareness of the problems besetting the kind of curriculum all of higher education will soon be involved with, namely one which centrally addresses change, complexity, and diversity. Our tasks remain challenging.

Nevertheless, FLC has had considerable impact upon students, faculty, Stony Brook, and upon other institutions of higher education. The implications of that success are many and diverse. Among the more important implications are the following:

1. It is not necessary to turn our backs on the values of the sixties in order to have a more coherent curriculum or a common learning experience.

2. The truly significant reforms in higher education are ones which complement the atomistic, transmission-dominated medium. If that medium does not change, as it is not changing in the general education movement, little will be accomplished. If it does change, all sorts of energies will be released and many people who were written off as deadwood will be engaged and renewed. The general direction of significant reform in higher education is that of building academic communities.

3. Relatedly, much of the passivity, illiteracy, lack of motivation and creativity which faculty complain about in their students is structurally induced by an unimaginative curriculum. Opening up spaces in a discovery-oriented curriculum invites and rewards the creative involvement of students. And the literacy appropriate to the situation develops naturally.[15]

4. The commitments of the industrialized West to both democracy and technological expertise have always been in tension. Our increasingly complex world exacerbates that tension and tempts us to abandon either the expertise or the participation of citizens in all the decisions which affect our lives. FLC is one curricular model in which the expertise is relied upon to illumine complex problems in a context where a) its strengths and weaknesses will be obvious; and b) citizens are educated to develop their own perspectives.

5. The one-half to three-quarters of a student's credits earned outside the major seldom cohere meaningfully, seldom relate to one's major interests, and hardly ever effect that expansion of horizons often sought by Pass/No Credit options and distributed requirements. Outside the major, one's education is a random affair. FLC offers one model wherein a significant portion of one's non-major study can be coherent, meaningful

and interest-expanding—even in subject areas which one had dismissed as unworthy of study. A specialized field of expertise may be necessary for meaningful participation in contemporary society, but our education need not constrict our potential and our identity to that one field.

6. Relatedly, the dichotomy between special and general education is a misleading one. The generally educated person ought to be defined, not in terms of some abstract skills or agreed upon exposures, but in terms of an experienced relationship between specialized knowledge and its function in a complex and diverse world. Educated persons of this mold are accomplished in one discipline and understand its strengths and weaknesses, most particularly the inherent partiality of its viewpoint. They have moved from passivity to active commitment in a relativistic world. They have immersed themselves in a communal, interdisciplinary study of one problem of social magnitude and have learned thereby the value—indeed, the necessity, of seeking many and diverse perspectives. They have developed skills in understanding and in integrating these diverse perspectives. They will themselves be able to conduct with their colleagues and to contribute their own expertise to subsequent social issues as the need arises in their lives. Tolerance of ambiguity, emphatic understanding, awareness of their own partiality, openness to growth through dialogue in plural communities—all those things have become virtually second nature to them.

7. Both economies and diseconomies of scale exist in large universities (and small colleges as well). Among the many economies are those which allow FLC to use already existing courses to address one contemporary issue after another without either a costly administrative structure or visiting faculty. The familiar diseconomies—impersonality, non-engagement, lack of community—can all be addressed without withdrawing into a small and allegedly more humane enclave. FLC is a dialectic of the large and the small, incorporating the strengths and avoiding the weaknesses of each scale.

8. Top-notch faculty and career-conscious students in an upwardly mobile, research-oriented university will still participate in experimental and demanding programs. The variety of institutional inducements for participants has not been described in this essay. I believe the essential inducement, the one which makes the others effective, is the continuity of the activity with one's major commitments. For faculty this means the use of already existing courses. For students, it means the incorporation of FLC programs into distribution requirements and the acceptance of FLC programs by eight or ten departments toward the requirements of the major.

NOTES

1. The first report of the Institutional Self Study was called *Stony Brook in Transition* (Stony Brook, 1974). *The Eclipse of Academic Community*, (Stony Brook, 1975), written by the author of the present essay, was one of several follow-up studies.

2. Major portions of FLC have been adopted by LaGuardia Community College, Queens College, SUNY at Plattsburgh, and the University of Nebraska at Lincoln. Three small liberal arts institutions, Dennison, Rollins, and Lesley, have started or will shortly start FLC programs.

3. Several people have provided significant assistance to me in framing this essay. Participants in a conference on the implications of FLC, held at Stony Brook in June 1981, all called attention to the need for an explanation of FLC less wedded to the context of Stony Brook and more rooted in a theory of academic community. In particular I wish to acknowledge the help of Susan Bordo, Lynda Glennon, Anita Landa, John Lane, Robert Marcus, Lee Miller, Marjorie Miller, Kenneth MacKenzie, Lynne Mitchnick, Steve Olsen, Robert Smith and Marshall Spector.

4. Quoted by Paul Goodman, *Compulsory Mis-education* and *The Community of Scholars*. (New York: Vintage Books, 1964), p. 277. Goodman's reference on this quotation is incorrect, as is its attribution to Theodore Newcomb. The more likely author was John Bushnell.

5. Ibid.

6. See John Dewey, *Democracy and Education* (New York: The Free Press, 1944), pp. 20–21.

7. In its first five years, FLC offered programs on the following topics: "World Hunger," "Cities, Utopias and Environments," Technology, Values and Society," "Social and Ethical Issues in the Life Sciences," a revision of the "World Hunger" program called "Hunger, Health and Poverty in International Perspective," a re-cycling of "Technology, Values and Society," "Ways of Seeing," "Human Nature," and "Science for Public Understanding." Fifty different faculty members (including ten graduate students) from nineteen different departments and three colleges participated in these programs.

8. Some members of the History department and the period-oriented English department resisted the development of FLC at Stony Brook because of the focus on contemporary issues. Over time, however, faculty from these two departments—along with philosophy and sociology—have been the most frequent participants in FLC programs.

9. Preliminary studies of the academic performance of FLC students in upper-level classes for which they do not have the usual departmental prerequisites do indicate achievement of an outstanding sort. But additional studies are in progress, none of which unfortunately will isolate the effect of federation alone.

10. Student perception of FLC as a refuge from the ordinary Stony Brook curriculum would be hard to maintain in view of the fact that FLC frequently federates the largest classes on campus, ones that enroll 600 or 1,200 students a semester.

11. These transformations are so numerous as to have led my colleague Lee Miller to describe FLC's emphasis on already existing courses as a fiction and to suggest that we speak instead of already existing interests. Nonetheless, the courses are already there in the catalogue when we start.

At institutions like Stony Brook, where three or four regularly offered courses serve as vehicles for transmitting one's scholarly research, the use of already existing courses engages the faculty's central commitments, lessening the possibility of artificial or non-engaging involvement. At smaller colleges where a faculty's commitment to good teaching may take precedence over the teaching of particular courses, it may be less important to use already existing courses.

12. The impact of FLC on students is described in "Significant Changes—I" and "Significant Changes—II," unpublished evaluation reports of Professor Anita Landa of Les-

ley College. A volume of essays by faculty participants in FLC is being readied for a 1983 publication.

13. The fullest treatment of the ML/MF role is in my "Communities of Learners. . . ," in *In Opposition to Core Core Curriculum*, ed. by James W. Hall with Barbara Keveles (Connecticut: Greenwood Press, 1982).

14. The simple criterion is adequate only as a rough measure of the existence of a genuine, intergenerational academic community. Epistemologically, the issues are far more complex, requiring the articulation of standards of excellence for interdisciplinary inquiries. In "Communities of Learners. . . ," I have outlined such standards, and I am currently working on a lengthier essay addressing this topic.

15. This point, which may appear as a startling and naive repetition of romantic errors of the sixties, is argued at length in my "Ethics of Helping; A Comparison of the Role of Self-Reliance in International Affairs and Pedagogy," in Metaphilosophy, Vol. 12, No. 2 (April 1981) pp. 181–205.

PART FOUR

The Roots of Contemporary Experimentation

Editors' Introduction

The views of John Dewey and Alexander Meiklejohn are in sharp conflict at the abstract level of educational philosophy. Indeed, in his *Education Between Two Worlds*, Meiklejohn appears to single Dewey out as his favorite devil's advocate ("The most striking defect in Dewey's 'general theory of education' is its disparagement of intelligence.") At the levels of pragmatic implementation, however, the progeny of these two great American philosophers have been observed to co-exist harmoniously. This has been clearly shown in the development of The Evergreen State College.

Many of the specific pedagogical expressions of Dewey's "progressive" educational philosophy became common features of many of the alternative colleges spawned in the 60's and 70's. These include coordination of academic study with related "hands-on" work in the community, independent study, student involvement in curricular planning, faculty participation in personal counseling and academic advising, self-paced learning, external degree programs, off-campus outreach programs, adult degree programs and narrative evaluation.

Before these features became commonplace alternatives they had been successfully experimented with at Goddard College under the critical scrutiny of Royce Pitkin, for many years in comparative obscurity, and then into the 50's as a model for an increasing number of small private colleges across the country.

Arthur Chickering's chapter traces this legacy.

Any history of the roots of the alternative education movement of the 1960's must also acknowledge the influence of Alexander Meiklejohn's ideas. Meiklejohn's vision spread to various educational institutions in the 1960's and 1970's—Old Westbury, The Evergreen State College, San Jose, Kenyon College, the University of California—Berkeley.

As Brown, Crawford, Crowley and Sapir note, Meiklejohn was committed to education which would prepare citizens for a free society. He believed that "our scheme of government and life can succeed only if, in their more mature years, men and women will engage in careful, enthusiastic, and guided study of common values, common dangers, and common opportunities." Looking at the curriculum of his time, Meiklejohn found it incoherent, divisively pitting students against one another, and failing to stimulate a sense of community. His solution was a required curriculum, respectful of students, progressive in pedagogy, and centrally based in ethics, which he saw as the "unifying foundation of the curriculum."

It is somewhat ironic that Meiklejohn's ideas would reappear in the politicized and individualistic 1960's and 1970's as the "elective system" reemerged with full force. The strains in this period resulting from the dual emphasis on individualism on the one hand, and community on the other, are evident throughout this volume, but Cadwallader's description of San Jose is perhaps most graphic in this regard. A number of the other institutions which worked with Meiklejohn's ideas also courted their opposite, a totally nonprescribed curriculum, and some of the institutions adopted the form but not the essential moral content of the Meiklejohn curriculum.

In the past decade the important question "knowledge for what" has again become central in higher education. Many institutions have attempted to answer the question through a revised general education curriculum. Few doubt the need for this reexamination. Recently, the Carnegie Commission issued on a new report on rising civic illiteracy. The report urges a vast educational commitment to civic education as the only solution.

> "One point emerges with stark clarity from all we have said: higher education and the nation's future are inextricably bound together. A new generation of Americans must be educated for life in an increasingly complex world. . . A ringing call today for colleges and universities to concern themselves with values and society's concerns seems, at first blush, almost ludicrously quixotic. Not only is the cultural coherence of an earlier day gone forever, but the very notion of cohesion seems strikingly inapplicable to the vigorous diversity of contemporary life. . . Within the academy itself, subject specialists seem increasingly fragmented, splintered into innumerable factions. . . America's colleges and universities need an inner compass of their own. They must perform for society an integrative function, seeking appropriate responses to life's most enduring questions, concerning themselves not just with information and knowledge, but with wisdom. In the end, education's primary mission is to develop within each student the capacity to judge wisely in matters of life and conduct."[2]

We would do well to reexamine the legacy of the alternative education movement in the 1960's and the thoughts of Alexander Meiklejohn as we confront this important and difficult challenge.

NOTE

1. *Education Between Two Worlds*, Alexander Meiklejohn, Atherton Press, N.Y., 1966, p. 152.
2. Carnegie Commission, "Higher Learning in the Nation's Service," Carnegie Foundation, Washington, D.C., 1981, pp. 55–60.

XVII. Alternatives for the 80's
The Goddard-Pitkin Legacy

by

ARTHUR W. CHICKERING

Many key issues of the 1980's were anticipated and addressed during the early 60's by a beleaguered band of adventurous administrators and faculty members at a few small private liberal arts colleges across the country. They were beleaguered for two reasons. Most were financially hard-pressed. Their ideas were outrageous to most institutions still comfortably complacent in the 50's, with steady enrollment growth as the early members of the World War II baby boom reached college age. Now that the bloom is off the boom, and now that much of higher education is becoming beleaguered and hard-pressed, the ideas and activities of these small colleges are surprisingly relevant to the concerns we face in the decade ahead.

One of the tiniest, most hard-pressed, and by all accounts, the most outrageous, was Goddard College. Started in 1938 by Royce Stanley Pitkin, a student of John Dewey and William Heard Kilpatrick, Goddard took the ideas of those philosophers seriously and was greatly influenced by the work of the Progressive Education Association. Kilpatrick chaired the intitial advisory committee which worked with Pitkin to conceptualize Goddard's basic orientation and program. In 1959, the point of departure for this paper, the College was a community of 120 students, 22 faculty members, and support staff. Most of Goddard's students came from the Boston-New York-Philadelphia strip. A Manor House and the renovated barns and out-buildings of a country estate in Plainfield, Vermont served as the campus. The physical location was beautiful, with rolling fields and woodlands looking off toward the main range of the Green Mountains to the west. Plainfield Village comprised 500 souls, two gas stations, a general store and Bill the Barber. Nearby Barre had a population of 13,000 and Montpelier, eight miles in the other direction and capitol of the state, had 8,000. Burlington, forty-five miles away with a population of 40,000, was the largest city within a 150-mile radius. The ideas and activities espoused and pursued by this small, geographically isolated, community of administrators, faculty, students and support staff, were as outrageous to many members of the local and larger Vermont community as they were to most members of the local and larger higher education community.

A comprehensive six-year "Experiment in College Curriculum Organization" was formulated during 1957 and 1958, funded by the Ford Foundation and begun in September 1959. This experiment was consistent with the educational philosophy which had dominated the institution since its founding; it built on several programs and activities which had already proven effective. Its final formulation grew out of extensive discussions which occurred during the regularly-scheduled faculty meetings held in the living room of the President's house over tea or sherry, from 3:00 to 5:30 every Friday afternoon when the College was in session.

The key ideas in which the Goddard program was, and would be, anchored were: (1) Students would develop increased self-reliance and strengthened capacity for social contribution. (2) They would develop increased intellectual competence and advance their understanding of other cultures. (3) The institution aimed to use more effectively the increasing store of knowledge without proliferating courses. (4) Ways would be found by which each teacher could work with more students without losing the values of close personal association. (5) The College would make the best possible use of new learning aids, and (6) it would use available knowledge concerning human growth and learning more effectively in the continued development of the College program. These basic aims and educational principles were consistent with practices and programs already in place.

Goddard made no use of crdits except for transfer purposes. For those purposes a semester's work was given 15 credits. A student was not permitted to take more than three courses; some took two and occasionally a student would concentrate on one course. Most students in their final semester spent all of their time on their senior study. The small faculty necessarily taught in broad subject matter areas.

All students were required to spend eight hours per week in an on-campus work program. The work program included a diverse collection of options, from para-professional assistance to faculty and administrators, to office work, to work on buildings and grounds which ranged from menial chores to sophisticated construction and repair jobs. Both faculty member and administrator taught. Each also had "counselees." The term was used to reflect a broader perspective than "advisees," which implied a more narrow focus on academic concerns. Weekly meetings between counselor and counselee were expected and were meant to be an important and regular part of the teaching and learning process.

Narrative evaluations were used rather than letter or number grades. These evaluations were completed by work program supervisors as well as by teachers. Student self-evaluation of each study area and of work program performance was required. The last week of the semester was spent preparing and discussing these evaluations. A final evaluation conference between each counselee and counselor reviewed the work of the semester, and considered the implications for future plans. This conference resulted in a recommendation concerning credit for the semester signed by both faculty member and student. When disagreement occurred it was referred to the Dean or to the President for resolution. In addition to the regular 16-week fall and spring semesters, students were required to complete a non-resident work term each year, normally during January and February, when no classes were scheduled. Evaluation of this work term by each student and counselor also became part of the record.

Students were admitted to the "Junior Division" which normally comprised the first two years of the four-year program. But admission to the "Senior Division" was not automatic, even if the work of the first two years had been successfully completed. Each student had to apply for Senior Division admission by designing a program of study for the last two years. This program was designed in consultation with appropriate faculty members. Approval was required by the faculty member identified as the counselor for that period and by the Dean or President. Admission to the Senior Division was withheld until a student could define a suitable program. On rare occasions, admission would be denied because the student was not judged capable of successfully completing Senior Division work, even though Junior Division studies had been satisfactory. Such students graduated from the Junior Division and were recognized as successful at that level.

Three programs had been developed to provide opportunities for off-campus work by students:

1. The *Educational Resources Project* aimed to test whether college

students could help small public schools by serving as assistants to teachers and thereby also advance their education and development. Students worked two days each week with teachers in the nearby small, rural, often "one-room" schools. They performed a variety of tasks and assumed teaching responsibilities in areas such as art, music, drama, French, science, and recreation. On-campus independent and group studies were tied to these responsibilities. Participants met regularly to examine their experiences in those settings, which were strikingly different from the urban and suburban schools from which most students had come.

2. The *Vermont Community Development Program* grew out of cooperation between Goddard and the Vermont Labor and Farm Council in a long series of conferences at the College and in northern Vermont communities. It was an adult education project which aimed to help citizens recognize and solve community problems and to establish cooperative relationships between the citizens, the students, and the College for their mutual benefit. An additional aim was to see if the "Rogerian approach" would be effective in encouraging community development.
3. The *Comparative Cultures Program* aimed to add meaning to the study of a foreign language by including study of the culture of which it is a part. It used the interest of students in the social sciences as an introduction to foreign languages and cultures. The proximity of French Canada provided an excellent resource. Students in this program devoted two-thirds of their time to the history, economics, social institutions, literature and language of French Canada for at least one semester prior to living and working in French Canada for a two-month nonresident term.

Faculty development activities to improve teaching by applying research findings in the behavioral sciences were also already underway. A three-day pre-semester faculty conference began the Fall semester in September 1959.* The experiment and what it implied for faculty and student behavior and for institutional development was thoroughly discussed. These pre-semester conferences persisted throughout the Experiment. The purposes and practices of the Experiment were continually part of the agendas for the weekly Friday afternoon faculty meetings in the President's living room. They were supplemented by small group meetings which pursued topics such as "The Workshop Approach to Teaching," "Evaluation in the Teaching-Learning Process," Extending

*Cadwallader and others also note the importance of explicit and continued professional development opportunities to discuss and develop "the experiment."

the Use of Learning Aids," and "Goal Directedness and Increased Depth and Focus."

During January and February, when students were on their nonresident work term, workshops on Psychoanalytic Concepts and Education and on Education and Behavioral Sciences brought persons from many institutions throughout eastern United States to join Goddard faculty in exploring concepts which might improve educational practices. There, before the brightly burning fireplace, under the leadership of resource persons like Carl Rogers, Brock Chisholm, Laurence Kubie, Ralph Tyler, Mike Giles, Dick Jones, and Ernest Boyer, thirty to sixty experienced professionals spent three-day weekends examining the implications of recent findings and long-standing principles from the behavioral sciences. With the added stimulation of plentiful "social hours" and fine food, these conversations ranged widely long into the winter evenings, through howling blizzards or through evening walks in crystal-clear, stone-still moonlight at twenty below. Goddard staff who shared these workshops were mightily enriched by the content and the friendships; they were strongly stimulated to test new insights in their own behavior as teachers, resource persons, counselors, colleagues, and as members of a vibrant educational community.

In addition, every teacher observed the classroom teaching of at least one colleague and was, in turn, observed by at least three colleagues. Each teacher also had the opportunity to tape and listen to several classes and to discuss them with others.

So the *Experiment in Curriculum Organization* was being undertaken by an institution which already was operating in many ways which were consistent with the key aims and educational principles of the grant proposal. The grant would lead to an enrichment of those earlier options, to a sharpening of those practices, and to an increased clarity concerning Goddard's purposes and principles.

Upon receipt of the grant, nine new staff were employed, enlarging the faculty by thirty-seven per cent. These staff additions helped provide released time for those already employed and created a core staff ready to respond to student enrollments which were expected to triple from 120 to 350 during the six years of the experiment. And, indeed, the College did grow steadily to an enrollment of 380 during these years.

These occasions for professional development were accompanied by periodic requests from the Coordinator of Evaluation. Faculty completed exercises which operationalized institutional goals in terms of desired student characteristics and measurable outcomes. They were enlisted in evaluation activities themselves, completing questionnaires concerning institutional practices, taking and reacting to tests used for student evaluation, examining and rating student records to assess change, and considering the implications of preliminary findings. At the same time, the Director of the Learning Aids Center was cajoling, exhorting and demonstrating the use of new learning aids. Faculty members were paid during the summers and non-resident terms to develop new resources and to incorporate these materials in their courses and independent study work with students.

While these basic human resources were being enriched, other resources were created. The print and micro-film resources of the library grew. The new Learning Aids Center was constructed, and, with faculty consultation and assistance, housed an increasing range of films, tape-slides and video materials, programmed books and other study guides. Off-campus opportunities for significant work by students were added. The *Vermont Youth Study* provided opportunities for participation in sociological research concerning rural delinquency. This involved direct observations, interviews with parents and children, and survey research. Most of the data collection was done by Goddard students. The *Big Brother-Big Sister Program* made possible more direct personal relationships with young children and early adolescents. The *Comparative Cultures Program* was extended to the study of Spanish. It followed the same model of cultural and language studies and used Puerto Rico as a site for working and living during the non-resident term. A *Rural School Community-College Counseling* project provided another arena for service and exchange between Goddard and its neighboring communities.

An *Adult Degree Program* restricted to students age 26 and older was begun in the summer of 1963. It was developed by Evelyn Bates who drew on her former experience as director of adult education and community services, as secretary of the Section on Residential Adult Education of the Adult Education Association of the United States, and on her study of adult education while a Fulbright lecturer at the University of New England in New South Wales, Australia. The Program involved six-month cycles which began and ended with two-week residential periods on campus, during which students were exposed to a rich mix of lectures, films, group discussions and individual conferences. During these residencies, independent studies were designed and evaluated. These studies were pursued during the months away using resources local to the student and with regularly-scheduled communication by phone and mail with the supervising faculty member. This "distance learning" was supplemented by occasional faculty visits and group meetings for clusters of students in geographic proximity to one another. Although many faculty members taught in this program, it grew so rapidly that six additional persons were employed, supplementing the staff available for the regular undergraduate activities.

The Experiment was backed by six years of empirical evaluative research. (For detailed reports see Beecher, G., Chickering, A. W., Hamlin, W. G., and Pitkin, R. S. *An Experiment in College Curriculum Organization*, Goddard College, 1966, Chickering, A. W., *Journal of Applied Behavioral Science*, Chickering, A. W., *Education and Identity*, San Francisco, Jossey Bass Inc., 1969.) The evidence clearly documents Goddard's success in developing and carrying out many innovations which are being adopted or critically examined in the 80's. Respecting and responding to individual differences in background, purposes and learning styles through contract learning, personalized systems of instruction, mastery learning, interdisciplinary studies and individualized majors or degree programs is becoming increasingly widespread. The use of "learning aids" and the application of new technologies, not only with films, video, and records but also with computers and micro-computers is gathering increasing momentum. The use of off-campus "experiential learning" as an integral part of academic studies, through field trips, volunteer activities, internships, and cooperative programs is increasing in both quantity and quality. The Council for the Advancement of Experiential Learning (CAEL) has more than 360 institutional members and a comprehensive publication program addressing key issues. Can we trace any connections? Are there any threads which connect Goddard's ideas, activities, and the persons associated with them in the early 60's to these current concerns? Can we discern any legacy which has persisted beyond those lively years in the life of a small, hard-pressed College off in the woods of Vermont?

OFFSPRING

Except in well-ordered families or specialized areas, it is difficult to trace ancestors. It is also the case that a good idea seems to have many parents and that less successful offspring seem to be orphans. These conditions certainly obtain for educational innovation. We are not so presumptuous, nor so ignorant of other innovative programs during the 60's, that we claim any chain of causality from Goddard's program to current innovative practices elsewhere. A more accurate metaphor would place the offspring that the College and Tim Pitkin helped conceive and nurture as threads in a tapestry of change which has grown in size, texture, and complexity in the twenty years since the Experiment began. In this perspective it is possible to identify some strands of association and influence that have made recognizable contributions to change in higher education.

One of these strands actually began to be spun in 1956 when Forest Davis called Pitkin's attention to a *Time Magazine* article which reported that Duane Hurley, then President of Salem College, in West Virginia, was organizing a meeting of small, nonaccredited private colleges. Pitkin went to the Palmer House in Chicago and found about 15 other presidents there who joined together to create the Council for Advancement of Small Colleges. The organization's primary purpose was to help members achieve regional accreditation. Three "Commissions" were established: Fund Raising, Administration, and Research and Experimentation. Pitkin, who was more interested in educational research and experimentation than in accreditation, became chairman of that Commission and served until the mid-sixties. In the summers of 1958, 1960, 1961 and 1962, Pitkin organized week-long "Case Study Workshops." Each of these workshops brought together knowledgeable small college faculty members and administrators from around the country to examine educational issues related to a CASC "Case College." Milligan, Malone, Nasson, and Messiah were the four "Cases" during those years. Resource persons were drawn from new and experimental institutions such as Monteith at Wayne State, New College at Hofstra, Stephens College in Columbia Missouri, Antioch, and, of course, Goddard. Among the resource persons were Dick Jones, then a counselor and faculty member at Brandeis, and Ernest Boyer, then Dean of Upland College outside Los Angeles. These workshops provided opportunities to examine critical issues concerning curricular design, teaching, evaluation, student-faculty relationships, educational environments, alternative scheduling, work-study arrangements and the like. They provided a forum for sharing not only the Goddard program and the Experiment, but also the creative thinking of other small college educators.

Boyer and Pitkin hit it off well and developed a lasting friendship. They recognized a strong mutual concern to improve teaching and educational practice in higher education. They shared an unusual capacity to ask fundamental questions, to get quickly to the heart of issues and to generate creative alternatives. And they were not only sharpshooters, but very fast on the draw, next to unbeatable in debate about educational issues. They thrived on the repartee and hot arguments that inevitably accompanied these case study workshops. In an effort to stimulate faculty to think differently about education and teaching, Boyer led Upland to create a month-long intersession when the whole College ceased its regular operation. Students and faculty together looked at a large complex issue through the perspectives of varied disciplines, using both internal and external resources. Mike Giles, Pitkin's long-time friend and colleague, helped design and lead the first of these. *The Problem of Russia* was chosen as the first topic, signaling Boyer's concern about international relationships, which continued to find expression during his later years as Chancellor of the State University of New York, as Commissioner of Education, and as co-author of *Educating for Survival*.

During 1960 and 1963, Boyer and Pitkin designed the *Project on Student Development in Small Colleges*. This project, carried out in collaboration with thirteen small colleges, was designed to stimulate change by collecting comprehensive information about the characteristics of entering students, the educational programs, and student experiences. This information was to be shared with faculty members and administrators of each institution as a basis for improving teaching and creating new alternatives. The hope was to reduce attrition and strengthen both "cognitive" and "affective" outcomes. Funding was obtained from the Applied Research Branch of the National Institute for Mental Health.

That spring Sam Gould, then Chancellor of the University of California at Santa Barbara, accepted the Chancellorship of the State University of New York system and invited Boyer to join him as Executive Dean. Boyer accepted that position and Art Chickering, who had been involved in the early deliberations and was completing his work on the Goddard Experiment, stepped in as Project Director.

The Project on Student Development was not very successful in stimulating change in the participating colleges. Chickering brought little sophistication about planned change in higher education, and with booming enrollments during the late sixties there was little outside impetus to make changes at institutions with little intrinsic motivation to improve their programs. The Project did result in numerous presentations and publications which were shared with higher education professionals around the country. The most significant of these was *Education and Identity* which drew not only on the Project but also on earlier research at Goddard. This volume turned out to be of significant value to student affairs professionals, serving not only those who worked in small colleges but those who staffed large institutions as well. The "seven vectors of student development," which were first formulated during the Goddard Experiment, provided a needed conceptual framework for designing services and activities to explicitly encourage student development. As such, it helped spawn the "student development approach" which became a major factor in training student affairs personnel and in program development activities of that profession.

At the end of the Project on Student Development, Chickering designed a follow-up project which would capitalize on the emerging research concerning organizational behavior and planned change which had been effectively synthesized by Ron Havelock in 1969. Called *Strategies for Change and Knowledge Utilization*, this project was similar to its predecessor in collecting comprehensive information about student characteristics, educational practices and student change in collaboration with eight participating colleges and universities. It differed in being much more explicit and intentional about institutional change and professional development. Bill Hannah, who had worked with Chickering on the earlier Project, was the first Director. Jack Linquist, employed as one of the three original staff members, became project director when personal circumstances forced Hannah's resignation. Lindquist brought substantial sophistication concerning organizational behavior and planned change from his prior experience and doctoral studies at the University of Michigan. Tim Pitkin was a member of the Advisory Board and a key resource person. The result was not only significant change in several participating institutions, but also one of the first major publications concerning planned change in higher education, *Strategies for Change: An Adaptive Development Approach*.[1] At the termination of that project, Lindquist spent two years leading a Kellogg Foundation project to disseminate and encourage the use of some fifty innovative programs which the Foundation had supported. Following this effort, Chickering and Lindquist designed and established the Institute for Academic Improvement as part of the Center for Higher Education in the College of Education at Memphis State University. This Institute draws on the experience and knowledge resulting from those earlier efforts to work with teams of faculty members and administrators at participating institutions to improve the quality of education for diverse adult students. Bill Hannah subsequently went to the University of New England in Armidale, Australia, where he helped provide leadership for a Center for Higher Education much like the Institute. The Center is a resource for program improvement in colleges and universities in Australia and the South Pacific. Lindquist subsequently became President of Goddard, which lends a certain symmetry to that chain of influence.

Meanwhile, Boyer had been busy with the State University of New York system. He became Vice Chancellor and played a key role in establishing a new SUNY at Old Westbury. Under the leadership of Harris Wofford, former Peace Corps Director and the first president, this College was to be anchored in one of the basic propositions underlying the Goddard Experiment. Students were to be directly involved in community action and service, which would be an integral part of the college program and their academic studies. Goddard professionals, graduates, and students were involved in the early planning sessions. Then, soon after he became Chancellor, Boyer created a task force to design yet another new addition to the SUNY system which was to become Empire State College. The task force report sounded much like Goddard's Experiment. This new institution was to meet the diverse educational needs of New York State citizens.* It was to develop programs tailored to their needs and purposes and provide flexible alternatives that would make use of diverse, already-available community resources for learning. It was to recognize the knowledge and competence they brought from prior learning and help them make useful connections between their academic studies and their responsibilities at work and in the community. The institution was to operate on a state-wide basis and provide education that was not restricted by time or place. Boyer employed Chickering as Empire State's first Academic Vice President and the result was an institution based on the key principles of the Goddard program and its Experiment. In consultation with one or more "mentors" each student designs an individual degree program which is approved by a faculty committee. The program is pursued through a series of "learning contracts" based on the student's purposes. Each contract includes diverse learning activities and educational resources, with evaluation methods and criteria established appropriate to its purposes. The time period for a given contract depends upon the purposes and activities specified; they are typically from one to six months long. Students use a wide range of community resources as well as the expertise of full-time faculty, adjunct faculty and tutors. Each student's knowledge and competence, derived from prior experiential learning as well as formal study, is assessed at the outset. A student's status with regard to degree completion and the particular areas for additional study incorporated in the degree program are based on this assessment.** In addition, extensive on-going work and life experience is used as an integral part of the academic studies included in learning contracts. The College recognized the power and flexibility of small units by establishing small "Learning Centers" throughout the state, which serve from 300 to 500 fulltime equivalent students. This design provides for the close

---

*Empire now serves some 3800 students through nine regional study centers.

**Thomas Edison College in New Jersey represents perhaps the logical full development of this approach. It exists solely to put together various forms of credit for degrees.

student-faculty contact which was of particular concern in the counselor-counselee and teacher-student relationships at Goddard.

This, then, is one major strand, or more like a loosely-woven web, contributing to the tapestry of change in higher education, which had its beginning in the Goddard program and Experiment in College Curriculum Organization carried out during the Early sixties.

A second major strand began to be spun in the winter of 1963 when, on the occasion of Goddard's 25th Anniversary, President Pitkin invited his counterparts from twelve experimental colleges around the country to a weekend conference on the Impact and Future of Experimental Colleges. Jim Dixon from Antioch, Bud Hodgkinson and Reamer Kline from Bard, Bill Fells from Bennington, Sister P. J. Mannion from Loretto Heights, Woodborn Ross from Monteith, Roger Gay from Nasson, Adolph Anderson and Henry Acres from New College, Hofstra, John Elmendorf, from New College, Sarasota, Dick Frost from Reed, Paul Ward from Sarah Lawrence, Joe Mullin from Shimer, and Seymour Smith from Stephens joined Tim and other Goddard faculty and administrators in front of the Manor House fireplace. They shared their sense of isolation and the varied obstacles they encountered as they tried to break new ground or simply maintain a foothold against the conservative forces of accrediting associations, state and federal agencies, graduate schools, professional associations, and their own internal dynamics. They criticized private and federal funding agencies which ignored them in favor of more prestigeous traditional institutions, despite their demonstrated accomplishments. And they considered whether some kind of association might help them to attract funds for further experimentation and also have a greater impact on higher education.

It is not hard for anyone who has been involved in educational innovation to imagine the feelings of warmth and fellowship which resulted when these presidents and chief academic officers from their lonely outposts around the country discovered their shared values and concerns in Goddard's convivial atmosphere. By the end of the weekend they had resolved to create a Union for Research and Experimentation in Higher Education. Jim Dixon, Bill Fells, Tim Pitkin and Paul Ward were named as a Committee to draft a statement of purpose. They convened again in January of 1964 and ratified articles of incorporation. Thus, the organization which later came to be known as the Union for Experimenting Colleges and Universities was born. Sam Baskin, director of research at Antioch, was employed full time as President in 1965 and the Union was off and running. A major grant from the U.S. Office of Education provided support for Project Changeover. From 1966 to 1969 this three-year undertaking supported a series of national conferences on research and experimentation in higher education, action planning for new program development by participating institutions and on-site consultation. The conferences provided opportunities for Union members to share their own developing activities and to bring together representatives from other experimental programs. During this period the Union also developed its University Without Walls (UWW) Program, modeled on Goddard's highly successful Adult Degree Program which had been operating since 1963. UWW programs, adapting various elements of that model, were created as added alternatives within a number of member institutions. The Union Graduate School was also created to serve students whose problem-oriented, thematic or interdisciplinary educational needs did not conform to the disciplinary or professionally-oriented traditional programs. This program also included the mix of experiences and resources which characterized the UWW programs for undergraduates and the Goddard Adult Degree program: individually designed degree programs based on student purposes, intensive residential experiences, core and field faculty selected for their expertise in relation to each student's program, independent study, and a culminating "Project Demonstrating Excellence."

The Union grew steadily; by the early 70's some thirty-five institutions were paying the $3,000 membership fee. During the late 60's and early 70's the Union flourished and was recognized nationally, even by the many who disagreed with its approach and philosophy, as a source of leadership and creative ideas for change in higher education. As a result of internal dynamics, management problems and external forces, the Union fell on hard times during the late 70's. But the patient is recovering and it survives as a continuing innovation in undergraduate and graduate education.*

Goddard's Adult Degree Program was adapted by other institutions. Virginia Lester took an administrative internship at Goddard as part of her Union Graduate School doctoral program. After a period of employment at Empire State, she became president of Mary Baldwin College and immediately moved to develop a similar program there. Dudley Luck, who helped get that program under way, now has a grant from the Fund for the Improvement of Post-secondary Education to help four other small private women's colleges develop a similar alternative. Purely by chance Chickering learned of the St. Mary of the Woods Women's

---

*See Michael Kirkhorn's brief comments in *Change*, April 1979, pp. 18–21 on the various problems facing Union and its steps to resolve them.

External Degree program when he went there to help lead a workshop on liberal education and work. The "Woods" administrators had earlier heard of Goddard's program, gone to visit the College and begun their own version. There are probably other examples around the country, unknown to us, whose ancestry would be difficult to trace.

Goddard itself created additional alternatives during the late 60's and early 70's. The Goddard Experimental Program in Further Education (GEPFE) was begun in 1967 to provide educational opportunities for low income persons working in the Head Start and Community Action programs of Lyndon Johnson's "Great Society." Although GEPFE was not originally designed for college-level work, in time it attracted persons interested in credentials and degrees. This program primarily serves Vermont residents who come to live on campus one weekend each month. During this weekend they hear lectures, see films, participate in group discussions and meet individually with faculty members who are supervising the independent studies they pursue through the course of each semester.

These are some of the identifiable contributions to higher education which are traceable to the Goddard Program, to the Experiment in College Curriculum Organization, and to the creative ideas and energy of Tim Pitkin and his associates during the 60's. It is important to recognize that the observations made here are constrained by the limited experiences and perspectives of the author. Undoubtedly other observers could identify contributions and strands of association and influence to supplement this collection, for many persons throughout higher education have been touched by that lively institution and by the adventurous administrators and faculty members who have been associated with it.

In closing, it is useful to consider the implications of the Goddard program and experiment for the 1980's. For in some ways the principles and practices explored and developed at that tiny, beleagured institution are highly relevant to the challenges currently confronted by many of our colleges and universities.

Implications for the 80's

A key Goddard principle has been to take students, their purposes and their characteristics, as the starting point for educational planning. A fair representation of the range of students pursuing higher education in the 80's would display an age group from 17 years to 69. It would also display a diverse array of backgrounds, motivations, financial capabilities, educational desires and educational needs. What problems do we need to solve to create a system which meets the needs of these diverse students? What are the key ways in which a constituency like this differs from our typical 18–25 year-olds? There are at least six major differences:

1. Their motives are more deeply rooted in personal, professional, or social concerns.
2. They have more constraints on their time, energy, emotion, and dollars; external demands resulting from responsibilities at work, at home and in the community; uncertainty about future plans and aspirations.
3. They bring much more wide-ranging knowledge and competence based on prior formal and informal education and prior life and work experiences.
4. They are involved in a richer array of on-going experiences relevant to their education.
5. They reflect a wider range of individual differences—differences which are more sharply etched, more solidly established.
6. They are more used to self-determination, to setting their own priorities, managing their own time, controlling their own scarce resources.

These six dimensions of differences mean that we must concern ourselves with educational purposes and student motives; issues of access which respond to external and internal constraints; assessment, advising and placement which recognize wide-ranging knowledge and competence; using on-going experiences as an integral part of teaching and learning; recognizing and responding to individual differences; and recognizing differing levels of self-determination.

Yet most institutions are greeting these diverse students with business as usual. They may tinker with calendars or course schedules and make more numerous offerings available evenings and weekends; they may expand correspondence study and televised instruction, or offer newspaper courses and the like, which package traditional curricula for off-campus distribution. But with perhaps half a dozen exceptions, colleges and universities have not yet taken seriously the significant individual differences and developmental needs of these students.

The major motives urging these persons into higher education—to prepare for more challenging, interesting, or better-paying work, to satisfy desires for personal development and enrichment—stem from changing circumstances, changing self-perceptions, and aspirations triggered by life-cycle challenges and developmental change.

These challenges and discontinuities stem from social changes that are here to stay. Since the turn of the century, the working life span has more than doubled. The average life expectancy of a man who reaches 50 is 78, of a woman, 83. These shifts have caused the dissolution of what Seymour Sarason calls "the one life, one career perspective."[2] Since World War II the center of the work force has become the "service worker" and the "knowledge worker," as the share of the total employment of goods-producing industries dropped from 45% to 33%. Meanwhile, services increased from 55% to 67%.[3] Producing effective service is much more difficult—and more frustrating—than producing goods. There are also changing sex role expectations. In 1920 married women comprised only 9% of the work force; by 1960, 60% of the female work force were married. A 1975 survey of students at eight east and west coast colleges found that 82% of the college women consider a career very important for their self-fulfillment. They put career above marriage and having children. And 86% of the men said that fathers should spend as much time as mothers in bringing up children.[4]

These cultural shifts in the world of work, in life span, in sex role expectations, and in other significant areas, create problems for individuals and for the institutions which serve them. Most current forms of higher education emphasize preparing for life rather than coping with current problems, aspirations and frustrations; they focus exclusively on the late adolescent with full-time on-campus study as the dominant model. They emphasize memorization of information given by authority, assessed by verbal performance on paper and pencil tests. These forms clearly will not serve the emerging motives diverse students will bring in response to life-cycle challenges and shifting social conditions. If additional alternatives are not created, exclusive reliance on these forms will aggravate the occupational and mental health of those seeking life-long learning, and will aggravate the health and morale of the faculty members, administrators and student personnel services professionals caught within them. But if the nation's colleges and universities can develop more subtle understanding of these students and the significant differences among them, and can develop alternatives appropriate to their varied motives and learning styles, major contributions to life-long learning and general social welfare will result.

To be effective, undergraduate education in the 1980's must be anchored in sound understanding of these diverse students: their motives, their shifting orientations toward family, work and citizenship, the life-cycle challenges they face, the ways they learn, the competence and knowledge they require.

These differences in purpose, prior knowledge and competence, on-going experiences, levels of self-determination, and personal constraints, are also powerfully present among any heterogeneous group of traditional students aged 17–25. The power of Goddard's program lay in its explicit recognition of this fundamental fact, in its capacity to recognize the educational principles which such facts of individual difference imply, and finally, in its ability to create institutional policies, programmic responses, and educational practices expressed in nuts and bolts behavior which recognized and respected each person in these important ways. This is why the Goddard program and its Experiment carried out in the early 60's suggests an institutional design and a collection of programmatic alternatives which are even more appropriate for higher education today than they were then. The increasing numbers of adults from all walks of life, the social pressures creating demands for life-long learning, and the drop in traditional college-age students are creating greater student diversity than we have ever faced before. Given this diversity, we can no longer afford the aristocratic or meritocratic orientations of the past where we emphasized careful selectivity to choose students which fit our colleges. Now we must forego the luxurious reliance on prediction equations and narrowly defined admission criteria. We must instead design programs and educational practices which recognize and respect the students to be served. The Goddard program of the 60's was a pioneering attempt to do just that. As such, it leaves a legacy from which many of us can learn.

NOTES

1. This publication is available from CASC, Washington, D.C.
2. Sarason, S., *Aging, Work, and Social Change*, Jossey-Bass, 1977.
3. Ginsberg, The Pluralistic Economy of the United States, *Scientific American*, December, 1976.
4. Katz, J., *Evolving Relationships Among Men and Women*, Paper presented at the Higher Education Research Institute Conference, Puerto Rico, February, 1976.

XVIII. Some Sources of the "Legacy"

by

ROYCE S. PITKIN

As Arthur Chickering says in his paper, it is often difficult to trace one's ancestry, yet Alex Haley demonstrated that a knowledge of one's roots can be revealing and sometimes helpful in understanding the present. And so it is with institutions. Goddard College may be regarded as a relevant case.

The late Vermont Governor Stanley Wilson once remarked that Goddard College was the spiritual heir of Goddard Seminar, a coeducational boarding school in Barre, Vermont which was founded by a group of Universalists in 1863, but which suffered a drastic enrollment drop in the 1920's and 30's because of the rise of public high schools. Like Colby Academy in New Hampshire and other private academies, it was do or die. Colby eventually became Colby-Sawyer College. Goddard Seminary closed in June 1938, but a new corporation was chartered and in July 1938 Goddard College began its life in Plainfield, Vermont.

H. Leslie Sawyer, who engineered the transition of Colby Academy to Colby Junior College in the late 1920's, perceived that the time to make significant changes in an institution is when conditions are bad. In other words, a school on the verge of collapse has nothing to lose and perhaps much to gain by change. That certainly was true for Colby. Its example encouraged those who supported the idea of a new Goddard.

As Governor Wilson, who was Chairman of the Seminary Board of Trustees, put it, Goddard College inherited the spirit of the Seminary. It can properly be said that its ancestry included the fruits of adversity, the influence of Colby Junior College and an undefined spirit.

If Goddard is a typical case, many of the elements that enter into the formation of an institution's character are fortuitous and serendipitous.

For example, while giving a course at Teacher's College, Columbia University, in the 1920's, University of North Carolina Professor Edgar W. Knight was persuaded to talk about his study of Denmark. This led to a reading of his book, *Among the Danes*, which in turn introduced the readers to the teachings of the famous priest and poet, Bishop N.S.F. Grundtvig and to the remarkable record of the Danish Folk Schools. Much of Goddard's philosophy was derived from this source.

Another illustration—in the summer of 1931 Professor Boyd Bode met with a group of educators at Yale University and introduced them to his *Conflicting Psychologies of Learning*. Seven years later that little volume was the basis for a series of discussions by Goddard teachers as they struggled to formulate an educational plan.

Goddard College also owes a lot to the work of two excellent progressive women's colleges, Sarah Lawrence which opened in the 1920's and Bennington in 1932.

Out of these influences and forces came a plan in 1938 for an experimental college that included most of the features that Chickering saw in 1959 when he came to coordinate the evaluation of the Experiment in College Curriculum Organization. One may properly ask why create an experiment if one with most of its elements had been going on for twenty years? There were two basic reasons. One, we had never done a thorough evaluation of the experiment as a whole as we had of the Educational Resources Project and the Comparative Cultures Project. Two, we had been told by foundation officers that because we regularly engaged in experimentation we should not expect to receive grants for experiments as they were a part of normal operations, and foundations didn't usually make grants for general support. Our problem then was to devise a proposal that was out of the ordinary for Goddard. With some help from some of its staff we produced a proposal which the Ford Foundation approved for a substantial grant.

To be candid, I should say that when the new college opened in 1938 those who were involved as faculty had big ideas but we were all neophytes when it came to putting these ideas into practice. We had to learn by experience in a new environment.

My recollections of the twelve experimental colleges who came to Goddard in 1963 and formed the Union for Research and Experimentation in Higher Education are that they were not as interested in being innovative as they were in engaging in real educational experimentation and research that leads to improvement in the conditions for learning.

It has seemed to me that some of the innovations that have taken place in the 60's and 70's were simply *innovations* and were not based on well defined psychological principles or educational philosophies.

XIX Alternative Education: Trends and Future Implications

by

CYNTHIA STOKES-BROWN
LISLE CRAWFORD
RALPH CROWLEY
MICHAEL SAPIR

We do not teach liberal understanding well chiefly because we do not know what it is. We are very much at home in the field of scholarship. If a student will limit his interest to some fields of intellectual abstraction, we can show him what the human mind has thus far done in that field, can build up in him the proper technique, can equip him, according to his ability, to take his place in the ranks of the craftsmen of that study.

But if the liberal question is asked, our skill and mastery vanish. If men inquire, "What should American life be; toward what end should it be guided and inspired; in terms of what scheme of ideas and values should it be interpreted and controlled?," the characteristic attitude of many of our ablest scholars is one of despair and utter incapacity. We have many sciences but little wisdom. We have multifarious and accurate information, but we have lost hope of knowing what it means. And to say this is to say in the most unmistakable terms that we are ourselves, for the time, beaten in the struggle for liberal education and therefore unable to lead our students into its activities.

—Alexander Meiklejohn, *The Experimental College*, *(1932), pp. 316–17.*

I.
ALTERNATIVE LIBERAL EDUCATION AT THE START OF THE 1980's

The major significance of the Evergreen Conference may well be its lively testimony that one segment of American education is *not* "beaten in the struggle for liberal education and therefore unable to lead our students into its activities." In fact, the overriding finding of the conference, that far more alternatives to traditional education exist and that these alternatives are more connected with the past ones than anyone had imagined, came as a welcome surprise to the participants. People had thought they were laboring alone, struggling within their specific institutions, without knowing there were many others or that a rich tradition of alternative education existed. This finding confirmed the purposes of the Conference's planners—to estimate the strength of alternative education, to encourage its practitioners, to analyze its problems, and to publicize its achievements.

The very range and diversity of programs described at the Conference caused consternation, as well as delight. Methods called "innovative" would be described, only to have it become apparent that they were at least as old as Socrates. Programs called "experimental" would be revealed as closely resembling the Experimental College at the University of Wisconsin from 1927 to 1932.

Would the experimenters never reach a conclusion? Would the innovations spin on ceaselessly in circles? Could any sense be made of the term "experimental," "innovative," and "alternative?" Did they denote any real differences among the programs? Could categories be made to differentiate alternative programs, or were these terms being used at random, or for purposes other than to describe the program?

The Conferees expressed these questions and the hope that some clarity could be found. But they did not attempt to make this analysis. Many programs, they knew, were not represented. Those represented were not all described systematically or in the same framework. The Conferees judged that some taxonomy of terms would be part of the follow-up of the Conference, when more complete lists of all programs would be collected by The Evergreen State College, which agreed to serve as a clearinghouse for this information.

One taxonomy of terms about alternative higher education was already in use before the Conference. Devised by Gerald Grant and David Riesman in *The Perpetual Dream: Reform and Experiment in the American College* (Chicago: University of Chicago, 1978), it distinguishes four kinds of reform: neo-classical, aesthetic-expressive, communal-expressive, and activist-radical. Grant and Riesman define the purpose of neo-classical programs as "to know the good," of aesthetic-expressive ones as "to foster creativity," of communal-expressive ones as "to achieve social harmony," and of activist-radical ones as "to generate radical critique" and "to train 'change agents.'"

The Grant/Riesman taxonomy uses the *purpose* of an alternative program as its determining characteristic and assumes that all other characteristics (constituency, staff, curriculum, methods, governance) will follow consistently from the purpose of the program's planners. We concur that the purpose of alternative programs does seem the most fruitful characteristic to use for classifying them. However, we suggest that Grant and Riesman's four categories might be usefully combined into two functional categories: individual expression and fulfillment, and social criticism and responsibility. The goals of neo-classical and aesthetic-expressive programs combined are to foster individual expression and fulfillment. The goals of communal-expressive and activist-radical programs combined are to generate social criticism and responsibility. The basic sorting of alternative programs could then be done in three categories: those aiming primarily for individual development, for social in volvement, or for a combination of the two.

These three categories for classifying alternative programs assume their most useful significance when compared with the goal of traditional higher education. This refers, of course, not to the tradition of the 19th century or earlier, but to the tradition of the 20th century, personified by Harvard University under President Charles William Eliot's administration (1869–1909).

The purpose of the 20th century university, which we are calling traditional to distinguish it from all forms of alternative higher education, is to train young people for graduate and professional schools. It uses a curriculum broken sharply into specialized academic disciplines, with a faculty responsible only for their own discipline. An elective system allows students to choose most of their own courses, usually with a few minimum breadth requirements. Grades and test scores are the determining criteria of success; lecturing is the approved method of instruction, with discussion encouraged only at advanced levels and only about the concerns of the discipline. Personal relationships among the faculty and the students are not encouraged. Current problems are avoided, especially any critical analysis of them. The accumulation of knowledge is stressed, rather than understanding that knowledge, and the students are trained in the basic point of view and the techniques used by the discipline they plan to specialize in. The product is young scholars-to-be or professionals-to-be, rather than citizens of a complex, free society.

We thus have in modern American higher education three major, sometimes competing purposes—individual expression and fulfillment, social criticism and responsibility, and professional training. We want briefly to describe an alternative program that kept itself clear about these three purposes. It firmly and consciously combined two, while postponing the third for the final two years of college and for graduate school. Consequently, this program provides a clear contrast between alternative and traditional education. Furthermore, this single program most nearly combines all the different alternative features represented at the Evergreen Conference and continues to be one of the most inspirational models for those devising alternative programs. And so we hope in this brief portrayal to summarize clearly what alternative-liberal education is and what its purposes are. The program to which we refer is the Experimental College created at the University of Wisconsin from 1927 to 1932 under the leadership of Alexander Meiklejohn.

Meiklejohn was fired as President of Amherst College in 1923 for, among other things, attempting to require some interdisciplinary courses, for encouraging discussion rather than lecturing, and for stirring up controversy about current issues and problems. Meiklejohn's ideas about what a college should be attracted Glenn Frank, the editor of the *Century* magazine. When Frank became President of the University of Wisconsin in 1926, he got the faculty at Wisconsin to agree to let Meiklejohn experiment with certain educational reforms by setting up an independent college within the University. The college would have the status of a department, but rather than reporting to the Dean of the School of Letters and Science, Meiklejohn would report directly to President Frank. This administrative arrangement promised independence, but was to cause no end of trouble.

Meiklejohn's purpose was to teach students to think critically, to understand the knowledge they possessed, and to create a framework for its social application. This framework also had to be an ethical one: how shall we understand and nurture all the dimensions of human life as it is properly lived. Thus he combined the goals of individual fulfillment and social criticism and responsibility.

The Experimental College took four classes of about 100 students each. It accepted all applicants; as the Depression deepened there was not an excess of applications. Because Meiklejohn wanted a common dormitory life for all students and for some of the staff, he chose to limit the College to men—since, at that time, co-ed dormitories were unthinkable to the university. He especially wanted to attract rural Midwestern young men, whatever their preparation, and to introduce them to the larger world of ideas and tolerance. He got these, but not in as large a proportion as the regular University did. His College and his reputation attracted a larger proportion of urban students, many from large eastern cities.

For his faculty Meiklejohn hired some he had known at Amherst, one or two from Wisconsin, and others from assorted places. They were all young, excited by the chance to work across disciplines and to share decisions about a new venture. Most of them afterwards considered the College a major positive influence in their lives and distinguished themselves in academic or public service.

For their curriculum Meiklejohn and his colleagues chose to study, in the first year, Greece in the fifth century B.C. and, in the second year, the United States in the 19th and 20th centuries. They chose not to divide this material into courses but to study each civilization as a whole. No part of this curriculum, which comprised the first two years of a student's University education, was elective. If a student wished to take an elective "subject," he could do so on the main University campus. But the curriculum at the Experimental College did not occupy a student's full time; he was strongly encouraged to choose from a wide range of extracurricular activities in which to express further his individuality

A third element in the required curriculum proved to be especially effective for students and for teachers. It consisted of a paper that students had to produce over the summer between the two years of study. Called the regional study, it was to be each student's analysis of his hometown or area, based on the Lynd's recently-published study, *Middletown*. This model for sociological investigation resulted, as Meiklejohn had planned, in close attention being paid to the various aspects of a society—including the economic and class factors. Students' eyes were opened when they looked at their own society with the tools they acquired in college, something that traditional education had never asked them to do.

As for methods, the faculty of the Experimental College rejected lecturing as the primary means. They chose weekly lectures shared by the whole College, weekly meetings of one faculty with 12 students, who rotated every six weeks, and weekly personal conferences between one student and one teacher. Grades were issued at the end of the year only because the larger University required them; final exams were omitted. Talking, reading, and writing were the chief activities of the College.

By the indicators of internal satisfaction and external success, the College proved extraordinarily effective. Most, though not all, faculty and students greatly valued the experience; many felt that it transformed their lives. The devotion of most members proved so great that 50 years later a number of them are still meeting regularly in local area groups and periodically for national reunions! Using scores on standardized tests, taken at the end of two years of college, as an external measure of success, students from the Experimental College performed better than did the students at the regular University of Wisconsin.

The faculty of the College of Letters and Science closed the Experimental College in 1932, ostensibly because the Depression had cut funds available to the University and had cut enrollment alarmingly. But by 1932, the majority of the faculty no longer wanted the presence of the Experimental College; it threatened their traditional enterprise too deeply. When their most acclaimed professor had ventured to teach in the Experimental College for one semester, he had returned humiliated—the students would not stop interrupting his polished lectures with questions he preferred not to deal with. The Dean of the College of Letters and Science felt humiliated by the refusal of the College to put on final exams, no matter how much pressure he applied. The Greek and Drama departments at the University were set back by the Experimental College's successful production of "Antigone," in a translation by one of their own students. The whole University was upstaged when the Experimental College students of the Free Speech Club arranged a place for Dora Russell (Mrs. Bertrand Russell) to speak. Nothing on campus or at the state capitol was available to her because she was known to believe in sexual intercourse before marriage. And so it went, with the total structure of the University education seemingly threatened by the questioning, the controversy, the sheer exhilaration, camaraderie, and freedom generated by the Experimental College.*

In light of this sketch of the pioneer model of experimental education, a look back over the programs described in this volume clearly reveals that alternative liberal education with all its rich diversity is still very much alive at the start of the 1980's. Not only that, but because of the Evergreen Conference, the people who believe in alternative higher education can now be more aware of its potential and the vitality and spirit of its heritage.

---

*For details of the Experimental College, see Alexander Meiklejohn, *The Experimental College*, now available in an abridged paperback edition: John Walker Powell, ed., (Cabin John, MD: Seven Locks Press, 1981). For an analysis of the College, see Cynthia Stokes-Brown, ed., *Alexander Meiklejohn: Teacher of Freedom* (Berkeley, CA: Meiklejohn Civil Liberties Institute, 1981).

II.
SOME IMPLICATIONS FOR THE FUTURE OF ALTERNATIVE EDUCATION

> Far deeper, then, than any question of curriculum or teaching method or determining conditions is the problem of restoring the courage of Americans, academic or non-academic, for the facing of the essential issues of life. How can it be brought about that the teachers in our colleges and universities shall see themselves, not only as the servants of scholarship, but also, in a far deeper sense, as the creators of the national intelligence? If they lose courage in that endeavor, in whom may we expect to find it? Intelligence, wisdom, sensitiveness, generosity—these cannot be set aside from our planning, to be, as it were, by-products of the scholarly pursuits. They are the ends which all our scholarship and our teaching serve.
>
> —Alexander Meiklejohn, *The Experimental College* (1932), p. 318.

The current reactionary trend in our society that is attempting to force retreat from alternative forms of higher education has appeared before—at Amherst in 1923, at Wisconsin in 1932 and at most universities in the 1950's. Traditional 20th century universities have learned that they can squash criticism by departmentalizing the thinking of students and faculty. By controlling the rewards of academic life, the departments keep the teachers in line, and by refusing to allow interdisciplinary studies they keep the students in line.

Fortunately, the proceedings of this Conference suggest that at the start of the 1980's alternative higher education has some flourishing constituencies. Bands of hardy souls, from diverse ethnic and social backgrounds, still believe in controversy and diversity, and they are not willing to abandon their beliefs. They may be suppressed, as tight economic circumstances give traditionalists the power of cutting "extra" programs, but they do not give up.

Most of the Conference time was devoted to consideration of professional papers about established programs, and to providing mutual support and counsel for surviving at a time of public retreat from alternative education. Consequently, there was little opportunity to think together about the ends toward which we intend our society to move, about what qualities of life it should have, about what would be the nature of the educational experiences that could nurture citizens desirous and capable of moving our society toward these goals. But since this chapter is a postscript to the Conference, it becomes possible to enumerate here some of the "essential issues of life" that must be faced by alternative education to be relevant in the 1980's, and to give consideration to some learning experiences that directly address these issues.

A Free and Intelligent Citizenry

All persons should be provided with life-long learning experiences which sustain a free citizenry—citizens free to question, to criticize, to learn, to reason, to value, to act and to reflect. Such freedoms and ways of learning are essential to an ever-changing society, if it is to develop and sustain individual and community growth. Some of these aspects of freedom and learning actually deteriorate under our traditional educational system. Both research studies and common observations show that children who start out asking several hundred questions a day end up in college with only the professor asking questions. These qualities of freedom and learning cannot be acquired or developed solely by reading or talking about them, especially in circumstances that provide few of the realities of life in which to practice them. This means that people must have self-governing, learning communities in which responsibility for making decisions, acting upon them, and dealing with the consequences while learning from them would be shared by all.

That it is possible for educators to begin to develop such self-governing, learning communities in our society is suggested by the programs described in the Evergreen Conference Proceedings. That such communities can have long-lasting effects was evident in the presence at the Conference of 13 alumni of the Meiklejohn Experimental College and seven of their spouses. Not only did their presence testify to a history that younger participants had no inkling of, but they also personified the very ideals the younger people were seeking. The men of the Experimental College, all over 65 and some in their mid-70's, were vigorous, curious, humorous, honest, diverse, and willing to let nothing go unexamined. It came as a surprise to many at the Conference that such people existed as a group, rather than as exceptional individuals. Their presence demonstrated as nothing else could the power of some alternative forms of higher education to develop learning communities that can nurture and sustain a free citizenry.

There are signs, other than the Evergreen Conference, that in this crisis period for liberal education the basic issues relating to developing a free and intelligent citizenry are being raised again. The Association of American Colleges in its January, 1982, annual meeting is quoted in *The New York Times* of January 17, 1982, as raising the student's and teacher's perpetual question: "What am I here for?" In consequence, the AAC has set up a national committee to reassess the bachelor's degree. One member of this committee observed that traditional undergraduate learning involves "little more than how to take notes, memorize facts for examination and deal with the registrar's office." He suggests, instead, that the student might better learn "investigative skills, gathering data, interviewing and laboratory experiments and integrative skills. The latter would include writing and speaking."

The same committee member points out that the baccalaureate degree "is a marvelous convenience for a mediocre society, putting passive acceptance ahead of questioning and propagating the dangerous myth that technical skills are more important than ethical teaching." The "key goal of education," he concludes, should be the teaching of "informed decision-making which recognizes there is a moral and ethical component to life."

Clearly, some leaders in traditional liberal education are considering "restoring the courage of Americans, academic or non-academic, for the facing of the essential issues of life"—as Meiklejohn advocated 50 years ago. Surely, alternative educators will respond to the relevance of their own heritage by getting on with the unfinished business of the Evergreen Conference.

Informed Ethical Decision Making and Action

The "key goal of education" set forth in the above report from the American Association of Colleges poses the next issue that alternative education must address, if it is to be relevant to the 1980's: All people must be provided with learning experiences that lead to informed, ethical decision making and actions. Now, you ask, "Why should alternative educators have to deal with ethics and morality? For generations the home, religious institutions, and traditional schools and colleges have been attending to this matter." But have they? A look at the conduct of a number of American leaders in recent times gives ample cause for concern over the state of ethics in high places. As reported in the press, the violation of public trust and the damage done to human rights and life by a recent American President and his staff, by some leaders of transnational corporations, giant engineering companies, prominent law firms, multi-million dollar religious enterprises, and by doctors who head up great pharmaceutical houses—all testify to a deterioration of ethical behavior.

Meanwhile, the stakes for risking unethical decisions and actions grow ever larger, for all are geared into power—economic-industrial, political, military, social control, and behavior manipulation. And these, in turn, grow by leaps with each new development in the technology of electronics, bio-chemistry, computers, automation, information and behavior control, and nuclear energy and bombs.

It is apparent that the concerns of the moral and ethical component of life can no longer be limited to the home town or the nation. Ethical concerns are now planet size. The old ways for determining what is most valuable and desirable in life and for protecting it with moral behavior and ethical codes will not do. These changing times—tomorrow's changing times—cannot be dealt with using yesterday's codes, no matter how patched up or tricked up with passing innovations. And no longer are the governing elite and the captains of great enterprises the only ones who should be making the major ethical or unethical decisions and acting upon them. Humankind—including the people of the Third World with their rising expectations—is demanding more of a voice in deciding between the hazards and the benefits of modern technologies.

If all this seems ambiguous and remote, consider for a moment some specific ethical situations adults face as voting citizens and as moral leaders of the young: Shall a block of deteriorated apartment buildings be torn down to clear the way for a needed city park, or expressway, or a university building, or a factory that could give work to hundreds of unemployed—when there is no other housing available in that area which these poor families can afford? Would you vote for a political candidate who refuses to approve the use of public funds for indigent women to have abortions? In your position with a production plant, would you approve, ignore or stop the use of a defective part or of a dangerous chemical that would make a product more lucrative but harmful to the environment and to the life of consumers?

When confronted with these ethical questions, and the even more difficult ones that our children will have to answer, it becomes evident that traditional accultural processes—including educational institutions—do not adequately prepare people to make today's moral decisions. It is time, then, to turn to some alternate directions which educators might explore for ways to cultivate and sustain appropriate moral and ethical behavior.

Some of the alternative programs described in this volume provide glimpses of some aspects of the kind of learning experiences that are needed. Here, we shall only re-emphasize the value of one component of the Meiklejohn Experimental College experience at the University of

Wisconsin (1927–32), the "Regional Study," which was referred to briefly in Part I of this chapter. The "study" was one of the culminating experiences of the civilizational approach to learning which characterized the two-year program. It was a self-selected, intensive and integrative investigation into the major aspects of the life of the student's home town or area. It came into being only after the student had spent a year to learn how to study and appreciate a whole society or civilization—its different aspects, achievements and values—and, thereby, come to some understanding of its way of life, of its ethos. Apparently the total Regional Study experience was an effective way to develop in students a desire to understand and appreciate a society's way of life and its particular values. For today, some 50 years later, many Meiklejohn Experimental College students and faculty testify to the continuing role of this creative learning experience in how they view and make fundamental decisions about their own lives and the life of the society about them.

Alternative Education and a Sense of Community

Throughout our considerations in the Conference, the term "community" was used in connection with some of the essential ideas set forth. A sense of community will not just come about because some people associate themselves around a learning situation.

It is ironic that our increasingly technological society, with its multiplying capacity by plane and television to juxtapose human beings in time and space, and to make people constantly aware of human happenings everywhere, appears to make us less capable or inclined, or both, to sense community with each other. A recent manifestation of this anti-social feeling was reported on *The Chicago Tribune* wire service on February 9, 1982. It summarized the results of a public opinion study, commissioned by the National Automatic Merchandising Association, to learn why Americans find vending machines so appealing that they feed 200,000 coins a minute into the automatic dispensers. Along with the predictable Americans who like vending machines because they save time and money, and are easy and attractive, 44 per cent said they liked the machines because "They help me avoid other people." That's almost half of those surveyed who would rather listen to the clink of quarters in a slot than to a human voice.

At times it would seem as if the anti-community forces at work in the world are greater than those that draw people together.

Just how formidable and complicated the task might be to develop a sense of *world* community is suggested by the following report based on recent United Nations data. It was published in the March 1982 *Newsletter* from the Unitarian-Universalist U.N. Office:

> "Of the 100 largest economic powers in the world, 53 are countries and 47 are corporations. The annual sales of the world's largest corporation, General Motors, exceed the Gross Domestic Product of at least three-quarters of the members of the United Nations.
>
> "As major agents in the transfer of technology and capital, transnational corporations (TNC's) are involved in commodities, industrialization, food, and energy. While governments debate the features of a New International Economic Order and U.N. agencies work for social and economic change, TNC's appear to be creating an order of their own. Critics view TNC's as amoral enterprises which in the name of profit bribe officials, destabilize governments, befoul the environment, and dump dangerous products on developing-world consumers. In contrast, other commentators hail TNC's as agents of economic growth, preservers of the peace, and torchbearers of a rational future."

Regardless of what view one takes of TNC's and their actions, they are a major force in the world scene and must be reckoned with in developing and maintaining any sense of world community. Despite the protests of traditional educators that "this is not the business of education," alternative education and teachers and students must confront the basic issues of community if they are to be relevant in the 1980's.

Obviously, cultivating and extending a sense of community is not a simple, short-term task. Nor is it one that can be accomplished mainly through the intellect by reading and talk. It must be experienced and practiced socially over a lifetime. In fact, we start out life seeking community with those about us. And, as we grow, we find that:

> "Learning . . . is, first of all, initiation into many social groups, and ultimately into the one social group (humanity). The teacher leads his pupils into active membership in a fraternity . . . (whose) motive force . . . is found in a common devotion to a common cooperative enterprise. Just as, in the home, each child learns, or should learn, to play his part in the family circle, so, in our schools and colleges, every citizen of the world should become 'at home' in the common 'state.' He should acquire a sense of what humanity is trying to do, and a will to join in doing it."[1]

When we look for learning situations that might nurture and develop a sense of community and turn to the traditional education, we find: "The curriculum has now become merely a vast collection of mutually-unintelligible subjects. The members of the faculty have, professionally, little if any intellectual acquaintance with one another. And pupils are encouraged to pursue each his own separate studies, without regard for or interest in what, in other classrooms, his friends may be doing."[2]

We find an entire learning system based on the divisiveness of pitting one person against another for a piece of the "common goal," a high grade. The struggle for this "intellectual" goal often degenerates into anticommunity attitudes and feelings. By contrast, as is evident in the reports of many alternative experiments, from the Meiklejohn College to the programs of coordinated study at The Evergreen State College, the pursuit of common learning goals tends to generate a sense of camaraderie and of shared risks and gains. As this process grows, the members learn to appreciate and to channel their diverse abilities and capacities. Out of these relationships grows a respect for each other's uniquenesses, and human differences become appreciated rather than feared. The drive to excel together toward a common goal provides a motivating force stronger than interpersonal competition.

The net result of these cooperative ways of learning is that each member, supported by others in the group, begins to build up a sense of community for increasingly larger groups. That this tendency can extend over whole life spans is revealed by the fact that the largest constituent group at the Evergreen Conference consisted of 13 alumni of the Alexander Meiklejohn Experimental College, who came to Olympia, Washington from 13 different directions of the country in order to participate—after 50 years!

NOTES

1. *Education Between Two Worlds* by Alexander Meiklejohn, as quoted by Cynthia Stokes Brown in *Alexander Meiklejohn: Teacher of Freedom*, p. 160, Berkeley, CA, Meiklejohn Civil Liberties Institute, 1981.
2. Cynthia Stokes Brown, ed., *Alexander Meiklejohn: Teacher of Freedom*, p. 115, (Quoting from Meiklejohn's address at the Experimental College Reunion at St. John's College, Annapolis, MD, on May 10, 1957.

XX. The Conditions For and Against Educational Experimentation in the Experience of Alexander Meiklejohn

by

CYNTHIA STOKES BROWN

We can only understand the conditions for and against Meiklejohn's educational experimentation if we keep clear about what his purpose was in experimenting. Throughout his life's work as a teacher, his purpose was to teach young adults to be free. To do this, he wanted to create a liberal college. For him, this meant a place where students and teachers could consider all the problems common to human beings. The purpose in doing this was to teach students to govern themselves in a free society. Meiklejohn's purpose was not to demonstrate that some method was better than another, some curriculum superior, some combination of faculty more effective.

Here is a statement by Meiklejohn of his purpose, as presented long ago at the annual meeting of the National Education Association in 1914, two years after he became president of Amherst College. Meiklejohn's language poses a problem for our ears; when he uses "men" he means "men and women," except when he refers to students—at Amherst they were all men.

> The fundamental principle of the liberal college, like that of all advanced education, technical or professional, rests on the opposition of action by custom and action by intelligence. All schools alike believe that activities

> guided by ideas are, in the long run, more successful than activities determined by habit and hearsay. The liberal college has, therefore, selected one group of activities for study. Just as the bridge builder studies mathematics and applied mechanics, just as the physician studies chemistry and biology, so the teacher in the liberal college studies those activities which are common to all men. We believe that human living can be made more successful if men understand it. We set our boys, or should set them, to the study of the religious life, the moral problems, the social and economic institutions, the world of physical and natural phenomena, the records of literature and history. Here are the features of human living common to all men. To understand them, to be acquainted with them, is to be liberally educated.
>
> There are men who would prefer that their sons be not educated with regard to religion, morals, social and economic problems. These men want all the new appliances in farming, all the newest devices and inventions in transportation and engineering, but they would prefer that the fundamental things of life be left to habit, tradition, and instinct. As against such men the liberal college is up in arms. There never was a time when men needed light on the great human affairs, the things we have in common, more than we need it now. Intelligence has improved our roads and bridges; it will improve ourselves, our living. The task of the liberal college is just as definite as that of any technical school. Its day is not ending; it is just beginning to dawn.

When Meiklejohn began his presidency at Amherst, the conditions for his work there included his choice as president by unanimous vote of the trustees. The old definition of Amherst—a place to train men of capitalist, Christian character by means of a fixed classical curriculum—was breaking down. The sheer bulk of knowledge and the number of academic disciplines needed to organize it were expanding at an explosive rate. Amherst's trustees were willing to give free rein to someone who could synthesize piety and knowledge and arrive at a new definition of a liberal college.

The conditions against Meiklejohn's work were more numerous. First and foremost, he was a newcomer and had no allies among the faculty, most of whom had hoped that the new president would come from within. The chairman of the math department had been their choice. Meiklejohn gradually chose his own faculty members who, by attracting more students, seriously threatened the older faculty. Meiklejohn wanted required, interdisciplinary courses and brought teachers able to create them. By the end of his presidency, eleven years later, the faculty deadlocked itself on every issue, half voting with Meiklejohn and half against him. In my attempt to understand the trustees, I believe this was probably the most pressing reason why they felt they had to fire Meiklejohn. He could not keep the faculty with him and therefore could not keep the college going.

Two other conditions against Meiklejohn were the provincialism of Amherst and World War I. Amherst was a small town of only 5000 people, almost entirely Congregationalists. This was a big change for Meiklejohn from Providence, Rhode Island—a large cosmopolitan city of people from various national, ethnic, racial and religious backgrounds. Meiklejohn and his family affronted the beliefs and customs of Amherst in many ways. His wife was from an Italian family and did not belong to the ladies' group of the Congregational Church. Meiklejohn did not attend town meetings. They brought guests from England and Scotland, including the great English socialist R. H. Tawney. When Meiklejohn noticed that students were not paying attention to the Bible in daily chapel, he substituted *The New Republic*. Meiklejohn encouraged the Intercollegiate Socialist Society on campus, and when Calvin Coolidge came to give a speech on preparedness for war, Meiklejohn insisted on having a speaker against war. When it came, the war practically shut down the campus for the duration.

By the time he was fired in 1923, Meiklejohn felt that what he envisioned as a liberal college could not be supported within existing U.S. universities. The basic conflict hinged on the fact that most people within colleges and universities did not share his purpose. The majority of teachers, administrators and trustees did not want to teach students to be free; they wanted to teach them to be professionals.

Reflecting his bitter experience at Amherst, Meiklejohn wrote in 1923 about one of his heroes, Benjamin Andrews, who had been president of Brown when Meiklejohn was a student there:

> Sometimes I think that no man should be allowed to have administration in his charge unless he loathes it, unless he wishes to be doing something else. I dare not trust the willing middlemen of life, the men who like arranging other men and their affairs, who find manipulation satisfying to their souls. These men if they can have their way will make of life a smooth, well-lubricated meaninglessness. . . . For him [Andrews] administration was Idea guiding and controlling circumstance. It was not, as many men demand it should be made, mere circumstances slipping smoothly past each other in the flow of time.

After Amherst, Meiklejohn no longer believed his work could be done within the old structures. He moved to New York City, wrote and spoke about his vision, and hoped he could set up a new college to provide the conditions necessary for his work. Glenn Frank, the editor of the *Century Magazine*, set up a committee to study the feasibility of a new college based on Meiklejohn's idea. But this plan never came to fruition. Meiklejohn went to Europe to bring back his fatally ill wife, who died within the year, and Frank, out of the blue, became president of the University of Wisconsin.

At Wisconsin the positive conditions for Meiklejohn's work included: a majority of liberal trustees, an extremely supportive president, a state with a progressive tradition, a period of growth and expansion, and expressed dissatisfaction from students over lectures as a method and over the content of the regular curriculum. President Frank was able to persuade the faculty of the College of Letters and Science to approve an experimental college separate from the regular university organization, and he was able to fund it with special bequests given with no specific purpose. It would be an independent college within the university.

Meiklejohn accepted these conditions because they seemed to promise genuine autonomy. He had just five years before the conditions against his work again became overwhelming, and he was discontinued once more. The negative conditions at Wisconsin proved to be highly similar to the ones at Amherst: departmentalism, provincialism, depression (instead of war), and a new one, the separateness of the experimental college.

The problem of departmentalism at Wisconsin played out in a different way than it had at Amherst. Meiklejohn had complete authority to choose his own faculty at Wisconsin, but by the arrangements set up by President Frank the faculty of the Experimental College taught two-thirds time in the Experimental College and one-third time in the regular department of their academic training. This arrangement created endless conflicts. The regular departments had to take on men chosen by Meiklejohn, in place of ones coming up in the ranks expecting these positions. Sometimes the departments felt that Meiklejohn's choices were not fully qualified academically; indeed, by their definition anyone who would teach both Greek and U.S. civilization could not be. Worst of all, from the departments' perspective, Meiklejohn set salaries in the Experimental College higher than those in the regular departments, so his men were not only crowding out the regulars, they were earning more. And, of course, these arrangements—new and different—were not always clearly understood by all parties.

Provincialism appeared in Wisconsin primarily as anti-Semitism. The Experimental College attracted a larger portion of Jewish students, about 40% the final year, than the regular university, which probably used a quota system to limit Jewish students to about 10%. These Jewish students were largely from large Eastern cities, and some of them were men of communistic and socialist sympathies. The school also attracted artists and free-thinkers. Possibly only one student in the Experimental College wore a cape, but he is the one depicted in the press, which constituted a fifth hostile condition to Meiklejohn's work in Wisconsin.

The coming of the Depression wrecked havoc on the Experimental College. Distribution of wealth was no abstract problem. Students had to drop out for lack of money. Many endured constant uncertainty about whether they could remain. Meiklejohn appealed to the wealthy students to set up a fund for the poor ones. Enrollment dropped each year. The faculty of the regular university suffered cutbacks and even waivers of their salaries.

When the faculty of the College of Letters and Science reviewed in 1932 whether it wanted to continue the Experimental College, it decided to set up a committee. The dean never named this committee, in view of the Depression. Because the Experimental College was separate, tacked on to the organizational chart, it could be easily lopped off—as black studies, ethnic studies, women's studies can be today, if they have not become integrated into the regular structure.

For his third experiment, Meiklejohn left the traditional university structure completely and started, in 1934, an independent school for adults in San Francisco, funded by private donations and foundations. The existence of the Depression was probably a positive condition for the San Francisco School for Social Studies—by making students more eager to study and private donors more willing to give. But we all know how desperate and frustrating it is to operate with this kind of uncertain funding. The school could plan only from year to year, and the coming of World War II put an end to it in 1942. By then, the faculty had concluded that adult education must be supported by some public funds, either through libraries or universities.

What can we conclude about conditions for and against experimentation in Meiklejohn's experience? At the most general, we can say that members of our society liked to say they believed in freedom, but they made no real provision for teaching it. In each of Meiklejohn's three experiments, whenever it became clear that he really believed in teaching all kinds of students to be free, the conditions for his work no longer existed within the college or the society. Meiklejohn's experience may not apply to all experimentation, since his purpose was specifically to make people capable of freedom, and many educational experiments have no such purpose. Meiklejohn was at odds with a capitalist society in which the majority did not want students to consider economic alternatives or to develop values that might challenge capitalism. Too many men preferred their sons not to be educated with regard to religion, morals, social and economic problems. Only in times of confidence, affluence, and economic expansion could traditional universities allow Meiklejohn's experimentation. When war, reaction to war, or depression occurred, his experimentation within traditional structures was cut off.

Meiklejohn seldom expressed discouragement at this. He expected it; he acknowledged it; he believed to go down with an idea is to make it live. He felt that the thinking power of people in the U.S. had diminished in his lifetime, that Madison Avenue was undermining our society more dangerously than the threat of the atomic bomb by undermining our ability to think, and that the U.S. experiment in free government may have run its course. But he never despaired that freedom would ever be completely crushed. He believed that at heart people desire freedom, dignity and excellence, that these inner qualities can never be crushed as long as people live. These qualities were to him closer to reality than space and time.

We may conclude with two paradoxes, one that Meiklejohn frequently told and one that summarizes his work.

In speaking of freedom, Meiklejohn often chose to quote a Greek slave, Epictetus, who said: "The state says that only free men may be educated, but wisdom says that only educated men may be free."

I believe that we can conclude that none of Meiklejohn's experiments survived for very long, and none of them ever died.

XXI. Experiment at San Jose

by

MERVYN L. CADWALLADER

This essay tells in some detail the history of a lower division experimental program that I directed at San Jose State College from 1965 to 1969. It is intended, however, to be more than a memoir. Because the coming decade will be a time of trials and troubles for higher education, it may be all too easy to forget the need for educational reform as we defend ourselves against declining enrollments and shrinking budgets by playing it safe. If there is a lesson to be learned from this particular experiment during the 1960's it is that we should redouble our efforts to reform the lower division, especially during the 1980's.

The San Jose program was based on the educational ideas of both Alexander Meiklejohn and Joseph Tussman, and resembled the Tussman experiment that ran its course from 1965 to 1969 at Berkeley. In 1969 the San Jose model, somewhat modified by four years of experiment and experience, moved to the State University of New York at Old Westbury. One year later, the idea took up residence in Olympia, Washington, at what was to become The Evergreen State College. Richard Jones has written an analysis of what happened to some of Meiklejohn's ideas at Evergreen, Joseph Tussman published an account of his program, *Experiment At Berkeley,* in 1969, and others have described and interpreted the Old Westbury experiment.[1] There is then no need to retell those stories, or to trace the migration of Meiklejohn's legacy from Madison to Berkeley and San Jose, then to Old Westbury, and finally to Evergreen. However, because neither my colleagues nor I published an account of the San Jose experiment, that story does need to be told, along with an account of the many lessons learned. It is especially useful to do so now as we attempt to assess the chances for successful reforms in the years to come.

In *The Perpetual Dream* Gerald Grant and David Riesman describe and interpret many of the reform movements and experiments in American higher education during the 1960's and early 1970's. They distinguish two kinds of reforms—*popular reforms*, which have brought about more autonomy and freedom of choice for the student (and I might add more autonomy and freedom for the faculty), and *telic reforms*, which have sought to redefine the purposes of contemporary education and create radically new ways of educating.[2] The fundamental differences between popular and telic reformers flow from their different attitudes toward the ideals and practices of the contemporary American research university.

Popular reformers accept the ideals and ethos of the research university with its enormous array of specialized courses, but want to make such universities more open and comfortable for students by making them less competitive and more flexible.

Telic reformers are opposed to many of the curricular and pedagogic practices of the research university and want to create something radically different. Their concern is usually with preprofessional and prevocational undergraduate education, and the institution that they hope to change is the college. For the telic reformers the unwitting enemy of the college is the research university which now trains all of the faculty for the colleges, and has come to define the goals of the colleges, and control the very criteria of their success and failure.

Alexander Meiklejohn's Experimental College at Madison, Tussman's experiment at Berkeley, and the experiment at San Jose were radical critiques of undergraduate education in research-oriented universities. These reforms were telic reforms undertaken in the hope of returning to some of the ideals and goals, though not the exact content and pedagogy, of the best of the American colonial colleges. All three experiments were predicated on the assumption that college teaching should nurture wisdom and shape character, that one of its goals was education for citizenship. All three sought to do this through a radical change in both the structure and content of the lower division.

THE MEIKLEJOHN IDEA BECOMES A PROPOSAL AND A PROGRAM AT BERKELEY AND AT SAN JOSE

Alexander Meiklejohn's Experimental College at the University of Wisconsin opened in 1927 and closed in 1932. Although it only lasted for five years it lives on in the lives of the men who have been fortunate enough to have been a part of it. Neither Joseph Tussman nor I had been among those lucky students, but in the fall of 1963 it seemed to us that a revival of the Experimental College would restore intellectual excitement and ethical relevance to the academic wasteland traversed by our freshmen and sophomores.[3]

Instead of a scattering of courses selected according to a distribution formula, why not offer our freshmen a coherent and fully prescribed liberal course of study? Instead of unrelated fragments, why not offer them an organic program organized around a theme? Instead of textbooks, lectures, and machine-graded tests, why not classics, discussions, and written essays?

On each campus a team of five or six faculty would teach in a two-year program of liberal studies that should satisfy the usual general education requirements. The program of reading, discussing, and writing would be organized around a controlling theme, much as Meiklejohn had organized his curriculum at Madison around the story of the birth and development of political democracy in classical Athens and colonial America. The faculty would be drawn from interested volunteers without regard for their academic disciplines because the experimental program was to be nondisciplinary. Teaching in the program would be the full responsibility, the one and only assignment, for each of the faculty for two whole years, and it would be collaborative teaching.

Approximately one hundred freshmen would be given the chance to volunteer for these experimental programs and, with the exception of one outside course each semester, the program would be a full-time commitment for each student. At the end of their sophomore year they would have satisfied their general education requirements and be ready to select a major in the upper division.

Both faculty and students would be totally immersed. Instead of teaching or taking lots of different courses, with their competing demands on time and attention, the faculty and students could concentrate and focus on one thing at a time.

The design of the program and actual development of the theme were to be continuous, always in process. Because the faculty were bound to be specialists in something else and very much in need of a chance to get ready to lead seminars about books outside of their field, there would be a weekly faculty seminar to discuss the books that were going to be read, talked and written about.

Finally, we would need a place, rooms of our own to give the program a home. An old house on the edge of the campus would be ideal. We would have to be able to develop our own weekly schedules without having to worry about space, bells and conflicts.

Joseph Tussman and I submitted proposals for our experimental programs in the fall of 1964, recruited faculty volunteers in the spring of 1965, and met our first students that fall. Alexander Meiklejohn was surprised and pleased by this unexpected reincarnation of his Experimental College.

At San Jose we called the integrating theme selected for the two-year program: *Four Crises in Western Civilization*. Each of the four semesters was to be focused on a subtheme with the first to be *Athens and the Peloponnesian War*. *The Rise of Science and the Modern State* was to give coherence to the second semester, *The Cultural and Social Revolutions of the 19th Century* to the third. The fourth subtheme was called *Contemporary Democracy in America* and we assumed that that final semester would be enriched by comparisons of democratic Athens confronted by the Peloponnesian War and democratic America enmeshed in Vietnam. It seemed obvious that the first semester reading list should be made up of paperback editions of: Herodotus, Homer, Aeschylus, Sophocles, Thucydides, Plutarch, Plato, Aristophanes, Aristotle, and Euripides.

President Robert D. Clark persuaded six departments to release six faculty volunteers and so in the summer of 1965 we gathered together for luncheons and planning sessions. After planning the first semester in some detail we picked a reading list for the second semester. No one noticed that it was made up of our favorite 16th and 17th Century authors, and was not a list demanded by a theme. We expected that the task of integrating some science into the third semester would be especially difficult and so planned to try to do it by using James B. Conant's case history approach. The team did not plan the fourth semester that summer, perhaps because it seemed a long way away and perhaps because each of us wanted to pick our own books about contemporary America.[4]

The program was to open in September, 1965, in an old residence owned by the college. It had been given faculty approval as a temporary experiment in general education and the program as a whole was to be worth forty-eight semester hours of credit and to substitute for all of the San Jose State general education requirements (except for two credits of physical education). Each faculty member was to assume responsibility for approximately twenty students each semester. We planned on four to six hours of seminar time each week for each student, a two to three-hour weekly assembly and at least one writing conference every other week.

Each member of the team had the responsibility of working out his own weekly seminar schedule and pattern of writing assignments. The weekly assemblies were to feature program or visiting faculty and were intended to augment the program but not to explain the books. We wanted our students to have a lot of time to read and reread the books, and a lot of time for discussion and writing. While most of our students signed up for one additional course outside of the program the experience was to be one of nearly total immersion. There were to be writing assignments, but no tests, and we planned to award letter grades while actively discouraging the discussion of grades. Finally, and perhaps most importantly, our weekly summer planning sessions were to become weekly faculty seminars. We agreed to meet every Friday and after lunching together to turn to a discussion of the books we were to be reading with our students. Collegial lunches and real faculty seminars, we discovered, were unanticipated rewards for planning the program.

So much for the early dream, the eager planning, and the way we started. There was, it turned out, much to learn when we met and started teaching our 112 students.

INTENTION AND DISCOVERY AT SAN JOSE

Underlying my commitment to the experiment were assumptions and intentions which, I came to realize, were not necessarily shared by my colleagues or students. My intention was to offer an experimental liberal curriculum in the lower division at San Jose State College and by that I meant the kind of education that a citizen of a democracy must have if he is to participate critically, creatively, and responsibly in the political process of self-government. Both the programs at Berkeley and San Jose were designed to teach young people to become intelligent, reasonable, and wise citizens. It was my assumption that the primary responsibility of a public college should be the liberal education of the citizen—for public life.

So much for my intention. I assumed that the idea of a liberal curriculum designed to prepare young adults for their political roles would be acceptable to faculty because American teachers had paid lip-service to similar sounding goals for decades. The form or structure of the program, on the other hand, I expected to appear quite radical because it was designed as a two-year, integrated educational experience taught wholly without courses.[5]

It seemed absolutely essential to get rid of courses and especially elected courses for this particular experiment because the students were to be totally immersed in one topic or issue at a time. A combination of ever multiplying specialized courses and the elective system has left general education a shambles of unrelated bits and fragments. The usual curricular building block is the course, and educational reformers usually advocate new courses or new combinations of courses. But the course by its very nature fragments, splinters, and disintegrates. If it were not for the narrow focus of courses, students might glimpse the organic wholeness of the real world, the whole world of the Athenian Republic, or at least the totality of Plato's *Republic*, before the specialists dismember those worlds into their specialized three-credit courses. The course may have its uses, but it is the enemy of wholeness and so the San Jose and Berkeley programs were to be two-year programs without any courses at all. Of course a program without courses was bound to run against familiar academic assumptions and settled professional work habits. Other obstacles were to come as real surprises.

The faculty was recruited with an eye for the teacher who liked to teach and had been popular with students, who was dissatisfied with the narrow limitations of his own academic specialty and wanted to branch out, who wanted to join something experimental and especially a program that sought to restore excitement and adventure to learning and to teaching. We had to find teachers who were willing to be cut loose from departments and courses for two years, and who would be willing to teach and study across the disciplines and across the curriculum. They were going to have to give up their disciplines, textbooks, lectures, scholarship, and research.

Certain great books were to be the heart of the program. I assumed that as the faculty selected the books semester by semester we would quite naturally create a liberal curriculum around the assumptions and propositions of Alexander Meiklejohn's political philosophy of education. I assumed that the students would notice that the books were relevant to their own lives and to the world they were confronting in the 1960s. I was wrong in both cases.

All of us had been exposed to growing student political involvement in the early 1960s. The new breed of student was lively, and we liked that. The free speech demonstrators at Berkeley were crying out for respect and attention and so we assumed that these lonely, pained, and angry students would like our reforms and would count us on their side. But, as we were to discover, we did not really understand the student revolt against the university. We assumed that if students were given respect, attention, and affection, they would be excited by a required liberal curriculum if it was taught properly. After all, we were excited. What we did not understand was that the students did not want any requirements, let alone a completely required curriculum, no matter how brilliantly taught. The popular demand was for more of the elective system, not less.

Let me emphasize that student discontent was always a side issue in my initial plans. Educational reform was to be carried on in behalf of the public welfare, for the body politic, not to pacify humiliated and angry students. Students would go along because they would no longer be anonymous. They would no longer be asked to read dull textbooks, listen to dull lectures or take machine-graded objective examinations. Their attention would not be scattered by an assortment of unrelated courses. They would be reading classics, discussing important ideas in small groups, and learning to write with clarity and style—under the guidance of enthusiastic teachers. I expected the students to be wildly enthusiastic about the books, the ideas, the opportunity to talk and to write. I really did expect that. I thought that there would be no holding them back once we offered freedom from the academic busywork that they had been complaining about and reacting against. I expected even the shy to catch fire when exposed to the excitement of their teachers.

So much for some of my assumptions about colleagues and students. But what were the students really like? What were their assumptions, wants and demands? Who were they? They were eighteen years old and from the suburbs south of San Francisco. These were the young adults that we had never known because we had been trying to turn them into chemistry, sociology, philosophy, and literature majors. When we got to know them, we discovered that they were not looking for a political education. They wanted a degree, or they wanted to satisfy the college's general education requirements as painlessly as possible, and this new experimental program seemed to be a means to that end. They did have a fantasy of what college might be and they assumed we understood their fantasy. We assumed they had understood ours; after all, they had volunteered for the program after reading a very clear description of it.

As it turned out, neither of us knew the other's fantasy. Those students who responded to the words "new" and "experimental" in the first announcement assumed that by some miracle a small group of adults had discovered what they thought was wrong with education and was actually going to do something about it. They did not have a clear idea of what they wanted, but they did know they wanted something different from high school. When they found themselves reading a lot, writing a lot, and being asked to discuss Plato and Hobbes, that did not seem to be different. Non-verbal communication, Yoga, polarity massage, seminars on Zen, or a political demonstration would have been different. The would-be revolutionary and the radical wanted to read Marx and Malcolm X, not Plato and Hobbes. The hip wanted to drop acid and listen to Bob Dylan. For some of the others the program looked better than the regular lower division because they might not have to work as hard as regular students. In the end most of the volunteers liked the program because they liked the teachers; some fell in love with the program—because they fell in love with the teachers. That was not exactly what we had had in mind either.

As students and faculty became friends, we began to understand what it was that they were objecting to. We felt the alienation, the cynicism, the aimlessness, the identity crises, the boredom, the testing, and the idealism of our students. We discovered that many of our young friends were deeply cynical about the baby-sitting apparatus called "school." Some were cynical about adults because they had never really found an adult they could trust. Most did not want to be like their parents. There were those who did not want to rush into adulthood and those who did. As different as they were, they shared a profoundly negative view of the state; politics seemed absurd and politicans corrupt. Military service was not a privilege, certainly not the moral obligation of the citizen; rather, it was involuntary servitude in an immoral cause. The shadow of Vietnam was everywhere.

These students were not convinced that a liberal curriculum with a big emphasis on political morality and on the arts of discourse, especially close reading, clear writing, and persuasive speaking, connected in any way with them, their lives, their problems, their needs. They were asking, in a hundred different ways, and incessantly, "Who are we and where do we fit in, and why can't we communicate with other human beings?" "How can we be honest with each other?" "Are all adults dishonest?" "Will we become dishonest?"

These questions opened up a host of problems that college professors were not used to thinking about, let alone talking about. Moreover, they were the questions of a generation that had turned its back on politics and politicians. Parents and college professors raised and schooled in the political and ideological 1930s were simply bewildered by some of the answers the young of the 1960s were creating out of their own experiences. Some of the solutions advanced in all seriousness were "pot, not politics," "make love, not war," and "do your own thing." A good many sons and daughters of the affluent white American middle class had weighed the Great Society and found it wanting. They asked why we were getting them ready to serve a greedy and hypocritical state. We tried to be candid and had to admit that we did not have easy answers. Was America so lost, confused, and arrogant that it was no longer the proper object of political loyalty, freely given? Was America so hopelessly flawed that it could not be expected to continue to move toward its own founding ideals? Was there anything the idealistic young citizen could do to alter the drift of his own country's history? What kind of an education was appropriate for the citizens of the United States during the troubled sixties? And what of the coming decades?

Our students finally forced us to face the fact that there was no point in devising new techniques for seducing them into reading Homer, Aeschylus, Thucydides, Plato, the Bible, Hobbes, Shakespeare, Montaigne, Locke, Rousseau, Goethe, Jefferson, and de Tocqueville, unless we could establish the relevance of those books to their lives as they were living them in the America of Selma and Vietnam, Father Berrigan and Billy Graham.

The faculty finally forced me to face the fact that we could not have a coherent program unless we all subordinated our individual fantasies to one common, dominant idea of what a liberal education should be. Whatever the curriculum was to be called, whether the liberal arts, or the political arts, or the moral curriculum, a controlling vision had to be there, it had to dominate our every decision about what to include in or exclude from the program. I had thought that the idea would sell itself but my faculty taught me that the dominant idea had to be sold, that faculty needed to be converted, that bringing individualistic college teachers together was not going to be easy.

The very nature of the program required each of us to subordinate our academic idiosyncrasies and our professional individualities to the idea of a common political curriculum. As I saw it, the common task was to be our investigation of the roots and rationale of our social and political life. We were to organize our teaching around the old and ever new questions of authority, power, legitimacy, obligation, and responsibility. We were to ask about community, justice, loyalty and obedience, and we were to follow the questions wherever they led. We were going to study the past to understand the present, and prepare for our uncertain future. From the Greek polis and the Roman civitas to the modern state we were going to be thinking, reading, talking, and writing about freedom and tyranny, peace and war, courage and cowardice, obligation and irresponsibility. Why? Because both teachers and students should have answers to certain persistent political questions: What should I do? What are my obligations? Should I join America? Should I obey? The political theme and personally relevant questions were to provide coherence, they were to provide a bright strong thread that would tie us together in a willing fellowship.

During the first two-year program the thematic thread never came through to the students. Most of the students told us at the end of the two years that they did not even know there was supposed to be an integrating theme. I thought it was obvious that we were reading and thinking about the individual, the state, and freedom as we studied four crises in western civilization. The common core of ethical questions seemed obvious. The theme seemed self-evident throughout the art and literature of 5th Century Athens and the story of the Greeks' attempt to create an ordered, just and democratic state. Surely it was obvious in the 17th Century English struggles and debates over law and order, freedom and authority, and it was absolutely central to 19th Century Europe confronted with the consequences of the industrial revolution. It all seemed so explicit. Clearly something had gone wrong.

Perhaps the biggest mistake was to assume that the faculty who made up the staff of this first program had really accepted the curricular theme and would easily switch to collaborative teaching. Because none of us knew the first thing about collaborative teaching, the book lists and teaching that emerged from our democratic deliberations never came together in a truly common effort. We worked well as a committee, but the theme was fuzzy and by the fourth semester it finally disappeared into very individualistic seminars. The curriculum fell apart because we had not recognized the necessity of teaching together as a team dedicated to a common theme, a common book list, and a common schedule. In this important respect Meiklejohn had succeeded at Madison in the twenties, while we had failed in the sixties.

ANOTHER ATTEMPT: THE CLASS OF 1967–69

In the spring of 1967 as the first program ended I was already planning the next. I had lost my innocence but not my faith in the rightness of a curriculum that was coherent and required. Campuses across the western world were being swept by an epidemic of student unrest, protest, and demands for relevance. Nothing seemed more relevant than a political education in the ethical dilemmas of citizenship, and yet that is exactly what was missing in movements of popular educational reform. In the popular movements students and faculty were joining together to abolish all requirements in the lower division, in the name of freedom of choice. This final victory of Eliot's elective system was quite simply an educational disaster because the elective system insured the dominance of the discrete course taught by the narrow specialist. The complete victory of the elective system meant the end of any chance for a coherent liberal education. In the face of the centrifugal force of the academic free market in courses, could Tussman at Berkeley and Cadwallader at San Jose State make required programs work that offered no courses at all?

There would be a new faculty and so I planned a few changes. I put the educational philosophy of the program in writing, discussed it with the prospective staff while recruiting them, and mailed it to prospective students. This time the faculty read Meiklejohn over the summer and talked about the integrating theme endlessly in staff seminars. That started us in the right direction. We read and talked about 5th and 4th Century Athens and 20th Century America, and underscored the contemporary relevance of Athens by reading and discussing books in pairs: something Greek and something contemporary.[6] While the contemporary titles varied somewhat from one faculty member to another, there was less resistance to keeping to a common book list and a common schedule. We were collaborating at last. The curriculum had a theme that we were developing and teaching together.

Finally, midway into the second two-year program we became a little community.[7] We were teaching, learning, reading, writing, and talking about political man, about our political problems and obligations, *and doing it together*. By the spring of 1969 the program was working. We could all feel it despite our occasional moments of doubt or periods of depression. The turning point came during the semester that we tried a frankly political approach to the creation of a curriculum in science that we called *political ecology*. The political thread was very much there.

What made the difference? There were several additions to the experiment that helped. We opened each semester with a retreat to the mountains to talk about the theme of the program, and we rounded off the program with a final retreat. We stressed communal activities within the program, sent the students out in teams to study small agricultural communities, and got students involved in planning our fourth semester. Finally, we encouraged informal writing and eliminated conventional grading. Let us look at some of these in more detail.

After two years of waiting for our commuting students to treat the experimental program as something more than just another class, we took the offensive. We believed that a community was essential and so despite the absence of residential bonds we took measures to build one. The first week the faculty and students moved off campus to a campground in the Santa Cruz mountains to talk about the program, the theme, and the books we would read. We were trying to get acquainted. The retreat was part of the program, *attendance was required*, and so everyone was there. The first retreat was so worthwhile we opened every succeeding semester that way and even ended the program in the mountains. The retreats were important because they helped our faculty and students agree to be bound together by a common intellectual purpose for two years. Slowly little cliques broke down and a loose assortment of individuals became a band of brothers and sisters.

To help build our community, we required students and faculty to see good films together: *Woman in the Dunes, Zorba, Red Desert, Black Orpheus, Marat-Sade, Ulysses, Chushingura, Winter Light, Gate of Hell*. These were films about the moral issues that we were discussing in seminar. Some of us began eating together regularly and only the lack of a dining hall prevented all of us taking a common meal together. By the second year we were meeting every Monday in a regular morning assembly in the college cafeteria so that we could be together, have coffee and breakfast together, and start the week together. The group became cohesive and as it did, everything improved; the seminars were better; we were doing more work together and enjoying it.

We asked small groups of eight and nine students to carry out anthropological surveys of several small agricultural towns in the Salinas Valley. One of the teams produced a documentary with a portable videotape recorder. Again the emphasis had shifted from independent study to cooperative study. These required studies of communities by student teams were much more successful than individual projects. Increasingly the students felt better about required work and required cooperation.

We experimented with a much greater variety of assignments. Students and faculty were required to keep journals and they filled them with informal writing about the books we were reading, the films we saw, reactions to each other, family crises, sex crises, and identity crises. We showed each other this informal writing and talked about form and content. Some made movies and did photographic essays. There was poetry, some fiction, and an occasional formal essay.

Conventional grades were finally eliminated in favor of a pass-incomplete system. With one or two exceptions the students all expressed satisfaction with the new grading system. It was difficult to assess the consequences of eliminating conventional grades because so much else was different in this particular program. Grades seemed unnecessary as our students committed themselves to the requirements of the fellowship. Toward the end of the program the students were required to write periodic evaluations of their own seminars, and of the faculty. These were included along with faculty evaluations of the seminars in a weekly paper published by the students. This was constructive criticism that was accurate, responsible, and public. We had substituted critiques for quizzes, and the public display of real work for letter grades.

The mistakes made in the first program were clear now. There was too much committee and not enough commitment. Accustomed to academic sovereignty in the classroom, the first faculty team continued to cherish and exercise that sovereignty despite the program. Someone was always spending an extra month on his favorite book while some books on the list were ignored and others added. We really did not want close collaboration.

The second time around we had a coherent program and a collegial faculty. The program had a clearly elucidated political theme and the theme was stated over and over again. The teachers collaborated as a team in the teaching of the theme all the way through the program, from beginning to end. The fact that the faculty had to plan and work together in a common educational enterprise, with a common book list, and on a common schedule was made clear in every discussion with every prospective teacher. It was never taken for granted. Each member of the faculty understood that he was a voluntary member of something that would become a fellowship, and that if he could not continue to accept the obligations of that fellowship, he must resign from it, rather than divide and destroy it.[8]

These, then, were some of the essential conditions satisfied in the second experiment, conditions which must be satisfied if this kind of lower-division, liberal arts program is going to be political, coherent, and collaborative.

An explicit theme and a committed faculty may ensure a coherent educational plan, but meeting these necessary conditions will not insure much of an educational experience for the students unless they too become active members of the program. Somehow they must be persuaded to join, to give up their hallowed but hollow individualism, and to accept the obligations of a peculiar but rewarding fellowship.

We discovered that there was a lot to learn about winning over students, signing them up as members, getting them to make the necessary commitment. Our students were constantly distracted by identity crises, family crises, sexual dilemmas and debacles, dates and drugs, beads and boots, cars and rock concerts, and even jobs, all more important than the books. The teacher is lucky if he is number ten on the list, and a successful antidote to these important distractions must be more powerful than a pop quiz. We decided to use the moral pressure of a cohesive community—if we could just get the students to join. We planned to conjoin the curriculum and the extracurriculum into a learning and living experience that would work powerfully. Back in 1965, at the start of the first experiment, we assumed that community would follow quite naturally from good discussion in seminar. We wanted our students to talk about ideas, the ideas of Sophocles or Goethe, Plato or Hobbes. Conversations were to have a beginning; someone, preferably a student, was to ask a question or locate a theme. The group was then to follow the question, develop the theme, explore implications, and make discoveries. The whole was to have an orchestrated quality, but with a minimum of direction from the teacher. The conversations were to be cooperative, creative, problem-solving.

What we wanted may have happened two or three times in the first year of the first program, but generally our discussions were unbelievably bad. Desperately we divided our groups, and then redivided them. We met in the daytime and then at night. We met on campus and off, with coffee and without, but nothing helped. Finally, at an angry session, a stubborn and hostile young lady spelled it out: "I never talk about anything important with people I don't like." That was it! Behind the cool, bored or bemused, and occasionally hostile looks of our students was fear and antipathy. They just did not want to discuss anything cooperatively, or in any way, except perhaps destructively, as long as they did not like or trust each other. We learned the hard way that for them the essence of good communication was trusting and being trusted. Neither trust, nor the lack of it have relevance for the traditional college course in which a distant professor lectures and dutiful student-stenographers take it all down. But trust is at the heart of a program built on a sense of community, and we realized that reconciliation had to come first, and good conversation about Plato or de Tocqueville could only come later, if at all.

The 1967–69 experiment was different because we became intimate. We talked about ourselves and the group. We wrote about ourselves in journals instead of trying to write term papers. We had fun going to retreats and the movies together. We began to like, trust and respect each other, and so we could talk about important things and sometimes fairly well. We were communicating a little in their sense, and a little in ours. The interaction felt better because we were discovering the lost art of cooperative conversation and some of the long-lost pleasures of community.

Let me end the story of this four-year experiment at San Jose. The last year was the best of all. It seemed a vindication of my faith in Alexander Meiklejohn. Two teams of faculty had worked on the art of teaching. For four years we had experimented with ways of making the liberal arts come alive in the lives of our students. We had learned to show freshmen how to marry morality and imagination, intelligence and experience. The most difficult task of all had been to enlist our students in a collaborative enterprise that was both intellectual and personal. Some of them understood, agreed, and enlisted. They found themselves members of a tight little educational community, a community that shaped and changed their lives. And, of course, much to our surprise and delight we found our own lives shaped and changed by that community.

REFORMS AND EXPERIMENTS: PAST AND PRESENT

Few American academics seem to realize that one hundred years ago there were three ideas of what an academic institution of higher learning should be. One was the Anglo-Saxon model established and disseminated by Oxford and Cambridge. Another was the Scottish pioneered by Saint Andrews, and then given a Calvinist cast by Edinburgh. The third was the German, especially as it took its peculiarly modern form at Berlin.

At Oxford the professor was both a moral and an intellectual teacher, a mentor for the sons of the ruling elite. The specific detail of what was taught was not as important as the teaching of mental discipline and the development of character. At Edinburgh many of the professors taught practical subjects and the Scots were proud of a literacy rate higher than that in England. Von Humboldt and the German professors committed themselves and their students to scientific research, even in theology, and their overarching goal became the expansion of knowledge through research. The German professor was primarily interested in teaching future scientists how to do research and how to publish the results of that research.

Although the first American colleges were mostly patterned on the Oxford-Cambridge model, the Scottish emphasis on useful subject matter had an early and strong appeal in an increasingly utilitarian country. The Scottish ideal helped pave the way for the introduction of practical subjects by the older colleges; Henry Tappan's innovations at Michigan in the 1850's, the Morrill Land-Grant Act of 1962, and, of course, the founding of Cornell in 1868.

However, it was the lodestone of the German research university that attracted the attention of ever larger numbers of American teachers, and over 9,000 of them followed George Ticknor there in the course of the 19th Century. It was the ideal of the German university that gave rise to the first graduate schools and the eventual dominance of the research university in America. The research university caused the decline in the importance and vitality of the liberal college. With the decline of the college, concern for character gave way to concern for subject matter. The rise of departments and disciplines and the adoption of the elective system meant that the liberal education of the whole student was increasingly left to chance.

It has been the mixing of these models and the mixing of a host of what seemed to be new and practical innovations, new and popular reforms, that have given us the kind of faculty and institutions that dominate American higher education today. The faculty is specialized and professional; the dominant institution is either the private research university with a departmentalized liberal arts college inside it or the conglomerate that Clark Kerr has called the multiversity.

The new academic prestige structure is increasingly one-dimensional as colleges and universities all across the land, staffed by the same kind of faculty, line up and play follow the flagship. Now that the American academic revolution has run its course, and most college professors are captives of the university ethos, America's colleges have lost both their identity and their calling, by default. While this historical development has given this nation a host of great universities it threatens to destroy the liberal college and liberal education altogether. Those who believe that at least some portion of higher education should be committed to the preparation of the citizen in the responsible practice of the civic arts must find some way of carrying out a radical reformation of the lower division.

Most of the popular reforms, past and present, will not provide the education that will transform America as long as the reformers, whether faculty or students, insist that "each individual must generate his own most vital questions and program his own education."[9] An individualistic education that actually takes pride in letting everyone, faculty and students, do their own thing cannot prepare future citizens to subordinate their private interests to the public need and the public good.

TELIC REFORMERS AND THE NEXT DECADE

What does the next decade hold in store for reformers? What should we do? Why should we do it? What strategy should we use? Finally, what are our chances of success? Is there a future for the anti-university reform movements?

Grant and Riesman conclude that the only reforms of the 1960's to have had any lasting impact were the popular reforms, not the telic reforms.

Only two out of the six neoclassical experiments they mention still exist—St. John's at Annapolis and Sante Fe, and St. Mary's of California. The San Jose experiment became almost exclusively an experiment in pedagogy after 1969 and closed down altogether three years later. Will neoclassical telic reforms do any better in the coming decade?

The decade of the 1980's already wears many forbidding faces: declining enrollments, shrinking budgets, demands for accountability from legislatures, tax revolts, layoffs, unionization, massive shifts in student demand, the end of geographical and vertical mobility for most faculty, and the prospect of intellectual stagnation for many of the campuses that survive. While the latter is one of the grimmest prospects of all, there may be in the midst of all this bad news opportunities to be seized, dark forces that we can turn to our advantage.

The rapid growth of American institutions of higher education between 1945 and 1970 was marked by the ascendancy of the arts and sciences disciplines and the death of the general education movement. The extension downward of that revolution into former teachers colleges and the acceptance throughout the academic world of the values of the departmentalized research university resulted in an enormous amount of research and publishing, a proliferation of specialized courses, and an upgrading of undergraduate curricula in the university-certified disciplines. By 1970 general or liberal education was virtually out of the picture.[10] The arts and sciences disciplines were riding high, and at first glance seemed quite in control of the whole of the higher academic system. But by 1970 the canny observer should have been able to spot a significant quickening in the relative rate of growth of the practical, the instrumental majors—both in the older programs like engineering, and in the somewhat newer ones like business and journalism. By 1980 it became clear that higher education was experiencing a massive shift in enrollments away from the arts and sciences disciplines and into the instrumental programs, at the very moment that many universities and colleges approached the threshold of a massive decline in overall enrollments.

The academic revolution that brought the disciplines and the departments to power is being followed by a counter-revolution driven by the job market and the market power of students.[11] Businessmen, legislators, public officials, and a tax weary and increasingly restive public are likely to see the decline of the arts and sciences disciplines and the proliferation and growth of the instrumental programs as a return to common sense, as an indication that a college education can be useful.

But for those who believe that neither the strictly disciplinary nor the strictly instrumental exhaust the meaning of a college education, this shift is a national disaster.

The decline of the arts and sciences disciplines is already leeching the significance, satisfaction, stature and status out of the work and lives of arts and sciences faculty on hundreds of campuses across the country. The loss of majors and a reversion to teaching service courses and despised general education courses will leave those faculty inert, parochial, and bored, or bitter, paranoid, and hostile, or all of these.

There is a way out of this mess and that is for faculty to find ways of making the teaching of a liberal curriculum in the lower division the most exciting, satisfying, and significant teaching there is at any level, on any campus. We must do something about college teaching to prevent it from becoming a bore, mere employment, an avenue to on-the-job retirement, and as dull as it is secure. I used to appeal to teachers to sign on to Alexander Meiklejohn's reform movement in order to save the souls of their students. My appeal now is for teachers to save their own souls through a new kind of teaching, and perhaps by doing so to serve their students and society.

During the decade of the 1980's there will be very few new faces on many of our campuses. We will have only ourselves; we will have to discover and create new sources of intellectual growth and vitality through our own efforts. In a decade of enrollment decline it will require an unusual kind of effort on the part of both faculty and administration, but it can happen.

In their 1932 report to the Faculty of Letters and Science at the University of Wisconsin, Meiklejohn and his faculty urged the reorganization of the lower half of the College of Letters and Science. Here are three of their concrete suggestions:

1. Student social life and student education might profit greatly if the thirty-six hundred freshmen and sophomores in the College of Letters and Science were divided into fifteen or twenty smaller colleges, each with its own social organization and social interests.
2. There would be very great gain if the teachers of the lower college could act, not only as one body, but also as fifteen or twenty smaller faculties, each considering the educational problem as a whole, each working out its own aims and methods in relative independence.
3. The experience of the Experimental College suggests a way in which college teachers might, much more satisfactorily than at present, be trained for the art of teaching.[12]

That was good advice in 1932; it is even better advice today. Grant and Riesman return to the very same solution forty-six years later—in 1978. Here is their modest proposal:

> In fact, one could argue that while the departments form a satisfactory community for groups of specialists and graduate students who choose to associate with them, they are not the best form of community for general undergraduate education. What, then, ought to be the basis of intellectual and social community for undergraduates? This is the heart of the debate that is being renewed with a gathering momentum.
>
> We favor a pluralism of core programs or subcolleges of which the early Santa Cruz represents an appealing ideal. . . . to serve as the basis of community, they should be integrating experiences, as was, for example, the early Cowell College at Santa Cruz or Meiklejohn's two-year Experimental College at the University of Wisconsin.[13]

There is something else that Grant and Riesman discovered: "A heightened sense of common purpose and common experiences are uniquely possible in such communities. Those who have taught in them have discovered that these experiences are as significant in the renewal of faculty as they are in fostering the growth of students."[14]

Reorganizing the lower division into small, thematically-based subcolleges would bring three very positive consequences: the return of extraordinary vitality and satisfaction to teaching in the lower division, the return of community for faculty, and the radical improvement of the intellectual and cultural ambiance of the campus. The liberal college would live again. But given the kinds of risks that come with great dislocating crises, what are our chances of success? If telic reforms did not fare well during good times, can we expect anything better during bad times? Finally, what strategy should we try?

OBSTACLES AND ASSETS

David Riesman, reflecting on a lifetime of research and experience, remains skeptical about the chances for telic reforms "except in the handful of overapplied institutions that can afford to turn students away by making greater demands on them for greater coherence."[15] Less naive today than in 1964, and much chastened by advances and setbacks at San Jose, Old Westbury, Evergreen, and the University of Wisconsin-Platteville, I am convinced that there is a way to plant reforms on unselective campuses. We know that there are formidable obstacles, and that there will be real resistance.

The first line of resistance to Meiklejohn's ideas will be the departments, because theme-based subcolleges really would end control of the lower division by the discipline-based departments. Today the power of the departments in all academic affairs is virtually absolute, and the departments are absolutely opposed to reforms that in any way threaten their sovereign power. The peculiar academic institution of tenure is already adding a special intensity to the defensive strategies of the departments as enrollments decline in the disciplines, but the custom of tenure itself is not a major obstacle even though it reinforces departmental power and rewards faculty commitment to the ethos of the research university.

The most formidable barrier to telic reform is the compelling and pervasive ethos of the research university, accepted uncritically by increasingly specialized faculty organized into sovereign departments. That barrier is reinforced by systems of faculty governance that give political expression to the values and structures of the academic revolution. Faculties have created Byzantine forms of governance that make it easy to add and multiply courses and options, and easy to block proposals that threaten departmental spheres of influence. Coupled to faculty acceptance of the values of the research university, there is grudging reverence for the multiversity as an ideal.

This general acceptance of the multiversity is in itself an obstacle because the multiversity thrives on and gives legitimacy to the overoptioned curriculum. The great public multiversities offer to be anything and everything to anyone and everyone, and every campus in the land feels the pull of that ideal and the threat of the coming competitive struggle for students.

Because there is no way of winning a head-to-head contest with the departments, the reformer will have to work around them while encouraging them to go on doing what they do best—in the upper division. This may not be as difficult as it seems. While many faculty still are teaching their specialties, an increasing number in arts and sciences departments are not. In fact, many are already spending most of their time teaching service courses and the inevitable growth of instrumental majors will relegate even more of them to a service function. This, in turn, will lead to an even greater degree of boredom, discontent, depression, and alienation. Faculty can escape this unhappy fate by leaving the departments to teach in a radically different lower division.

But why would faculty ever leave the rewards and security of the established and specialized disciplines and departments for cross-disciplinary teaching in the lower division? There are at least two reasons.

First, idealism is found in high concentrations on college and university campuses. Faculty idealism may be submerged, even laced with skepticism; nevertheless, it is there waiting to be mobilized and energized. There is an inner ambivalence and an inner tension about the present state of the academy in the minds of many faculty, and that means there are some out there waiting for a compelling vision of something better. I have known many college teachers who have a job, and tenure, but who want to feel called to something significant. Just teaching is not as exciting as being committed to a reform movement. It is exhilarating to stand with David against Goliath. Second, many faculty hunger for a kind of collegiality that is broader and deeper than anything provided by a department and its discipline. Many are ready for an education that they never had because they were so busy becoming chemists or sociologists. Many are ready for membership in an intellectually stimulating community of scholars, the kind of community so many of us dreamed of belonging to when we were graduate students. Such faculty would respond with relish to the intellectual adventure and the close-knit community that accompany the collaborative teaching of a coherent liberal curriculum. Anyone who resonates to the myth of a golden age that resembles, even though faintly, the "academical village" of Thomas Jefferson is a potential convert.

To know young American students is to discover their latent idealism, and that they too want and need community. Some students are already ready to admit to teachers that they feel a need for commitment, coherence, unity and meaning. They want support for their curiosity, creativity and seriousness. They would like someone to look up to, adult friends and teachers to depend upon. They would like adults to take their personal lives seriously enough to give them some good advice, models to follow, even outright leadership. Many need a halfway house on the way to adulthood and others are even ready to apprentice themselves to a master teacher. Yes, I am talking about the job-serious students of the 1980's. Instead of trying to talk them out of their interest in instrumental majors, we must have the vision and the courage to tell them that they must take a required, faculty-designed first program first.[16] If we are persuasive, they will listen; if we lead, they will follow.

Why not give students the chance for commitment and guide that commitment? Why not give them a chance to search for unity, coherence, and synthesis alongside committed teachers? There is the potential power of youthful idealism just waiting to be used for good ends. There is the potential power of an educating community just waiting to be used. Fortunately, the American system of higher education still has a lot of variety in it, and that variety, along with a desire to be different and to be better, will give some the opportunity and the courage to march to a different drummer.

Enough historical evidence is now available for us to pass judgment on the consequences of the academic revolution and the telic reforms opposed to it. Instead of drifting with the popular tide I believe that we should follow and build on the ideas and experiences of Alexander Meiklejohn at Madison, Stringfellow Barr and Scott Buchanan at St. Johns, Robert Hutchens at the University of Chicago, John Rice at Black Mountain, Joseph Tussman at Berkeley, and Richard Jones at Evergreen.[17] Having said that, there is still the question of strategy.

Here, sketched in very broad strokes, is one suggestion for a grand strategy. Let those who believe in thematic coherence and collaborative teaching convert a few presidents and enough faculty on enough campuses to start a movement and make it visible. A lot of push from a president and a lot of work by a small band of enthusiastic faculty will make it possible to set up and operate one or two subcolleges on any campus. The coalition or alliance of the president and faculty enthusiasts is essential—neither can launch a program without the other. One president and five faculty could start an experimental program on almost any campus in the land.

Reformers should look for likely campuses and then get in touch with the president and likely faculty. Someone should publish and preach and start a missionary movement. Once converted it will be up to the converts to start something on their own campus, and the reformers can move on. There ought to be a demonstration campus to which we could invite interested presidents and faculty for short workshops. We ought to run model programs in the summer for teams of presidents, faculty, and students. We ought to persuade one or more foundations to support a traveling team made up of a small number of those who have taught in successful programs. This team of experienced first program teachers could visit campus after campus, traveling in a caravan of Airstream trailers as a mobile demonstration of what we are talking about. Before we dismiss these schemes and others like them as too fanciful for the prosaic foundations, reflect for a moment on the millions of dollars that have been wasted on the heady dreams of an electronic revolution in teaching. We could put a demonstration program on the road for $200,000 a year and visit 20 campuses a year. Whether there is a team on the road or one that operates on a demonstration campus, someone must carry the message to presidents and faculty, to students and parents, to regents and politicians in a host of articles, news stories, and lectures. Someone must organize a society to sound the alarm and propagate the best ideas we can think of.

If only a few work at it, I believe that it will be possible to plant thematically integrated experiments in college teaching on a good number of campuses during the decade of the eighties. If this happens, I expect the programs to flourish and to form in the aggregate a significant telic reform movement that will help redefine the American undergraduate college and rescue hundreds of able teachers from a life embittered by boredom.

NOTES

1. Richard M. Jones, *Experiment At Evergreen* (Cambridge: Schenkman, 1981); Joseph Tussman, *Experiment At Berkeley* (New York: Oxford University Press, 1969); and Gerald Grant and David Riesman, *The Perpetual Dream* Chicago: University of Chicago Press, 1978).

2. Ibid., p. 15.

3. Alexander Meiklejohn, *The Experimental College* (New York: Arno Press, 1971). I would like to acknowledge an important intellectual debt. Alexander Meiklejohn was over ninety when I first met him. Small, frail, and happily intense, he quite simply bowled me over. I then searched for and read his books, and have never been the same since.

4. The volunteer staff of the 1965–67 program was made up of Gary L. Albright, philosophy; Harold J. DeBey, biochemistry; John A. Galm, English; David K. Newman, psychology; Richard G. Tansey, art history; and Mervyn L. Cadwallader, sociology. The Berkeley and San Jose reading lists were almost identical for the first semester and then diverged as the two programs developed in slightly different ways.

5. I was to discover that while teachers and students found a program without courses, lectures, and tests to be a bit unfamiliar, they were quicker to accept that than the wholly unfamiliar idea that the public college should be the democratic state's instrument for the liberal education of its citizens and that this should be a principal concern of the public college. Teachers, it turned out, were harder to educate in these matters than students.

6. The students were enthusiastic about the familiar contemporary titles on the book list but by the end of the program most agreed that the moderns just did not hold their own against the ancients. Later, students in an Evergreen program were to ask me to eliminate the modern authors.

7. The word "community" is peculiarly susceptible to misunderstanding. I am using it to denote a group of individuals who come to share certain assumptions, values, understandings, and expectations because they have agreed to join the group, accepted its conditions of membership, worked together on common tasks, talked together about common experiences, and grown together for a considerable period of time. This kind of a community takes a lot of time and joint effort to crystalize. It cannot be decreed into existence. Wishful thinking and memos addressed "To the community:" will not do it. Encounter groups are not what I call communities.

8. Later I learned to ask for a written compact because tacit understandings all too easily turned into misunderstandings.

9. This typical expression of the popular reform movement is from the *Catalogue of the Free University of Palo Alto*. (Stanford, 1968)

10. "The college is everywhere in retreat, fighting a dispirited rearguard action against the triumphant university." Tussman, *Experiment At Berkeley*, p. xiv.

11. I am heavily and thankfully indebted to the stimulating ideas and analysis of Roger L. Geiger in "The College Curriculum and the Marketplace," *Change*, Nov./Dec., 1980.

12. Meiklejohn, *The Experimental College*, pp. 246–247.

13. Grant and Riesman, *The Perpetual Dream*, p. 369.

14. Ibid., p. 370.

15. David Riesman, *On Higher Education* (San Francisco, Jossey-Bass, Inc., 1980), p. 292.

16. For the definition of a first program see Tussman, *Experiment At Berkeley*, pp. 18, 19.

17. The books to start with are: Meiklejohn, *The Experimental College;* Robert M. Hutchins, *Education For Freedom* (New York: Grove Press, 1963); Grant and Riesman, *The Perpetual Dream;* Tussman, *Experiment At Berkeley*, Richard M. Jones, *Experiment At Evergreen;* Martin Duberman, *Black Mountain: An Exploration in Community* (New York: Dutton, 1972); and, Harris Woffard, ed. *Embers of the World: Conversations With Scott Buchanan* (Santa Barbara: Center for the Study of Democratic Institutions, 1970).

Selected Bibliography on Alternative Education

PREPARED BY ROBERT DANA AND MALCOLM STILSON

Books:

Abbs, Peter and Graham Carey, *Proposal for a New College*. London. Heinemann Educational, 1977.

Baskin, Samuel. *Higher Education: Some Newer Developments*. New York, McGraw Hill, 1965.

Bear, John Bjorn. *The Alternative Guide to College Degrees and Non-Traditional Higher Education*. Grosset/Stonesong Press, New York, New York.

Boyer, Ernest L. and Martin Kaplan. *Educating for Survival*. Change Magazine Press, New Rochelle, New York, 1977.

Brick, Michael and Earl J. McGrath. *Innovation in Liberal Arts Colleges*. Teacher's College Press, New York, 1969.

Carnegie Commission on Higher Education. *Toward a Learning Society: Alternative Channels to Life, Work, and Service*. New York. McGraw-Hill, 1973.

Chait, Richard P. and Ford, Andrew T. *Beyond Traditional Tenure; A Guide to Sound Policies and Practices*. Jossey Bass, San Francisco, 1982.

Chance, Charles W., and Denis J. Curry. *The Evergreen Study: Report and Recommendations on The Evergreen State College*. Olympia, WA., State of Washington Council for Postsecondary Education, 1974.

Connecticut. Committee on Alternate Approaches for the Delivery of Higher Education. *Improvements of Opportunity in Higher Education: Alternative Modes for Earning Undergraduate* Degrees and

College Credit. Hartford, Conn. Commission for Higher Education, 1973.

Coyne, John and Tom Hebert. *This Way Out: A Guide to Alternatives to Traditional College Education in the United States, Europe and the Third World*. New York, Dutton, 1972.

Duberman, Martin. *Black Mountain: An Exploration in Community*. New York. Dutton, 1972.

Elmendorf, John. *Transmitting Information About Experiments in Higher Education; New College as a Case Study*. New York. Academy for Educational Development, 1975.

Gaff, Jerry, *The Cluster College*. Jossey Bass, 1970. San Francisco.

Gould, Samuel and Patricia Cross (eds). *Explorations in Non-Traditional Study* Jossey Bass. San Francisco, 1977.

Grant, Gerald and Riesman, David. *The Perpetual Dream: Reform and Experiment in the American College*. Chicago. University of Chicago Press, 1978.

Guide to Alternative Colleges and Universities. Boston, Beacon Press, 1974.

Hall, Laurence. *New Colleges for New Students*. San Francisco, Jossey-Bass, 1974.

Henderson, Algo Donmeyer. *The Innovative Spirit*. San Francisco, Jossey-Bass, 1970.

Higher Education Alternatives. Edited by Michael D. Stephens and Gordon W. Roderick, New York, Longman, 1978.

Implementing Innovative Instruction. Roger H. Garrison, Issue Editor. San Francisco, Jossey-Bass, 1974.

Individualizing Education by Learning Contracts. Neal R. Berte, Issue Editor. San Francisco, Jossey-Bass, 1975.

Interdisciplinarity and Higher Education. Edited by Joseph J. Kockelmans. University Park, Penn State University Press, 1978.

Jones, Richard M. *Experiment at Evergreen*. Schenkman, Cambridge, MA., 1981.

Learning and Living; Proceedings of an Anniversary Celebration in Honor of Alexander Meiklejohn, Chicago, May 8–10, 1942.

MacDonald, Gary B. edit. *Five Experimental Colleges: Bensalem, Antioch-Putney, Franconia, Old Westbury, Fairhaven*. New York, Harper and Row, 1973.

Martin, Warren B. *Alternative to Irrelevance; a Strategy for Reform in Higher Education*. Nashville, Abingdon Press, 1968.

McHenry, Dean and Associates. *Academic Departments*. San Francisco: Jossey Bass, 1977.

Meiklejohn, Alexander. *The Liberal College*. New York, Arno Press, 1969.

Milton, Ohmer. *Alternatives to the Traditional*. San Francisco, Jossey-Bass, 1972

Owens, Graham. *The Module: A Democratic Alternative in Education*. SLD Publications, 1978

Powell, John Walker (ed.). *The Experimental College*. Washington D.C., Seven Locks Press. 1981.

Schaer, Walter A. *The Utilization of Experimental Design Awareness in Undergraduate General Education Programs*. 1976.

Thelin, John R. HIGHER EDUCATION AND ITS USEFUL PAST, Cambridge, MA., Schenkman, 1982.

Tussman, Joseph, *Experiment at Berkeley*, Oxford University Press, New York, 1969.

Washington (State) Select Commission on Non-Traditional Study. *Dynamics of Change: Alternative Educational Opportunities*. Report of the Select Commission on Non-Traditional Study to the Council on Higher Education. Olympia, WA., Council on Higher Education, 1974.

Periodical Articles

Allen, Sheilah. "An Experiment in Field Based Education: A Description of the Program at the University of Lethbridge." *Education Canada;* 20(3): 11–13 Fall 1980.

American Civil Liberties Union. "Academic Freedom in New Colleges." *School and Society:* 94:144 Mar 19, 1966.

Andrews, Grover, and John Harris. "A Perspective on the Accreditation of Nontraditional Higher Education," *Peabody Journal of Education;* 56(3); 167–73 Apr. 1979.

Andrews, Tec. F. "An Experimenting College of Environmental and Applied Science." *Community College Frontiers;* 3(2): 17–22 Winter 1975.

Anthony, John H. "Reflections on the Cluster College." *New Directions for Community Colleges;* 4(1): 11–24 Spr 1976.

Axelrod, J. "Experimental College Model." *Educational Record:* 48:327–37 Fall 1967.

Baker, J. J. W. "College of Science in Society; Wesleyan University." *American Biology Teacher;* 38:494 Nov 1976.

Bartell, Shirley Miller. "A Model for Crosscultural and Interdisciplinary Teaching." *Improving College and University Teaching;* 27(1):34–37 Win 1979.

Baskin, Samuel, and Edwin F. Hallenbeck. "Nontraditional Program of Undergraduate Learning: University Without Walls, Redesigning the Halls of Ivy: Innovations in Higher Education." *Compact* 6(5):21–25 Oct. 1972.

Benson, D. "Communal University Model Gives Students Educational Freedom, Self Support System." *College and University Business;* 51:77+ Sp. 1971.

Berth, Donald F. "Where Students Shape Their Education. Redesigning The Halls of Ivy: Innovations in Higher Education." *Compact;* 6(5):9–11 Oct. 1972.

Binzen, Peter. "Penn's College of Thematic Studies." *Change:* 6(7):17–19 Sept. 1974.

Black, Bob, and Blair Hamilton. "The Spirit of the Free Universities." *Change in Higher Education;* 1(1): 54 Jan–Feb 1969.

Black, Sidney J. "Utopia as Reality." *College English;* 33(3):304–16 Dec. 1971.

Bloch, Peter, and Nancy Nylen. "Hampshire College: New Intents and Old Realities." *Change:* 6(8):38–42 Oct. 1974.

Bobowski, R. C. "College Model for the Grass Roots." *American Education;* 12:14–19 Jun. 1976.

Bragg, S. M. "St. Olaf and the Paracollege; A Case Study of Planned Curricular and Organizational Change in Higher Education." *Journal of General Education;* 29:152–71 Summ. 1977.

Bromell, Henry. "The Great Experiment at Hampshire." *Change;* 3(7):47–51 Nov. 1971.

Brown, W. E., and O. B. Adams. "Design for Independent Study: An Experimental Program at Columbus College in Georgia Supports the Value of Independent Study in Junior Colleges." *Junior College Journal;* 36:29–31 May 1966.

"Campus-free College." *Edcentric;* 22:16–18 Mar. 1973.

Ciporen, Marvin. "Threads: Humanities in a Union Setting." *Alternative Higher Education: The Journal of Nontraditional Studies*, v6. p. 1 p. 30–39 Fall.

Cobb, Gerald T. "Developing a Six-Year High School-College Learning Model." *Notre Dame Journal of Education;* 6(4):349–52 Win 1975.

Coughlan, Reed. "The Mentor Role in Individualized Education at Empire State College." *Distance Education*. v1 n1 p1–12 Mar.

Coy, Harold, and Mildred Price Coy. "Educational Commune: The Story of Commonwealth College." *Harvard Educational Review;* 42(2): 264–68 1973.

Coyne, John. "Bensalem: When the Dream Died." *Change:* 4(8):39–44 Oct. 1972.

Coyne, John. "College Without a Campus." *Change:* 5(7):18–21 Sep. 1973.

Cross, Ronald. "The Other Open University, Part 1." *Planning for Higher Education,* v7 n1 p9–19 Aug.

Cross, Ronald. "The Other Open University, Part 2." *Planning for Higher Education,* v7 n1 p25–36 Aug. 1978.

Cudhea, David. "California's "Free" Universities." *Change:* 6(7):19–22 Sep. 1974.

Danilov, V. J. "Exciting Experiments in Higher Education." *Phi Delta Kappa;* 41:221–4 Fall 1960.

Day, Mildred L. "Strategies for Teaching the Non-Traditional Student." 10 p: Paper presented at the Annual Meeting of the National Council of Teachers of English (70th, Cincinnati, OH, November 21–26, 1980). Nov. 1980.

Drake, Christopher. "Nova University: The Controversial Dream." *Change*. v11 n4 p16–18. May–Jun. 1979.

Draves, Bill. "The Free University Network." *Lifelong Learning:* 3(4):4–5 Dec. 1979.

Egerton, John. "The Uncommon College." *Change;* 6(3):14–17 Apr. 1974.

Ekstrom, Ruth B. "Evaluating Women's Homemaking and Volunteer Work Experience for College Credit." *Alternative Higher Education: The Journal of Nontraditional Studies;* 4(3): 201–11 Spr 1980.

Ellert, Jo Ann C. "The Bauhaus and Black Mountain College." *Journal of General Education;* 24(3):144–52 Oct 1972.

Experimental College. United States. Office of Education. Division of Higher Education. (OE-50010; New Dimensions in Higher Education. No. 3); 13 p. 1960 Supt. of Documents.

Farber, Robert H. "The Free University". *School and Society;* 97(2319); 356–58 October 1969.

Freiman, Arnie, and David Morris. "Communitas." *Edcentric;* p. 12–14 Jan. 1973.

Gaff, Jerry G. "Cluster Colleges and Their Problems." *Journal of General Education;* 23(1):21–8 Apr. 1971.

Gamson, Zelda F., et. al. "Experimental College Grads: Getting Theirs." *Change;* 9(9):48–49 Sep. 1977.

Gehret, Kenneth G. "Washington's Evergreen College." *Change:* 4(4):17–19 May 1972.

Gellhorn, Alfred, and Ruth Schever. "The Experiment in Medical Education at the City College of New York." *Journal of Medical Education;* 53(7):574–82 Jul 1978.

Gibbs, O. B., and H. C. Lee. "Colleges Without Walls; the Status of Non-Traditional Learning in California Community Colleges." *College and University;* 49:267–74 Spr 1974.

Gilbert, A. N. "Academic Free Enterprise; a Proposal." *Improving College and University Teaching;* 21:188–9 Summ 1973.

Goldberg, Richard. "Goddard's Adult Degree Program." *Change:* 5(8):15–20 Oct. 1973.

Goldberser, Nancy, "Simon's Rock: Meeting the Developmental Needs of the Early College Student." *New Directions for Higher Education, No. 29 (Educating Learners of All Ages)* v8 n1 p37–46. 1980

Goodman, Denise. "The First 'Ecology College'." *Change:* 5(7):21–23 Sep 1973.

Grant, Gerald. "Let a Hundred Antiochs Bloom!" *Change;* 4(7):47–58 Sep 1972.

Greenberg, Elinor, "The University Without Walls (UWW) Program at Loretto Heights College: Individualization for Adults.", *New Directions for Higher Education,* No. 29 (Educating Learners of All Ages) v8 n1 p-47–61.

Hall, James W. "Regional Accreditation and Nontraditional Colleges; A President's Point of View." *Journal of Higher Education;* 59(2):171–77 Mar–Apr 1979.

Hamilton, E. "Black Colleges; Opportunity for Non-traditional Study." *Journal of Negro Education;* 46:254–63 Summ 1977.

Hammons, James O. "Burlington County College: A Success Story." *Community College Review;* 4(2):48–56 Fall 1976.

Harding, Gene, and Schuyler Houser. "The Centennial Educational Program." *Interface Journal;* 1(1):23–29 Win 1974/75.

Hassler, Donald M., and Helga E. Kaplan. "Student Evaluations of Experimental University Classes." *Journal of General Education;* 29(2):97–104 Summ 1977.

Hassler, Donald M.; Kaplan, Helga E., "Experimental University Classes and "The Best That Has Been Thought." *Alternative Higher Education: The Journal of Nontraditional Studies,* v5 n2 p126–34 Win. 1980.

Hawkridge, David, "The University of Mid-America: An Open University Analogue?", *Teaching at a Distance*, n13 p37–44 Win 1978.

Hayward, S. "Beloit Plan." *Liberal Education:* 50:335–48 Oct. 1964.

Hechinger, F. M. "Academic Counter-Revolution: The New Collegiate Seminar Program." *Saturday Review World;* 2:63–64 + Nov 16, 1974.

Heiner, Harold G. "An Experiment in Educational Freedom." *Improving College and University Teaching;* 23(4):243–4 Fall 1975.

Helfgot, Steven R. "Student Development Faculty in the Interdisciplinary Learning Center." *Community College Frontiers;* 4(1):4–11 Fall 1975.

Hill, James W. "Prospectus for a New Type College." *Improving College and University Teaching;* 19(4):314–16 Fall 1971.

Hoffman, Jonathon. "Widening the Concept of City as Teacher." *College Management;* 7(8):32–33 Aug 1972.

Horowitz, Irving Louis, and Joshua Feigenbaum. "Experiment Perilous: The First Years of Livingston College of Rutgers University." *Urban Education;* 15 (2):131–68 Jul 1980.

Houghton, Raymond W. "Founding a Peoples' College." *Educational Leadership;* 28(4):347–50 Jan 1971.

Hull. W. F. "Development Ideal: Higher Education Reform." *Improving College and University Teaching;* 21:279–81 Aug 1973.

Jacobsen, E. E. "Goddard College." *Christian Scholar;* 50:91–5 Summ 1967.

James, Bernard J., and Robert P. Fagaly. "Organizational Marginality and Opportunity in University Outreach Education." *Journal of Higher Education;* 44(8):646–56 Nov 1972.

Janaco, Richard Paul. "Micronizing the Humanities: A Communal Approach." *New Directions for Community Colleges;* 3(4):67–77 Win 1975.

Jerome, Judson. "Friends World College, Bensalem, The College of the Potomac: Portrait of Three Experiments." *Change;* 2(4):40–54 Jul–Aug 1970.

Jerome, Judson. "The Living-Learning Community." *Change:* 3(5):46–55 Sep 1971.

Johansson, Charles B., and Robert L. Dey. "Assessment of an Experimental College." *Research in Higher Education;* 1(1):71–78 1973.

Johnson, Jeffrey N. "Community Faculty in the University Without Walls at the University of Minnesota: A Preliminary Description." *Alternative Higher Education;* 1(1):5–13 Fall 1976.

Director of Higher Education Programs in Experiential Education. *Journal of Experimental Education*. v2 nl p17–27 Spr. 1979.

Karr, P.J., "An Exploratory Study: The Need, Scope, and Ramification of an Alternative Education Program and Curriculum". *Education*, v99 n2 p136–40 Win 1978.

Kelly, Dorothy A. "Serving Adult Learning at the College of New Rochelle." *New Directions for Higher Education*, No. 27 (Building Bridges to the Public) v7 n3 p21–29 1979.

Killack, Cecil James, and Joseph K. Rippetoe. "Community Education in Kansas, A Challenge to Community Colleges." *Alternative Higher Education;* 1(1):51–60 Fall 1976.

Killian, C. Rodney, and Catherine M. Warrick. "Steps to Abstract Reasoning: An Interdisciplinary Program for Cognitive Development." *Alternative Higher Education: The Journal of Nontraditional Studies;* 4(3):189–200 Sp 1980.

Kirkhorn, Michael. "Union for Experimenting Colleges and Universities, Back From the Brink." *Change*. 11(3) 10–21. April 1979.

Koehnline, William A. "Learning Clusters: A Creative Alternative." *Community College Frontiers;* 4(1):26–31 Fall 1975.

Koehnline, William A., and William C. Brubaker. "Trends in Community College Planning and Design." *Community College Frontiers:* 6(4):28–35 Summ 1978.

Kornfeld, Milton. "A New Opportunity for General Education." *Alternative Higher Education: The Journal of Nontraditional Studies:* 3(4):254–59 Summ 1979.

Kowalski, Joanne and Others, "Does Alternative Higher Education Need an Alternative?", *Alternative Higher Education: The Journal of Nontraditional Studies*. v4 n4 p299–307 Sum 1980.

Kreps, Alice Roelofs, and Jan L. Balck. "The College for Living: Self Reliance Through Experiential Learning." *Humanist Educator:* 16(3):98–102 Mar 1978.

Kirkhorn, Michael. "Union for Experimenting Colleges and Universities: Back From the Brink." *Change:* 11(3):18–21 Apr 1979.

Lauter, Paul, and Florence Howe. "What Happened to the 'free university'." *Saturday Review;* 53(25):80–82 and 93–94 June 20, 1970.

Lawler, Nancy. "Teaching in a Cluster College." *Community College Social Science Journal;* 1(2):52–56 1977.

Lawson, Katherine, "John Wood Community College Brings the Common Market to the Midwest." *Community College Frontiers;* 5(2):28–33 Winter 1977.

Leff, L. "Pep Rally at the O.K. Corral". *Change*. 11:22–23 Nov–Dec 1979.

Leggett, Stanton. "Diary of a New University. At Athabasca University, The Students are Stimulated, But the Plans are Real." *College and University Business;* 52(5):72–77 May 1972.

Leppert, William A. "Alpha College Today." *Community College Frontiers;* 7(4).15–17 Summ 1979.

Leppert, William, and Joan Koenig. "Alpha-College for Exploring." *Community College Frontiers;* 4(4):14–17 Summ 1976.

Levensky, Mark. "Trying Hard: Interdisciplinary Programs at The Evergreen State College." *Alternative Higher Education;* 2(1):41–46 Feb 1977.

Levine, Arthur, "An Unheralded Educational Experience: Brookwood Remembered." *Change*, v13 n8 p38–42 Nov–Dec 1981.

Lieberman, J.E., and J.C. Millonzi. "Institutional Change: Four Factors of Reform." *Community College Frontiers;* 7:46–49 Spr 1979.

Lindquist, Jack. "Empire State College: Can There be an Experimenting College?" *New Directions for Higher Education;* 15:83–94 Aut 1976.

Lombardi, John. "An ERIC Review: Update Report on Noncampus Colleges." *Community College Review;* 4(3):57–64 Winter 1977.

London, Herbert. "Questions of Viability in Non-traditional Education." *College Student Journal;* 7(3):90–93 Sep/Oct 1973.

Longsworth, C.R. "Experimental Colleges: Agents of Change." *Today's Education;* 65:73–76 Jan 1976.

Losty, Barbara P. and Broderson, Deborah D. "Who Succeeds? A Comparison of Transcripts of Graduates and Inactive Students of a Nontraditional Bachelor of Arts Degree Program." *Alternative Higher Education: The Journal of Nontraditional Studies*, v5 n2 p91–99 Win 1980.

Lyon, David N. "Embryo: A Radical Experiment in Learning." *Journal of Higher Education;* 50(1):48–62 Jan–Feb 1979.

Magada, Virginia, and Michael Moore. "The Humanities Cluster College at Bowling Green State University: Its Middle Years." *Liberal Education;* 62(1):100–112 Mar 1976.

McDonnell, Pia, "A Student Perspective on Nontraditional Graduate Education." *Alternative Higher Education: The Journal of Nontraditional Studies*, v4 n1 p70–76 Fall

Moore, Dorothy G. "Student Perceptions of Traditional vs. Non-Traditional Pursuit of Undergraduate Degrees." *Journal of Negro Education*, v50 n2 p182–90 Spring 1981.

McNeil, Donald. "UMA: Progress of An Experiment." *New Directions in Continuing Education:* 5:47–53 1980.

Meister, Joel S. "A Sociologist Looks at Two Schools: The Amherst and Hampshire Experiences." *Change*, v14 n2 p26–34 Mar 1982.

Miller, Jerry W. "Credit for Nontraditional Education: A Conceptual Framework for Recognition." *Educational Record;* 55(3):188–92 Summ 1974.

Munser, Paul David; Priest, Douglas M. "Planning the Integration of Nontraditional and Traditional Postsecondary Education." *Planning for Higher Education*. v7 n4 p14–20 Feb 1979.

Murray, Donald M. "The Good Ship Lollipop." *Today's Education;* 65(3):32–37 Sep–Oct 1976.

Nolan, Donald J. "State Leadership in Experiential Learning: The New York Experience." *New Directions for Experiential Learning*, n4 p71–77 1979.

"Opening College Doors to Senior Citizens." *College Board Review;* 93:29 Fall 1974.

Oski, Katharine, "Problems and Issues Raised by Returning Adults." *Alternative Higher Education: The Journal of Nontraditional Studies*, v5 n2 p100–05 Win 1980.

Nontraditional Education: State-Level Issues and Concerns. A Conference Held at Harvard University Graduate School of Education (May 16–18, 1976). Association of Governing Boards of Universities and Colleges, Washington, D.C. George Washington University, Washington, D.C. Inst. for Educational Leadership; Harvard Univ., Cambridge, Mass. Graduate School of Education. 24 p. 18 May 1976.

Palola, Ernest G., and Timothy Lehmann. "Evaluating External Degree Programs." *Peabody Journal of Education:* 56(3):174–85 Ap 1979.

Pennypacker, Malcolm. "A Trustee's Role in Changing Instruction." *New Directions for Community Colleges;* 5(1):31–36 Spr 1977.

Perry, W. "Locked Into An Outdated Philosophy of Learning." *Chronicle of Higher Education:* 17:72 Nov 27, 1978.

Poppenhagen, Brent W. and Byxbee, William E. "Experiential Education at the Graduate Level: A Perspective on Faculty Role and Development." *Alternative Higher Education: The Journal of Nontraditional Studies*, v5 n2 p135–43 Win 1980.

Potter, George T. "Innovation, Experimentation, and Higher Education: Is The Perpetual Dream A Nightmare?" *Liberal Education*, v66 n3 p307–14 Fall 1980.

Purdon, Tom. "Another Store Down the Street." *American Education;* 14(1):21–26 Jan–Feb 1978.

Rapson, Richard L. "The Little College That Might: New College in Its Second Year." *Educational Perspectives;* 11(2):21–25 May 1972.

"Rethinking the Dream at Santa Cruz." *Science;* 207(4427):157–60 and 162 Jan 1980.

Riesman, David. "New College." *Change:* 7(4):34–43 May 1975.

Riesman, David. "A Conversation with Simmons College." *Journal of General Education*. v31 n2 p79–108 Summ 1979.

Rosenman, Mark, "Empowerment as a Purpose of Education." *Alternative Higher Education: The Journal of Nontraditional Studies*, v4 n4 p248–59 Summ 1980.

Rosenstein, Paul; Stick, Hal, "Models of Union University Cooperation." *New Directions for Experiential Learning*, (Building New Alliances: Labor Unions and Higher Education) N10 p13–15 1980.

Ryan, M., and J. Bills. "Middle Tennessee State University Experimental String Program." *School Musician:* 37:56–58 Fall 1966.

Schatz, A.E., et al. "Business Education in Nontraditional Settings." *National Business Education Yearbook;* 17:40–53 1979.

Scheuerle, William H. "New College of the University of South Florida." *Alternative Higher Education: The Journal of Nontraditional Studies;* 3(3):154–60 Spr 1979.

Schöen, W.T. "Educational Experimentation: Hofstra University's New College Plan." *Journal of Higher Education;* 36:336–8 Jun 1965.

Schöen, W.T. "Hofstra's New College: The Student View." *Improving College and University Teaching;* 13:210–13 Aut 1965.

Schmitt, Kara Lynne. "New Options for College Study." *Personnel and Guidance Journal;* 53(10):739–45 June 1975.

Schroth, Raymond A. "College as Camelot." *Saturday Review: Education;* 55(46):52–57 Dec 1972.

Sharp, Laura M.; "External Degrees: How Well Do They Serve Their Holders?" *Journal of Higher Education*, v50 n5 p615–49 Sep–Oct 1979

Sievert, William A. "The College of Rock and Roll." *Change:* 5(4):19–21 May 1973.

Smith, David. "Deep Springs Is Far Out." *Change;* 4(8):20–21 Oct. 1972.

Stafford, Roger A. "Green Bay's Interdisciplinary Faculty." *Change;* 4(3):20–22 Apr 1972.

Stein, Bernard H. "College Without Walls: A Teacher's View." *Liberal Education;* 59(4):480–89 Dec 1973.

Sullivan, H. "Experimental College: A Cool Medium." *Improving College and University Teaching;* 21:265–8 Aut 1973.

Swift, Betty. "Public Awareness of the Open University." *Teaching At A Distance*, n19 p79–84 Summ 1981.

Taafee, Thomas and Litwak, Eleanor "A Union Campus." *New Directions for Experiential Learning*, (Building New Alliances: Labor Unions and Higher Education) n10 p37–52 1980.

Thompson, Lyle. "Johnston College: An In-depth Description of a Successful Experiment." *AAUP Bulletin;* 59(4):411–18 Dec 1973.

Thrash, P.A. "Eureka! Factor: An Inquiry Into Educational Alternatives; Evaluation of Nontraditional Institutions and Programs." *The North Central Association Quarterly;* 52:455–63 Spr 1978.

Trembley, William. "Don't Call It 'Kayak College'." *Change;* 4(7):15–17 Sep 1972.

Tyler, R.W. "American Needs the Experimental College." *The Educational Forum:* 28:151–7 Jan 1964.

"Union of Experimental Colleges." *School and Society;* 93:239 Apr 17, 1965.

Veysey, Laurence. "Black Mountain: An Exploration in Community." *Harvard Educational Review;* 43(2):258–64 1973.

Walters, J.C. "Searching for Atypical or Non-mainstream Colleges." *Journal of Research and Development in Education;* 6:15–20 Fall 1972.

Wilson, R.C.L. "The Open University." *Geotimes;* 16(8):16–19 Aug 1971.

Wish, John R. "Beachhead College." *Improving College and University Teaching;* 23(4):249–51 Fall 1975.

Wolfe, Alan. "The Experimental College—Nobel Contradiction." *Change Higher Education;* 2(2):26–32 Mar–Apr 1970.

Wolman, M. Gordon. "Interdisciplinary Education: A Continuing Experiment." *Science;* 198 (4319):800–804 Nov 1977.

Woodley, Alan; McIntoch, Naomi "The Door Stood Open: An Evaluation of the Open University Younger Students Pilot Scheme." *Teaching at a Distance*, n19 p72–79 Sum 1981.

A SAMPLE OF ALTERNATIVE COLLEGES AND PROGRAMS

Institution

1. Wayne State University
   Monteith College
2. Wesleyan University
   College of Social Studies
   College of Letters
3. University of the Pacific
   Raymond College
   Elbert Covell College
   Callison College
4. University of California Santa Cruz
   Cowell College
   Stevenson College
   Crown College
   Merrill College
   College Number Five
5. Goddard College
   Greatwood
   Northwood
6. Hofstra University
   New College
7. Michigan State University
   Justin Morrill College
   Lyman Briggs College
   James Madison College
8. Nasson College
   New Division
9. Oakland University
   Charter College
   New College
   Allport College
10. University of California San Diego
    Revelle College
    Muir College
11. Fordham University
    Bensalem College
12. University of Michigan
    The Residential College
13. Western Washington State College
    Fairhaven College
14. City University of New York, Kingsborough Community College
    Brighton
    Darwin
15. Rutgers—The State University of New Jersey
    Livingston College
16. Colby College
    Program in Human Development
    Program in Intensive Studies in Western Civilization
    Program in Bilingual and Bicultural Studies
17. Grand Valley State College
    Thomas Jefferson College
18. University of Nebraska
    Centennial Education Program
19. State University of New York, College at Old Westbury
    Urban Studies College
    Disciplines College
    General Program
20. Redlands University
    Johnston College
21. St. Edwards University
    Holy Cross College
    Maryhill College

22. St. Olaf College
    The Paracollege
23. Sonoma State College
    Hutchins School of Liberal Studies
24. University of Vermont
    Experimental Program
25. Western College
    Miami University
26. Goodrich Program
    University of Nebraska-Omaha
27. William James College
    Grand Valley State College
28. ADAPT Program
    University of Nebraska
29. DOORS Program
    Illinois Central
30. STARS Program
    Seminole College
31. PATH Program
    William Rainey Harper College
32. CREATE Program
    Surry Community College
33. STEPPE Program
    Joliet Junior College
34. LIFT Program
    Allegheny College
35. RISE Program
    Prarie State College
36. The Evergreen State College
37. Stockton State College
38. Ramapo College
39. Southern Minnesota State College
40. Hampshire College
41. New College, Florida
42. Montieth College
    Wayne State University
43. State University of New York
    Empire State College
44. State University of New York
    Federated Learning Communities
    Stony Brook
45. University of California
    Los Angeles
    Program in Medicine, Law and Human Values
46. University of Alabama
    New College
47. Bard College
    General Education Program
48. Boston University
    College of Basic Studies, Division of Social Science
49. Bucknell University
    Program in Social Theory and Human Action
50. California State University—Hayward
    Program in Human Development
51. University of California—Irvine
    Program in Social Ecology
52. Connecticut College
    General Education Program
53. David & Ilkins College
    Division of Integrated Studies
54. Earlham College
    Human Development and Social Relations Program
55. Eastern Kentucky University
    Central University College
56. Hobart-William Smith College
    General Education Program
57. Kenyon College
    Integrated Program in Humane Studies
58. Maharishi International University

59. Mars Hill College
    Program of General Education
60. Northeastern Illinois University
    Program for Interdisciplinary Education
61. Northwestern University, Mathematical Models in the Social Sciences
62. San Francisco State University
    NEXA and several others
63. St. Cloud State University
    Department of Interdisciplinary Studies
64. St. Joseph's College (IN)
    Core Curricular Program
65. SUNY—Geneseo
    Time-Flexible Degree Program
66. University of Virginia
    Political and Social Thought Program
67. Wayne State University
    University Studies & Weekend College Program
68. University of Wisconsin—Green Bay
69. New College
    San Jose State University
70. Strawberry College
    University of California
    Berkeley
71. The Experimental College
    University of Wisconsin
    Madison
72. Unit One
    University of Illinois
73. Antioch University
74. The Grassroots Project
    Craftsbury Common, Vermont
75. University Without Walls
76. Union Graduate School
77. Whatcom Community College
    Bellingham Washington

LIST OF CONTRIBUTORS

Arthur Chickering
Memphis State University
Memphis, TN 38111

Mervyn Cadwallader
University of Wisconsin
Platteville, WI 53818

C. DeLisle Crawford (Lisle)
Meiklejohn Foundation
16176 Roselawn
Detroit, MI 48221

Ralph M. Crowley
Meiklejohn Foundation
16176 Roselawn
Detroit, MI 48221

J. Peter Euben
University of California
Santa Cruz, CA 95062

Jonathan Fairbanks
St. Mary's College of Maryland
St. Mary's City, Maryland 20686

Diane Gillespie
Goodrich Program
University of Nebraska—Omaha
Omaha, NEB 68105

Charles Grubb
S.W. Minnesota State College
Marshall, MN 56258

Jeanne Hahn
Member of the Faculty
The Evergreen State College
Olympia, WA 98505

Patrick J. Hill
Provost
The Evergreen State College
Olympia, WA 98505

Frank Holmquist, Associate Prof. of Politics
Hampshire College School of Social Science
Amherst, MA 01002

Virginia Ingersoll
Member of the Faculty
The Evergreen State College
Olympia, WA 98505

Richard M. Jones
Member of the Faculty
The Evergreen State College
Olympia, WA 98505

Robert H. Knapp, Jr.
Member of the Faculty
The Evergreen State College
Olympia, WA 98505

William H. Newell
Western College Program
Miami University
Oxford, OH 45056

Laura Nisonoff, Assistant Prof. of Politics
Hampshire College School of Social Science
Amherst, MA 01002

John Perkins
Academic Dean
The Evergreen State College
Olympia, WA 98505

Royce Pitkin
R.F.D. 1
Plainfield, VT 05667

Robert M. Rakoff, Associate Prof. of Politics
Hampshire College School of Social Science
Amherst, MA 01002

H. Michael Sapir
Retired Economist—Alumnus of Alexander Meiklejohn Experimental College at Wisconsin
63 Arguello Circle
San Rafael, CA 94901

Philip Secret
Goodrich Program
University of Nebraska—Omaha
Omaha, NEB 68105

Barbara Leigh Smith
Academic Dean
The Evergreen State College
Olympia, WA 98505

Cynthia Stokes-Brown
Antioch University
1019 Oxford Street
Berkeley, CA 94707

Charles Teske
Member of the Faculty
The Evergreen State College
Olympia, WA 98505

Paul von Blum
University of California—Los Angeles
2038 Louella Avenue
Venice, CA 90291

George Von der Muhll
University of California
Santa Cruz, CA 95064

Frederick S. Weaver
Dean of Social Sciences
Hampshire College
Amherst, MA 01002

Byron L. Youtz
Member of the Faculty
The Evergreen State College
Olympia, WA 98505

Malcolm Stilson
Head of Reference, Library
The Evergreen State College
Olympia, WA 98505

Index